' for Work and Pensions

The Development of Welfare States in Europe and America

The Development of Welfare States in Europe and America

Edited by
PETER FLORA
and
ARNOLD J. HEIDENHEIMER

Transaction Publishers
New Brunswick (U.S.A.) and London (U.K.)

Fifth printing 1995
Paperback edition 1982
Copyright © 1984 by Transaction Publishers
New Brunswick, New Jersey 08903.

This book is printed on acid-free paper that meets the American National Standard for Permanence of Paper for Printed Library Materials.

Library of Congress Catalog Number: 79-65227
ISBN: 0-87855-920-5
Printed in the United States of America

Library of Congress Cataloging-in-Publication Data

Main enter under title:

The Development of welfare states in Europe and America.

Includes bibliographical references.
I. Civilization, Modern-1950–
  1. Welfare state—Addresses, essay, lectures.
I. Flora, Peter, 1944–   II. Heidenheimer, Arnold J.
HN17.5D48
ISBN 0-87855-920-5

To the Memory of
STEIN ROKKAN
1921-1979

Contents

List of Tables

List of Figures

Preface

This book is the fruit of a joining of efforts by two research groups that were active during the 1970s. One was constituted by the Study Group on Historical Indicators of West European Democracies (HIWED Project), which worked as a cohesive body under Peter Flora's leadership at the Universities of Mannheim and Cologne. The other group was a more loosely structured American-based body of researchers whose members constituted the Social Policy Research Group of the Council for European Studies, of which Arnold J. Heidenheimer was cochairman.

The man to whom we owe the stimulus for bringing the two groups together is Stein Rokkan. It was Rokkan who first mentioned the goals of the HIWED group to Heidenheimer when the latter was a visiting professor at the University of Bergen in 1973. Rokkan's work was an important inspiration for the comparative research efforts especially of Peter Flora, but also of others in our groups. It was with great sorrow that we received reports of his declining health, and then, in July 1979, the news of his death. We dedicate this volume to Stein Rokkan, and our memories of him as a friend and scholar.

The conference for which most of us wrote the papers that evolved into the chapters of this book was held in a splendid setting by the shores of Lake Lucerne in July 1977. It was the first time that most of the contributors had met each other, and the quality of both the encounter and the papers led us to pursue the long and arduous road toward joint publication. We were stimulated not only by what we learned from each other, but also by the comments of these other participants in the conference: Christa Altenstetter, of the City University of New York; Richard Eichenberg and Kurt Seebohm, members of the HIWED project; Rudolf Klein, of the University of Bath, an active member of the Social Policy group; and Richard L. and Anna J. Merritt, from the University of Illinois.

It was evident to the editors that while the Lucerne papers covered a very broad spectrum of historical data analysis and interpretation, there were lacunae. But we decided not to aim for "completion"—as we might have by commissioning complementary papers on policies—such as social services and housing, which were not extensively treated. Rather, we sought to maximize congruence and complementarity among the existing papers, particularly by urging several of the contributors to provide more systematic comparative treatment of the West European and North American developments. We trust, also, that the abbreviated geographical referents in the book title are not taken amiss by readers. There was no way in which we could select a brief title that exactly circumscribes the geographical areas we cover. Both the Americas south of the Rio Grande, and Western Europe south of the Pyrenees, were excluded from coverage largely because the area and linguistic interests and expertise of our members did not extend to these countries. We can only hope that colleagues may profit from our experience to undertake somewhat similar studies comparing welfare state development in areas like Eastern Europe, Iberia, and Latin America.

Numerous institutions made available support that was indispensable for our efforts. Thus the HIWED Project was generously financed by the Volkswagen Foundation, and was provided extensive facilities by the Universities of Mannheim and Cologne during the period 1974-79. Alber, Kohl, and Kraus are other contributors who collaborated in the HIWED Project. The large task of establishing comparability between available European national statistics for the policy areas covered in this book, as well as several others, has led to the publication of numerous reports and a comprehensive handbook.

The activities of the Social Policy Group were supported in the period 1975-78 by the German Marshall Fund through the Council for European Studies. Theodore Marmor was cochairman of the group with Heidenheimer, while Heclo, Kudrle, and Wilensky were other group members who are contributors to the present volume. Richard Rose was another charter member of the group, who took the lead in organizing some of its other activities.

It will be evident that the other contributors did not seek to subscribe to a common conceptual framework and data base in the way that the HIWED authors have. Their research styles and methodologies vary more, both as among the Social Policy Group members and as between the articles of Hartmut Kaelble and Stein Kuhnle, who joined in our enterprise. Ours was of course very much a cross-disciplinary effort, with a historian and several economists relating their work to those of political scientists and sociologists. Among other colleagues, we would like to acknowledge especially the helpful criticisms of Alfred Diamant, Dietrich Gerhard, Werner Hochwald, and Peter Sturm on various draft chapters.

The editors have wrestled mightily with the contributors, as well as with each other, in the attempt to render the chapters more comprehensible and readable. We were very lucky to be assisted in this endeavor by Michele Prichard, a superb editing coach. Her careful paring and punctilious editing has improved many of our chapters. Part Five also benefitted from the editing suggestions of Carol Leff, while Richard Eichenberg provided invaluable advice at the Cologne end. Our project editor, Kerry Kern, provided patient and continuous care toward the production of a volume that would be in consonance with its title. Emma Danoski extended invaluable help in proofreading as well as preparation of the tables.

Peter Flora   Arnold J. Heidenheimer
European University Institute   Washington University
Florence   St. Louis

Introduction

Peter Flora and Arnold J. Heidenheimer

Welfare and *state* are among the most ambiguously employed terms in contemporary English political vocabulary. In the latter 1970s, the welfare state concept has been enmeshed in embattled slogans that have raised the level of public anxiety, even as it has also been utilized in the more dispassionate analyses of social scientists.

The dimensions of the contemporary discussion can well be described as being focused on the growth and crisis of the variety of publicly financed programs that have come to be placed under the welfare state rubric. Even if one controls for opinion cycles, it is evident that symbols fused and generated in one sociocultural setting have taken on differing connotations as they have been diffused around the world.

Scholars who seek to deflect energies from heat to light in this setting can attempt to grapple with the following kinds of questions. Is there really a crisis? If so, what is its character and extent? Is the crisis a product of program growth and can scaling it down put an end to it? Or is it rather a crisis within growth? Can we even identify the presence of some of the crisis-producing elements at the very origins of welfare state growth?

It is clearly true that, when measured in terms of the relevant public expenditures, the growth of welfare states in the past quarter century has been unprecedented in Western history. In the mid-1970s the nations of Western Europe were on the average allocating almost 25 percent of their national resources to public social expenditures. In North America the ratio has also surpassed the 20 percent level.

It is not only that resources allocated are vast by any measure, but that the functions they perform have become indispensable in the attempts to maintain stability in Western economies. As welfare state programs have had an increasing impact on the month-by-month lives of major parts of the population, they have assumed more visible and more direct significance for the operation of political systems. The consequences of these processes have propelled the complex labeled "the welfare state" away from the role of an auxiliary mechanism and moved it into the institutional core of Western societies. There it has augmented, usurped, and made consonant with modernity many functions previously performed by the family, the church, the guild, and the local community.

In many of the continental countries examined here this process has been proceeding intermittently for a longer time. Bismarck's measures made much less of a "splash" with German public opinion than did Lloyd George and Beveridge later in England; in fact, he scarcely mentions "his" social reforms in his memoirs. To place issues near the top of the public discussion agenda requires visible policies, articulate intellectuals and sensitized publics.

Particularly in the "stagflation" setting of the late 1970s, there are few significant social groups who are not highly sensitized to issues that experts and intellectuals link to the crisis of the welfare state. But, of course, the diagnoses of the commentators differ significantly as to the nature and severity of the problems, their historical origins, structural roots, and causal relationships.

Typical social scientific interpretations have focused on the interrelationships between the slackening economic growth levels of the 1970s, the higher levels of inflation and unemployment, and the fiscal problems engendered by rapidly expanding public sector spending. These have been elaborated either by postulating a process of increasing social costs exacted by the institutional structure of the modern capitalist economy, such as discussed by O'Connor, or by visualizing a "revolution of rising entitlements" engendered by an earlier "revolution of rising expectations," such as presented by Bell. Or, again, the welfare state is perceived as an organism whose crisis is due to its failure to generate political, social, and intellectual bases for transforming itself, as charged by Janowitz. In the concluding chapter of this book Hugh Heclo assesses some of these interpretations. He, too, diagnoses problems that make some redefinition of the democratic welfare state seem likely, but he questions the line of analysis that is couched in terms of "democratic excesses" and "overloaded governments."

If most of the other contributors to this volume refrain from joining the discussion at this level of generality, it is only because we have differentiated our labors. Our more detailed research has caused us to be more conscious of the limits of our knowledge. Aware though we are of general issues, we feel that our individual efforts can best be focused by matching theories with empirical data in delimited areas. In joining together in this endeavor, we have followed these precepts about the characteristics that make sound scholarship feasible even in the context of embattled slogans:

1. It is apparent that any significant analyses of Western welfare states and their "crises" must link knowledge of both broad developmental trends and important program details shaped by economic systems, political institutions, and social structures. An attempt to cope with the challenge of assessing the achievements and shortfalls of welfare states thus necessitates interdisciplinary collaboration.

2. We attempt to analyze welfare states in developmental terms, but even if we did not, such concepts as "stages," "recurrence" and "trend" require careful calibrations over several time periods. Thus, the question of whether the situation of the 1970s represents a threshold or a different stage for the welfare state requires historical analysis.

3. Complementary to this is the comparative analysis, based on the experiences of 15 nations on two continents, which all of us have pursued in varying degrees. Comparison engenders appreciation of contextual interrelationships. The assessment of uniformities and differences in national programs is also a prerequisite for testing and developing causal explanations. Finally, comparative analysis can help surmount the ideological fixations developed in particular places and times.

In this sense, then, our volume seeks to contribute to an interdisciplinary, comparative, and historical study of Western welfare states. It attempts to link their historical dynamics and contemporary problems in an international perspective. Building mainly on collaboration already developed within two established research groups, we have elicited and coordinated contributions by economists, political scientists, sociologists, and historians. The developments they analyze cover a period from the initiation of significant national social policy at the end of the nineteenth century to the present. The experiences of all the presently existing West European systems except Greece, Spain and Portugal are systematically encompassed in many of the articles, with comparisons made selectively to the experiences of the United States and Canada. The development of the social security systems and public expenditures, of public education and educational opportunities, and of income inequality are described, compared, and analyzed for varying groupings of the Western European and North American countries.

We believe that the possible merit of the volume lies mainly in its comparative and historical dimensions and in the attempts to pursue analysis in a systematic empirical fashion. Much of the welfare state literature contrasts particular policies with quantitative indicators regarding expenditure and coverage that are not checked and adjusted for comparability across countries and time. Much of it focuses disproportionately on phases of policy initiation or controversy without carefully assessing data pertaining to program development and adaptation. Much of it discusses crucial variables in a more impressionistic manner than is necessary or useful. We hope that readers and reviewers will find that our interpretations are usually more broadly validated.

This volume, therefore, addresses itself to two audiences with slightly different interests. The first and most obvious group includes all students of policy problems of the welfare states who seek to gain a more comparative perspective and historical understanding. However, there is also a second group who may be more interested in the theory and empirical analysis of long-term societal developments concerning the question of how our societies have become what they are today. In this context, the growth of the welfare states emerges as a major development along with the development of national states and capitalist economies, of industrial societies and mass democracies. We interpret the welfare state as a general phenomenon of modernization—as a product of the increasing differentiation and the growing size of societies on the one hand and of processes of social and political mobilization on the other. It is an important element in the structural convergence of modern societies and at the same time a source of divergence from variations within its institutional structure. Thus, the welfare state must be assessed in any study of growth and change of our societies.

The Structure and Contents of the Volume

What is the essence of the welfare state? This introductory question is answered in Part One. There it is argued that the concept of the welfare state cannot be defined by relating its meaning too closely to the specific reform-minded spirit of Britain in the 1940s, which was characterized by an unusual situation of war and austerity creating a high degree of solidarity among its citizens. Nor should the concept be defined, without regard to historical context, by a mere designation of policy boundaries and their underlying principles. Rather, the concept is defined by interpreting the welfare state as an answer to basic and long-term developmental processes and the problems created by them. From the perspective of a theory of political development, it is interpreted as an answer to increasing demands for socioeconomic equality in the context of the evolution of mass democracies. The theory of modernization or structural differentiation, on the other hand, leads us to understand the welfare state as an answer to the growing needs and demands for socioeconomic security in the context of an increasing division of labor, the expansion of markets, and the loss of "security functions" by families and other communities. In this sense, the basic goals and legitimizing principles of socioeconomic security and equality are interpreted as the core of the welfare state.

But the welfare state does not distribute benefits only as compensatory measures for those who have less. It also interacts with the labor market so as to make it possible for those who utilize public programs to raise or maintain their social status. Meritocratic criteria are employed to select these and other beneficiaries of educational opportunities, but this consideration should not cause one to separate the educational system from the other components of the welfare state. Rather we can perceive national programs constituting trade-offs between benefits presented usually as a means for the realization of individual opportunities, as in advanced education, or benefits made available through categorical entitlements, as in family allowances. Welfare states can further be classified by the ways in which they relate their educational systems to other social programs through established requirements for work positions and other entitlement instruments that differentiate candidates for more or less desirable positions in labor markets, as well as to provide varying benefits.

In accord with this understanding of the essence of the welfare state, Parts Three, Four, and Five of this volume are entitled Social Security, Economic Equality, and Educational Opportunities. Parts Two and Six explicitly refer to the two major objectives of the book: to study the historical dynamics of the welfare states and to link it to an analysis of their current problems. Accordingly, Part Two is entitled How and Why Welfare States Grew and Part Six, An End to Growth?

The two chapters of Part Two try to present a broad picture of the historical development of the Western welfare states and to investigate the underlying forces that may explain uniformities as well as differences. They make it possible for the reader to compare the development of welfare states in Europe and North America without losing sight of the important variations within both areas. Security and equality are defined in Part One as two basic values underlying the evolution of the welfare states and relating to two long-term developments of the Western societies: structural differentiation and democratic political development. Pursuing this analysis, Peter Flora and Jens Alber in Chapter 2 start with the explication of a theoretical framework composed of a more general theory of modernization, on the one hand, and Stein Rokkan's more specific model of European political developments, on the other. The chapter then proceeds to a broad comparison of the development of the Western European welfare states and tries to specify differences between countries as well as to relate these to a higher level of generality. The description, in quantitative and qualitative terms, focuses on the social security systems. In the final part, the attempt is made to explain differences in the establishment of these systems by comparing socioeconomic processes, such as industrialization and urbanization, and variations in the development of mass democracies and by investigating the possibility of "internal dynamics" and "diffusion processes."

In Chapter 3 entitled "The Development of Welfare States in North America," Robert T. Kudrle and Theodore R. Marmor attempt to identify both the different characteristics of Canada and the United States as well as the common features setting them apart from the Western European systems. They confirm the view that Canada and the United States lag behind Europe even when private and subnational programs are included in the analysis, but, nevertheless, they come up with some interesting exceptions. They present a detailed comparison of the development of old age security, unemployment insurance, other income maintenance schemes, family allowances, and health care in both countries. In an attempt to explain the differences between them, they analyze the meaning of federalism and of "crisis" in relation to the development of social policy in both societies, as well as to the differences in the ideological traditions and the structures of trade unions and party systems. Finally, the question of whether the factors explaining past differences between the U.S. and Canada and between North America and Europe will produce different answers to the common problems of the 1970s is examined particularly with respect to income maintenance and health care.

In describing and analyzing the general evolution of welfare states in the Western world, the two chapters of Part Two lean heavily on the examination of the development of social security. Because of the importance of social security in welfare states, the two chapters of Part Three study it closely, on the one hand, by limiting the number of countries and the time span covered to Scandinavia between 1880 and 1910 and, on the other hand, by concentrating on one social security system, unemployment protection. The difference in focus may give the reader an idea of the possibilities and limitations of different but complementary approaches.

In Chapter 4, Stein Kuhnle focuses on the early phase in the creation of the modern welfare state. He compares the responses of Denmark, Finland, Norway, and Sweden to the issue of the role of the state in the protection and the development of social rights of citizens, originating from—or at least strengthened by—Bismarck's large-scale social insurance schemes in the 1880s. Investigating parliamentary discussions and legislative activities, he first examines whether the creation of social insurance systems in the four Nordic countries could be interpreted as a process of diffusion, a process emphasized in several studies in comparative social policy. He then examines the differences in the development of social insurance systems until about 1910 by relating them to differences in the "macrosetting" of the four countries that defined the constraints within which legislators and administrators had to act. He considers, also, the questions of whether relatively high levels of political and socioeconomic mobilization led to an earlier introduction of social insurance programs and whether a stronger liberal ideology and/or the existence of relatively extensive private insurance organizations strengthened the principle of voluntary insurance.

In Chapter 5, Jens Alber deals with only one social security system, but he includes all Western European countries and covers the whole time span from the beginnings of modern national unemployment insurance systems until today. The innovative aspect of his study lies above all in the detailed analysis of the various legislative provisions found in the introductory and contemporary laws on unemployment insurance. Using this standardized information, he studies the change and the interrelations among the complex characteristics of the insurance systems, their generosity and control, the participation of the state and its redistributive or non-redistributive character. The variations of the unemployment insurance systems among countries and over time are then explained by three major factors: the impact of the past in terms of starting levels and age of systems, the pressure of unemployment problems, and the influence of different party governments.

The question of whether, and to what extent, welfare state development has contributed to an equalization of incomes, the topic of Part Four, has been the subject of especially intensive debate. Studies addressing themselves to this problem therefore need to devise and employ carefully established measures and criteria, a standard which the contributor to this section has tried hard to meet. In Chapter 6, Franz Kraus compares the potential and present state of knowledge about the changes in income inequality in Western Europe. He evaluates the main official statistical sources, assesses their coverage and reliability, and shows that comparative studies covering periods before World War II are limited to the upper income strata and are confined to pretax incomes.

Kraus attempts to improve and enlarge Kuznets' data collection, and identifies a long-term decline in the share of the richest decile since the turn of the century, which is most pronounced immediately after the two world wars. The decline in overall inequality, which can be traced only for the post-1945 period, seems to have levelled off during the mid-1960s in most European countries, and in a few cases the trend has even been reversed. The equalizing effects resulting from increasing shares for the lower deciles have been counterbalanced by a steadily increasing share of the upper middle class. Subsequently, the most important statistical analyses are critically reviewed and compared. The most important cross-sectional studies suggest that the process of democratization and the growth of state activity are key determinants of changes in income inequality. In the few longitudinal studies, however, the management of aggregate demand and changes in the structure of the labor force are the major explanatory factors.

In Part Five, a historian and a political scientist apply their skills to the problem of how the development of educational opportunity can most fruitfully be related to the growth of welfare states as a whole. Public education institutions, like taxation systems, are much older than the welfare state. But certain new departures, like the implementation of progressive income taxes and the establishment of mass postprimary education, occur in conjunction with its development. As broadened political opportunities extended effective citizenship, access to educational institutions came to be seen less as a privilege and more as a right. But recognition on the basis of credentials, the securing of which was often class-conditioned, differs greatly—especially between America and Europe, but also among the European countries.

In Chapter 7, "Educational Opportunities and Government Policies in Europe in the Period of Industrialization," Hartmut Kaelble examines how access to secondary and higher education was controlled and altered in three large European nations in the period up to 1914. He seeks to ascertain whether the education systems of Britain, France, and Germany significantly modified the prevailing socially elitist selection criteria during the period that marked the advent of welfare state institutions. To this end he compares data pertaining to education opportunities in secondary and higher education, examines the social origins of both kinds of students in the three countries, and develops measurements of the social distribution of opportunities for the six decades of rapid industrialization prior to 1914. He finds that during the latter part of the period there was a gradual reversal of the preceding trend toward growing inequality in the social distribution of opportunities, and examines four determinants that produced rather similar outcomes in the three countries. He attributes some indirect effect to government policies, which enhanced demand for university graduates through their social and health programs. However, the rate of change was modest, and he finds that governmental policies were aimed primarily at adapting educational institutions to the requirements of industrializing societies, and were not yet concerned with reducing inequalities in educational opportunities.

Arnold J. Heidenheimer, in Chapter 8, "Education and Social Security Entitlements in Europe and America," expands both the time and policy area frames by examining how access and entitlements to social security benefits and education services came to be so differently extended on the two continents. Focusing on Germany and the United States, he explains policy divergence at the start of the welfare state era in terms of the dominance of bureaucratic and pluralist traditions. The former inhibited educational expansion in Germany, so that most credentials were less accessible than in the American setting, which stressed a widening of educational opportunity. The European strategy emphasized economic security at the end of the life cycle mainly because there citizenship, as manifested in take up of education entitlements, operated as a stronger instrument of social stratification. In Germany most social security benefits were also more class-stratified than were the later American programs. From the 1930s, the author identifies a gradual pattern of convergence that builds up to more similar patterns of social security and education entitlements for Germans and Americans by the 1970s. American social welfare benefits become more uniform and less discretionary, German education opportunities more abundant. In his concluding section, Heidenheimer compares American and German social security and education entitlement growth with data pertaining to Britain and Sweden, and presents policy profiles that illustrate how entitlements were extended in the century since the 1880s.

In the concluding Part Six of the book entitled "An End to Growth?", an economist, a sociologist, and a political scientist address themselves directly to the contemporary problems and crises of the welfare state. They analyze interrelationships central to resolving many of the recent political and academic disputes. What is the relationship between the growth of welfare expenditures and increasing deficits? To what extent is expansion of the public sector linked to the control of governments by particular kinds of parties or to the nature of party competition. How convincing are the arguments that public sector expansion has limited economic growth? All three authors draw on conventional data bases, but analyze them in fairly novel ways. In order to help establish to what extent the experiences of the 1970s are unique, they carefully examine trends and convergences in previous eras, especially those of the post-World War II period.

The question of how voter demands are catered to by governments composed of parties with different social and ideological bases is analyzed in Chapter 10 by Harold L. Wilensky, who here builds on earlier studies that have helped structure the field of inquiry. He does not simply match party control of governments with expenditure growth, but introduces two variables—the interest group structure associated with the "democratic corporatism" model and classification of taxation modes—that have come to loom larger in recent social scientific discussion. Controlling for these factors, he finds that when one compares the records of Catholic and left government parties, it is the former that are linked more closely to expenditure growth. Few are aware that the Netherlands has in recent years overtaken Sweden as the biggest European spender, but those who are can find an explanation in Wilensky's analysis. He also shows that left party governments spent more if subjected to intense Catholic competition, but where left parties were more continuously in power they tended to "slow the adoption of new programs or the rapid expansion of the old, while simultaneously keeping high hopes in check."

The author of the concluding Chapter 11, Hugh Heclo, seeks to pull together many of the broader themes and questions that have been addressed in more limited contexts in preceding sections. Does the current situation, seen in the light of historical developments as well as today's debate about policy, represent a threshold and different stage for the welfare state? Or is it one of the recurrent phases in a basically continuous line of development? To help answer these questions, Heclo assesses the current situation in the light of several common stages through which most Western welfare states appear to have passed during the last century. He argues that while a redefinition of the democratic welfare state is likely, the result will probably bear little relationship to the currently fashionable emphasis on "democratic excesses" and "overloaded governments." Rather, he predicts that Western nations are entering a new period of experimentation in which many of the traditional aims of the welfare state will be pursued by novel means. During the coming decades we may well experience a situation mirroring that prevalent in the late nineteenth century. He foresees a situation in which defenders of the status quo will be aligned behind an activist social policy, while the advocates of radical change will demand dismantled programs and limited government.

Part One

What Is the Welfare State?

Chapter 1

The Historical Core and Changing Boundaries of the Welfare State

Peter Flora and Arnold J. Heidenheimer

I. British Experience and the History of the Concept

The question of the nature of the welfare state can be related to the process of its "discovery" and labelling. In one way it is strange that, according to the chronology which has now become conventional, the welfare state should have been growing for several generations before it was recognized and labelled by this name. But from a broader perspective on the historical introduction of new political concepts it is not so strange. Even an entity with seemingly clear-cut delineations, like the British Empire, took several centuries to become recognized and labelled for what mapmakers then informed all school children it had come to be.

The German Empire, by contrast, appeared on maps rather suddenly in 1871, largely as the culmination of several successful European wars. In 1878 it initiated a governmental campaign to destroy the growing social democratic movement, and then the emperor, in his Social Message of 1881, laid the basis for the subsequent innovative social security legislation. Reviewing this accomplishment in a 1915 volume celebrating the five hundredth anniversary of the establishment of the Hohenzollern rule in Brandenburg-Prussia, Otto Hintze admitted that it had not succeeded in shifting working class loyalties, as Bismarck and Emperor William had hoped. Still, he concluded, "it provides the government with a good conscience, and enables it to take a strong and decisive position vis-à-vis the lower classes and their demands, as is befitting the traditions of the Hohenzollern state."[1]

It would have been very dissonant with those traditions if the Prussians had referred to their creation as a "Wohlfahrtstaat." The terminology they employed was strictly bureaucratic and by implication reserved to the emperor the power of setting larger national and societal goals. Thus, the German Interior Ministry mounted an exhibition at the 1904 St. Louis World's Fair under the title, "The German Worker Insurance as a Social Instrumentality." When conservatives depreciated it as a "social-political carnival," German officials pointed out that their pioneering effort had won not only worldwide attention, but also widespread imitation. They claimed that "imitation would doubtless have been even more widespread had not initiatives in various states been retarded by prevailing social political ideas—and, as in Switzerland, France and England, by far-reaching concessions to the attitudes of the voting masses. What this illustrates are the advantages of the monarchical government in Germany, which provides the strength for the resolute implementation of necessary social reforms despite the opposing powers of political shortsightedness, heartless insensitivity, sluggish routine or economic recklessness."[2]

Empirical analyses pertaining to the diffusion or imitation of the German model will be presented below, particularly in Chapters 2 and 4. Our concern here, however, is to identify divergences and convergences between the growth of social security institutions and their recognition in political vocabulary and symbolism. For this purpose we will contrast developments in Germany—the institutional innovator—with those in Britain, the country from which the term welfare state came to be diffused around the world in the 1940s. One can see how overseas recipients who did import terms like "kindergarten" might boggle at adopting Wilhelmine concepts like "social monarchy" or other terms that draped citizen entitlements with hierarchical condescension. But why was the term, which has come to be generalized, coined in Britain, and why in the 1940s?

A good scout to follow in this quest is Winston Churchill, who in 1906 entered the Liberal cabinet to help prepare the initial British social insurance laws. In those years he was telling the voters that, "In Germany they have a very much wider national system of safeguards, of bulwarks against accidents and against all the dangers and all the chances of those who are engaged in industry. . . ." We find Churchill the wordsmith avoiding bureaucratic terminology, and attempting to coin political phrases which will catch on. One term that recurs is that of the need for "averaging machinery"; another is that of "the left out millions" who are "miserable," even as the fortunate in Britain are "more happy than any other equally numerous class have been in the whole history of the world." Assisted by experts like William Beveridge, Churchill and Lloyd George prepared the

Liberal government's National Insurance Act. By the time of its passage in 1911, Churchill was talking of "bringing in the magic of averages to the aid of the millions."[3]

It was to be another thirty years until the insurance metaphors were replaced by the "welfare state" metaphor. Again the stimulus came from Germany, but this time the causal chain followed a more complex dialectic. The Germans had pioneered again in 1919 by anchoring social rights in the Weimar Constitution. But their experiences in the 1920s did not invite replication elsewhere. In 1930 deep divisions over the magnitude of unemployment and other benefits led directly to the fall of the last democratic government based on a parliamentary majority. In Britain the unions also failed to prevent cutbacks in unemployment insurance. But then they helped depose Ramsay MacDonald and salvaged the Labour party, whereas the German unions sought to avoid repression by adopting a lower political profile. They were unable to counterattack when Chancellor von Papen prepared the ideological transition to fascism by sharply attacking the Weimar Republic "Wohlfahrtstaat" in June 1932.[4] He accused his predecessors of inducing the "moral exhaustion" of the German people by "creating a kind of welfare state" that burdened the state with tasks which were beyond its capability.[5] When they took power the next year, the Nazis cleaned out the union-supported sickness funds even before they dissolved the unions themselves. Then they reduced unemployment problems by initiating an armaments drive.

Public usage of the "welfare state" term in Britain began in 1941, during a period when Britain was holding out virtually alone against threats from the German war machine. While Churchill was heading the wartime coalition government, a clergyman, Archbishop Temple, coined the phrase in an attempt to characterize a polar contrast to the "power" and "warfare" state of the Nazis.[6] Thus launched to sustain morale and discipline during a period of wartime crisis, the term subsequently came to be more closely associated with the social benefits that democratic governments hoped to offer once the war was over. It was after the publication of the Beveridge Report in 1942 that the term became increasingly linked to the kinds of definitions employed in this book. This linkage was to the liking of neither Churchill nor Beveridge, who had gone different ways since their collaboration in the period from 1908 to 1911.

World War II reinforced these differences, "for it confirmed Churchill in his fundamental commitment to traditional values, whereas it induced in Beveridge an almost extra-sensory consciousness of revolutionary change." Accepting advice to give his report a Messianic tone, Beveridge aimed his proposals at promoting solidarity and "bringing institutions and individuals into partnership with the state, in a common condemnation of 'the scandal of physical want.' " In lecture tours he promoted his plan as a

practical embodiment of the Atlantic Charter's guarantees of freedom
from want, but Churchill and other ministers refused to commit themselves
to its implementation. Later, as a Liberal member of the House of Lords,
Beveridge was embarrassed by his reputation as "chief architect of the
welfare state in the English-speaking world." He disliked the phrase and
never used it because of what he called its "Santa Claus" and "brave new
world" connotations, preferring the term "social service state."[7]

Britain in the 1940s and 1950s was exceptional in the history of European
welfare state development in that intellectual conceptions formulated primarily by academic social scientists had an important impact on the development of social policy institutions. Especially important were the contributions of T. H. Marshall and Richard Titmuss, both affiliated with the
London School of Economics and Political Science, of which Beveridge
had been director in the interwar period. In his famous lecture on "Citizenship and Social Class," Marshall argued that political development in
Britain had induced the realization of increments of citizenship rights, with
civil rights becoming universalized in the eighteenth century, political
rights in the nineteenth, and social rights in the twentieth.[8]

Marshall also elucidated why the convergence between institutional
development and conceptual change occurred in that particular decade. He
argued that in certain periods in the history of a society an exceptionally
strong consensus may develop with regard to "key points" of the social
system—a consensus favoring the growth of collective self-awareness. For
Marshall, the 1940s in Britain were such a period, and the term "welfare
state" took shape also as the antithesis to the old poor law situations in
which "welfare" recipients, the paupers, lost their personal freedom and
their right to vote because social dependency implied the sacrifice of
citizenship rights.

For Marshall, the growth of the new consensus was explained by the
coincidence of repudiation of a discredited past, with a specific historical
constellation containing two interrelated elements. Firstly, the war created
a national solidarity that formed the foundation for new institutions—and
at the same time was strengthened by it. Secondly, the social reforms were
carried out in a time of economic austerity, when public regulation of
consumption and control of markets was commonplace and when society
felt committed to "fair shares" in redistributing real income. "It [the welfare
state] was born at a time when the sense of national solidarity created by the
war coincided with the enforced restraints on consumption and the régime
of sharing imposed by post-war scarcity. . . . the Welfare State reigned
unchallenged while linked with the Austerity Society and was attacked
from all sides as soon as it became associated with the Affluent Society."[9]

Janowitz acknowledges that British social historians "have produced a
richer and more interpretative analysis of the expansion of the welfare state

than have American specialists."[10] Indeed, the detailed and sensitive studies produced by British writers about their own society may be unmatched in quality in other European countries as well. But many readers familiar with this rich literature can agree with an Indian critic who has noted that

> English analyses, in spite of their descriptive richness, are in a curious sense, "culture-bound." In emphasizing the unique British historical development in the matrix of which the British welfare state was born, they help us little in understanding developments in the direction of welfare states elsewhere. Most of the definitions of the welfare state are heavily overlaid with facts and circumstances peculiar to British historical development.[11]

Indeed, it would appear that the conceptual and ideological problems encountered by this generation of British social historians and analysts in critically probing their own society may have limited the energy they devoted to comparative studies. The fruits of such efforts are a small number of incisive essays, several of them devoted to particular subaspects of welfare state development.[12] Representative of the way in which the British scholars circumscribed their efforts may be the fact that Richard Titmuss' only large-scale attempt at cross-national institutional analysis was his brilliant study of the operation and financing of blood banks.[13]

The assumptions and methodologies of contributors to this volume are in contrast with some of the tentative conclusions articulated on the basis of this British corpus of analysis. Thus we deviate from Marshall's Britain-centered conceptualization when he wrote that "perhaps we should conclude that France and Germany pressed on into the Affluent Society without ever pausing to establish a Welfare State."[14] Also we lay the basis for questioning assertions, like that by Janowitz, that "British experience can be taken as the prototype of welfare institutions under parliamentary governance."[15]

Experiences since Marshall wrote have reinforced the impression that intensive study of the British case is not the optimal way of starting to grasp the general characteristics of welfare state development. With regard to many important determinants, the British experience is unrepresentative of Western Europe as a whole. The labor relations and management traditions shaped in the course of its longer antecedent industrialization experience have proved more resistant to change. The tempo with which social security measures were extended between 1909 and 1946 was quicker than in countries like Germany and Sweden, as is shown in Chapter 2. The manner in which social welfare legislation was linked to the rhetoric of a period of wartime crisis was more dramatic and direct than elsewhere. Its ability to restabilize its international political and economic position in the post-1945 period has been more problematic than in the case of any other larger or post-imperial nation. Its economic growth rate has been lowest in

Europe. These considerations make it more understandable that the welfare state should have become more vulnerable to attack in Britain than in most other countries.

For those who seek to predict the future, as for those who want to understand better the past, this volume seeks to distill some answers from the century that has elapsed since the German emperor delivered his social message in 1881. But to encompass the broad analyses required by such a task makes it necessary to incorporate the experiences of individual nations—be it Germany the innovator, or Britain the adapter and propagator—into the larger body of experience.

II. The Welfare State as an Answer to Developmental Problems

We can try to define the core of the welfare state and to delineate its changing boundaries by seeing it as a more or less conscious or reactive response to long-term processes and basic development problems. But what were these developments and problems? To this fundamental question of classical macrosociology we of course find different answers in the works of de Tocqueville or Weber, Marx or Durkheim. But they would agree that, in the context of European history, the growth of the modern welfare state can be understood as a response to two fundamental developments: the formation of national states and their transformation into mass democracies after the French Revolution, and the growth of capitalism that became the dominant mode of production after the Industrial Revolution.

The prehistory of the modern welfare state, the "Poor Law Period,"[16] was closely related to the early state building efforts of fifteenth- and sixteenth-century Europe. The later consolidation of the absolutist state was accompanied by a gradual, though by no means continuous, "nationalization," differentiation, and extension of welfare institutions. National differences within Europe in the creation of absolutist states with strong bureaucracies and paternalistic traditions may explain the earlier or later beginnings of the welfare states (for example, Germany versus Great Britain or Sweden versus Switzerland).

The real beginning of the modern welfare state, however, had to await the transformation of the absolutist state into mass democracy in the last third of the nineteenth century, after a variable intermediary period of liberal democracy with restricted suffrage. In thus linking welfare state development with the evolution of mass democracy, one may interpret the welfare state as an answer to increasing demands for socioeconomic equality or as the institutionalization of social rights relative to the development of civil and political rights.[17]

But the welfare state is far more than the mere product of mass democracy. It implies a basic transformation of the state itself, of its structure, functions, and legitimacy. In a Weberian tradition, the growth of the welfare state may be understood as the gradual emergence of a new system of domination consisting of "distributing elites," "service bureaucracies," and "social clienteles."[18] With the structural transformation of the state, the basis of its legitimacy and its functions also change. The objectives of external strength or security, internal economic freedom, and equality before the law are increasingly replaced by a new raison d'être: the provision of secure social services and transfer payments in a standard and routinized way that is not restricted to emergency assistance.

At this point, however, the welfare state is no longer primarily interpreted as a response to the demand for socioeconomic equality, but to the demand for socioeconomic security. We turn from the evolution of mass democracy and the transformation of the nation state to the second fundamental development in modern European history: the growth of capitalism. In the Marxist tradition, the welfare state is seen as an attempt to deal with specific problems of capitalist development, class conflict and recurring economic crises: welfare measures represent an effort to integrate the working classes without fundamental challenge to the institution and distribution of private property. As with the early state building efforts, the prehistory of the welfare state is also tied to the emergence of capitalism in sixteenth-century Europe—to a growing labor market, agrarian capitalism, rural unemployment, and overpopulation. And as with the democratic transformation of the state, the creation of the modern welfare state did not precede the aggravation of business cycle effects and the intensification of organized class conflict in the last decades of the nineteenth century.

Both perspectives—that of political sociology in the tradition of de Tocqueville and Weber, and that of political economy in the tradition of Marx and others—do not necessarily contradict one another and may in fact be complementary. They are an expression of the historical constellation in which the European welfare state emerged, a constellation of growing mass democracies and expanding capitalist economies within a system of sovereign national states.

In Chapter 2, it will be shown, however, that the most democratic and capitalist of the European societies at that time were not the first to develop the institutions and policies of the modern welfare state. Furthermore, the fascist states after World War I did not completely change these institutions and even developed them to some extent. Finally, the experience of Russia after 1917[19] illustrates that nondemocratic and noncapitalist societies have established very similar institutions. Thus, the welfare state seems to be a far more general phenomenon of modernization, not exclusively tied to its "democratic-capitalist" version.

The generality of this phenomenon may be illuminated by some of

Durkheim's ideas and concepts. Using his perspective, the welfare state may be understood as an attempt to create a new kind of solidarity in highly differentiated societies and as an attempt to respond to problems in the division of labor, which for him is the basic process of structural change in modernizing societies. Division of labor weakens old associations and intermediary powers and thus increases the opportunities for individualization. Responding to the need to regulate the manifold new exchange processes, social life is centralized. These fundamental processes are reflected in the institutions of the welfare state; public bureaucracies take over many of the functions formerly filled by smaller social units, and their services and transfer payments tend to become more and more individualized.

In Durkheim's view, the integration of highly differentiated societies is threatened by two main problems: anomie and inequality. His famous concept of anomie refers to a lack of normative or moral regulation that manifests itself on two levels: social relationships and individual personalities.[20] He first applied this concept to the unregulated socioeconomic relationships produced by the growth of the capitalist market economy that resulted in recurring economic instability and increasing industrial conflict. He later extended it to define an imbalance between individual needs and wants and the means of satisfying them.

From a Durkheimian point of view, the contemporary welfare state represents' only a partial, and to some extent inadequate, answer to the problems of anomie. The democratic welfare states have met with only limited success in attempting to institutionalize industrial relations and conflicts and to stabilize markets. Although they have developed institutions of income maintenance and tried to secure the provision of specific services, they still respond primarily to material needs and have remained somewhat helpless in shaping and defining those needs themselves. Thus the welfare state would here represent an answer not to the more general problem of anomie in modern societies, but rather to the limited problem of economic insecurity. This limitation may explain some of the more recent problems of the welfare states in creating feelings of security and satisfaction.[21] The fact that economic security is usually called social security is perhaps a hint of this underlying difficulty.

For Durkheim, the answer to the problem of anomie was normative regulation. In order to create solidarity, however, such regulation had to be considered just, which for him meant equality of opportunity and just contract on the basis of an equality of exchange conditions. In the Western cultural tradition as a whole, however, the concept of equality is broader and has two different meanings that are at least partially contradictory.[22] The first is a major component of the socialist ethic, often called equality of result. It implies an equalization in the disposal of resources, commodities, and services, a redistribution according to needs. In interpreting the welfare state as a response to equality demands of this kind, one must distinguish between efforts to establish national minima (poor relief, minimum wage, national pensions, compulsory education, certain social services) and efforts at redistribution in a stricter sense (above all, progressive income taxation). This distinction has been of great historical importance and still has institutional consequences. The second meaning, a major component of liberal ethic, is equality of opportunity and is most relevant in the field of public education. The development of comprehensive secondary education would be an example of an attempt to realize this principle. In its emphasis on merit, however, equality of opportunity inherently legitimizes inequality, mainly in the form of income and status differences. This is most obvious in income-related social insurance programs and the higher levels of public education financed by general taxes.

Security and equality are here seen as the two fundamental dimensions of the welfare state. These dimensions may be shown graphically, in Figure 1.1. This schematic view, however, does not answer empirical questions about the relative importance of these two objectives or the degree to which they have been realized. Has the goal of security always been more important than the goal of equality? What were the different priorities among the Western nations and how have they changed over time? Furthermore, both objectives may interact to supplement as well as contradict one another. Thus, as soon as social security develops into a security of social status, it contributes to the stabilization of inequality. But in so doing, even such a stabilization modifies inequality in that the poorer parts of the population have usually been the most insecure.

There are three basic means by which the welfare state pursues its goals: the direct payment of cash benefits, the direct provision of services in kind, and the indirect extension of benefits through tax deductions and credits. The essential function of transfer payments, the first of these means, is income maintenance for typical phases of nonemployment in the life cycle (maternity, childhood/parenthood, education and training, old-age, widowhood), typical situations of employment incapacity (sickness, injuries, invalidity), and unemployment among the active labor force. These benefits may be financed either with earmarked taxes or general revenues. In addition, benefits in cash and kind such as public assistance may be given in less standardized situations of need that are not covered by differentiated income maintenance schemes. An analysis of transfer payments must also take into account family allowances and subsidies for specific goods and services ("vouchers").

The direct public provision of services in kind is the second basic instrument of the welfare state. In interpreting and evaluating this means, one has to see it in close connection with governmental intervention in

Figure 1.1
Dimensions of the Welfare State

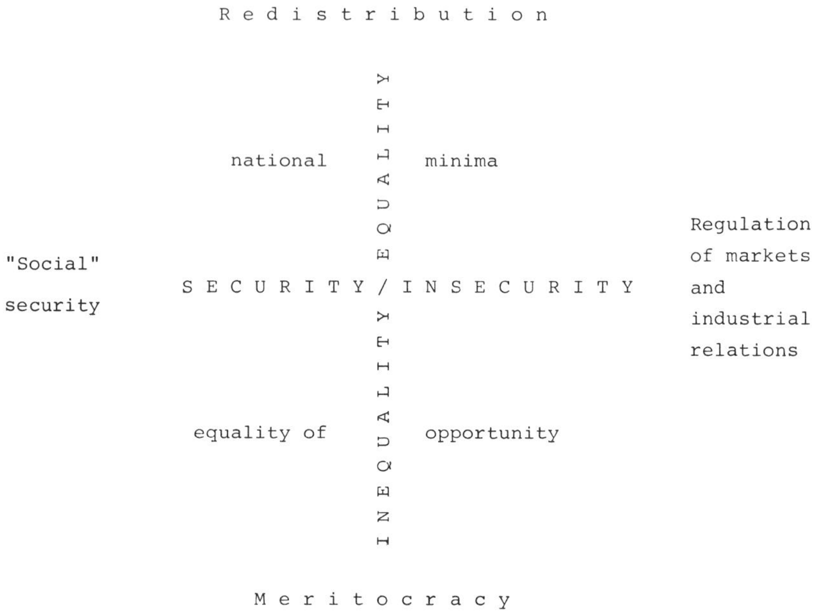

```
              R e d i s t r i b u t i o n


                          Y
                          T
                          I
        national          L     minima
                          A
                          U
                          Q                        Regulation
"Social"                  E                        of markets
                S E C U R I T Y / I N S E C U R I T Y    and
security                  Y                        industrial
                          T                        relations
                          I
                          L
                          A
        equality of       U     opportunity
                          Q
                          E
                          N
                          I


              M e r i t o c r a c y
```

private markets, like the housing market, and subsidization of market goods, like food supplies. Today, four such services predominate: education, medicine and medical care, social care and advisory services, and housing. Of course, the "social service basket" varies a good deal among the Western welfare states, and it has naturally changed in the process of political and economic development. The regulation of food supply was formerly an essential public function,[23] and in the future new services, such as recreational facilities, may be more important on a continuing basis.

Finally, tax credits, the third and often neglected method, may serve as a functional equivalent to direct benefits in cash or kind.[24] In a still broader perspective, the more indirect instruments of economic policy and protective legislation would have to be added to these three basic tools, insofar as they are concerned with security and equality.

The objectives and instruments discussed above provide the conceptual elements and coordinates for a definition of the welfare state. In themselves, however, they do not define the historical core of the welfare state or describe how its boundaries change in the process of development. It has become usual to identify the beginning of the modern welfare state with the innovation of social insurance. Should we therefore define the historical core of the modern welfare state by its attempt to "insure" the working classes against the danger of losing their income through industrial injuries, sickness, or old age?

Let us look at the case for doing so. In comparison with earlier poor relief, social insurance had several new traits:

- its main intention was not to help destitute people in cases of emergency, but to prevent destitution through routine measures;
- it was a differentiated institution aiming at the maintenance of earned income in specific situations;
- it focussed on the male laborer rather than on women and children, the main beneficiaries of previous poor relief;
- it usually compelled potential beneficiaries to contribute to its financing, thus strengthening their legal claim to benefits.

A major distinction of the social insurance mechanisms, however, lay in how the internal dynamics of its routine procedures differed from those of poor relief. By its very nature poor relief covered only a small part of the population, although it could be extended and become more widespread. Social insurance, on the other hand, is characterized by a double dynamic. One tendency has been to extend income maintenance schemes to additional contingencies, most obviously to unemployment. These extensions may also have contributed to generalizing demands for public income guarantees through other methods, such as price regulations for agricultural products.

Probably even more important, is that social insurance resembles suffrage to some extent. Once the right to vote is given to one population group, other groups will sooner or later also be enfranchised; usually, in the modern context, there is no way back other than to abolish elections altogether. The extension of social insurance is a similar process, though differing in two respects. Whereas the right to vote was extended from the top to the bottom of the social ladder, social insurance usually was broadened in the other direction. And whereas elections have been abolished in modern societies, social insurance institutions scarcely have.

But one can entertain reservations about regarding social insurance as the historical core of the welfare state. From the very beginning it was surrounded by other institutions and policies, both old and new. Some of these became more and more important and certainly have changed the boundaries of the welfare state; they may even have shifted its core. For example, the old institution of poor relief remained significant, even though it changed its nature and name. Protective legislation and factory inspection preceded social insurance in many countries, as did the freedom of association and the development of trade unionism and collective bargaining. Furthermore, the institution of other policies with related objectives fall into the same period as social insurance legislation: the introduction of income taxation for higher income levels; the extension of public primary education in some countries and reform of secondary education in others. National policies dealing with housing and employment usually did not develop before World War I, but communal efforts started much earlier.

III. Changing Welfare State Boundaries

The difficulty in defining the boundaries of the welfare state lies at least as much in how to formulate the question as it does in how to interpret measurements that would provide a tangible answer. Should the question be posed in terms of the goals of policies and programs, the reach of bureaucratic institutions, the magnitude of budgets or of the needs of social groups and their power to elicit governmental response to them?

This problem came to be faced in Germany in the 1920s, after the core institutions had been established and legitimated through the inclusion of social rights in the Weimar constitution. In 1929, shortly after the last of the four basic social insurance programs had been put into place, the economist Eduard Heimann addressed himself to the question of defining the boundaries of what he called social policy. He answered that there could be no such boundaries: "The diminution of capitalism which social policy brings about does not create a vacuum, but the creation of something new and different in those areas which are extricated from the sphere of pure capitalism. But everywhere these structures attach themselves to the remaining capitalist institutions. . . . In general, the boundaries of social policy can only be related to the existing boundaries of social power, but this sentence is itself tautological if one refers not to the institutions as such, but to the social forces that operate through them."[25]

Up to 1914, and to a large extent through the interwar period, the social forces most relevant to welfare state development were those of the working class. But in the post-1945 period the benefits of both social insurance and social services were extended on a massive scale to increasing proportions of the middle classes. This was done either by universalizing income transfer programs and public services or by adding middle-class beneficiaries in incremental steps. The main instruments for this expansion were mass political parties, and Wilensky demonstrates in Chapter 10 that European Catholic parties competed very effectively with Social Democratic ones in "blanketing" these strata into the security guarantees of public programs.

The social insurance mechanisms that buttressed the security goals of the working class had by the 1950s become institutionalized, with the support of unions, so as to constitute a sphere distinguishable from the core capitalistic institutions. But the inclusion of middle class beneficiaries again complicated the boundary questions, especially as regards the relationship between public and private programs. The affluent middle classes already possessed extensive security supports, and their organizations were frequently sharply divided over how the private and public programs should complement each other. Where middle class providers and client organizations were relatively stronger, as in the United States, the share of many education, health, and income maintenance guarantees supplied through private organizations remained larger. This complicates the boundary questions because functionally similar structures may be classified as belonging, or not belonging, to the welfare state complex, depending on the degree of public control, which is usually clear-cut, but sometimes a matter of degree.

In 1961, after the middle classes in Britain and elsewhere had become beneficiaries of many welfare state guarantees, Asa Briggs ventured a definition of what a welfare state is:

> A "Welfare State" is a state in which organised power is deliberately used (through politics and administration) in an effort to modify the play of market forces in at least three directions—first, by guaranteeing individuals and families a minimum income irrespective of the market value of their property; second by narrowing the extent of insecurity by enabling individuals and families to meet certain "social contingencies" (for example, sickness, old age and unemployment) which lead otherwise to individual and family crises; and third by ensuring that all citizens without distinction of status or class are offered the best standards available in relation to a certain agreed range of social services.[26]

This definition can be used to delineate more clearly the question of welfare state boundaries.

The attempt to circumscribe more precisely the kind of governmental activities encompassed by the welfare state has provoked two kinds of border disputes, one related to definitions of minima, the other related to range of services. The disputes over minima flared up as the consequence of the redefinitions of poverty that were articulated in all countries during the late 1960s and early 1970s. Critics applied concepts like relative deprivation to identify demands for equalization of resources for much larger population groups than those who had up to then benefited from the implementation of national minima, as established in the Beveridge and similar plans.

This led proponents of the older, more limited definitions of poverty and welfare state goals to expostulate heatedly that

> the new formulation appears to be that everyone who is not able to enjoy middle-class standards is assumed to be living in poverty and must be rescued from his state of relative deprivation. . . . The new definition makes inequality

the cause of poverty, and those who would cure it must inevitably advocate the socialist doctrines of egalitarianism. The national minimum concept has been a cornerstone of welfare state policy and the welfare state can scarcely accept so fundamental a change in aim in order to overcome the handicaps of "the new poor," who by previous standards would in many cases not be living in poverty.[27]

The boundary issue relating to what range of public services are to be encompassed within the welfare state has been addressed most directly by Harold L. Wilensky. He has held that, "The essence of the welfare state is government-protected minimum standards of income, nutrition, health, housing and education, assured to every citizen as a political right, not charity." But he then tries to distinguish those policy areas whose programs have a central thrust of furthering "absolute equality" from those that primarily further "equality of opportunity." The core of the welfare state for him is a nation's health and welfare effort that constitutes "clearly and directly a contribution to absolute equality." By contrast, he perceives a "nation's educational effort, especially at the higher levels, as chiefly a contribution to equality of opportunity—enhanced mobility for those judged to be potentially able and skilled." He concedes that the ideological underpinnings of the welfare state reflect everywhere a tension between meritocratic and egalitarian values. "But the mix varies from program to program, with the meritocratic component for education far more prominent than it is for the rest of the welfare state."[28]

How equality of opportunity is juxtaposed to equality of results crucially affects how the discussion of welfare state boundaries is cast, and how countries are compared with regard to attainment of its goals. Those who presume that meritocracy is inevitable within systems that stress equality of opportunity, tend to disregard education efforts as extraneous. But others who perceive equality of opportunity more in terms of removing the accidental handicaps of birth and condition, adduce plausible reasons for classifying services like education as furthering equality goals. When they utilize aggregate data to rank countries on their achievement of welfare state outputs, scholars can arrive at startlingly different sequences, as is borne out in a comparison of Wilensky's rankings with those of Castles.[29]

Among the problems encountered when trying to juxtapose measures of equality of opportunity against those of equality of results, is that the two concepts do not anchor the same dimension in sociological terms, much as they seem to in common sense labelling. Many would agree with Parkin that, "Inequalities associated with class system are founded upon two inter-locking but conceptually distinct, social processes. One is the allocation of rewards attaching to different positions in the social system; the other is the process of recruitment to these positions."[30] The concept of opportunity is most directly applicable to functions like recruitment and role assignment, selection and "dropping out." The concept of results, on the other hand, is associated more with processes of allocation and renumeration, with social rewards and punishments. The closeness of linkage between educational, occupational and social security systems determines how the two kinds of social processes are interrelated in specific societies. But usually they do encompass rather distinct aspects of experience. Equality of opportunity is associated more with "becoming," the attainment of statuses over a life-cycle or intergenerational development. Equality of results tends to reflect "being" more in terms of measures of income and "levels of living."

Another perspective on the "opportunity v. results" dichotomy is suggested by findings about historical welfare state development. As articles in this volume by Flora, Alber, Wilensky, and others bear out in fine detail, the shaping role of Liberal, Social Democratic and Catholic parties on the development of social policies has varied subtly by time and place. Liberal governments were marginally stronger promoters in certain periods, Social Democratic ones in others. But the predominant lesson is how much the values of the major Western political currents have mingled to create and shape the welfare state. How much analytical sense does it make then, to juxtapose a more Liberal-colored concept, equality of opportunity, against a more Socialist-colored concept, equality of results, in order to identify boundaries and thresholds of welfare state development? If one did so, one could indeed identify "islands" of socialism, "bands" of liberalism, more restrictive Socialist and more inclusive Liberal boundaries. But while some will link results with socialism, others like Parkin read the evidence to show that "Social Democrats have been more able or willing to broaden the social base of recruitment to privileged positions than to equalize rewards attached to different positions."[31]

The modern welfare state was a product of capitalism. If the earning and learning capacities of capitalism are entering a phase of stagnation, then the limits of welfare state development may become apparent through a series of crises. It is worth trying to analyze whether, and which, of the objectives of welfare state social policy are "in central conflict with the distributive rules and economic mechanisms of capitalism"[32] under present and foreseeable conditions. But neither demographic, nor economic, nor political "laws" would seem to dictate that welfare state adaptability will necessarily be lower in its mature phases than it has proved to be during preceding eras.

The difference between the industrial welfare state and its predecessors is that the costs of security which were formerly internalized are now externalized. The costs of health care are removed from the family unit, and reintroduced as social costs borne by the economy. But to what extent should the welfare state limit citizens' liberty to purchase security guarantees which substitute or complement the publicly provided ones? One principle enunciated here has been based on "the abolition of the power of money outside its sphere . . . a society in which wealth is no longer convertible into social goods with which it has no intrinsic connection."[33] Health care has been widely acknowledged as an example of such a social good, while education has as frequently been cited as an area where the prohibition of private school opportunities would violate the liberties of the more well-to-do. It is around the back-door gates that party differences have focussed. Left wing parties have sought to abolish "pay-beds" in public hospitals, right-wing parties have sought to support and legitimate fee-paying private schools by endowing them with publicly funded scholarships.

Normative disputes at the front-door to the welfare state have centered around the question of the degree to which compensatory equality of opportunity shall be furthered to achieve selective equality of condition. Here the goal is less one of aiming for equality of results at one time point for the needs of an entire population, as one of gradually advancing the equalization of conditions between particular sub-groups. Equality is here less measured only in terms of income, and more in terms of status and authority. Cast generally, the discussion has centered around what Dworkin, building on Rawls, has identified as the rights of individuals "to equal concern and respect in the design and administration of the political institutions that govern them." This abstract right can be interpreted in various ways. One utilitarian interpretation of welfare state goals would require the political system to manifest "equal concern and respect" by aiming at improving "the average welfare of all citizens counting the welfare of each on the same scale."[34]

Typical disputed boundary questions concern how the state shall utilize its power to determine linkages between education credentials and the labor market, or between housing conditions and the access to public and private services. Reducing which range of inequalities will do most to further "equality of concern and respect" for whom? From the perspective of the more privileged, the granting of easier access or subsidies to individuals whose grandparents were the victims of discrimination, appears as an unjust reduction of their liberties. From the perspective of the less advantaged, the granting of special benefits is often disappointing, because the more privileged usually find ways of discounting, if not stigmatizing, the benefits which were intended to reduce inequalities. This does not mean that the politicians and bureaucrats who direct the welfare state are the hapless cogs of processes that lie outside their ability to influence. Rather, it illustrates that after several generations of welfare state development, all groups concerned have developed more sophisticated expectations, more alternative strategies and fewer notions of ignoring or opting out of the system.

Notes

1. Hintze 1915, p. 671.
2. Die Deutsche Arbeiterversicherung 1905, p. 150.
3. Churchill 1974, pp. 1083, 1146.
4. Some scholars believe this was the first time the term "Wohlfahrtstaat" was employed in German political discussion. One finds it employed in Edwin Erich Dwinger's *Wir Rufen Deutschland* (Jena: Eugen Diederichs, 1932) in which war veterans ruminate about developments since 1918. One of them foresees the arrival of a conservative era, partly because "the liberalism has so eviscerated this *Wohlfahrtstaat* that it will surely break up in the hard times ahead" (p. 518).
5. Huber 1966, p. 486.
6. Bruce 1961, ix.
7. Harris 1977, pp. 369, 418, 448, 459.
8. Marshall 1963, pp. 67-127.
9. Marshall 1963.
10. Janowitz 1976, p. 32.
11. Kini 1966, p. 180.
12. Briggs 1961; Abel-Smith 1972.
13. Titmuss 1971.
14. Marshall 1963, p. 302.
15. Janowitz 1976, p. 32.
16. Rimlinger 1974.
17. Marshall 1963.
18. Baier 1977.
19. Rimlinger 1974.
20. Durkheim 1960a; Durkheim, 1960b.
21. Janowitz 1976.
22. Bell 1973.
23. Tilly 1975.
24. Titmuss 1974 was among the first to stress the importance of "fiscal welfare."
25. Heimann 1929, p. 154.
26. Briggs 1961, p. 228.
27. Robson 1976, p. 58.
28. Wilensky 1975, pp. 6-7.
29. Wilensky 1975, p. 30; Castles 1978, p. 69.
30. Parkin 1971, p. 13.
31. *Ibid.,* p. 121.
32. Westergaard 1978, p. 95.
33. Bell 1978, p. 268, citing Michael Walzer, "In Defense of Equality," *Dissent,* Vol. 20. No. 4 (Fall, 1973), 399-408.
34. Dworkin 1977, p. 180.

References

Abel-Smith, Brian. 1972. "A History of Medical Care." In E. W. Martin, ed. *Comparative Development in Social Welfare.* London: Allen & Unwin.

Baier, Horst. 1977. "Herrschaft im Sozialstaat. Auf der Suche nach einem soziologischen Paradigma der Sozialpolitik." In *Soziologie und Sozialpolitik,* ed. by Christian von Ferber and Franz Xaver Kaufmann. Special number 19 of *Kölner Zeitschrift für Soziologie und Sozialpsychologie.*

Bell, Daniel. 1973. *The Coming of Post-Industrial Society: A Venture in Social Forecasting.* New York: Basic Books.

Bell, Daniel. 1978. *The Cultural Contradictions of Capitalism.* New York: Basic Books.

Briggs, Asa. 1961. "The Welfare State in Historical Perspective." In *European Journal of Sociology,* 2, 221-258.

Bruce, Maurice. 1961. *The Coming of the Welfare State.* London: Batsford.

Castles, Frank. 1978. *The Social Democratic Image of Society.* London: Routledge & Kegan Paul.

Churchill, Winston S. 1974. *Complete Speeches,* 1 (1897-1908). New York: Chelsea House.

Durkheim, Emile. 1960a. *De la Division du Travail Social.* 7th ed. Paris: Presses Universitaires de France.

Durkheim, Emile. 1960b. *Le Suicide: Etude de Sociologie.* New ed. Paris: Presses Universitaires de France.

Dworkin, Ronald. 1977. *Taking Rights Seriously.* Cambridge: Harvard.

Harris, José. 1977. *William Beveridge: A Biography.* Oxford: Clarendon.

Heimann, Eduard. 1929. *Soziale Theorie des Kapitalismus: Theorie der Sozialpolitik.* Tübingen: J. C.B. Mohr.

Hintze, Otto. 1915. *Die Hohenzollern und ihr Werk: Fünfhundert Jahre vaterländischer Geschichte.* Berlin: Parey.

Huber, Ernst R. 1966. *Dokumente zur deutschen Verfassungsgeschichte.* Vol. 3. Stuttgart: Kohlhammer.

Janowitz, Morris. 1976. *Social Control of the Welfare State.* New York: Elsevier.

Kini, N.G.S. 1966. "Approaches to a Theory of Comparative Welfare Policies." In *Perspectives on the Welfare State,* ed. Sadashiv Ayar. Bombay: Manaktalas.

Marshall, T. H. 1963. *Sociology at the Crossroads and other Essays.* London: Heinemann.

Marshall, T. H. 1964. *Class, Citizenship, and Social Development.* New York: Doubleday.

Parkin, Frank. 1971. *Class Inequality and Political Order.* New York: Praeger.

Rimlinger, Gaston V. 1974. *Welfare Policy and Industrialization in Europe, America, and Russia.* New York: John Wiley & Sons.

Robson, William. 1976. *Welfare State and Welfare Society.* London: Allen & Unwin.

Tilly, Charles. 1975. "Food Supply and Public Order in Modern Europe." In *The Formation of National States in Western Europe,* ed. by Charles Tilly. Princeton, N.J.: Princeton University Press.

Titmuss, Richard. 1971. *The Gift Relationship: From Human Blood to Social Policy.* New York: Pantheon.

Titmuss, Richard. 1974. *Commitment to Welfare.* 4th ed. London: Allen & Unwin.

Westergaard, John. 1978. "Social Policy and Class Inequality: Some Notes on Welfare State Limits," *Social Register 1978.* London: Merlin Press.

Wilensky, Harold. 1975. *The Welfare State and Equality.* Berkeley, Calif.: University of California Press.

Part Two

Why and How Welfare States Grew: Determinants and Variations

Chapter 2

Modernization, Democratization, and the Development of Welfare States in Western Europe

Peter Flora and Jens Alber

Introduction

The evolution of the welfare state is obviously related to a great variety of social developments and changes. One of our main tasks thus consists in attempting to construct a theoretical framework that systematizes and relates these processes. In Part I of this chapter the concept of modernization is examined since it emphasizes the multidimensionality and interrelatedness of developmental processes. From this analysis of modernization, a sectoral model is developed that poses some relationships among socioeconomic and political developments and the evolution of welfare state policies and institutions. More specific hypotheses are then elaborated on the basis of Stein Rokkan's theory of European political development.

The modern European welfare states really began in the last two decades of the nineteenth century. Part II of this chapter describes these beginnings through examining the introduction of social insurance systems throughout Europe and the growth and structural change of public social expenditures in three countries. The later growth of the European welfare states is compared mainly through the evolution of the social insurance systems that are of central fiscal and institutional importance.

Finally, Part III here attempts to explain the emergence of these systems through the socioeconomic processes of industrialization and urbanization as well as through the political developments of suffrage extension and parliamentarism. In addition, the possibility of diffusion processes, an idea studied in more detail in Chapter 4, is analyzed.

I. Theoretical Considerations in the Development of the Welfare State

A. Classical Concepts and an Analytical Framework of Modernization

The concept of modernization has largely replaced the traditional concept of development as well as superseded more specific concepts such as industrialization and democratization.[1] Despite its vague and ambiguous meaning, modernization has one salient characteristic that makes it interesting for our analysis: an emphasis on the multidimensionality of societal development, or the assumption of causal interrelationships among economic and population growth, social and psychic mobilization, political development, cultural change, and the transformation of the international economic and political order. Figure 2.1 illustrates the relationships among some of the basic concepts of modernization. The main distinction is between general growth processes and structural changes, which are institutional as well as organizational. Growth processes are related to two different capacities: the capacity to grow, the core of which is the economy, and the capacity to change structures, the core of which is the polity. This may be understood as a generalization of Marx's distinction between the growing and relatively flexible forces of production and the relatively inflexible relations of production. The rigidity of social organization may either encourage or impede the growth of the productive forces, thus producing strains and conflicts.

In the tradition of Durkheim, structural-functional differentiation is the fundamental process characterizing modernization. This increasing specialization and fragmentation is intimately related to the processes of growth and affects all social structures, activities, and individual lives. Fundamentally, differentiation involves a loosening of ascriptive bonds and a growing mobility of men, goods, and ideas. It leads to the development of extensive networks of exchange and greater disposable resources.[2] As differentiation advances and breaks down traditional forms of social organization, it changes and exacerbates the problem of integration, which was Durkheim's main interest. He suggested two types of solutions to this problem: integration through mechanical solidarity based on affinity of values, beliefs, and sentiments and through organic solidarity that simultaneously weakens the impact of social segmentation and strengthens the impersonal interdependence of individuals. We follow here Parsons' cri-

Figure 2.1
An Analytical Framework of Modernization

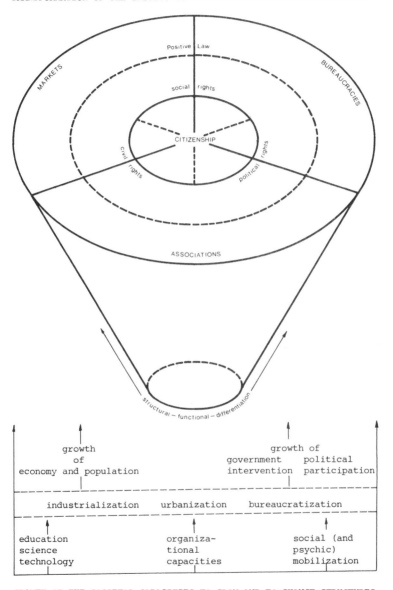

TRANSFORMATION OF THE INSTITUTIONAL AND ORGANIZATIONAL STRUCTURES

STRUCTURAL CHANGES

Positive Law

MARKETS

BUREAUCRACIES

social rights

CITIZENSHIP

civil rights

political rights

ASSOCIATIONS

structural – functional – differentiation

PROCESSES

| growth of economy and population | growth of government intervention | political participation |

industrialization   urbanization   bureaucratization

| education science technology | organiza- tional capacities | social (and psychic) mobilization |

GROWTH

GROWTH OF THE SOCIETAL CAPACITIES TO GROW AND TO CHANGE STRUCTURES

tique of Durkheim[3] that these two solutions to the problem of integration do not represent two distinct stages of development, but coexist in modern societies.

In modern, highly differentiated societies the mechanical element of integration lies in the core institution of citizenship. This has been formulated most clearly by T. H. Marshall: "Citizenship is a status bestowed on those who are full members of a community. All who possess the status are equal with respect to the rights and duties with which the status is endowed."[4] Marshall distinguishes between three elements of citizenship: a civil element, providing the rights to ensure individual freedom; a political element, centered in the right to participate in the exercise of power; and a social element, primarily constituted by the right to share a minimum level of economic welfare, social security, and cultural heritage. The process of differentiating the basic rights and the institutions giving access to them has been accompanied by geographical integration, or a "nationalization" of the specialized institutions. "Citizenship is by definition national."[5] Of course, the sequence, form, and degree of institutionalization of citizenship rights have varied widely from country to country and still do.

Besides the core integrative institution of citizenship, modern Western European societies have developed three regulating organizational structures: markets, which organize the exchange of economic resources and commodities; associations, which organize the articulation, aggregation, and representation of interests; and state bureaucracies, which organize the fulfillment of collective tasks. There are specific relationships between these three organizational sectors of modern societies and the basic rights of citizenship (see Figure 2.1). Civil rights are related to markets (the right to own property and to enter valid contracts, free choice of work and residence) as well as to associations (freedom of speech, thought and faith, right to assemble, and freedom of association). They guarantee a sphere of public opinion, that together with political rights forms the legal basis for the development of interest groups and political parties and for the evolution of parliaments symbolizing the associative character of society itself. But political rights are also related to state bureaucracies, since the right to participate in the exercise of political power only has meaning when the governing power of parliament is established. Finally, social rights are also related to state bureaucracies and to markets. Originally, they were provided through membership in local communities or functional associations. On the national level, the right to a minimum level of economic welfare and social security developed successively through the regulation (labor legislation), supplementation (social security systems), and replacement (social services) of markets by state bureaucracies. With respect to the social right to share in the cultural heritage market elements usually were replaced much earlier through the establishment of public schools and the institutionalization of compulsory education.

Within this framework then, the development of the welfare state may be analyzed according to at least the following three aspects:

1. the processes of differentiation (the differentiation of individual and household income, of working and living place) creating specific labor market problems that must be solved by the state;
2. the evolution of social rights as a consequence of (or compensation for) the institutionalization of political rights;
3. the increasing control, substitution and supplementing of markets (and to some degree of associations) by state bureaucracies.

B. Modernization and the Welfare State: A Sectoral Model

1. Problem Pressure: Changing Socioeconomic Conditions and Political Mobilization

The distinction between markets, associations, and state bureaucracies as the three main organizational sectors of society is used now to draft a sectoral model of the development of welfare states (see Figure 2.2). In the model, markets and associations are further divided into two subsectors. In the first subsector of markets (I) those developmental aspects creating specific welfare and security problems are summarized. The second subsector of markets (II) includes the developmental aspects assumed to lead to social mobilization processes. In the first associative subsector (I), associations in the widest sense are included that are concerned with welfare and security problems independently of the state. The second subsector (II) embraces those associations that mobilize political support and articulate demands for welfare assurances from the state.

Under Markets I four main problems generated by industrialization and urbanization and affecting the immediate associations of family and household are specified:

1. changing working conditions (for example, industrial accidents);
2. the development of a free or unrestrained labor contract (for example, child labor, working hours);
3. income security for disabled persons without property (sickness, invalidity), for those not or no longer engaged in the productive process (children, housewives, old persons) or for the unemployed;
4. the provision of certain (public) goods by controlling, supplementing or substituting for private markets (housing, health, to some degree education).

These problems are in turn assumed to create an objective problem pressure. To assess the intensity of the pressure directly exerted on the government, however, the activities of those associations that respond to

Figure 2.2
A Sectoral Mode of the Development of Welfare States

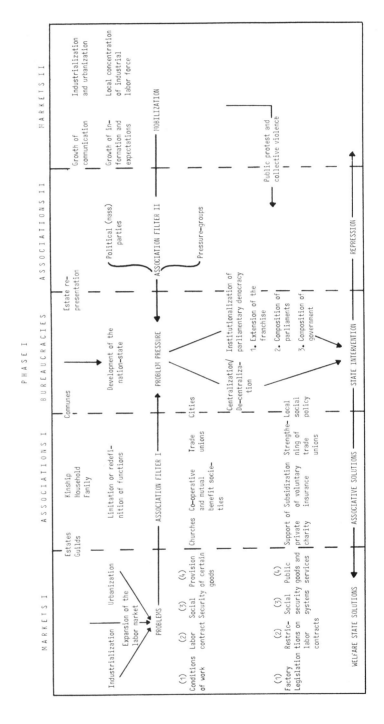

these problems, such as churches and private charity organizations (poor relief), mutual benefit and cooperative societies (insurance, housing) and trade unions (unemployment assistance) must be considered. This association filter will often greatly modify and typically diminish the objective problem pressure. For example, the countries with strong Protestant state churches developed early a notion of state responsibility for public welfare, whereas in the religiously mixed and Catholic countries the tradition of private charity and the principle of subsidiarity, giving priority to the responsibility of smaller collectivities, remained strong. Thus, differences in the existing associative structures and their historical development may explain some of the differences in the development of the welfare state.

Under Markets II, at least two developments may have been responsible for mobilizing major parts of the population: (1) the concentration of the labor force in cities, industries, and enterprises as a consequence of industrialization and urbanization and (2) the growth of information and expectations as a consequence of expanding communication. This social mobilization may find its political expression in various unstructured forms such as public protest and collective violence or in institutionalized forms like voting, unionization, and the creation of political parties and interest groups.

Since the origins of the modern welfare states are closely related to the "social question" and the labor movement, differences in the strength and coherence of working class parties and trade unions are most important for explaining variations in welfare state developments. To some extent, differences in the strength of labor movements are a function of religious, linguistic and/or ethnic cleavages that might have deflected attention and support from class issues and retarded the development of welfare states: Alternatively, strong working class internationalism may have also impeded welfare state developments by factionalizing the working class movement, above all by dividing socialists and communists and thus decreasing opportunities to gain executive power.

The problem pressure thus consists of two elements: the objective problem pressure and the pressure generated by social and political mobilization. The distinction between these two aspects is not merely analytical, since the effects of both can vary widely as discussed in Part III. Nor does this suggest that governments simply act in response to pressures; they may not act at all or they may anticipate some of the problems and act to prevent their full realization.

2. The Shaping of State Intervention: Bureaucracy and Democracy

The intervention of governments in response to or in anticipation of the problem pressure historically involved several alternatives. One concerned the relationship between welfare state policies directed toward solving social problems and police state policies designed to repress political mobilization processes. In practice, of course, these alternatives were often combined. Their clear differentiation is possible only with the establishment of modern welfare and police institutions compared to the earlier institutions of a poor police and a health police. A second major alternative lies in the way governments tried to solve social problems. They could choose between direct intervention through labor legislation, factory inspection, the establishment of compulsory insurance systems, and the provision of public goods (housing, health, education) on the one hand and associative solutions through subsidizing private charity and voluntary insurance and strengthening trade unions on the other. The result was probably greatly influenced by the political strength of existing associations and the efficiency of their programs.

At a more general level, government intervention has probably been shaped predominantly by two basic developmental processes: first, the creation of state bureaucracies and thus administrative capacity. An early and strong bureaucratization and centralization may have promoted welfare state development because of greater government resources and strong paternalist traditions. It may also have thwarted efforts to institutionalize democracy and thus impeded welfare state development. Second, the creation of mass democracies reflected by constitutional developments (the introduction and extension of suffrage and the legal or de facto enactment of parliamentary responsibility) and power shifts (composition of parliaments and governments) are of major importance in the development of government intervention. Of course, additional factors to explain differences in the development of welfare states could be cited, particularly cultural values underlying the definition of welfare responsibilities and standards and the long-term growth and cyclical fluctuations of economic resources and public revenues.

In following sections, we are primarily concerned with the relationship between the growth of mass democracies and welfare state policies, since sufficient information on the growth of state bureaucracies is still largely missing for most European countries. Furthermore, it is important to note that while this model points to possible relationships between factors influencing the development of the welfare state, it does not sufficiently specify their extent and character. This is especially true for the relationships between the objective problem pressure and the associative structures, and their combined impact on government responses. There is hardly any theory from which to formulate a systematic set of hypotheses about the relationships between socioeconomic development and the evolution of welfare states. With respect to the processes of political mobilization, organization and institutionalization (see columns 3 and 4 in Figure 2.2), however, we can utilize Stein Rokkan's theory of European political development to formulate more specific hypotheses.

C. Rokkan's Stage Model and the Evolution of the European Welfare States

Stein Rokkan's theory[6] attempts to integrate various approaches to the study of political development to explain the growth of the European national states, their external consolidation,and their internal restructuring (or consolidation). It essentially consists of two parts: first, a theoretical conception of stages of political development; second, empirical typologies which try to explain variations in these respective stages (for example, in territorial consolidation, the introduction and extension of suffrage, cleavages, and party systems).

1. Stages of Political Development

Rokkan distinguishes four stages or problems of political development that may form relatively distinct phases or may coincide and even cumulate to cause developmental crises. The first two phases are primarily thrusts from the center toward the periphery, attempting to subject it to military-economic (state formation) and cultural (nation building) control and to create subjects (of the king and later the state). The last two stages originate predominantly from the periphery toward the center and are aimed at an internal restructuring through the extension and redefinition of citizenship (participation and redistribution):

1. *State Formation* or the development of fiscal and military states. This phase involves political, economic and cultural unification at the elite level, the creation of organizations for the mobilization of resources (tax bureaucracies), the consolidation of the territory (armies) and the maintenance of internal order (police and army).
2. *Nation Building* or the building or growth of national states. This phase refers to the establishment of direct contacts between the elite and larger sectors of the peripheral population through conscript armies, schools, mass media, religious and linguistic standardization.
3. *Participation* or the development of mass democracies and the establishment of citizenship through the equalization of political rights. This phase includes growing participation of the peripheral population, the institutionalization of civil and political rights (franchise, parliaments), and the creation of political parties.
4. *Redistribution* or the development of welfare states and the establishment of social citizenship through the redistribution of resources, goods and benefits. This phase involves the creation of public welfare systems (social security, health, education, housing) and public policies for the equalization of economic conditions through progressive taxation and transfer payments.

A primary question is how the development of the first three stages has created general conditions that either promote or retard the development of welfare states. The relationships posed in the preceding section can be viewed now with respect to variations in these phases: these include variations in the early creation of state bureaucracies that are closely related to the problems of territorial consolidation (state formation); variations in old cultural cleavages (nation building) that later may have detracted from "welfare issues"; and variations in the structure of party systems, particularly in the strength and coherence of working class parties (participation).

2. Institutional Variations

We are particularly concerned with the growth of mass democracies and their consequences for the evolution of welfare states. In general, the introduction and extension of the franchise and the legal or de facto enactment of parliamentary responsibility will probably create a setting promoting the development of the welfare state. This is because opportunities increase for economically disadvantaged groups to articulate, aggregate, and represent their interests and demands, and eventually to gain executive power. More specific hypotheses about the establishment and nature of welfare institutions, however, seem dependent on the interaction between these variables:

Table 2.1
Enfranchisement, Parliamentarism, and Social Rights

Parliamentary regime	LIBERAL DEMOCRACIES	MASS DEMOCRACIES
	Public assistance as disqualifying alternative to political (and civil) rights	Social rights as democratic corollary of political rights and as consequence of party competition for votes
Non-parliamentary regime	CONSTITUTIONAL–DUALISTIC MONARCHIES	
	Poor relief as paternalistic responsibility for needy 'subjects'	Social welfare as authoritarian defense against (full) political citizenship and as consequence of a competition for loyalty
	Limited (manhood) suffrage or estate representation	Extended (manhood or adult) suffrage

Hypothesis (1) Constitutional-dualistic monarchies with a limited suffrage or an estate representation are likely to develop relatively undifferentiated and localized systems of poor relief in the paternalistic tradition of bearing responsibility for needy and obedient subjects. Benefits are based on charity, not entitlement. They usually are in nonmonetary form and restricted to persons unable to work. These regimes maintain or even extend poor relief in response to growing social needs, but they do not introduce more differentiated systems based on entitlement.

Hypothesis (2) Liberal democracies with a limited suffrage based on property, tax, or social status tend to restrict government intervention in general and public assistance in particular. They may even reduce welfare expenditures despite growing social needs. They are likely to maintain or develop relatively undifferentiated and localized systems with benefits usually restricted to persons unable to work. They oppose obligatory schemes, but may subsidize voluntary mutual benefit and other associative efforts. Public assistance receivers are disqualified as political citizens.

Hypothesis (3) Mass democracies are more likely to develop extended, differentiated and centralized welfare systems based on social rights and obligatory contributions. They are more predisposed to do so than liberal democracies or monarchies with limited suffrage because they face a stronger and more organized working class and a greater competition for the votes of economically disadvantaged groups and because working class parties have greater opportunities to gain executive power. Within mass democracies, however, great variations may result from differences in the party system, above all the strength and coherence of the working class movement, as well as from differences in the development of state bureaucracies.

Hypothesis (4) Constitutional-dualistic monarchies with extended suffrage are most likely to develop more extended, differentiated and centralized welfare systems based on obligatory contributions and entitlements because of stronger paternalistic and bureaucratic traditions and greater autonomy from middle-class pressures opposed to public welfare activities. They face greater organized pressures from the working class that lead to the development of welfare institutions as a defense against full participation rights and as a means to strengthen working class loyalty for the authoritarian state.

This fourfold classification thus produces a simple typology of institutional settings that may promote or retard the development of welfare states and produce specific variations in public welfare institutions. Since all European countries in the last hundred years can be associated with more than one of these types, their welfare institutions at any given point will show the influence of varying developments. These hypotheses will be tested, at least partially in Part III, since variations in the institutional development of mass democracies are probably most relevant for explaining the different beginnings of the European welfare states until World War I. Thus, we shall now turn to a descriptive discussion of these early differences.

II. A Comparative Description of European Welfare States

A. The Beginnings of the Modern Welfare State

While the modern welfare state is a product of the last ninety years, it has an important early history. Gaston Rimlinger[7] has convincingly demonstrated the need to distinguish between two phases of this "pre-history": the "Poor Law" period from the sixteenth to the eighteenth and nineteenth centuries and the "Liberal Break" of the nineteenth century. Poor relief became a matter of national concern in the sixteenth century with the emergence of national states and economies. It was a "relief of the poor within a framework of repression." However, the poor laws contained an element of reciprocal social responsibilities, but they were much more reliant on punishments than on relief. The reciprocal social responsibilities mainly referred to the relationship between individuals and their local communities, since the execution of the national poor laws was left to local authorities.

Whereas the old European welfare states developed very similarly during the poor law period, the liberal break produced many divergences. The core ideas of liberalism — individualistic freedom, equality, and self-help — were antithetical to the former concepts of dependence and protection. The importance of this second phase lies primarily in the coincidence of new social problems created by industrialization and urbanization with an emerging philosophy that facilitated the destruction of old protective institutions.

1. The Take-Off Period

The take-off of the modern welfare state occurred in the last two decades of the nineteenth century. We use two measurements to delimit this breakthrough: the increase and structural change of public expenditures with respect to social welfare (social expenditure ratio), and institutional innovations (above all, the institutionalization of social insurance systems). Here, the long-term development of public social expenditures can only be illustrated for three countries for which longitudinal studies are already available: Germany, the United Kingdom, and Sweden.[8] However, they reflect the average level and variation in Europe at the turn of the century, since Germany then had a comparatively high ratio of public social expenditures to GNP and the United Kingdom one of the lowest.

Figure 2.3
The Development of Public Expenditures in Germany,
the United Kingdom, and Sweden

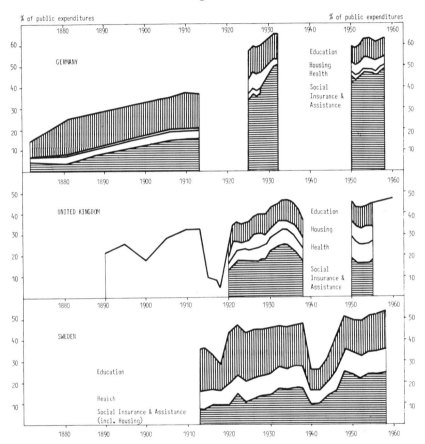

Between the turn of the century and the end of World War II, the ratio of public expenditures to GNP roughly tripled in the three countries. As Figure 2.3 illustrates, social expenditures disproportionally shared in this tremendous increase: in Germany the proportion of social expenditures in the budget rose from about 30 percent to 62 percent, in the United Kingdom from about 20 percent to 47 percent, and in Sweden from about 30 percent to 53 percent from the beginning of the century to 1960. This steady increase was curbed only in times of war, and accelerated during economic depressions.

The trend and time pattern of social expenditures has been predominantly shaped by social security outlays in the sense of transfer payments for social insurance and public assistance. Although the structure of expenditures cannot be given for a common base-year at the start of the century for all three countries, Figure 2.3 illustrates that these payments have absorbed an ever increasing share of the budget. The widening scope of income redistribution through social transfer payments thus seems to be the most significant structural change in the development of social expenditures and of public expenditures in general.

This may justify our concentration on social insurance legislation as the basic institutional breakthrough of the modern welfare state. Four main social insurance (or security) systems developed in relation to different risks: industrial accidents; sickness (and invalidity); old age (and invalidity, survivors); and unemployment.

2. The Break with Liberalism

Although there is no uniform sequence in the establishment of these four systems, in general, social insurance for industrial accidents came first, unemployment insurance last, with the other two systems in between. This can be shown by determining the sequence of the first laws establishing compulsory systems for each of our twelve countries. Table 2.2 summarizes the total and average ranks, as well as the first, last, and average year of introduction (see also the list of laws in Table 2.4). The year of the first law establishing a compulsory or voluntary subsidized system appears in brackets.

Table 2.2
Sequence of Introduction for the Four Social Insurance Systems

	Sequence of introduction: ranks					Non-compulsory	Year of introduction		
	1.	2.	3.	4.	average		first	last	average
ACCIDENT INSURANCE	7	2	1	2	1.8	–	1884	1971	1914
	(6)	(4)	(2)	(-)	(1.7)		(1884)	(1911)	(1898)
SICKNESS INSURANCE	2	4	5	1	2.4	1	1883	1963	1923
	(5)	(2)	(3)	(2)	(2.2)		(1883)	(1963)	(1906)
OLD–AGE INSURANCE	3	5	3	1	2.2	–	1889	1946	1922
	(1)	(4)	(5)	(2)	(2.7)		(1889)	(1946)	(1912)
UNEMPLOYMENT INSURANCE	–	1	3	8	3.6	4	1911	1967	1930
	(-)	(2)	(2)	(8)	(3.5)		(1906)	(1934)	(1917)

This sequence may tentatively be explained by the degree to which the introduction of each system represented a break with the liberal ideas concerning the assignment of guilt and responsibility among individuals, groups, and the state. The break with liberalism lay above all in the principle of compulsory insurance as well as in the recognized amount of state (financial) responsibility. In comparison, the break with patrimonial traditions was much less vivid, lying primarily in the principle of individual legal entitlements that is from the liberal tradition.

The introduction of accident insurance or workmen's compensation constituted the least radical break with liberalism since it could be rationalized by redefining the old idea of liability for individually caused damages. Two aspects of employers' liability, however, represented a clear break rather than a mere redefinition. The first was that industrial accidents were increasingly viewed as an inevitable element of industrial production, thus weakening the notion of guilt (with its reliance on court trials) and introducing the principle of automatic compensation for the loss of earnings through work injuries. The other aspect was that the individual liability of employers usually was replaced by a pooling of risks among all employers of an industrial branch. Of our twelve countries, five introduced workmen's compensation schemes first (Belgium, Denmark, France, Sweden, the United Kingdom) mandating employers to provide relief, while the other seven started with compulsory insurance schemes (Austria, Finland, Germany, Italy, the Netherlands, Norway, Switzerland) that, today, all countries possess.

Providing security against risks of nonoccupational origin (sickness and old age) that could not be viewed as individually caused damages constituted a much deeper break with the liberal tradition. Both of these risks at that time were the main causes of poverty and destitution, and their mitigation required the commitment of much greater financial resources than were needed for the compensation of industrial accidents. The primary object of sickness insurance, whether compulsory or only subsidized, was to provide cash benefits in the event of lost earnings due to nonoccupational sickness. The degree of substitution between private (subsidized) and public (compulsory) schemes seems to have been somewhat higher for sickness insurance than for old age insurance. This is suggested by the fact that six countries introduced subsidized voluntary sickness insurance schemes that usually were retained for long periods and reached comparatively high coverage (high coverage: Denmark 1892-1933, Sweden 1891-1947, Switzerland 1911 ff; low coverage: Belgium 1894-1944, France provisional 1852-1930, Italy 1886-1928), whereas only three countries introduced subsidized voluntary old-age insurance (Belgium 1900-1924, France provisional 1856-1910, Italy 1898-1919) with only Belgium reaching a higher level of coverage. Pension insurance schemes usually group together three different risks of long-term character: invalidity, old age, and the death of the family breadwinner (survivors). Of these, old age has generally been the first (together with invalidity) and by far the most important. Besides controlling and subsidizing voluntary schemes, the state intervened primarily in establishing either compulsory public insurance schemes or demogrant (noncontributory) universal pension schemes financed by general revenues.

Unemployment insurance was usually introduced last because the notion of state support for the "undeserving poor" required the most radical break with liberal and patrimonial principles. Due to the special difficulties of solving unemployment through insurance techniques (see Chapter 5), public assistance programs persisted with subsidized voluntary and compulsory insurance schemes. Three countries still have only subsidized voluntary schemes (Denmark, Finland, Sweden), whereas five others have retained such schemes for a long period (Belgium 1907-1944, the Netherlands 1906-1949, Norway 1906-1938, France 1905-1967, Switzerland 1924-1976). Only four countries introduced compulsory insurance systems from the outset (Austria, Germany, Italy, the United Kingdom).

B. The Development of Social Insurance Systems

1. Steps in the Extension of the Social Insurance Schemes

The expansion of social security systems may be described qualitatively by the risks and social categories successively covered, as well as in quantitative terms by the number of insured persons. In general, the sequential steps of extension within each system have followed a similar pattern in including new groups of persons and new types of benefits. Initial provisions for industrial accidents were frequently limited to workers in a few especially dangerous industries. By 1911, when Switzerland introduced its program, all twelve countries had workmen's compensation schemes of some kind, and by the outbreak of World War I all had extended them to the majority of industrial workers. In a second step, the schemes were extended to additional groups, primarily agricultural workers and later to the majority of all employed persons. This step usually was completed between the wars, although Norway and Switzerland did not extend their schemes to agricultural workers until the 1950s. The third step was marked by widening the concept of industrial accidents to include new risks such as occupational diseases. With the exception of the United Kingdom and Switzerland that had broad definitions of industrial accidents from the very beginning, this step was made after World War I. A last step of extension, which largely did not begin before the 1950s and which is not yet complete, consists in the extension of coverage to self-employed persons.

Sickness insurance, at the time of its introduction, was usually limited to industrial workers and a few categories of employees below an income limit. By 1913, when the Netherlands passed a law on compulsory insurance, all countries had taken legislative action to provide some kind of insurance scheme. In the next step coverage was extended to groups such as agricultural workers or higher paid employees. In the countries with compulsory schemes, this step usually occurred in the 1920s. The consolidation of the schemes through the provision of medical benefits, either introduced for the first time (the Netherlands 1941) or improved and extended to new groups, represents a third step. With the exception of the pioneer Norway (1909), medical benefits were generally extended to family members between 1930 and 1945, while their extension to pensioners usually came about a decade later, between 1941 (Germany) and 1955 (Italy). As in the case of industrial accidents, the extension to self-employed persons marks the last and fourth step, mainly in the years after 1950.

In the introductory phase of pension insurance, coverage was usually limited to workers and certain groups of employees, with benefits limited to old age and/or invalidity payments. A first major modification occurred when survivors' benefits were included: Germany was first in 1911 with most countries following by 1930. However, introduction in Switzerland and Sweden did not occur until 1946, with other Scandinavian countries following as late as the 1950s and even 1960s. Another consolidating step consisted in the inclusion of self-employed persons. Here, the old age insurance schemes in Scandinavia covered the entire population from the very beginning, while the other countries moved toward this goal only after World War II. The introduction of periodic adjustments of pensions to price or wage levels, and the combination of fixed (national minimum) benefits with earnings-related pensions may be understood as a fourth and last significant step. Most countries introduced pension adjustments only after World War II and between 1955 and 1965. While countries with earnings-related pension programs moved towards supplementary flat-rate pensions, such as the Netherlands (1956), Italy (1965), and, in a sense, also Germany (1972), countries providing flat-rate pensions, such as the Scandinavian countries and the United Kingdom, introduced supplementary earnings-related pensions in the period of 1959 to 1966.

Unemployment insurance initially was typically limited to industrial workers or specified industries. After the differentiation between insurance benefits of limited duration and unlimited assistance benefits independent of contributions, the major consolidating steps of the insurance systems consisted in the extension of the schemes to wider groups, including agricultural workers, and the introduction of dependants' benefits.

2. Stages in Social Insurance Legislation

Considering the general chronological development of all these schemes, it is possible to distinguish four phases or stages of social insurance legislation[9]:

1. A classical introductory phase from the early German legislation until 1914. By the outbreak of World War I, all twelve countries had some kind of workmen's compensation schemes, ten had introduced either compulsory or subsidized voluntary sickness insurance programs, eight countries provided for old age, while only five had established some kind of unemployment insurance.

2. A phase of extension between the two World Wars. Social insurance was adopted in additional countries and was extended to cover new risks (especially unemployment and occupational diseases) as well as new groups (particularly nonemployed persons such as family members and pensioners), thus adding the idea of a national minimum to the older concept of just wage substitution. At the start of the second World War, the majority of the twelve countries had made accident and sickness insurance compulsory, all countries had introduced some kind of unemployment insurance, and, with the exception of Switzerland, they all provided for old age.

3. A phase of completion immediately after World War II. In this phase, extensive reforms in several countries (Belgium, France, Sweden, Switzerland, the United Kingdom) made the catalogue of covered risks complete, so that by 1950 all nations had rather comprehensive programs for all the four main risks. All countries had a compulsory pension insurance or demogrant scheme; eleven possessed compulsory accident insurance, nine had compulsory sickness insurance, while seven had adopted compulsory unemployment insurance.

4. A phase of consolidation and reorganization after 1950. Two major changes occurred in this phase. The first consisted in extending social insurance to self-employed persons, often accomplished through the establishment of universal insurance systems. This step was to some degree related to Lord Beveridge's idea of national solidarity as the core principle of social security. The second change was constituted by a coordination, and even unification, of existing schemes based on a more comprehensive conception of social security. By 1965, all countries except Germany had extended their pension and sickness insurance schemes to some categories of self-employed, and, beginning in the 1960s, several countries tried to reorganize and unify their social security systems (particularly Italy from 1965, the Netherlands from 1966, Norway from 1970, Belgium from 1970 and Germany from 1972).

3. Measuring the Scope of Social Insurance Systems

Quantitative data on the extension of social insurance coverage partly reflect these broad legislative phases. In order to facilitate a comparison of national scheme extensions, an index of social insurance coverage has been developed that consists of a weighted average of the percent of the labor force covered by the four systems. The weights given to the four systems, tentatively derived from their varying financial as well as sociological significance, are: 1.5 for old age insurance coverage, 1.0 for sickness and unemployment insurance coverage, and 0.5 for accident insurance cover-

Figure 2.4
The Growth of Social Insurance Coverage in Western Europe

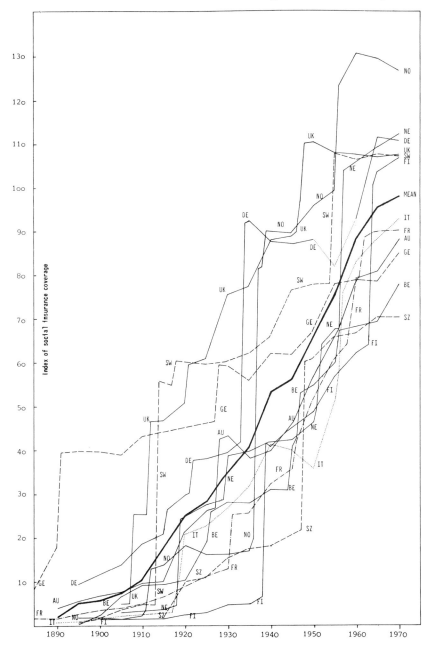

Table 2.3
Parameters of the Growth of Social Insurance Coverage

	1890	1895	1900	1905	1910	1915	1920	1925	1930	1935	1940	1945	1950	1955	1960	1965	1970
Mean index values	2.0	5.1	5.8	7.3	10.4	18.1	25.2	28.4	35.0	40.9	53.2	56.2	66.2	75.1	88.2	95.3	97.8
Mean percentage growth per quinquennial period		3.0	0.7	1.5	3.1	7.7	7.1	3.2	6.6	5.8	12.3	3.0	9.7	8.2	13.1	7.1	2.5
Median percentage growth		0.5	0.7	0.8	1.0	1.3	4.6	2.1	4.2	1.4	5.1	2.7	5.7	6.6	9.5	2.6	1.7
No. of countries above mean percentage growth		2	6	5	3	3	5	4	5	2	2	5	4	5	5	3	6
Range	17.8	39.8	39.5	38.9	43.1	53.8	57.5	58.0	70.7	87.4	71.4	68.7	74.5	56.0	65.4	60.1	56.1
Standard deviation	4.9	10.8	10.7	10.2	12.2	18.6	17.4	18.2	20.9	25.1	23.6	22.6	21.4	18.9	19.6	17.9	15.6

age. The percent covered by subsidized voluntary systems only is divided by 2. Figure 2.4 shows the growth of social insurance coverage between 1890 and 1970 in each country compared to the European mean.

The mean index value demonstrates a steady rise in social insurance coverage over this period. After a gradual and modest increase up to 1910, coverage expands quickly in the interwar period and after World War II up to 1960 and then levels off. Judging from the mean and median quinquennial percentage growth of coverage in the twelve countries, the period from 1945 to 1960 stands out as the phase of major extension. The years from 1925 to 1930 and from 1935 to 1940 also witnessed rapid growth, but only the decade from 1950 to 1960 has seen a major and general extension of social insurance coverage. In single countries, the growth of coverage in general has been relatively steady, with only a few periods of very rapid extension (Germany 1885-1891, the United Kingdom 1906-1911, Sweden 1913, Italy 1919, Denmark 1933, Norway 1936-1940, Finland 1939, Belgium 1944-1946, Switzerland 1947-1948, the Netherlands 1951-1957, Sweden 1955, Norway 1956, Italy 1955-1960, and Finland 1963-1964).

Looking at the differences among the European countries and judging from the standard deviations of the country index values, we can see that the classical introductory phase before World War I was relatively homogeneous. Most countries kept the initial scopes of the systems limited, and only Germany and Denmark stood out as pioneers. The second phase of extension between the two world wars witnessed the greatest divergence with the Scandinavian countries of Sweden, Denmark, and Norway, as well as the United Kingdom, extending the scope of their systems, while Finland, Switzerland, France, Belgium, and Italy lagged far behind. The greatest divergence occurs in 1935. The phases of completion and consolidation after World War II demonstrate a slow convergence still characterized by the lead of the Scandinavian countries and the United Kingdom that all have national insurance schemes in at least one of the four systems. This group is followed by five countries with index values close to the mean with compulsory insurance systems of a more limited coverage (Italy, France, Austria, Belgium, Germany). Switzerland, which still mainly relies on subsidized voluntary insurance, is last with an extraordinary low index value. The international differences began to diminish especially in the 1960s, when several countries approached complete coverage of the resident adult population. Given this nearly complete extension of the scope of social insurance schemes, further developments are better revealed by the expenditure data in Chapter 9.

III. Determinants of Social Insurance Legislation

In this closing part, we attempt to explain the great variations in the introduction and institutional development of social insurance systems.

From all major social insurance laws, we selected seventy-four that appeared to establish the institutional core of the four insurance systems in each of our twelve countries (see Table 2.4). In general, a core law is defined as the introduction of a compulsory system covering a majority of industrial workers. Subsidized voluntary systems were counted as functional equivalents if they persisted for longer periods or had a high coverage. An important subset of these seventy-four laws is formed by the first forty-eight laws (4 insurance systems x 12 countries) establishing a compulsory or subsidized voluntary system (excluding insurance schemes for very limited and special groups).

A. The Key Variables

Three independent variables are used in our attempt to explain the variations in social insurance in Western Europe. Considering the great time span and the large number of countries to be analyzed, these variables must be simple. The first two variables refer to the basic elements of problem pressure, socioeconomic development and political mobilization, whereas the third refers to constitutional development that shaped government intervention. All three variables define broad societal contexts in which social problems arise, political demands are formulated, and institutional solutions are sought.

1. Socioeconomic Development

This variable includes the two fundamental developmental processes of industrialization and urbanization. The underlying assumption is that these processes generate and intensify social problems leading to the introduction of social insurance (security) systems, especially in the context of a capitalist organization of production. Industrialization (I) is measured by the percentage of the labor force employed in the secondary (industrial) sector, and urbanization (U) by the percentage of the total population living in cities of twenty thousand or more inhabitants (a criterion facilitating international comparison and a sharper distinction between urban and rural population than the standard definition).[10]

2. Political Mobilization of the Working Class

Since social insurance legislation was predominantly directed toward industrial workers until World War II, the electoral participation of the working class is considered the main political variable. The underlying assumption is that working-class mobilization is a measure of the political pressure for introducing social insurance systems, even though working-class parties did not always demand their introduction. It does, however, imply that social insurance legislation was partly a defense against working-class mobilization. This is measured by the percentage of votes in national elections for working-class parties.[11]

Table 2.4
Core Social Insurance Laws in Western Europe

Country	Industrial Accident Insurance		Sickness Insurance		Pension Insurance		Unemployment Insurance	
	employers' liability	compulsory ins.	subsidized voluntary	compulsory	subsidized voluntary	compulsory	subsidized voluntary	compulsory
AUSTRIA		1887		1888		1906 (employees) 1927 (workers)		1920
BELGIUM	1903		1894	1944	1900	1924	1907	1944
DENMARK	1898	1916	1892	1933 (semi-compuls.)		1891 (national pensions) 1922 (national pensions rev.) 1933 (invalid./old age insur.)	1907	
FINLAND	1895	1917		1963		1937	1917	
FRANCE	1898	1946		1930		1910 1930		1914 (unempl. assistance) 1959 (collective labor agreements) 1967
GERMANY		1884		1883	1898	1889		1927
ITALY		1898	1886	1928 (collective labor agreements) 1943		1919		1919
NETHERLANDS	1901	1921		1913 1929		1913	1916	1949
NORWAY	1894			1909		1936	1906	1938
SWEDEN	1901	1916	1891 1910			1913	1934	
SWITZERLAND		1911	1911			1946	1924	
UNITED KINGDOM	1906	1946		1911 1946		1908 (national pensions) 1925		1911 1920

3. Constitutional Development

This variable is only used to explain social insurance legislation until World War I and consists of two dimensions. The first is the extension of suffrage with respect to social stratification or social class, so that sex and age are held constant. This is calculated as the number of enfranchised males expressed as a percentage of the male age group defined by the respective electoral laws.[12] The second dimension of constitutional development refers to parliamentarism. Here, the political regimes before World War I are simply classified as constitutional-dualistic monarchies or parliamentary democracies.[13]

We shall now turn to an examination of these internal factors that might explain variations in the introduction and evolution of the social insurance systems. First, however, we examine whether external factors, primarily a diffusion process in which countries imitate and adopt institutions from an innovative pioneering country, might not have played a significant role.

B. Examining the Diffusion Process Concept

That the introduction and evolution of social insurance systems in our twelve countries might be interpreted as a kind of diffusion process is suggested in Reinhard Bendix's conception of modernization: "a basic element of modernization is that it refers to a type of social change since the eighteenth century, which consists in the economic and political advance of some pioneering society and the subsequent changes in the follower societies."[14] In this case, Germany obviously was the pioneering country. However, the mere fact that other countries followed chronologically is not sufficient proof that these countries were decisively influenced by the German example.[15] The crucial question is whether and to what extent the development in other countries would have been different if Germany had not established its social insurance systems in the 1880s. We should first note that in several other European countries, similar projects were discussed at the same time or even earlier. Thus, the idea was not completely new, and it is reasonable to expect that another country besides Germany could have pioneered. Furthermore, we would have to know whether the German institutions were really viewed as a model by the public, the legislators, and administrators in other countries. This question is analyzed in Chapter 4 with respect to the Scandinavian countries, and the results are ambiguous. Unfortunately, we are not able to conduct a similar analysis for all Western European countries, but we can develop an alternative test of whether the development in these countries would have been significantly different without the German example.

The diffusion concept, as related to Bendix's conception of the modernization process, is a far-reaching one. It holds that because one country pioneered in introducing a specific institution at a certain level of development, other countries will adopt this institution in general at a lower level of development. Thus, if we define here level of development as the level of socioeconomic development on the one hand and the level of political mobilization on the other, we could hypothesize that the follower societies that introduce these institutions later in chronological time establish them earlier in developmental time, i.e. at lower levels of socioeconomic development and political mobilization.

This hypothesis is clearly rejected by examining the two scatterplots in Figures 2.5 and 2.6 in which all seventy-two[16] core laws are recorded with respect to the year of enactment, the level of socioeconomic development reached in that year (Figure 2.5), and the level of working-class mobilization in the same year (Figure 2.6). The follower societies established their systems usually at a slightly higher level of socioeconomic development and generally at a much higher level of political mobilization.

Figure 2.5
Social Insurance Legislation and Levels of Socioeconomic Development

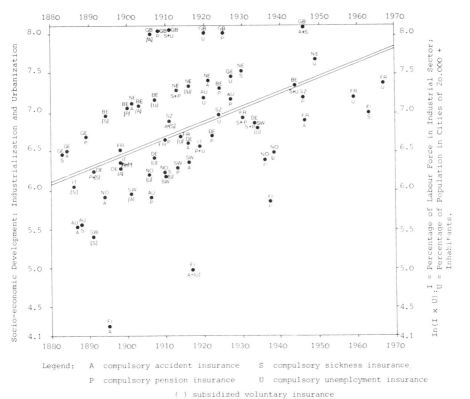

Legend: A   compulsory accident insurance   S   compulsory sickness insurance

P   compulsory pension insurance   U   compulsory unemployment insurance

( )   subsidized voluntary insurance

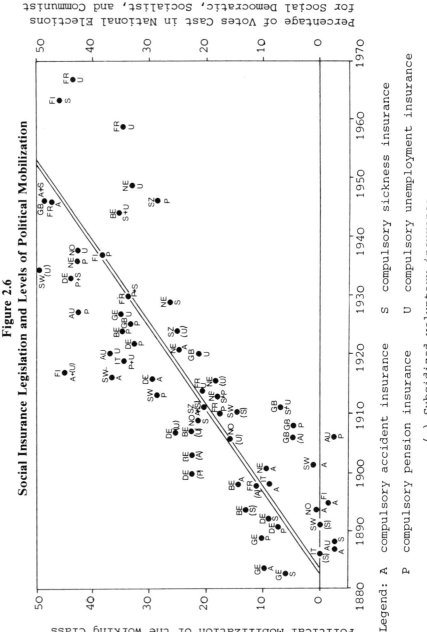

Figure 2.6
Social Insurance Legislation and Levels of Political Mobilization

Legend: A   compulsory accident insurance   S   compulsory sickness insurance

P   compulsory pension insurance   U   compulsory unemployment insurance

( )   Subsidized voluntary insurance

To test the hypothesis in more detail, the whole set of seventy-two social insurance laws has been subdivided into eight subsets: the first laws and all core laws for each of the four social insurance systems. The relevant coefficients for these subsets are presented in Table 2.5. The standardized regression coefficients show that the general conclusion holds for all subsets: 12 of the 16 coefficients are clearly positive and the other 4 are practically zero. In general, these coefficients and the percentage of explained variance are much lower in relation to socioeconomic development than in relation to political mobilization.

In Western Europe, the follower societies have thus introduced social insurance systems at consistently higher levels of political mobilization and at slightly higher and rather similar levels of socioeconomic development. A similar pattern was earlier found by David Collier and Richard E. Messick with respect to the timing of the adoption of the first social security program in each country. Among the European nations, they found a "moderate but consistent tendency" for late adopters to adopt programs at successively higher levels of modernization as indicated by the labor force in the agricultural sector.[17] In contrast to Collier and Messick who take this pattern as evidence for a diffusion process "up a hierarchy of nations," we interpret this result as evidence that diffusion processes alone cannot account for the establishment of national social security programs. Although diffusion processes may have affected the course of national decision making, the example set by a pioneer country does not apparently provide sufficient incentive to adopt social insurance schemes independent of internal socioeconomic problems and political mobilization. We therefore turn our attention to the analysis of some internal prerequisites for social security legislation.

C. The Importance of Socioeconomic Development and Political Mobilization

Do thresholds of socioeconomic development or political mobilization exist that make the establishment of social security programs highly probable or even mandatory? Looking first at the range of socioeconomic development at the time of adoption, one can see that the three lowest ranking countries (Finland 1917, Sweden 1891, Austria 1887, neglecting the exotic value of Finland 1895) introduced their first social insurance schemes at a mean level of 5.29 (= 1n I × U) corresponding to a level of 17.5 percent industrialization and 11.5 percent urbanization. Britain, as the highest ranking country on the other hand, established its first systems between 1906 and 1911 at a level of 54 percent industrialization (probably the maximum) and around 60 percent urbanization (a level reached in Europe in 1970 only by the Netherlands). With respect to the level of political mobilization of the working class, the range of variation is similar with extreme values at 0 percent and 50 percent of total votes.

Table 2.5
Diffusion of Social Insurance Legislation

(1) With respect to socio-economic development: x = chronological time (year of introduction), y = socio-economic development (ln Ixl) at the year of introduction

		n number of laws	x̄ mean year of introduction (round fig.)	ȳ mean level of socio-economic development	s_x standard deviation in chronological time (years)	s_y standard deviation in socio-economic development (ln Ixl)	b regression coefficient	r = B regression coefficient of standardized scores	r^2 percentage of explained variance
Accident Insurance	First Laws	12	1898	6.36	7.5	0.94	0.06	0.52	0.27
	All Laws	18	1908	6.48	17.3	0.96	0.03	0.46	0.21
Sickness Insurance	First Laws	12	1906	6.58	22.9	0.75	0.02	0.50	0.25
	All Laws	17	1914	6.76	23.8	0.77	0.02	0.63	0.40
Pension Insurance	First Laws	12	1912	6.65	18.4	0.63	-0.0005	-0.02	0.0004
	All Laws	19	1917	6.81	16.1	0.60	0.01	0.14	0.02
Unemployment Insurance	First Laws	12	1917	6.81	8.6	0.77	0.01	0.11	0.01
	All Laws	18	1927	6.99	18.2	0.72	0.01	0.26	0.07
All 4 systems	First Laws	48	1908	6.60	16.8	0.77	0.01	0.32	0.10
	All Laws	72	1917	6.76	19.8	0.78	0.02	0.44	0.19

(2) With respect to political mobilization: x = chronological time (year of introduction), y = political mobilization (%of votes for 'working class parties') at the introduction

		n number of laws	x̄ mean year of introduction (round fig.)	ȳ mean level of political mobilization	s_x standard deviation in chronological time (years)	s_y standard deviation in political mobilization (% of votes)	b regression coefficient	r = B regression coefficient of standardized scores	r^2 percentage of explained variance
Accident Insurance	First Laws	12	1898	8.5	7.5	7.7	0.08	0.08	0.01
	All Laws	18	1908	18.5	17.3	16.7	0.79	0.82	0.67
Sickness Insurance	First Laws	12	1906	14.6	22.9	14.3	0.58	0.93	0.86
	All Laws	17	1914	20.2	23.8	16.3	0.64	0.94	0.88
Pension Insurance	First Laws	12	1912	19.0	18.4	13.6	0.57	0.77	0.59
	All Laws	19	1917	25.4	16.1	14.0	0.70	0.80	0.64
Unemployment Insurance	First Laws	12	1917	27.9	8.6	12.5	1.01	0.69	0.48
	All Laws	18	1927	30.4	18.2	11.6	0.38	0.60	0.36
All 4 systems	First Laws	48	1908	17.5	16.8	13.9	0.65	0.79	0.62
	All Laws	72	1917	23.6	19.8	15.2	0.63	0.82	0.67

First Laws = all first laws establishing a compulsory or subsidized voluntary system (excluding systems for very limited groups, such as e.g. miners)

Even if the extreme values are disregarded, the spread remains very wide. We may thus conclude that the variation in developmental levels at the time of the establishment of social insurance systems is too great to allow any generalization about thresholds. Of course, it is obvious that predominantly agricultural societies probably will not adopt social insurance systems, just as highly industrialized and urbanized societies will have such schemes. Given the weak explanatory power of the threshold concept with respect to single developments, it is important to analyze whether socioeconomic change and political mobilization combine to influence social insurance introduction.

If this is the case, we would expect that countries that introduce social insurance schemes at relatively low levels of socioeconomic development are characterized by relatively high levels of political mobilization of the working class pressing for such institutions. Similarly, countries that introduce social insurance schemes at relatively low levels of political mobilization are characterized by relatively high levels of socioeconomic development producing social problems that necessitate the introduction of such institutions. In either case, countries introducing social insurance schemes at relatively low or relatively high levels of both socioeconomic development and political mobilization, should be the exception, rather than the rule.

Figure 2.7
Socioeconomic Change and Political Mobilization as Influences on Social Insurance Introduction

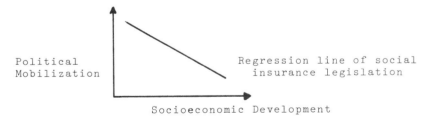

The scatter plot in Figure 2.8 is used to examine this hypothesis. The horizontal axis refers to the levels of socioeconomic development, the vertical axis to levels of political mobilization. Each point represents the introduction of one (or more simultaneous) social insurance laws at the respective levels and is marked by the country name, the year of introduction, and the type of law. The regression lines show that, in its general formulation, the hypothesis must be rejected. With respect to social insurance legislation, the two developmental dimensions seem to be completely independent.

Figure 2.8
Social Insurance Legislation in the Context of
Socioeconomic Development and Political Mobilization

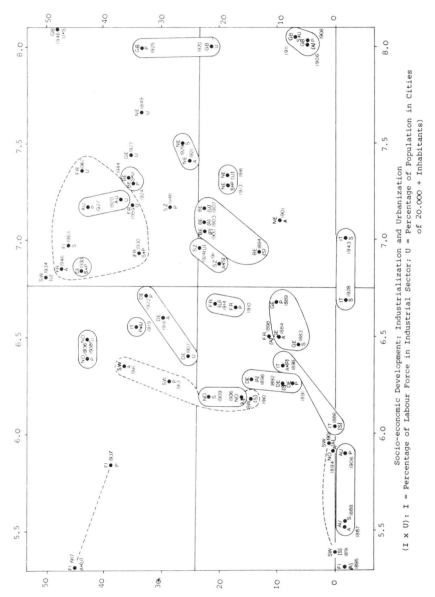

It could be, however, that the above hypothesis is meaningful only in relation to various subsets of the 72 laws, the combination of which may obscure the hypothesized relationship. This is made probable by the fact that all countries developed their systems not in one, but in several steps. The differentiated hypothesis, therefore, would look like Figure 2.9.

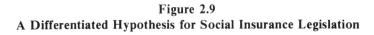

Figure 2.9
A Differentiated Hypothesis for Social Insurance Legislation

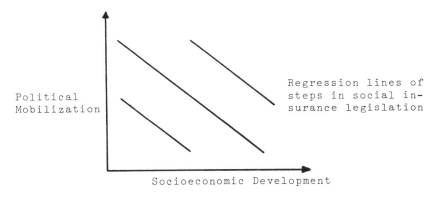

In order to identify the possible subsets, we first simplify the analysis by combining two or more laws of each country (in the first scatter plot surrounded by lines) that are characterized by similar levels of development and mobilization and/or temporal proximity (the problematic groupings have dotted lines). This reduces the number of cases to 33 insurance legislation periods for which the mean values of the combined laws are then considered. To test now the more differentiated hypothesis, three subsets are constructed:

1. by grouping together those insurance legislation periods which are comparable among the countries with respect to their sequence in the national evolution of social insurance legislation and to time periods;
2. by calculating the respective regression lines for the three subsets, starting with those insurance legislation periods for which the hypothesis seems to fit best;
3. by maximizing the percentage of variance explained by the regression lines in a procedure of trial and error, including and/or excluding those steps with a relatively greater distance from the regression line. This procedure proved that the inclusion and/or exclusion of the values did not essentially change the regression coefficients but only the coefficients of determination.

Thus, three subsets have been constructed that represent approximately three time periods (with few exceptions):

Figure 2.10
Social Insurance Legislation in the Context of Socioeconomic
Development and Political Mobilization

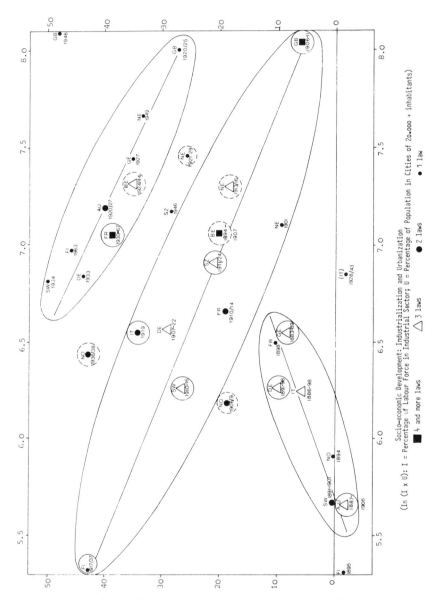

Subset	Time-Period	Mean Level of Socioeconomic Development	Mean Level of Political Mobilization	Regression Coefficient	Coefficient of Determination	
I.	1880-1900	6.12	5.3	12.07	0.85	7
II.	1900-1920	6.77	22.7	-13.49	0.81	10
III.	1920-	7.25	38.8	-16.19	0.86	9

The main period of social insurance legislation in each county is surrounded by a line (dotted lines for countries with two such periods).

Figure 2.11
**The Sociopolitical Paths of Social Insurance Legislation
in Three Time-Periods**

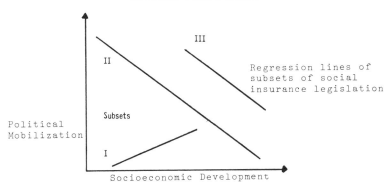

Simplified, the three subsets yield the structure in Figure 2.11. For our argument, the middle subset (II) is the central one, since it includes the main social insurance legislation periods of five countries (Finland, Sweden, Italy, Switzerland, the United Kingdom) in addition to two countries with the first of two main legislative periods (Belgium, the Netherlands). With respect to this group of countries, the differentiated hypothesis seems to have some validity. This means that we should here consider the introduction of social insurance schemes as a function of the combined effects of growing social problems (socioeconomic development) and an increasing political pressure (mobilization of the working class). Although differing widely in levels of industrialization and urbanization on the one hand and political mobilization on the other, these countries enacted social insurance laws at similar levels of sociopolitical development. We are not able here to explore the differences in the interaction of socioeconomic and political development in greater detail. An explanation will probably have to be sought in the consequences of a "late" versus an "early" industrialization and urbanization (Finland, Sweden, Italy versus the United Kingdom, Belgium, the Netherlands, Switzerland)

for the mobilization of the working class, but also in the impact of cultural cleavages upon the labor movement (Switzerland, Belgium, the Netherlands). The plausibility of the differentiated hypothesis for this group of countries is not undermined by the fact that some introduced minor social insurance schemes earlier (Finland, Sweden, Italy) or later added some laws to supplement the established systems (Sweden, Finland, the Netherlands, the United Kingdom).

In need of explanation, however, are those cases where the main periods are characterized by relatively low or relatively high levels of both developmental dimensions (Subsets I and III). Group I is of special interest, since it includes those introductions of social insurance schemes that, compared to the central Group II, definitely came "too early." The different slope of its regression line suggests that the hypothesized relationship is irrelevant here. In the following part, therefore, we shall attempt to explain the "deviance" of these cases by referring to differences in constitutional developments.

D. The Role of Constitutional Developments

With respect to these early developments, we can hypothesize that the constitutional-dualistic monarchies tended to introduce social insurance schemes earlier (in chronological and developmental time) than the parliamentary democracies for several reasons. First, they had a greater need to solidify the loyalty of the working class since they were competing with a growing and hostile labor movement that threatened the legitimacy of the nonparliamentary political regimes. Second, the constitutional-dualistic monarchies had already developed stronger state bureaucracies capable of administering such systems and preserving a paternalistic heritage. Finally, these regimes were dominated by landed interests that were able to shift the costs of social expenditures to the urban upper and middle class by taxes on income and profit and employers' insurance contributions and to the working class itself by indirect taxes and compulsory insurance contributions.

In Table 2.6, three levels of enfranchisement are distinguished in the vertical axis (0 - 35 percent, 40 - 70 percent, 75 + percent, representing the percentages of the respective male age group who could vote), and the two types of regimes are differentiated in the horizontal axis. This produces six different political settings in which the various countries are located for the corresponding years. The period stems from 1883, when the first law in Germany was enacted, to 1914, excluding the specific impact of World War I. The first social insurance laws introduced in this period are distinguished according to their importance (major, medium, minor) and relocated with respect to the political setting at the time of their passage. In order to measure the "propensity to introduce social insurance schemes," a "ratio of social insurance realization" was calculated by dividing the number of

Table 2.6
Constitutional Development and Social Insurance Legislation

CONSTITUTIONAL – DUALISTIC MONARCHIES

MALE SUFFRAGE	First Social Insurance Laws (major / medium / minor)	Ratios of social insurance realization
0 – 35	AU 1883–1906: major 1888 Sw 1883–1910: medium 1887, 1906; minor 1891, 1901	5 laws / 8 potential laws 52 years = 1,20 %
40 – 70		
75 –	AU 1907–1914: major 1891 DE 1883–1910: major 1883 GE 1883–1914: major 1889; medium 1892, 1884; minor 1898 Sw 1911–1914: major 1913	7 laws / 11 potential laws 63 years = 1,01 %

	countries	actual laws	potential laws
	4	11	16
	4	10	16
	4	12	15 (= 16–1 of DE)

Ratios: 11/16 = 69 %   10/16 = 63 %   12/15 = 80 %

Ratios of sub set I

18 % = 5/28   (Ratios of period until 1901) 21 % = 6/28   (Ratios of period until 1914) 76 % = 22/29

PARLIAMENTARY DEMOCRACIES

Ratios of social insurance realization	First Social Insurance Laws (major / medium / minor)	MALE SUFFRAGE
3 laws / 16 potential laws 64 years = 0,29 %	BE 1883–1893: II 1883–1912: minor 1886, 1898, 1898	0 – 35
7 laws / 12 potential laws 54 years = 1,08 %	NO 1884–1893: NE 1883–1896: NE 1897–1914: 1913 NO 1894–1899: 1908, 1911, 1911 GB 1885–1914: medium 1901, 1894, 1906	40 – 70
12 laws / 17 potential laws 124 years = 0,57 %	BE 1894–1914: medium 1900, 1903, 1907, 1907, 1898, 1910, 1914; minor 1894 DE 1901–1914: FR 1883–1914: II 1913–1914: NO 1900–1914: 1909; medium 1906, 1911, 1911 SZ 1883–1914:	75 +

	countries	actual laws	potential laws
	7	5	28
	7	6	28
	8	22	29 (= 32–3 of DE)

actual laws by the number of potential laws, assuming that each country could have introduced four first laws (one in each of the four insurance systems).

Comparing the ratios, the following conclusions may be drawn:
(1) In subset I, the propensity to introduce social insurance schemes was much higher in the constitutional-dualistic monarchies (Austria, Denmark, Germany, Sweden) than in the parliamentary democracies. The respective ratios are 69 percent to 18 percent. The difference remains even if one defines the subset in strictly chronological terms as the period until 1901. Here, the ratios are 63 percent to 21 percent. Furthermore, three of the five laws in the category of democracies were enacted in Italy, which poses problems in being classified as a parliamentary democracy at that time. It was only later, not until 1914, that the democracies compensated for the advance of the authoritarian regimes and narrowed the gap in ratios (80 percent to 76 percent).

(2) This difference in the propensity to introduce social insurance schemes seems to be primarily a function of the type of regime and not the level of enfranchisement. In order to compare the two types of regimes at various levels of enfranchisement properly, one has to weigh the respective ratios of actual laws to potential laws by the number of years that a country remained in the respective category, thus calculating an annual average ratio of social insurance realization. The ratios show that at both levels of enfranchisement for which comparisons can be made (0-30% and 75+% male suffrage) the propensity to introduce social insurance was considerably higher in authoritarian than in democratic regimes (1.20 to 0.29 and 1.01 to 0.57). Only the category of parliamentary democracies with 40 to 70 percent male suffrage disturbs the picture, but this is because of the heavy influence of Great Britain that introduced all four systems. If this category is combined with the 75 percent and more suffrage, the ratios become 1.01 to 0.37.

(3) In the parliamentary democracies the extension of suffrage clearly increased the propensity to introduce insurance systems. Although it seems difficult to generalize about a "suffrage threshold," the propensity increased where suffrage was over 50 percent of the male population. In the constitutional-dualistic monarchies, however, the influence of the suffrage level is not clear. On the one hand, the ratio is higher in the category with a lower suffrage (1.20 to 1.01), while on the other, the countries with a higher level of enfranchisement generally introduced more important and comprehensive systems.

The greater propensity of the constitutional-dualistic monarchies to introduce social insurance schemes is even more remarkable considering the differences in socioeconomic development. Calculating the average level of socioeconomic development for each category (mean ln I x U for all years in which social insurance laws were enacted) shows that parliamentary democracies introduced social insurance not only later, but usually also at relatively higher levels of industrialization and urbanization:

Male Suffrage	Constitutional-Dualistic Monarchies	Parliamentary Democracies	
0 - 30	mean ln I x U = 5.66	mean ln I x U = 6.22	
40 - 70		7.49	7.00
75 +	6.39	6.72	
All	6.09	6.89	

If the establishment of social insurance systems by the early adopters is related to constitutional developments, the question as to what influenced the "deviant" group that introduced their schemes in the period after 1920 (Subset III in Figure 2.11) remains. In contradiction to our hypothesis on the combined effects of socioeconomic developments and political mobilization, these countries established their insurance programs at relatively high levels of both types of problem pressure. This is especially true for France, to some degree for Belgium, but maybe also for the Netherlands which falls outside the group.[18]

To explain the late adoption of social security in these countries, it is probably necessary to consider such variables as government instability and cleavage structures, especially within the labor movement. Frequent government turnovers probably account for much of the French history of delayed social security legislation, whereas cross-cutting cleavages would probably help to explain the developments in Belgium and the Netherlands. We should be aware, however, that categorizing countries as late adopters simply because of the timing of their legislation may be misleading. It is very possible that the laggards in the establishment of insurance systems were in fact pioneers with respect to the adequacy of protection. Thus, the latecomers may have initiated systems at higher levels of coverage and/or compensation, whereas the early adopters may have only gradually extended their schemes. An analysis of the more recent period would therefore require the inclusion of much more refined dependent variables describing the scope, the level and duration of benefits, and so forth for the systems. To do this for all insurance systems here is impossible, but Chapter 5 attempts to describe at least the most recently established system—unemployment insurance—in these terms.

Table 2.7
Active Members of Occupational Injuries Insurance

Year	GE	AU	NO	FI	DE	FR	IT	NE	SW	BE	UK	SZ	Year
1880	18 7												1880
1885													1885
1890	70 28	9 5											1890
1895	81 33	14 8	15 6	8 3									1895
1900	75 31	18 9	13 5	8 3	15	10 5							1900
1905	72 31	20 10	12 5	8 3	20	13 7	5	25 10	17 7	23 11	76		1905
1910	87 38	25 14	16 6	8 4	40	20	10	27 11	20 8	24 11	76		1910
1915	78 34	27	31 13	15 7	40	20	12 5	28 11	22 9	25	76		1915
1920	75 38	32 15	33 13	19 9	50	20	15	36 14	56 25	25	77	33 16	1920
1925	72 37	30	29 12	33 16	50	50	50	47 19	51 23	35	77	32 16	1925
1930	75 38	40 23	29 12	32 16	50	50	50	51 21	55 26	45	77	38 18	1930
1935	77 38	49 24	30 13	31 17	50	55	50	41 16	57 27	45	77	31 15	1935
1940	88 44	50	34 15	34 18	50	55	50	44 18	62 29	45	78	34 16	1940
1945	90	50	34 15	43 21	50	55	50	45	70 32	57 24	75	40 19	1945
1950	91 42	54 26	40 17	49 23	50	55	50	58 23	73 32	55 23	90 42	43 20	1950
1955	100	87 42	42 17	56 26	51 24	58 29	56 23	64 24	79 36	60 25	89 43	48 23	1955
1960	92 44	94 45	76 30	68 31	61 29	65 28	66 27	67 24	76 36	59 24	92 44	55 26	1960
1965	96 44	89 42	76 30	75 34	60	70	65	71 26	76 37	60	92 44	61 28	1965
1970	98 43	94 41	77 31			80	65	75	74 36	60	93 43	60	1970

Number of members of compulsory occupational injuries insurance or employer's liability (workmen's compensation) schemes in percent of the economically active population and in percent of the total population. Missing percentages of the population usually indicate estimates (or, in a few exceptions, missing population data).
Source: HIWED archive.

⌐ ⌐ employer's liability scheme in effect

⌐ compulsory insurance scheme in effect

Table 2.8
Active Members of Public Sickness Insurance

Year	FR	GE	II	AU	SW	DE	BE	NO	UK	SZ	NE	FI	Year
1880													1880
1885	5 2	26 10											1885
1890	5 2	36 14	5 3	12 7									1890
1895	8	39 15	6	15 8	4 2	15 7	3 1						1895
1900	9	44 18	6	18 10	13 5	25 13	6 3					3 1	1900
1905	13 7	46 20	6	20 11	21 8	40	8 4					4 1	1905
1910	17 8	51 22	6	23 12	27 11	55	12 6	38 15	75 35			4 2	1910
1915	15 8	50 22	6	22	24 10	70 31	12 5	51 21	79 36	22 10		4 2	1915
1920	17 9	56 28	6	40	28 13	91 40	21 9	48 20	83 38	44 21		4 2	1920
1925	21 11	57 29	6 3	47	29 13	100 43	28 12	48 20	89 41	49 24		4 2	1925
1930	33 17	59 29	8 3	59 28	35 17	104 47	33 15	51 22	89 42	68 33	40	4 2	1930
1935	35 17	53 26	23 10	49 24	32 15	135	34 15	67 29	105 48	79 37	40	5 2	1935
1940	46 22	58 29	50	50	49 23	137 71	31 13	64 28	111 51	86 40	40	5 3	1940
1945	52 27	60	60 27	55	84 38	142 71	48 20	72 31	160	100	45 18	5 3	1945
1950	75 38	77 36	65 29	85 41	99 44	145 70	63 26	79 32	155	113 52	58 22	7 3	1950
1955	79 37	91 43	85 36	92 45	162 74	146 71	64 26	184 72	155	121 57	76 29	8 4	1955
1960	92 39	87 42	115 46	102 49	158 76	157 72	67 27	180 72	155	134 63	80 29	9 4	1960
1965	124 51	85 39	125 47	108 50	161 78	157 74	79 31	178 72	160	150 70	83 30	158 72	1965
1970	120 50	97 43	141 51	128 56	160 78	160 75	98 40			155 74	83 30	162 74	1970

Number of active members of compulsory or subsidized voluntary sickness insurance schemes in percent of the economically active population and of the total population. Missing percentages of the population usually indicate estimates (or, in a few exceptions, missing population data). Source: HIWED archive.

⌐ law on subsidized voluntary scheme in effect

⌐ law on compulsory scheme in effect

Table 2.9
Active Members of Public Pension Insurance

Year	FR	GE	IT	BE	SW	NE	DE	UK	AU	NO	FI	SZ	Year
1880													1880
1885	6												1885
1890	6												1890
1895	8	53 21					(20)						1895
1900	8	51 21	0 0	4			(20)						1900
1905	8	49 21	1 1	9 11			(20)						1905
1910	8	52 22	2	23 14	136 57		(25)	(55)	2				1910
1915	9 5	58 24	2	30	132 58	50	(25)	(55)	3				1915
1920	14 8	58 27	20	30	132 60	55 22	(25)	(55)	4				1920
1925	14 7	61 30	25	30	131 62	55	91 39	(55)	5				1925
1930	15	64 31	32	51 24	135 64	60 24	95 43	90 41	40 19				1930
1935	37 18	64 32	35	47 21	136 64	65 26	132 63	91 42	36 17				1935
1940	47 23	68 33	40	55	143 64	66 27	112 56	104 47	40	160	95 51		1940
1945	52 27	65	25	44 18	138 61	64 25	111 55	109 50	50	160	105 56		1945
1950	70	69 30	25	57 23	140 64	72 27	111 54	101 47	51 25	160	111 55	102 47	1950
1955	89 42	78 35	45	69 28	140	169 61	94 45	100 48	54 26	160	129 61	110 52	1955
1960	93 40	82 37	95	89 36	140	170	114 52	99 47	75 36	160	140	107 50	1960
1965	100	79 35	100	90	135	170	160	99 47	76 35	155	140	110	1965
1970	100	81 74	100	90			160	98 46	78 74		140	110	1970

Number of members of compulsory or subsidized voluntary pension insurance schemes in percent of the economically active population and of the total population. Missing percentages of the population usually indicate estimates (or, in a few exceptions, missing population data). Figures in brackets are beneficiary ratios under semi-demogrant schemes. Source: HIWED archive.

⌐‾ ‾ law on subsidized voluntary scheme in effect   ⌐‾ law on compulsory scheme in effect

Table 2.10
Active Members of Unemployment Insurance

Year	FR		NO		DE		BE		UK		NE		FI		IT		AU		SZ		GE		SW		Year
1880																									1880
1885																									1885
1890																									1890
1895																									1895
1900																									1900
1905	0	0																							1905
1910	0	0	2	1	9	4	4																		1910
1915	0	0	4	2	12	6	5	2	11	5															1915
1920	1		11	4	21	9	5	9	22	9	13	5	1		25		30								1920
1925	1		4	2	19	8	18	8	59	26	9	4	1		25		35		8	4					1925
1930	1	0	4	2	19	9	17	8	59	27	14	6	1		26	11	34	16	17	8	44	22			1930
1935	1	1	5	2	23	11	25	11	65	30	16	6	2	1	28	12	25	12	28	13	36	18	2	1	1935
1940	-		35		26	13	30		70	31	15	6	4		30		25		27	13	45	22	7	3	1940
1945	-		37	16	29	14	34	14	62	29	5		7	4	36		30		26	12	45		27	12	1945
1950	-		50	21	31	15	58	24	85	39	5		7	3	16	7	40	20	27	12	43	20	35	16	1950
1955	-		56	23	32	15	57	23	81	39	54	20	10	5	26	11	46	22	27	13	53	26	37	17	1955
1960	50		59	23	35	16	57	23	79	38	55	20	14	6	41	16	55	26	25	12	59	28	37	18	1960
1965	50		59	23	35	17	60	24	77	37	63	23	24	11	45		57	26	21	10	62	29	42	20	1965
1970	50		57	23	34	17	63	26	74	35	78	28	38	17	48		60	26	18	9	72	32	55	27	1970

Number of members of compulsory or subsidized voluntary unemployment insurance schemes in percent of the economically active population and of the total population. Missing percentages of the population usually indicate estimates (or, in a few exceptions, missing population data). Source: HIWED archive.

- - law on subsidized voluntary insurance in effect
— law on compulsory insurance in effect

Notes

1. See Flora 1974.
2. See Parsons 1971.
3. See Parsons 1960.
4. Marshall 1965, p. 84.
5. Marshall 1965, p. 72.
6. The elements of Rokkan's theory are scattered in various publications. The most important are: Lipset and Rokkan 1967; Rokkan 1970; Rokkan, Saelen, and Warmbrunn 1973; Rokkan 1974a, 1974b, and 1974c.
7. Rimlinger 1971, p. 59.
8. For Germany, cf. Andic and Veverka 1964; and Weitzel 1968; for the United Kingdom, Peacock and Wiseman 1961; and for Sweden, Hök 1962.
9. Cf. Perrin 1969.
10. An indicator of socioeconomic development is constructed by taking the natural logarithm of the product of both percentages: $\ln (I \times U)$. The product instead of the mean is used, because we assume that the impact of medium levels of industrialization and urbanization on the generation of respective social problems is higher than the impact of relatively high industrialization with relatively low urbanization (e.g., Switzerland) or vice versa (e.g., the Netherlands). The raw data can be found in Flora 1975.
11. A major problem lies in the simple addition of the votes for the various parties. Further explanatory attempts will certainly have to account for the relative homogeneity of the labor movement and also to include more indicators measuring different aspects of the mobilization of the working class. The data on election results have been taken from Mackie and Rose 1974. The following parties have been included:

Austria: Social Democrats (1907-1971), Communists (1945-1956).
Belgium: Workers Party/Socialist Party (1894, 1900, 1912, 1919-1971), Liberal-Worker Party Cartels (1894, 1912, 1946, 1950-1958), Communists (1925-1971).
Denmark: Social Democrats (1884-1971), Communists (1920-1971), Social Peoples Party (1960-1971), Left Socialists (1968-1971).
Finland: Social Democrats (1907-1970), Communists (1922-1970), Social Democratic League (1958-1970).
France: Socialists/Socialist Party (1893-1968), Radical Socialist Party (1967), Independent Socialists/Socialist Republicans (1906-1936), Communists (1924-1968), United Socialist Party (1962-1968).
Germany: Social Democrats (1871-1969), Communists (1920-1953), Independent Socialists (1919-1928).
Italy: Socialist Party (1895-1968), Reformist Socialists (1913-1919), Independent Socialists (1913-1921), Communists (1921-1968), Social Democrats (1948-1968).
Netherlands: Social Democrats (1888-1967), Communists (1918-1967), Social Party (1918-1925), Revolutionary Socialist Party (1929-1933), Pacifist Socialist Party (1959-1967).
Norway: Labour Party (1894-1969), Social Democratic Party (1921-1924), Communists (1924-1969), Socialist People's Party (1961-1969).
Sweden: Social Democrats (1902-1970), Left Socialists (1917-1921), Communists (1921-1970), Socialists (1936-1944).

Switzerland: Social Democrats (1896-1971), Communists (1922-1971).
United   Independent Labour Party (1895), Labour Party (1900-1970),
Kingdom: Communists (1922-1970).

12. These age groups have been reconstructed using the data of the population censuses and estimating the age distributions for the intercensus years. The raw data on the enfranchised male population can be found in Kohl 1977.
13. The data on the political regimes are taken from von Beyme 1970. The difficulties of classification have an institutional and a chronological aspect. As to the first, Italy and Switzerland are classified as parliamentary democracies, although they may be seen as representing a "mixed type" and a "third type" (of directorial democracy). As to the second, difficulties arise when the parliamentary responsibility of government was introduced de facto but not de jure (Norway 1884 and Denmark 1901 seem to be clear cases, but Sweden 1917 may be disputed). The following classification has been used: (1) constitutional-dualistic monarchies: Austria, Denmark until 1901, (Finland), Germany, Norway until 1884, Sweden until 1917; (2) parliamentary democracies: Belgium, Denmark since 1901, France, Italy (?), Netherlands, Norway since 1884, Sweden since 1917, Switzerland, United Kingdom.
14. Bendix 1967, p. 331.
15. For this reason, the analysis by Collier and Messick 1975 is not very convincing.
16. Seventy-two instead of seventy-four laws are used in the analysis because two laws passed under the fascist regime in Italy are excluded since they could not be classified with respect to the level of political mobilization.
17. Collier and Messick 1975, p. 1310.
18. Norway seems to be a special case, since one of its two main periods came "too early" (1906-09), and the other "too late" (1936-38) with respect to the combined levels of problem pressure.

References

Andic, Suphan and Veverka, Jindrich. 1964. "The Growth of Government Expenditure in Germany Since the Unification." *Finanzarchiv*, N.F. 23: 169-278.
Bendix, Reinhard. 1967. "Tradition and Modernity Reconsidered." *Comparative Studies in Society and History* 9: 292-346.
Beyme, Klaus von. 1970. *Die parlamentarischen Regierungssysteme in Europa.* Munich: Piper.
Briggs, Asa. 1961. "The Welfare State in Historical Perspective." *Europäisches Archiv für Soziologie* 2: 221-258.
Collier, David and Messick, Richard. 1975. "Prerequisites versus Diffusion: Testing Alternative Explanations of Social Security Adoption." *American Political Science Review* 69: 1296-1315.
Flora, Peter. 1974. *Modernisierungsforschung. Zur empirischen Analyse der gesellschaftlichen Entwicklung.* Opladen: Westdeutscher Verlag.
Flora, Peter. 1975. "Quantitative Historical Sociology." *Current Sociology* 23: 2.
Hook, Erik. 1962. *Den offentliga sektorns expansion. En studie av de offentliga civila utgifternas utveckeling aren 1913-1918.* Stockholm: Almkvist and Wicksell.
Kohl, Jürgen. 1977. "Elections I - Enfranchisement and Electoral Participation." HIWED Report No. 6. Cologne. Mimeographed.
Lipset, Seymour M. and Rokkan, Stein, eds. 1967. *Party Systems and Voter Alignments.* New York: Free Press.

Mackie, Thomas T. and Rose, Richard. 1974. *The International Almanac of Electoral History.* London: Macmillan.

Marshall, T. H. 1965. *Class, Citizenship, and Social Development.* Garden City, N.Y.: Anchor Books.

Parsons, Talcott. 1960. "Durkheim's Contribution to the Theory of Integration of Social Systems." In *Emile Durkheim 1858-1917,* ed. K. H. Wolff, pp. 118-153. Columbus: Ohio State University Press.

Parsons, Talcott. 1971. *The System of Modern Societies.* Englewood Cliffs, N. J.: Prentice Hall.

Peacock, Alan T. and Wiseman, Jack. 1961. *The Growth of Public Expenditure in the United Kingdom.* Princeton, N. J.: Princeton University Press.

Perrin, Guy. 1969. "Reflections on Fifty Years of Social Security." *International Labour Review* 99: 249-292.

Rimlinger, Gaston V. 1971. *Welfare Policy and Industrialization in Europe, America, and Russia.* New York: John Wiley & Sons.

Rokkan, Stein. 1974a. "Cities, States, and Nations." In *Building States and Nations,* ed. S. N. Eisenstadt and Stein Rokkan, 1: 73-97. Beverly Hills. Calif.: Sage.

Rokkan, Stein. 1974b. "Dimensions of State Formation and Nation Building." In *The Formation of National States in Western Europe,* ed. Charles Tilly, pp. 562-600. Princeton, N. J.: Princeton University Press.

Rokkan, Stein. 1974c. "Entries, Voices, Exits: Towards a Possible Generalization of the Hirschman Model." *Social Science Information* 13: 39-53.

Rokkan, Stein, Saelen, K. and Warmbrunn, J. 1973. "Nation Building." *Current Sociology* 19: 3.

Weitzel, Otto. 1968. "Die Entwicklung der Staatsausgaben in Deutschland. Eine Analyse der öffentlichen Aktivität in ihrer Abhängigkeit vom wirtschaftlichen Wachstum." Dissertation. Erlangen-Nürnberg.

Wilensky, Harold L. 1975. *The Welfare State and Equality: Structural and Ideological Roots of Public Expenditures.* Berkeley, Calif.: University of California Press.

Chapter 3

The Development of Welfare States in North America

Robert T. Kudrle and Theodore R. Marmor

Introduction

Many discussions of the development of the welfare state have con-
trasted the experience of the United States with that of Western Europe.
The commonplace claim is that the United States has been a "laggard" in
the development of programs found elsewhere.[1] Various factors have been
cited as contributing to the difference: the absence of feudalism, a democratic political system that emerged prior to a large working class, a
relatively low level of status differentiation, and high per capita income.[2]
The other major North American state, Canada, has received little attention in the growing comparative literature on welfare state policy. In recent
years, however, American policy analysts have begun to investigate the
Canadian experience to extract policy lessons for the United States. This
has usually involved areas in which policies have been implemented in
Canada before being debated and introduced in the United States. Other
investigators have argued that a more careful look at Canada can illumi-
nate the past development of U.S. public policy.[3]

Our comparison of Canadian and U.S. welfare state developments will
attempt to identify both what unique characteristics distinguish the two
North America countries and what common features set them apart from
the countries of Western Europe. The first section of the paper will place
the introduction of major social programs in an international perspective.
The second discusses some of the major Canadian-American differences in

the making of social policy. The succeeding section briefly outlines developments in the two countries of major social policies: pensions, unemployment insurance, other income maintenance policies, and health insurance. An interpretive overview is presented, and the future of the North American welfare state in an international context is the subject of some concluding comments.

I. The Timing of Policy Initiation

If judged only on the basis of the date of social program introduction, Canada and the United States would certainly fit the "laggard" hypotheses, as all European countries, including the European "laggards" Italy and France, had introduced national programs earlier.[4] Even when the relatively greater scope of private and subnational programs in North America is taken into account, the picture is little changed. Because of the greater reliance on subnational programs in both countries, comprehensive data for the earlier periods are difficult to obtain, and this has necessitated inference from known data in one country to the other. However, throughout this century, the United States and Canada can be thought of as virtually one economic region. Rates of inflation, economic growth, and unemployment differ somewhat, but they are often quite similar in magnitude and tend to move together.

Table 3.1 shows the dates of introduction of national North American programs and those in several major European countries. Although estimates indicate that perhaps as much as 30 percent of the U.S. work force was covered by state workman's compensation laws by 1915,[5] only about 2 percent had retirement pensions[6] before the passage of the Social Security Act, and only about two-tenths of one percent had unemployment insurance. The figures for Canada, where urbanization and industrialization were similar but somewhat lower, are not precisely known but cannot be very different. Workmen's compensation plans in North America covered about three-quarters of the labor force by the mid-fifties,[7] and the number has increased in subsequent years.

Canada provided universal but means-tested old age support beginning in 1927 while the United States introduced both Old Age Assistance and insurance in 1935. Sickness insurance of the kind known in most other industrial countries has never been part of the U.S. welfare state. Heclo cites 1965 as the introduction of the first national U.S. program, presumably because in that year disability benefits were relaxed to cover those not permanently and totally disabled. Nevertheless, to qualify an applicant had to be unemployable for the last six months with the expectation of another one year of the condition[8]—an extremely severe test by international standards. In Canada the standards for disability were relaxed over the years under general income maintenance schemes, but only in 1971 did the

Table 3.1
Dates of Introduction of Selected Social Programs

	Industrial Accident Insurance	Sickness Insurance	Pension Insurance	Unemployment Insurance	Family Allowances	Health Insurance
Germany	1884	1883	1889	1927	1954	1880
U.K.	$\dfrac{1887^1}{1906^2}$	1911	1908	1911	1945	1948
Sweden	1901	1910	1913	1934	1947	1962
Canada	1930	1971	1927	1940	1944	1972
U.S.	1930	----	1935	1935	----	----
France	$\dfrac{1898\#}{1946\#\#}$	1930	$\dfrac{1905^1}{1910^2}$	1905^1 1914* 1959** 1967	1932	1945
Italy	1898	$\dfrac{1928^1}{1943^2}$	1919	1919	1936	1945

---

^{1}Heclo   #employer liability   *unemployment assistance
^{2}Flora   ##compulsory   **collective labor agreements

Source: Hugh Heclo, "Income Maintenance: Patterns and Priorities," in Arnold
         Heidenheimer, Hugh Heclo, and Carolyn Teich Adams, Comparative Public
         Policy: The Politics of Social Choice in Europe and America
         (New York: St. Martin's Press: 1975), p. 189.

         Peter Flora with Jens Alber and Jürgen Kohl, On the Development of the
         Western European Welfare States (Mannheim, 1976), (Mimeographed.), p. 51.

         Gaston Rimlinger, Welfare and Industrialization in Europe, America and
         Russia (New York: John Wiley & Sons, Inc.: 1971), pp. 194-95.

         Robert J. Myers, Social Security (Homewood, Illinois: Richard D. Irwin,
         Inc., 1975), p. 537.

         Statistics Canada, Social Security: National Programs (Ottawa: Statistics
         Canada, 1976), p. i.

government amend unemployment insurance to provide the kind of sickness and maternity benefits familiar in many other countries. The United States has no direct family allowances, nor does such a scheme appear imminent. The reasons for this divergence between the two North American countries will be briefly discussed in a later section.

In their study of the development of the welfare state in Western Europe, Flora and his collaborators develop an index of coverage of industrial accident, sickness, pension, and unemployment insurance. The index weights accidents at 0.5, pensions at 1.5, and sickness and unemployment at 1.0.[9] In Figure 3.1 an approximation of the scores for the two North American countries at a few time points have been superimposed upon a simplification of a diagram used by Flora. The similarity in development between the two countries is striking. The differences up to 1970 are due mainly to a different history of pension development.[10] The positions of both countries were much lower than virtually all European countries in the early part of the century, rose considerably after 1930 (largely but not exclusively because of the depression) when European countries also expanded their programs, and climbed rapidly in the postwar years, only to stagnate in the years prior to 1970. The score for Canada soars in the early seventies (after the Flora material ends) with the introduction of sickness and maternity benefits.

The index approach, while obviously limited, does allow the identification of some important characteristics of the development of welfare states. In this case, it shows rather vividly that although North America was a laggard in introducing programs, their subsequent development was extensive. The American New Deal and a series of Canadian initiatives from 1928 to the beginning of World War II not only expanded the North American welfare state very rapidly but by this measure, put it temporarily "ahead" of several European countries, including France and Italy.

The timing of the introduction of welfare state programs and the extent of their coverage are two entirely defensible criteria by which one might identify leaders and laggards. But at least one other standard of appraisal demands attention: the levels of expenditure on the programs in relation to total national resources. By this measure both the United States and Canada are unambiguously laggards. Calculations made on the basis of the nonhealth care related programs to be discussed in this paper—programs in which the national government plays at least some role—yield an estimate of 7.0 percent for Canada in 1974-75 and 6.9 percent for the United States. These figures somewhat underrate each country's effort, as is suggested by the data in Table 3.2 that include more expenditure by subnational units. As the rankings for the countries indicate, both the United States and Canada remained near the bottom of the group in 1962 and held exactly the same relative positions in the entire distribution ten years later. This was so despite a 35 percent growth in the share of GNP devoted to income maintenance expenditures in both countries. The elasticities with respect to both total and per capita income were only about average, and this, coupled with the moderate rate of economic growth of both countries by international standards, suggests that in terms of expenditure the laggard position is likely to persist.

Concentrating as it does on the earliest measures that countries typically take in developing a welfare state, the Flora study does not explicitly consider the issue of national health insurance. Nevertheless, it is a policy of the utmost contemporary importance, and a consideration of the postwar experience would be seriously incomplete if health care were ignored. Column 6 of Table 3.1 presents the dates of introduction of the major

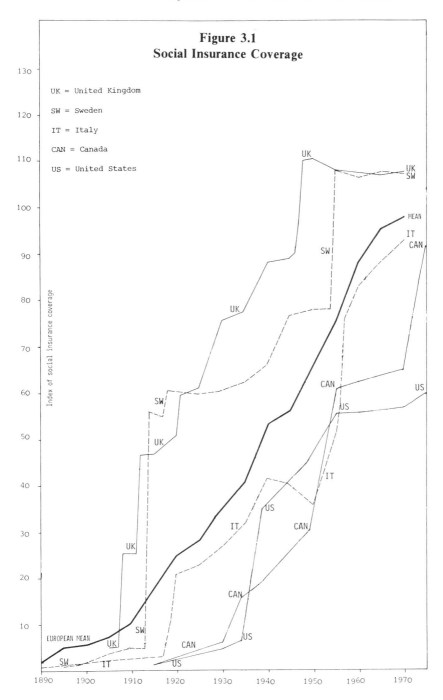

Figure 3.1
Social Insurance Coverage

UK = United Kingdom

SW = Sweden

IT = Italy

CAN = Canada

US = United States

Sources for Figure 1:

Adapted from Peter Flora with Jens Alber and Jürgen Kohl, On the Development of the Western European Welfare States (Mannheim, 1976), (Mimeographed.), p. 27.

John G. Turnbull, C. Arthur Williams, Jr., and Earl F. Cheit, Economic and Social Security (Third Ed.: New York: The Ronald Press Company, 1967), p. 262.

Gaston V. Rimlinger, Welfare Policy and Industrialization in Europe, America, and Russia (New York: John Wiley & Sons, Inc., 1971), pp. 194-196.

Arthur H. Reede, Adequacy of Workmen's Compensation (Cambridge: Harvard University Press, 1947), p. 17.

Dorothy McCamman, "Workmen's Compensation: Coverage, Premiums, and Payments," Social Security Bulletin, July 1950, pp. 3-10.

Ben J. Wattenberg, The Statistical History of the United States (New York: Basic Books, Inc., 1976), p. 342.

Statistical Abstract of the United States, 1977 (Washington: U.S. Government Printing Office, 1977).

Statistics Canada, Social Security: National Programs (Ottawa: Statistics Canada, 1976), pp. 98-99.

Statistics Canada, Annual Report on Benefit Periods Established and Terminated Under the Unemployment Insurance Act, various calendar years.

Health, Welfare, and Labour, Reference book of the Dominion-Provincial Conference on Reconstruction (Ottawa: King's Printer, 1946), p. 62.

Canada, Parliament, Joint Committee on Old Age Security, Report (Ottawa: King's Printer, 1950), p. 7.

No official estimate for Canadian Workmen's Compensation is available for any year. As a very rough approximation, the covered percentage for the United States was used. This may exaggerate the level of Canadian coverage in some years and underestimate it in others. The U.S. estimate for 1975 was 72 percent; this is several points below the estimated minimum Canadian coverage for that year. The latter estimate was provided to the writer by Mr. Wong of the Workers' Compensation Branch, Labor Canada.

national action in health care coverage. North America is once again the lagging area internationally. Canada's 1972 program is later than any other date, and the United States still has no health care system that combines universality and a central public role.

Table 3.3 records the experiences of the same set of countries with health expenditure in recent years. Although the role of government in directly mobilizing these resources varies by country, the extraordinary annual growth of medical expenditures has become one of the major concerns of the managers of welfare states.

Table 3.2
Public Income Maintenance Expenditure (YME) for 1962 and 1972
(or near dates)

	In percent of "trend" GDP at current prices		Implied elasticity of: Total YME with respect to GDP (at current prices)	Implied elasticity of: Per capita YME with respect to per capita income (at constant prices)
	1962	1972		
Australia (1961/62–1971/72)	4.7 (16)	4.0 (16)	.74 (17)	.50 (17)
Austria (1962–73)	14.1 (1)	15.3 (1)	1.13 (13)	1.34 (12)
Belgium	11.7 (4)	14.1 (2)	1.35 (11)	1.61 (11)
Canada	5.4 (13)	7.3 (13)	1.64 (6)	2.15 (7)
Denmark	6.5 (9)	9.9 (7)	1.82 (4)	2.35 (4)
Finland (1962–73)	6.7 (8)	9.9 (7)	1.63 (8)	1.99 (8)
France	11.8 (3)	12.4 (4)	1.09 (14)	1.14 (15)
Germany (1962–73)	11.9 (2)	12.4 (4)	1.09 (14)	1.29 (13)
Ireland (FYs 1961–71)	5.3 (14)	6.4 (15)	1.32 (12)	1.93 (9)
Italy	7.5 (7)	10.4 (6)	1.63 (8)	1.90 (10)
Japan (1962–73)	2.1 (17)	2.8 (17)	1.42 (10)	1.27 (14)
Netherlands (1962–73)	8.6 (5)	14.1 (2)	1.90 (3)	2.31 (5)
New Zealand (FYs)	7.6 (6)	6.5 (14)	.78 (16)	.51 (16)
Norway	5.1 (15)	9.8 (9)	2.55 (1)	3.05 (1)
Sweden	6.0 (10)	9.3 (10)	1.93 (2)	2.43 (3)
United Kingdom	5.7 (11)	7.7 (11)	1.68 (5)	2.85 (2)
United States	5.5 (12)	7.4 (12)	1.64 (6)	2.19 (6)
Dispersion[b]	3.1	3.4	.44	.71
Average[c]	6.8	8.6	1.42	1.63
Average EEC[c]	8.2	10.6	1.45	1.85

a. YMEs have been deflated by the consumption expenditure national deflator.
b. Measured by standard deviation.
c. Geometric mean.
( ) Rank.

Source: OECD, Studies in Resource Allocation, Public Expenditure on Income Maintenance Programs (Paris: 1976), p. 36.

Table 3.3
Total Expenditures for Health Services in Seven Countries
in Selected Periods from 1961 to 1969

	WHO Estimates[a]		SSA Estimates[b]		Average Annual Rate of Increase in Health Expenditures[c]	
	Year	Percentage of GNP	Year	Percentage of GNP	Year	Rate of Change (percentage)
Canada	1961	6.0	1969	7.3	1961-69	13.2
United States	1961-62	5.8	1969	6.8	1962-69	10.1
Sweden	1962	5.4	1969	6.7	1962-69	14.0
Netherlands	1963	4.8	1969	5.9	1963-69	16.1
Federal Republic of Germany	1961	4.5	1969	5.7	1961-69	10.3
France	1963	4.4	1969	5.7	1963-69	14.9
United Kingdom	1961-62	4.2	1969	4.8	1962-69	9.5

[a]Brian Abel-Smith, An International Study of Health Expenditure, WHO Public Paper No. 32 (Geneva: 1967).

[b]Joseph G. Simanis, "Medical Care Expenditures in Seven Countries," Social Security Bulletin (March 1973), p. 39.

[c]Office of Health Economics, London, "International Health Expenditure 11," Information Sheet No. 22 (May 1973), Table 2.

Source: The Report of the Health Planning Task Force prepared under the auspices of the Research and Analysis Division of the Ontario Ministry of Health.

The final section of this paper will discuss the relevance of the North American experience to this international health care cost explosion as part of a more general discussion of the future of the welfare state. The relative similarity of the timing of program initiation, index values, and aggregate levels of expenditure in the classic welfare state areas typically leads to a summary bracketing of the United States and Canada for comparative purposes.[11] In fact, differences between the two countries are just as interesting as their similarities. In the following sections we shall discuss both.

II. The United States and Canada: Explaining the Differences

The United States and Canada are certainly "most similar" societies. All of the factors mentioned earlier that distinguish the United States from Western Europe also hold for Canada. Nevertheless, there is a considerable literature attempting to explain the remaining differences. Only a part of this literature is relevant for our purpose: that which promises to explain the differential development of social policy. Three explanations can be identified: one concerns the nature of Canadian society by contrast with the United States; one stresses differences in the electoral and party systems; and the third emphasizes the profound differences in federalism between the two countries.

The first factor is noted in nearly all Canadian discussions of differences from the United States. Canada was originally settled by people with a different structure of values from the Americans, and the distinctions persisted. Hockin's explanation is typical.

> Canada outside of Quebec, will unfold in ways not only somewhat dissimilar from Europe but dissimilar also from the United States, because socialist and tory sentiments are admissible and natural, if far from all-commanding, in Canada. These sentiments and styles . . . continue to distinguish English Canadians from Americans. French Canada developed differently from France . . . and . . . escaped many of the anti-corporatist and libertarian ideals of the French Revolution. Based on these beginnings, it can be suggested perhaps that Canadian political mentality is much more open and supportive to the notion of state action for national and provincial development than is the American.[12]

The historical observation is borne out by contemporary Canadian political ideology: not only is there a significant socialist party, but there is also a distinctly un-American strain of paternalist thought on the right. A spokesman for the Conservative party advocating the welfare state in the early sixties, for example, blamed liberalism for encouraging the growth of communism by permitting "rugged individualism" to run rampant, resulting in a "class war in unrestrained competition."[13] Horowitz asks: "Can one conceive of a respected philosopher of Republicanism denouncing rugged individualism as foreign to traditional Republican principles?"[14]

The party and electoral systems are vastly different in Canada from those in the United States. The Canadian system is essentially the Westminster model applied to a federal system in which the regional diversity of interest is virtually as great as in the United States. This has led to a greater proliferation of political parties than in most other countries. The major national parties are replicated in the provinces, but at both levels party discipline forces those who disagree with the policies of the two major parties to form new political groups. Furthermore, local and regional issues are of such importance and the power of the provinces in certain areas so great that intraparty discipline between provincial and national parties scarcely exists. A very high percentage of all Canadians vote for one party in provincial elections and another in federal elections (those elections almost never take place at the same time, so there is little sense of "ticket-splitting").[15] By contrast, in the U.S. voters tend far more often to vote for only one party at a given time, although in different parts of the country the ideological and policy meaning of that vote is regarded differently. And this is entirely appropriate. The lack of party discipline gives each legislator an opportunity to represent his own constituency in a way that is impossible in Canada. The same holds at the subnational level. Hence, the formation of new parties is strongly encouraged in Canada and greatly retarded in the United States.

Leman has argued that the Canadian system "gives a parliamentary foot hold to regionally-based third parties, and hence provides a platform for their proposals."[16] The party he is concerned with is the socialist Cooperative Commonwealth Federation, whose prairie image was part of the reason for its transformation into the New Democratic Party in 1962. The implication is that leftish innovations that might be submerged in the U.S. system are presented as options to the public more sharply and dependably in Canada. (Other regionally-based parties such as Social Credit in Alberta, British Columbia, and later in Quebec, have been important provincially without becoming an important force at the national level.)[17]

The third explanation concentrates on federal power-sharing differences between the two countries. In Canada, the provinces are large and have greater explicit reserved power than the American states. Not only are there only ten provinces, but two, Ontario and Quebec, contain over 60 percent of the national population. Quebec with 28 percent of the national population is in many ways virtually a nation apart, and the maintenance of its special identity has been one of the principal causes of the complicated constitutional structure evolving since the British North America Act of 1867. Under this act and subsequent judicial interpretation, powers are shared in a way that has caused almost continuous conflict in recent decades. The federal government is given broad taxing powers. But specific policy responsibilities—including health and social welfare—are provincial responsibilities.[18] Many of the provinces—not just Quebec—have historically resisted federal encroachment. In recent years, however, Quebec nationalism has provided the greatest barrier to any increase in federal power; indeed, by most measures, federal power has diminished.[19] In Canada, the issue of provincial secession has never been settled; in sharp contrast to the United States, it appears to be an option for any province.

There is great centralization of power within the federal and provincial levels of government of Canada. The provincial premier speaks for the province, and he essentially holds a veto power over proposed power-sharing schemes with the federal government. A satisfactory outcome has historically been assured by the commitment of virtually the entire national and provincial elite to the continuance of the national state (a situation now seriously threatened by some influential elites in Quebec). This has led to a condition of permanent negotiation that Simeon refers to as "Federal-Provincial Diplomacy," a pattern of relations which he claims has more features in common with the European Community than with the United States.[20]

The second and third explanations just outlined underlie a recent claim by Leman[21] that the United States and Canada have very different patterns of social policy development. According to Leman, Canada proceeds in a steady deliberate fashion in the social political area whereas the United States tends to move only with a "big bang." In this dimension the Canadian experience appears at least superficially quite similar to that observed by Heclo in some European countries. The bilateral focusing of power coupled with innovative thrusts from minor parties and the necessity to avoid breakdown has made possible much considered, compromised policy innovation in Canada. By contrast, the United States is so divided through vertical and horizontal power sharing that innovation is more rare, although when it does come it is usually legitimized well enough for its managers to have considerable developmental leeway. Leman suggests that the diffusion of power in the United States makes innovations in social policy possible only under conditions of acute crisis.[22]

The very similar figures presented for total North American spending for nonhealth related welfare programs make it obvious that the U.S. and Canadian differences will arise in the timing and composition of those expenditures. The three explanations, singly or in combination, suggest the following hypotheses:

1. Welfare state developments should generally be earlier in Canada; the only exceptions should be when a "crisis" more severely affects the United States than Canada or where objective circumstances are similar but major constitutional problems prevent an immediate Canadian policy response and the provinces are not in a position to respond independently.
2. Canadian programs should usually be more advanced in terms of program development, coverage, and benefits.
3. Canadian programs should exhibit a steadier development in the sense of the number of major changes in each program.[23]
4. U.S. policy innovation should take place only in response to acute "crisis."
5. Canadian financing of welfare state measures may be more egalitarian. This is a hypothesis offered more tentatively than the others because the ideological difference from the United States is not simply that Canada is more left-wing; the tory socialist element is also there.

An evaluation of the explanatory power of the three general factors will be presented following an examination of welfare state development.

III. Components of the North American Welfare State

A. Old Age Security

An average retiring Canadian in the 1970s would have government pension benefits quite comparable in terms of earlier income to that of his

American counterpart.[24] Nevertheless, both the present pension programs and the chain of developments leading to them are strikingly different.

The difference in timing of the introduction of national pensions can scarcely be regarded as accidental. In Canada, the introduction took place at a time of relative prosperity, while in the United States it came only with the depths of the depression. The Liberals, the dominant party in Canada in the twentieth century, went on record as favoring national pensions in 1915, and although a means-tested flat grant pension scheme was not actually introduced until 1927 by the Liberal Government of Mackenzie King, the idea had encountered little opposition. In contrast, only Theodore Roosevelt's 1912 campaign presented social insurance as a national issue in the United States, and until the passing of the Social Security Act in 1935, pensions as a national policy were actively opposed by virtually all major politicians and trade union leaders. This was largely because the state appeared to be competing with the unions as the agent of economic improvement for the working class.[25] It was not until the twenties that organized labor declared its willingness to work at the state level for public pensions to protect the needy poor.

In Canada, rather than being part of the firm ideological commitment of a large part of the population, the existing opposition stemmed largely from specific vested interests, such as private insurance. After World War I there was considerable discussion in the provinces about setting up pension schemes, but, as in the United States, a major new tax program at the subnational level was held to be destructive of the unit's competitive position in the economy. From the mid-twenties onward, various types of pension schemes were discussed in Canada by all major political groups, but only a flat-rate means-tested program was regarded as both constitutional and of reasonable expense.[26] Several provinces favored a joint federal-provincial scheme, and this was provided by the 1927 plan. In fact, it was the first jointly funded program in Canada and the first activity of the federal government in the field of social welfare. After the Liberals introduced the program with Socialist support (the CCF/NDP was later to argue that "J.S. Woodsworth had wrested old age pensions from Mackenzie King . . . when he and a colleague held the balance of power in the House of Commons"[27]), the Conservatives moved to increase their strength by pledging to increase benefits.[28] Thus, the hypothesis of earlier enactment by Canada is certainly supported by the pension case and appears to be explained by a strong Liberal and Socialist thrust that met with no ideological resistance from the Conservatives.

It is more difficult to see that Canadian pension development was at all times more advanced and steadier than the American. The maximum pension was first set at $20 and was reduced by the amount of outside income between $125 and $365 a year, at which point a person became ineligible. By 1950 the basic payment had been gradually increased to $40, but there was widespread dissatisfaction with the means test and its assumption that a person could live comfortably on a bit over a dollar a day. Furthermore, per capita income by this time had made the pension scheme increasingly irrelevant for a large part of the population. As early as 1931, the Conservative party had favored contributory pensions, and the Liberal Party government of the early forties "had always been for the contributory principle."[29] But despite both popular and party sentiment, this reform was by no means imminent.

The Liberals anticipated contributory pensions in the reform of 1951 but were thwarted, instead witnessing the passage of the Old Age Security and Old Age Assistance Acts. The former simply took the maximum benefit level from the existing means-tested scheme and made it a demogrant for those over seventy, while the Assistance Act retained the old system for those between sixty-five and sixty-nine. The immediate appeal of demogrant pensions as proposed by the tiny CCF was a factor leading to this compromise legislation. Also important, however, was the apparently insoluble constitutional problem of a contribution scheme. According to the deputy minister, "Pensions, financed out of general revenues clearly were *intra vires* and contributory pensions clearly were not, while earmarked taxes constituted a grey area."[30] Thus, a constitutional amendment had to be developed that explicitly allowed for a sharing of power between the provinces and the federal government in the area of old age pensions.

For another decade and more, struggles persisted for the enactment of some kind of earnings-related scheme: the Canadian Congress of Labor continued its attack on the inadequacy of the demogrant plan, while the Conservatives won a landslide victory in 1957 by campaigning on a platform that included the introduction of earnings-related pensions. Massive electoral pressure might then have contributed to reform, were it not for John Diefenbaker's determination that any revision should include survivors' and disability benefits that had not been allowed by the 1951 amendment. Not until the Liberals returned to office and after several provincial-federal conferences at which pensions were only one of several major issues was the earnings-related scheme including survivors' and disability benefits introduced in 1965. The contributory Canada and Quebec Pension Plans were thus established as another tier on top of the already existing programs. Quebec demanded a greater level of funding than the "till cash" American approach, after which the pension plans were largely modeled, so that surplus funds could be used for provincial development. Its pension scheme was finally just coordinated with the federal government, while the plans for all other provinces were handled completely at the national level, although interim funds could be used by the provinces. Subsequent pension developments included the phasing out of Old Age Assistance (OAA) as the eligibility age for Old Age Security (OAS) was lowered to sixty-five and the enactment of the Guaranteed Income Supplement that provided a means-tested increase of up to 40 percent over the Old Age Security payment.[31]

In contrast to the changing Canadian scene, the original plan of the U.S Social Security Act of 1935 remains basically intact. Under pressure from the vast success of the grassroots Townsend Movement,[32] the Roosevelt Administration put in place a system that included means-tested Old Age Assistance run jointly with the states and the contributory, self-financed pension scheme. In 1939, coverage of the self-financed scheme was expanded to include the survivors and dependents of those insured.

The contributory part of the Old Age Security Income system had a very long gestation period. It was not until the early fifties that half the aged in the United States got any benefits at all from the programs initiated in 1935. And Old Age Assistance (OAA) about two-thirds financed by the federal government from general revenues with the rest from state taxes— provided for a larger number of the aged in the United States than did OASDI until about the time of Canada's 1951 reforms. During most of this period, the average payment per beneficiary in the two U.S. programs was similar. The change in beneficiary numbers since the early fifties, however, has been dramatic. By 1975, support of some kind for the old was virtually universal, and Supplementary Security Income (SSI), the entirely federal successor to OAA introduced in 1971, provided full support for only a few percent of the elderly population.

In 1975 the United States spent $62.6 billion on OASDI and an estimated $3.3 billion for the support of the aged under SSI. This was 4.6 percent of GNP, and was up sharply from 3.7 percent in 1972. In Canada the payments from the Old Age Security and Guaranteed Income Supplement Program totalled $3.4 billion in 1975 and the Canadian and Quebec Pension Plans in that year paid $.5 billion; the total percent of 1974-75 GNP was 2.8 percent by comparison with 2.6 percent three years earlier. A detailed comparison of benefits per recipient reveals little average difference between the nations; two factors, however, explain the far greater U.S. total expenditure. First, the Canadian population is younger. Had Canada 10.7 percent of the population 65 and over as in the United States instead of only 8 percent, the Canadian pension share of GNP would have been 3.8 percent in 1975.[33] Virtually all of the rest is explained by the additional beneficiaries under the OASDI system: the survivors and the disabled; 32 million people received some benefits from the system in 1975 although only 22.7 million were 65 or over.[34]

Confirmation of the hypotheses that Canadian program development was more advanced and steadier would thus seem misleading since the Canadian scheme provided greater breadth of coverage of the aged, but offered no disability or survivors' benefits until the mid-sixties when the earnings related system was introduced. In the absence of these three features the overall Canadian social insurance program is not obviously more advanced than the American one. Moreover, it should probably be emphasized that the stated reason for the Canadian changes in 1951 and in 1965 was the fundmentally unsatisfactory nature of the previous plans. As Christopher Leman states, "The prospect of constitutional conflict foreclosed consideration of a contributory insurance program in 1927 and 1951, shunting pressures first into a means-test program and then into a demogrant program."[35] This may be a more important point about the development of pension policy in Canada than the fact of change itself: policies emerged and were retained that did not reflect the intentions of the government but rather the exigencies of the immediate situation, deflecting major revisions into the future. A plan that did not reflect the popular desire for the protection of relative social and economic status was, from the beginning, inherently unsatisfactory. If pension policy efforts had initially dealt directly with constitutional issues and had been more in line with both popular and political intentions, the apparently major changes might not have appeared any more substantial than those which occurred in the United States.

The hypothesis that American innovation will only take place in conditions of crisis is certainly confirmed in the pension case, in that the Social Security Act that immediately followed the Depression set the fundamental format for pension coverage and benefits that were only modified and expanded in later years. The hypothesis about more egalitarian financing in Canada is similarly verified. It must be remembered that OAA, financed about two-thirds from federal general revenues and the rest from the states, was exceeded in importance by the contributory OASDI pensions only in the fifties. Yet it is true that the contemporary Canadian system relies more heavily than does the U.S. system on progressively raised taxes. Furthermore, the Canadian plan is more egalitarian since its benefits are more equal across before-retirement earning classes than is the American.

B. Unemployment Insurance

In the United States the pattern of development of unemployment insurance looks very much like that of old age support: an original thrust followed by increases in coverage with only minor modifications. The system was established in 1935 by the Social Security Act to be operated by the states with federal coordination. With the exception of federally financed temporary extensions of benefits during periods of high unemployment since 1958 and the 1975 introduction of a temporary special unemployment assistance (SUA) program for unemployed workers who were not enrolled in the system, the initial format has remained basically unchanged.

The contrast in the Canadian development of unemployment insurance is marked. The original Employment and Social Insurance Act passed by the federal legislature in 1935 was declared by the Supreme Court to be beyond the power of the national government. The British North America Act was amended through the waiving of powers in the area by all of the provinces, and the scheme was finally begun in 1941.[36] Thus, even though only constitutional problems prevented Canada from introducing unemployment insurance virtually simultaneously with the United States, the hypothesis of earlier Canadian enactment is not supported in this case.

From the very outset, the Canadian plan differed from the American in its financing, purpose, and conception of the unemployment problem; these differences led to major innovations throughout the next three decades. It explicitly equalized nominal cost sharing between employer and employee, while in virtually all American states only the employer nominally pays the tax,[37] and the Canadian federal government provides 20 percent of the amount provided by the private sector, plus administrative costs.[38] Furthermore, by the early postwar years it became clear that the managers of the unitary Canadian system were determined to use it in part as an income maintenance scheme. In 1950 the unemployment fund began to be used explicitly to aid workers in winter months when their earned benefits had legally expired, and major revisions in 1955 allowed for support of self-employed fishermen on the basis of their catches during the season.[39] In 1971 the system was substantially changed again, with the federal government contribution greatly increased to provide for all expenses attributable to national unemployment over 4 percent and programs for special groups, while the private sector would pay for ordinary benefits up to the 4 percent rate. These amendments led to the federal government paying a 61 percent share of the total cost of unemployment insurance in 1973,[40] a huge increase from the previous system. Overall, unemployment insurance payments went from 0.8 percent of GNP in Canada in 1970 to 1.5 percent in 1974 and 2.1 percent in 1975, while in the United States they declined from 1.5 percent in 1972 to 1 percent in 1975.[41] When compared to the nearly static American experience then, Canadian unemployment insurance development underwent successive and continual reforms starting from the date of initiation, supporting the hypothesis of steadier social welfare development.

Attempting to determine the more advanced system is somewhat more difficult, since the two countries rank differently on our indicators of level of benefits and extent of coverage. Between 1949 and 1971, Canadian benefits varied between 24.2 and 31.5 percent of average wages and were not taxable, while there was a much higher average payment in the United States: at least one-third and often as high as one-half or more. Beginning in 1972, Canadian payments jumped to above 40 percent where they have remained. The new program also considerably increased the percentage of the population covered from an initial level of about 80 percent of all workers to about 96 percent. This can be compared with only 43 percent of the U.S. labor force covered in 1940, 59 percent in 1950, and 81 percent in 1974.[42] The new levels of Canadian remuneration are now subject to tax, and it is clear that Canada has opted for a modest, universal system by contrast with the much spottier and varied U.S. program. Thus, while the Canadian plan has been broader in scope and historically covered a greater percentage of the work force, American benefits have typically been higher.

The egalitarian or income redistributive properties of the two systems are dramatically different. The American system is intended to be minimally redistributive; this intention was an historical argument for forcing the system to operate on a relatively low ceiling of covered wages per employee.[43] By contrast, Canada has disproportionately supported certain occupations and regions very heavily over others and relied increasingly on general revenues for these activities. While many have questioned both the fairness and the long-run viability of such objectives,[44] it is clear that the Canadian system has been very strongly redistributive. The recent Unemployment Insurance Review claimed that individuals earning over ten thousand dollars received only 5 percent of the total benefit expenditure in 1975, but provided 54 percent of total program revenue.[45]

One of the central problems facing both systems is that of work disincentives. It is widely held that unemployment compensation dampens a worker's determination in the job search process. While the replacement level of wages in the United States may be close to the earned wage level because benefits are not taxed,[46] the Canadian system, with its much more generous qualifying period of insured work and a generally longer benefit period as well, is even more vulnerable than the much attacked American system.[47] Econometric studies have estimated that the increased benefits of the 1971 amendments have inflated the Canadian permanent unemployment rate by as much as one percentage point. Nevertheless, in keeping with its apparently greater commitment to redistribution, the most recent Review of the Unemployment Insurance Program recommends only minor reforms. It defends the income maintenance function of the program and regards much of the increased care in job searching as entirely appropriate. It attacks the United States practice of "experience rating," which gives special advantages to employers with a low use of the system, for three reasons: it is difficult to implement in a system of employer-employee cost-sharing; it diminishes the redistributive impact of the program; and it adversely affects some marginal firms and industries.[48]

Another feature of the new Canadian system is almost certain to gain greater American attention over time. The recent U.S. Supreme Court decision that private employers' fringe benefits need not provide pregnancy benefits highlighted the fact that the United States is virtually the only major industrial country without officially mandated sickness and pregnancy benefits. Canada too was an international laggard in this area and only introduced the change with the 1971 legislation. The Canadian experience may not, however, encourage U.S. policymakers to take the same path. By 1974, the last year for which complete data are available, and after only three years of operation, illness and maternity benefits were already 8.4 percent of the total unemployment insurance expenditures and appeared to be rising at a very rapid rate.[49]

C. Family Allowances

The Canadian system of family allowances introduced in 1945 is wholly without an American counterpart. There is unfortunately no very satisfactory account of the genesis of the law, although the discussion of family allowances in the British Parliament over a year earlier was undoubtably influential. The usual rationale for family allowances is simple enough: an income sufficient for a single person or a couple may not be sufficient for raising of children. Furthermore, by the end of the war very few were working. As William Beveridge had explained, "it would be absurd and even dangerous to give subsistence benefits on a family basis, to try to abolish want when earnings were interrupted by sickness or accident, unemployment or old age, without taking steps to see that want was abolished also for all people when earning."[50]

However compelling the Beveridge argument might have been, several sources claim that it was not the principal reason for the introduction of family allowances in Canada. Rather, family allowances were "seen as a socially desirable means of distributing resources collected for war purposes in a way that might stimulate the purchase of available consumer goods when other forms of semidurable and durable goods were in short supply and when the release of tax resources to other members of the community might have set up inflationary trends."[51] This original intent was wholly unnecessary as it turned out, but in keeping with the underconsumptionist fears of the simple Keynesian thinking that dominated policy circles in both the United States and Canada. This explanation is consistent with the extent to which real benefits per child were allowed to fall over the coming years. The $6 per month payment for the youngest age group was retained from 1946 to 1972.[52] What was never a very generous payment was almost halved by inflation.[53] The official justification was that the allowances had become increasingly unnecessary with the growth in real incomes and the increasing level of other social services—particularly Medicare (government health insurance) and the Canada Assistance Plan (income support).[54]

By the early seventies, many Canadian observers were predicting the virtual demise of the family allowance through neglect. Expert federal opinion strongly favored such an abolition because of the seeming irrationality of paying without regard to need and then taxing back only part of the payment even for the wealthiest families.[55] Instead, The Family Allowances Act went into force in 1974 and boosted payments from $7.48 to $20 per child. What explains the sudden and unexpected change? First, the payment figures overstate the fiscal reality; the new scheme provides taxable benefits while the older grants were largely tax free. Second, the entire family allowance program is federally funded, yet has always had greatest popularity in the province of Quebec. To view the introduction of the family allowances as a "gesture to French Canadians," as Moynihan does,[56] may be overly simple, but pronatalism has always been a powerful sentiment in French Canada. Quebec is the only province that uses the fixed total of federal support to give increasing allowances for each successive child, and only Quebec and tiny Prince Edward Island provide additional family supplements out of provincial funds.[57]

If the ruling Liberal party turned around on family allowances to shore up its political strength in Quebec, as many Canadians believe, it would scarcely have been the first time.[58] The details of the decision to change government policy are not yet known. Whatever the causes, the fiscal impact of family allowances is now substantial. In 1974-75, they amounted to 1.3 percent of Canadian GNP.[59]

While the impact of family allowances on the birth rate has never been firmly established, a desire to increase the population has often resulted in program initiation and revision in other countries.[60] The possible increase in the birth rate of the poor was a factor causing the family allowance to be regarded with suspicion in the United States, although its fiscal inefficiency, which taxation reduces but cannot eliminate, was a more important reason for opposition. Even many favoring family allowances over the negative income tax as the beginning (or the end) of a solution to America's poverty problem did so mainly because of its greater political acceptability—the logical complement of its inefficiency.[61]

D. Other Income Maintenance Programs

The development of other income assistance programs provides another sharp contrast between the two countries. Again, the 1935 Social Security Act remains the central legislative basis in the United States that set the federal role by authorizing the payment of grants to the states for the blind and needy children. In 1950, the "Aid to Children" program became "Aid to Families with Dependent Children" (AFDC) that allowed benefits for one parent in a family where children were already beneficiaries. In the same year aid was extended to the permanently and totally disabled. In 1961 payments to families with two parents who were both unemployed were made possible, but fewer than half the states implemented them. Amendments in 1972 removed responsibility for the aged, blind, and disabled categories from the states and set up the federal uniform system of Supplemental Security Income (SSI). Thus, only one major cash program, and by far the least popular, AFDC, was left to joint federal-state funding and influence.[62]

In Canada the means-tested pension plan was the only federal welfare program prior to the depression, since low income support was chiefly a provincial responsibility. The Employment Bill of 1935 was the only major piece of depression legislation to set against the massive legislative thrust of the New Deal. Assistance to the blind was given in 1937 by lowering their pension eligibility age to forty,[63] but this was shortly superceded in 1951 when all blind persons became eligible for the means-tested pensions that were available to those aged from sixty-five to seventy. Disability allowances became a federal-provincial cost-shared program in 1954, and in 1956, the Unemployment Assistance program for unemployed adults and their dependents began with equal cost-sharing between the provinces and the federal government. But, only a decade later, it was replaced by the Canada Assistance Plan that eliminated separate programs for the blind and disabled and introduced low income support for the able-bodied and fully employed.[64] No province or municipality actually implemented this latter provision until the seventies.[65]

Considering these various income-related cash programs, Canada would appear the policy laggard and America the leader. Just as constitutional problems plagued the efforts of Canadian policymakers to introduce contributory pensions at the federal level, so too were income-related survivors' and disability benefits blocked. Survivors' insurance, an integral part of the U.S. system since 1939, did not become a national program until the passage of the Canada Pension Plan and contributed significantly to the postponement of the introduction of the entire plan. Another extremely important consideration, however, is that Canadian welfare responsibilities have been constitutionally interpreted to reside with subnational units. Thus, the absence of national programs has not necessarily meant the neglect of income maintenance measures, nor inadequate provincial funding that only the introduction of national programs changed dramatically.

Following the crash, the Canadian government aided the provinces in a way somewhat similar to the support given states in the United States. But where the New Deal consolidated these grants into categorical programs,[66] the Canadian federal government continued to provide only loosely conditioned grants to the provinces, much as it had been doing since 1913. Thus, Canadian federal authorities entered the depression already accustomed to providing very substantial support for programs over which they had virtually no control. This was an unsatisfactory situation for Ottawa politicians, but no solution was developed, and during the war all efforts ceased. In fact, no permanent solution was ever found. But in the postwar years a series of agreements between the federal government and the provinces emerged that ceded certain provincial taxing powers to coordinated federal schemes that did not hurt any province's competitive position and allowed a number of joint programs. The Canada Assistance Plan represents a refined example of such measures.

Whereas the federal government attempted in later years to remedy disparities in provincial tax bases through redistributional formulae,[67] it was clear that the provinces as a group were not starved for revenue, and the welfare state did not languish. It is difficult to find meaningful comparative material by program, but Table 3.4 shows the percentage of GNP spent on low income assistance in the United States and Canada for selected years. In 1950 Canada was spending a greater percentage of its GNP on welfare than America, even five years before the development of the Unemployment Assistance Act. The provinces were simply providing low income support in the absence of a formal national program. Sometimes this involved special provincial programs, such as Ontario's disability plan of the early fifties, but more often undifferentiated programs of low income assistance were used.

The substantial extent of subnational activity in Canada makes the testing of our hypotheses very difficult. The longer period of largely nonfederal support makes it nearly impossible to date the introduction of help for special groups and therefore to determine whether Canada fits the hypothesis of earlier enactment. In the case of income-related support for survivors, Canada was clearly a laggard. In disability insurance, too, the general support offered until 1966 only provided for absolute need while income-related benefits were added to U.S. Social Security in 1954. In other areas, however, there is little evidence that Canada lagged behind the United States. Special aid to the blind was widespread provincial policy before it was first added as a national responsibility in 1937. "Mother's allowances" or "mother's pensions" (similar to the original intent of ADC in the United States which was principally to aid widows) started in the United States in the twenties but became more widespread in Canada before the depression and continued to grow at the provincial level after the introduction of the U.S. national program.[68]

Leman[69] draws a very important political point from the relative lack of

Table 3.4
Expenditures for Low Income Assistance by all Levels of Government as a Percentage of GNP

	Canada		U.S.
	Social Assistance	Family Allowances	Public Aid
1950	1.2%	1.6%	.9%
1955	.4	1.3	---
1960	.7	1.3	.8
1965	.9	1.0	1.0
1970	1.3	.9	1.7
1974	2.0	1.3	2.3

Sources: Canada–Munro, 1970, Table 1: FPCMW, 1975a, Table 4; Statistics Canada, 1973-5a, "Family Allowances" includes Youth Allowances and Quebec Family Allowances; "Social Assistance" includes all aid funded under the Canada Assistance Plan. GIS for the aged included in 1970 and 1974; OAS pensions not included in any year.

U.S.-Skolnick and Dales, 1977, Table 3. "Public Aid" includes AFDC, SSI vendor payments, food stamps, social services and work relief.

(Entire table from Christopher Leman, The Collapse of Welfare Reform: Political Institutions, Policy, and the Poor in Canada and the United States (Cambridge, Mass.: MIT Press, 1980).)

differentiation among Canadian low income assistance programs. He argues that the absence of a special program for families with female heads has contributed to a remarkable absence of Canadian "welfare backlash" by comparison with the United States. In the early seventies, the new Minister of National Health and Welfare, Marc Lalonde, launched a two-year federal-provincial Social Security Review without any discussion of excessively rising costs or any other kind of "crisis." Many federal and provincial authorities hoped that the cool, insulated world of federal-provincial diplomacy would make it possible to hammer out yet another joint thrust—this time to help the working poor. The conference ultimately failed to produce a satisfactory outcome, but the defeat arose from disagreement over various fiscal details, not the overall goals of welfare reform. This stands in sharp contrast to the fate of the Nixon administration's welfare reform plans, a direct and calculated response to the "welfare backlash" that foundered on ideological criticism from both the left and the right.

Given Canada's persistant constitutional difficulty in developing national income-related insurance, it is hard to argue that its low income assistance programs have been consistently more advanced than those of the United States. It is easier to make the opposite case until the mid-sixties with the adoption of the Canada Assistance Plan (CAP). At that point, however, aid for families with two unemployed parents was provided— something half the states in the United States still fail to do—and the need to support some working poor families was formally recognized. In this sense, Canadian schemes for nonpension support have moved "ahead" of U.S. policy.

The hypothesis that Canadian programs will experience more steady change than those in America appears correct, but the test is weak. The replacement of the Unemployment Assistance Plan with the considerably broader Canada Assistance Plan after only a decade is evidence of a kind of flexibility in underlying program parameters[70] without a U.S. counterpart. The development of the SSI program was almost undeniably a more modest measure. Furthermore, serious consideration was given to changing the system yet again only a few years later in the absence of any great difficulty with CAP. This vividly contrasts with the American context where the Nixon administration sought massive reform in response to popular outcry against the "welfare mess."[71] Thus, that the United States will innovate only when there is an acute crisis seems largely borne out by the nonaged income maintenance experience, although the definition of "innovation" is critical. None of the policy changes—except the unsuccessful Nixon Family Assistance Plan—were in response to strong popular feeling, yet none were very fundamental policy innovations either.

The hypothesis that Canadian programs will be more progressively financed than those in the United States is virtually impossible to test. Both provincial and federal governments rely on a wide variety of taxes, and there is considerable variation among the provinces themselves. The same is true of cost-shared U.S. programs. The tax systems of both national governments, relying heavily on corporate and personal income taxation, are generally progressive or at least proportional.

E. Medical Care

Evaluating international developments in government health policy is complicated by the widely varying medical care systems of the countries compared. In U.S. and Canadian health policy comparisons, however, the striking underlying similarity of the medical care systems prior to introduction of major government action simplifies the task. American and Canadian hospitals are largely "voluntary," not publicly owned; physicians in both are typically paid under a free-for-service system. The similarities even extend to the training and outlook among physicians and nurses. As one Canadian national official put it, the principal hospital officials and physicians belong to "sister associations. They read the same journals, attend the same meetings, (and) prescribe the same drugs."[72]

A developmental similarity between the two systems has been the pattern of the government taking over the model of private health insurance and socializing its costs. While most Western European health insurance was part of the social insurance institutions labor unions helped to manage, the North American pattern differed markedly. Private health insurance set the example for what the government might more equally distribute.

In the United States the anticipated outcry from conservative sections of the populace and organized medicine in particular caused President Roosevelt to delete any mention of national health insurance in the original Social Security Act. In the early postwar years, the Truman administration tried to revive national health insurance, but the proposal met with strong Congressional resistance. The American Medical Association, starting in earnest with the congressional elections of 1950, conducted a sustained campaign against "socialized medicine," one which appears to have been extraordinarily successful. Supporters of government health insurance were obliged to shift their attention to an especially attractive subgroup, the aged, but even this change of tactics was unsuccessful until the Kerr-Mills Act of 1960 that provided federal and state cost sharing for the medical expenses of the indigent elderly.

Throughout the early sixties pressure for more comprehensive medical coverage of the aged continued, along with concern about improved access for the poor. After the Democratic landslide of 1964, these demands were translated into the legislation creating Medicare and Medicaid. The former was an entirely federal effort that provided hospitalization insurance for the elderly under Social Security and heavily subsidized, but voluntary, coverage for outpatient services. Both subplans involved patient cost sharing. Medicaid was to provide for the poor and retained the joint federal and state control, financing, and varying benefits characterizing the federal and state AFDC program. Most state programs employed minimum cost sharing.[73] The American debate still rages over whether partial government health insurance (now paying for some 40 percent of health expenditures) should become universal in population coverage.[74] The absence of national health insurance scarcely meant that the U.S. federal government was idle in the health field during the fifties. There were a number of research, construction-subsidy, and categorically specialized disease and population programs: the National Institutes of Medicine, the Hill-Burton Hospital construction and modernization program, and poor mothers and children (Title V of the Social Security Act).

In Canada, public policy, as well as popular and professional opinion developed somewhat differently. It is difficult to find the complete rejection of government action in the health insurance field among virtually any group in post-war Canada. The American Medical Association, which had in the early part of the century briefly considered the idea of public health insurance,[75] stood in firm opposition to virtually any government action in the field for fifty years.[76] In sharp contrast, the Canadian Medical Association began issuing policy statements quite favorable to government action as early as 1934. A 1943 statement supported a plan that would be "compulsory for persons having an annual income below a level which proves to be insufficient to meet the cost of adequate medical care," and that "payment of a premium should be made by the employee, employer, and government."[77]

There is striking similarity between this early Canadian thinking and the AMA's Medicredit national health plan introduced in the U.S. Congress in the 1970s. Medicredit "would have astonished AMA critics a decade ago and generated complaint within the medical profession for its encouragement of more third party medical financing."[78] Canadian physicians, it should be said, shared many of the same concerns as their counterparts to the south: third party control, the freedom of relation between doctor and patient, adequate remuneration, and fears about the impact of government participation on quality. What differed, however, was the timing and tone of their response.

The extent to which these differences reflect the differing views of Canadian doctors or a different reading by the profession of political realities cannot be known; surely both have played a part. As Canadians, Canadian doctors presumably have a lower level of anxiety about the negative consequences of state action; as doctors, they surely realized the inevitability of major government health insurance as early as the 1935 Employment and Social Insurance Act, which, while found to be unconstitutional, envisioned health benefits financed by compulsory premiums as part of a general improvement in social security.

In the immediate postwar years—again in vivid contrast to the American situation—several provinces began to develop health insurance schemes. By 1947 CCF-controlled Saskatchewan, a particularly left-leaning province for which there is no U.S. analogue, had almost universal, compulsory hospitalization insurance. By the mid-fifties, there was strong provincial pressure for the federal government to move into the hospital insurance area. In April of 1957, the federal parliament passed the Hospital Insurance and Diagnostic Services Act without the opposition of organized medicine. Hospital insurance was recognized by virtually everyone as being but a first step. Following the 1964 report of the Hall Commission, the government proposed to the provinces in 1965 the outlines of the Medical Care Act involving a comprehensive range of medical services jointly financed with federal government guidelines. It was passed in the following year with only two votes opposed and was fully implemented by 1972.[79] While the medical profession was opposed to many aspects of the 1966 legislation, Saskatchewan's abortive doctors' strike[80] several years earlier made that opposition cautious and largely ineffective.

As the United States considers the future of government health insurance, it is naturally drawn to consider the Canadian experience, especially since the full operation of its "Medicare." Until very recently both countries appeared unable to control the astronomical growth of what is called the medical care industry. All the measures pointed in the same direction: more real resources devoted to medical care, a higher rate of inflation in that sector, increased utilization by patients, and greater intensity of services, particularly in the hospital. The rates of overall health expenditure increases during the 1960s were remarkably similar: between 1960 and 1971 total Canadian health expenditure rose by 11.8 percent per year, while the comparable U.S. rate was 11.1 percent per year. Furthermore, the North American countries were the leading spenders among all of the industrial countries until 1969.

What is striking is the differential response of Canada and the United States to the apparent problem. From the vantage point of 1971, both countries were spending leaders. Only five years later, however, the picture had changed considerably. Canada spent a smaller share of its GNP on health in 1976 than in 1971: roughly 7.1 percent versus 7.3 percent. The United States, on the other hand, spent approximately 8.6 percent of GNP in 1976 as opposed to 7.6 percent in 1971. The final section of the paper will discuss and evaluate the differing recent experience.

In health policy we have a very easy test of our hypotheses. Canadian developments come out "ahead" by all criteria. They were both earlier and broader—partial U.S. coverage for the elderly and poor was being passed at the same time complete coverage was being planned for Canada. They showed strong development through change: hospital insurance was scarcely in place before the government was preparing a major new thrust that was far more than a mere extension of the earlier scheme. More progressive financing is also confirmed in this case for Canada. The larger of the two subprograms in Medicare, hospitalization insurance, is financed in the same relatively regressive manner as is the Social Security program in general. Furthermore half of the cost of the elective Supplementary Insurance program is paid for by patient premiums and the rest from general revenues. Medicaid is financed about half from the federal government and half from the states whose share is almost certainly regressive. The present financing of the Canadian scheme is very much like Medicaid. In the early years of hospitalization insurance, many provinces relied on compulsory premiums—the most regressive measure of all. For various reasons, including the difficulty and expense of premium collection as well as income distribution consequences, virtually all provinces moved to financing their share out of general provincial revenues. Furthermore, copayment is virtually absent from the Canadian system.

The introduction of new programs in the United States was not in response to a discrete crisis as was Social Security, but to the rapidly increasing cost of medical care. Crisis can, of course, be defined to include a problem that is gradually but steadily worsening. But in the case of the policy innovations of the mid-sixties, the "cure" produced a growth in the disease such that the elderly's out-of-pocket payments mandated by Medicare began to exceed what they were paying before the system began. Thus, the United States might be viewed to be still crisis but a crisis of aggregate cost more than individual privation. This is not, however, the kind of public outcry defined by Leman as exclusively stimulating major policy innovation in the United States, implying that such fundamental reform is not imminent.

IV. Hypotheses and Explanations:
An Interpretation of U.S. and Canadian Differences

The development of the North American welfare state is presented in summary form in Table 3.5. The most salient feature about the U.S. experience is that, with the exception of the food stamp program, every measure is an amendment to the original Social Security Act. This, of course, says virtually nothing about the substance of policy because of the unusually broad scope of the original legislation. The Canadian experience on the other hand has largely been one of new or completely revised programs.

The expenditure on the various programs discussed in previous sections at selected times is presented in Table 3.6.

Table 3.7 summarizes the results of the hypothesis testing. Hypothesis 1

Table 3.5
The Development of the North American Welfare State

	U.S.	Canada
1925		Old Age Pensions Act 1927
1930		
1935	Old Age Insurance 1935 Old Age Assistance* 1935 Unemployment Compensation* 1935 Aid to Dependent Children* 1935 Aid to the Blind * 1935 Survivors & Disability Insurance 1939	
1940		Unemployment Insurance Act 1940 Family Allowances Act 1944
1945		
1950	Aid for permanently and Totall- Disabled* 1950	Old Age Security Act 1951 Old Age Assistance Act 1951 Blind Persons Act 1951 Disabled Persons Act 1954
1955		Unemployment Assistance Act 1956 Hospital Insurance & Diagnostic Services Act 1957
1960	Medical Assistance for the Aged* 1960 Maternal and Child Care Planning* 1963	Youth Allowances Act 1964
1965	Health Insurance for the Aged* 1965 Medical Assistance for the Poor* 1965	Canada Pension Plan 1965 Canada Assistance Plan 1966 Medical Care Act 1966
1970	Supplementary Security Income for the Aged, Blind, & Disabled 1972	Unemployment Insurance Act 1971

---

*Aid to States

Table 3.6

Government Expenditures as a Percentage of GNP in the U.S. and Canada for Selected Programs and Years

	CANADA						UNITED STATES				
	Old Age Security		Unemployment Insurance	Family Allowances	Other Income Maintenance Programs	Health Care	Old Age Security		Unemployment Insurance	Other Income Maintenance Programs	Health Care
	Means Tested	Non Means Tested					Means Tested	Non Means Tested			
1950	.5	0	.5	1.7	1.2	—	.6	.3	.8	.3	.8
1955	.1	1.3	.8	1.3	.4	1.4	.4	1.2	.5	.4	.8
1960	.1	1.5	1.3	1.3	.7	3.0	.4	2.2	.6	.4	.9
1965	.1	1.7	.6	1.1	.9	2.6	.3	2.6	.5	.7	1.0
1970	.3	2.0	.8	.7	1.3	4.0	.3	3.2	.4	1.4	1.7
1974	.6	2.0	1.5	1.3	2.0	5.5	.2	4.1	.5	2.2	2.0

Sources: Statistics Canada, _Social Security: National Programs_ (Ottawa: Statistics Canada, 1976).

Canada Year Book, 1974.

Alfred M. Skolnick and Sophie R. Dales, "Social Welfare Expenditures, 1950–75," _Social Security Bulletin_, January 1976, pp. 3–20.

is presented both in its simplest form as "Canada will be first" and in the modified form of "Canada will be first, unless." The hypotheses appear to be a useful way of understanding North American welfare state development. Of the 24 scores, 16 or 67 percent are confirmations (A), 6 or 25 percent are either undetermined or subject to differing interpretation (Cs) and only 2 or 8.3 percent are disconfirmations (Bs). It is clear that if the developments are weighted in some rough way by the amount of expenditure involved, the results are even more strongly in the direction of confirming Canada's lead.

Table 3.7
Summary of Hypotheses Tests

Hypothesis 1A — Welfare state developments should generally be earlier in Canada.

Hypothesis 1B — 1A + The only exceptions should be when a "crisis" more severely impacts the U.S. than Canada or where objective circumstances are similar but major constitutional problems prevent an immediate Canadian policy response and the provinces are not in a position to respond independently.

Hypothesis 2 — Canadian programs should ususally be more advanced in terms of program development, coverage, and benefits.

Hypothesis 3 — Canadian programs should exhibit a steadier development in the sense of the number of major changes in each program.

Hypothesis 4 — U.S. policy innovation should take place only in response to acute political outcry.

Hypothesis 5 — Canadian financing of welfare state measures should be more egalitarian.

	1A	1B	2	3	4	5
Pensions	A	A	C	C	A	A
Unemployment Insurance	B	A	C	A	A	A
Income Maintenance	C	C	A	A	A	C
Health	A	A	A	A	B	A

A - Confirmation

B - Disconfirmation

C - Undetermined or subject to varying interpretation

Particular note should be taken of Hypothesis 4, Leman's contention about U.S. innovation only in situations of crisis. In fact, although there are four cells, there are only two pieces of legislation, and one of them disconfirms the hypothesis. Furthermore, the predictive power of the hypothesis for future welfare state development appears extremely limited. Would the successful passage of national health insurance legislation by a second Carter administration likely take place under conditions of widespread popular outcry? Would this be the likely atmosphere surrounding a major change in the funding of social security? The problem with scaling down the causal factor in Leman's hypothesis to something like "widespread recognition of an important problem" or even less sharply to "strong pressure from influential groups" is that the hypothesis can easily become virtually a tautology.[81]

The complete absence in the United States of family allowances also deserves some comment. The United States remained throughout the period one of the only major countries without such a scheme. Should this weigh as an additional factor in its "laggardliness?" We are inclined to minimize its importance. As our Canadian discussion points out, family allowances are an extremely inefficient way of supporting needy families. Moreover, the difference between U.S. practice and that of many others is more apparent than real. Tax deductions for dependents—a very instructive example of what Stanley Surrey calls "tax expenditures"—have served a virtually identical function in the United States and are subject to the same criticism as family allowances.

The hypotheses together confirm a great deal about Canadian and U.S. developmental differences. The hypotheses themselves, however, stem from three differences between the two societies already discussed: ideology, party and electoral system, and constitution. How can we assess the relative importance of each?

First, the importance of the ideological difference seems completely sustained. In every policy area it appears that general public as well as elite opinion was at least as supportive of state action in Canada as in the United States at a given time and often, as in the case of public health care, considerably more supportive.[82] This support appears to underlie not just the typically earlier enactment of policy in Canada but also subsequent changes: the rapid development of Medicare after hospital insurance and the substitution of the Canada Assistance Plan for the Unemployment Assistance program. The more progressive financing of the programs also appears to reflect general ideological differences between the two countries because the NDP did not play a pivotal role in the design or passage of most of them.

The constitutional explanation is also important and explains why some policy thrusts that appeared earlier in U.S. unemployment insurance would have been five years earlier in Canada had it not been for constitutional complications. Earnings-related pensions with survivors and disability benefits would certainly have appeared far earlier in Canada without constitutional problems.

What explanatory role is left for the electoral system? First, the role of the system should be distinguished from the ideological content of pivotal parties. Lipset has recently argued that the greater degree of leftism in Canada is more apparent than real because the nature of the Canadian system produces distinct parties while the same forces in the United States operate within the Democratic party.[83] He sees this as the answer to the question he first asked in 1944: why socialism in Canada and not in the United States?[84] Yet Lipset may take the argument too far. Is 15 to 20 percent of the U.S. electorate not completely supportive of capitalism? That is the range of popular vote of the New Democratic Party in Canada.[85] The claim that the reason for the high vote is merely that the national union movement in Canada supports the small left party, rather than the more left of the two major parties, simply highlights another ideology-laden difference between Canada and the United States. The Canadian trade union movement, historically heavily influenced by the British Labor party, is more socialist than is the U.S. labor movement and always has been.[86] It may thus be a mistake to attribute all of the influence of the NDP in Canada to the electoral system: a real but unknown part of that strength may be reflecting a different underlying distribution of values from the United States. Whatever the exact causal factors, there are at least two instances in which the socialists' role as an independent group speaking to a national public seriously affected welfare legislation: gaining the original pension legislation in 1927 and forcing some form of universal pensions in 1951. The success of the public hospital insurance in Saskatchewan developed by the NDP government there undoubtedly hastened federal health initiatives, although it seems as fitting to attribute this development to ideology as to the party system.

In sum, the ideological difference—slight by international standards—between Canada and the United States appears to have made a considerable difference in welfare state development. Constitutional problems have sometimes delayed the introduction of programs in Canada, but provincial-federal bargaining mechanisms have often allowed steadier and more advanced policy development once initial jurisdictional problems have been overcome. In welfare matters the party and electoral system appear more important as a means whereby power is focused at the federal and provincial levels for bargaining purposes than as a vehicle for remarkable influence by a minor party.

V. The North American Welfare State in International Perspective

The striking fact about the development of the welfare state in Western Europe and North America is its diversity. The timing and sequence of programs, the extent of coverage, and the proportion of national income expended all vary significantly. The striking fact about the 1970s, by contrast, is the similarity in the concerns about the welfare state expressed across national borders—concerns with dwindling energy supplies, aging population bases, and diminishing economic growth rates.[87]

Forecasted strains have already inspired programmatic review. Income support programs started earlier typically expanded their coverage to include a larger proportion of the general population. Among the factors creating these margins for expansion were rapid economic growth with relatively stable prices, an abundance of readily exploitable natural resources and primary products, and state fiscal resources freed by the absence of severe unemployment. By the last quarter of this century, these margins have begun to fill up. Interstices between any income support policy and private contractual arrangements, taxation, or other social programs have narrowed appreciably. In the face of such pressures, will the Canadian and United States developments diverge, or will they jointly remain laggards?

From an international perspective, the prospects of similar North American responses to the strains of the 1970s are most plausible. OECD studies of public income maintenance expenditure indicate both nations now spend approximately the same proportion of national income for "maintenance" purposes. As Table 3.2 indicated, both were near the bottom of the distribution in 1962 and held the same relative positions ten years later. In the absence of unlikely relative changes in economic growth, the laggard position of North America is likely to persist for cash transfer programs.

This forecast arises partly from the fact that the main income maintenance programs in both countries are now stably institutionalized. That does not mean argument has disappeared regarding social security and public assistance programs, or unemployment insurance, for that matter. But the main disputes are marginal, not fundamental. They are directed at the degree to which inflation indexing should be used, how the tax burden for such programs should be distributed, and how income transfer programs should be linked to levels of unemployment and economic growth. They are not about a repudiation of the welfare state's main programs, nor are they about a dramatic expansion of them. The concerns of the Canadian Social Security Review were very similar to those worrying the numerous groups now analyzing the social security system in the United States. Commentators refer to the tradeoff between efficiency and equality, treating the welfare state's programs as competitive with resources directed at economic growth and improved productivity. And where there is discussion of seemingly bold programmatic departures—as with welfare reform in both Canada and the United States—the discussion is far more intense than the probabilities of great change would warrant.

It is not the case, however, that the North American prospects are identical. The two largest components of the welfare state, health care and pensions, are not treated similarly in both countries. While pension outlays make for similarities in income maintenance efforts, the same is not true for health. Canada embarked on its comprehensive national health insurance program before the constrained perspective of the 1970s was commonplace. The result is paradoxical. On the one hand, North American health care patterns and costs are strikingly similar. Not only is medicine practiced in much the same way, but for much of the postwar period, the pattern of expenditure growth was practically identical. On the other hand, the current differences in the government's fiscal role in medical care may lead to important divergences. Current Canadian policy is to have the administratively responsible provinces pay for health outlays that rise more rapidly than GNP growth. Even before this policy change, medical care competed sufficiently with other governmental outlays so that cost control measures produced actual reductions in the proportion of national resources devoted to medical care. So, whereas both countries spent roughly the same proportion of GNP on health at the beginning of the decade, by 1976 Canada was spending some 7.6 percent and the United States some 8.6 percent.[88]

The continuing rapid escalation in U.S. medical care prices and expenditures reinforces the demands for a government solution to the problem while simultaneously making the result of insurance expansion through public financing more expensive. The result is a striking difference between the North American nations regarding the role of health insurance in the welfare state. Canada has a stable system in place; disputes are at the margin. As in many European countries, there is worry about the large share of national resources devoted to medical care and uncertainty about the marginal impact on health of increased expenditures. But while there is concern about continuing disparities in access among some social and geographic groups, it proceeds from the premise that the financial barriers to care have been largely eradicated. It is on this issue that differences between the United States and the rest of the OECD countries is likely to widen.

A major expansion of U.S. welfare state programs in the early 1980s seems unlikely. In that respect, the common inflationary experience of the 1970s may have produced a distinctive impact for the United States. Do North American developments together point to different or even divergent political responses from those of Europe?

The differences among Western welfare states, measured by public expenditure, are, in our view, likely to lessen somewhat over time. The past differences between Europe and North America arose substantially from the later introduction of welfare state programs and the more limited coverage of those programs. These historical measures highlight divergence at the outset; such separateness persists as pension programs differentially mature. But as countries experience decades of universality in both pensions and medical care (the United States excepted), the remaining differences are likely to become narrower. The differences in origins, in short, are muted by arrival at some common points of maturation.

Measuring modern welfare state development by public expenditure, however, presents some serious difficulties. In the case of medical care— between 6 and 10 percent of GNP in all the nations under review in this volume—public expenditure is an ambiguous indicator of a country's commitment to welfare state goals. While North American and European expenditures on medical care have grown rapidly in the post-World War II period, what cannot be claimed is that this common phenomenon means convergent redistributive experiences. Spending more can exacerbate as well as reduce economic and social inequalities. This would be the case where relative inflation in medical care increased public budgets, but not delivered services. Equally, lower expenditures increases need not mean inegalitarian health results, as the British example illustrates. Levels of spending can also be deceptive. It would be misleading to suggest that Canada, for instance, has become a leader in medical care by advancing beyond Britain in the proportion of GNP devoted to public medical care expenditures. This point, then, suggests that measuring laggardness in the welfare state's service sector by levels of public expenditure may be misleading over time.

Another issue here is whether the different historical development of social programs will continue to separate North American from European experiences. The forces for convergence are very substantial. The aging of Western societies, coupled with the common commitment to large, universal pensions, means that social security expenditures will converge. As the common demographic trends become social facts the pension programs will consume larger shares of public expenditure and make welfare states more similar.

Are there pressures to distinguish North America from Europe? Are there other bases for new sources of divergence? Here we think the differences will show up less in new programs differentially foregone than in continued differences in how welfare state programs are managed. The North American welfare state arrived later and was less corporatist in both management and ideology. The trade union movement—so central in Europe to the administration of social insurance—plays a different role in North America. As a supporter of universalist social programs, the North American trade union movement is not a party to the administration of the programs whose enactment it heralded. In European pensions, unemployment, and health insurance, unions are involved both as political supporters and participants in governance. This development has not been exported to nearly the same degree as has the conception of what problems the modern state should try to solve collectively.

Finally, one should add that the political debate over the welfare state will continue to have a distinctive North American as opposed to European flavor. Without the prospect of a social democratic government ruling in North America, the welfare state programs are open to criticism on both the extreme left and right. Those who want to return to a nineteenth-century utopia of individualistic self-help play a much larger role in the political discourse of North America than in Europe. But the absence of socialist parties as major governing coalitions in North America also means that the issues of welfare state development amidst fiscal strain appear different on the west side of the Atlantic. Common features include the major programs dealing with health, education, pensions, and social help. A critical difference is the place on the political spectrum of those groups likely to win political power. The result is that tax limitation victories—like those of Proposition 13 in California—engender both fears and hopes about change that the bureaucratic inertia of the modern welfare state will almost surely frustrate. And it does mean that we shall have more extreme discussions of choices to reduce the welfare state than are at all likely to be reflected in policy. Further, even choice without change can be frightening to those whose interests are most threatened by the movement to reduce the North American welfare state. In sum, North America is likely to remain a laggard more in the language of welfare than in the substance of the welfare state that it more slowly adopted in the course of the twentieth century.

Notes

1. For an excellent study centrally concerned with an explanation of why the United States is in this position as well as empirical examination of some broad dimensions, see Wilensky 1975.
2. These are among the frequently noted characteristics of the United States. See Lipset 1976, p. 20.
3. A fine example is Leman 1977, pp. 261-291.
4. Even if a case can be made that the "real" date for, say, French unemployment insurance ought to be 1967, the fact that a much earlier date can be considered suggests significant national attention to the problem by that time.
5. Reede 1947, p. 17.
6. Computed from data presented in Rimlinger 1971, pp. 195-196.
7. This is a moderate estimate drawn from Somers and Somers 1954, p. 38.
8. Turnbull, Williams, and Cheit 1967, pp. 34, 370.
9. Flora with Alber and Kohl 1976, p. 26.
10. The reader will recognize that there are a number of obvious ambiguities in the construction of such indexes. We note only one that would change the North American score rather considerably during the interwar period: how should old age protection be calculated? If there is a national scheme (or at least a scheme with national minima) protecting every aged person whose income falls below a certain level (and meets other uniformly administered criteria), is this universal (if contingent) coverage? Is it better to count only

beneficiaries of such a scheme in relation to the total aged population? Or finally, should only those persons be counted who are beneficiaries of at least a nominal "insurance" scheme on the grounds that in such a system "right" is far more firmly established than otherwise? At the suggestion of Dr. Jens Alber of the Flora group the authors have employed the following procedure. The means-tested Canadian pension scheme passed by Parliament in 1929 is counted as a genuine "pension" scheme because it was so regarded by the Canadian public. Beneficiaries are calculated in relation to the population of seventy years and older. In the United States, however, the introduction of Old Age Assistance as part of the Social Security Act was regarded rather more as a "welfare" than a pension measure, despite its formal similarity to the Canadian "pension" scheme. This is almost certainly due to the introduction of contributory pensions at the same time. Thus, neglecting Old Age Assistance that actually benefitted more Americans than did the contributory plan until well after World War II could be interpreted as biassing our results "against" the United States. On the other hand, our treatment of the contributory scheme cuts the other way. Following the practice of the Flora group wherever possible, we have taken the number of people enrolled in the United States scheme as a fraction of the labor force rather than the percentage of beneficiaries to the target age group: those over sixty-five.

11. See, for example, Wilensky 1975, Chapter 3.
12. Hockin 1975, p. 10. More complex discussion of some of the same considerations can be found in Lipset 1968.
13. Horowitz 1968, Chapter 1, p. 21. The conservative writer is W. L. Morton.
14. Horowitz 1968, p. 21.
15. An excellent comparative discussion of the functioning of parties at the national and subnational levels in Canada and the United States appears in Glaser 1969, pp. 3-4, 30-46.
16. Leman 1977, pp. 280-281.
17. Leman 1977.
18. Simeon 1972, p. 40.
19. Simeon 1972, p. 300.
20. Simeon 1972.
21. Leman 1977.
22. Leman 1977.
23. Coverage and benefits may be relatively complete at the very outset of the program in which case the observation will be of limited relevance.
24. Material in this section is drawn from Bryden 1974.
25. Rimlinger 1971, pp. 80-81.
26. Bryden 1974, pp. 77-78.
27. Zakuta 1964, p. 48.
28. Bryden 1974, p. 74.
29. Bryden 1974, p. 115.
30. Bryden 1974, p. 123.
31. Bryden presents a very detailed discussion of the pattern of negotiations and the positions taken by several of the provinces. Bryden 1974, pp. 129-146.
32. For a discussion of the free pension movement, see Rimlinger 1971, pp. 195-196.
33. See Canada Year Book 1974, pp. 140-143; and Statistical Abstract 1975, p. 10.
34. Council of Economic Advisers 1976, p. 11.
35. Leman 1977, p. 283.
36. Statistics Canada 1976, p. 97.
37. Most economists believe that, regardless of the statutory requirements,

payroll taxes are absorbed either through a reduction in wages or an increase in prices, but not by the employer.

38. Unemployment Insurance Commission, 1977, p. A-17.
39. Morgan 1969, p. 117.
40. Statistics Canada 1976, p. 97.
41. Unemployment Insurance Commission 1977, pp. H-11, A-20; Skolnik and Dales 1976, pp. 7, 12.
42. Statistics Canada 1976, pp. 98-99; Turnbull 1967, p. 262; Economic Report 1976, p. 108.
43. Turnbull, Williams, and Cheit 1967, p. 247.
44. See Morgan 1969, p. 116; such criticism is implicit in Feldstein 1975, pp. 51-61.
45. Unemployment Insurance Commission 1977, pp. H-10, H-12.
46. Feldstein 1977, pp. 90-92.
47. Unemployment Insurance Commission 1977, Chapter C.
48. Unemployment Insurance Commission 1977, p. J-21.
49. Statistics Canada 1976, p. 132.
50. Quoted by Eleanor Rathbone 1949, p. 274.
51. Morgan 1969, p. 113; Bryden 1974, p. 110; Willard 1968, p. 113; this explanation is also offered in Joint Economic Committee 1968, p. 70, which cites material from House of Commons debates of the period.
52. A slightly higher payment was made for older children from 9 to 16 (and 17 and 18 year olds were added to the scheme in 1964).
53. Statistics Canada 1976, p. 249.
54. Willard 1968, p. 66.
55. Leman 1980, p. 59.
56. Moynihan 1973, p. 48.
57. Statistics Canada 1976, pp. 211, 214.
58. Statistics Canada 1976, p. 247.
59. Statistics Canada 1976, p. 247.
60. Marmor and Rein, with the assistance of Sally Van Til, 1969, p. 273; Moynihan 1973, p. 48.
61. Moynihan 1973, pp. 125-126.
62. For a discussion of the growth of the AFDC program, see Council of Economic Advisers, 1976, pp. 96-101.
63. Bryden 1974, p. 79.
64. Material in this paragraph is from Morgan 1975, p. 121 and from Statistics Canada 1976, p. 302.
65. Leman 1977a, 1980, pp. 38, 119.
66. Leman 1977a, 1980, p. 35.
67. For a discussion of the growth of "fiscal federalism" in the Canadian context, see Van Loon and Whittington 1971, pp. 192-220.
68. Bryden 1974, pp. 75, 85, 86.
69. Leman 1977, pp. 174-78.
70. For a detailed discussion of the changes in income maintenance policy in Canada, see Lehman 1977, pp. 33-41.
71. See Moynihan 1973, pp. 156-174.
72. LeClair 1975, p. 11.
73. For an exhaustive account of U.S. Developments, see Marmor 1973.
74. On the current debate, see Marmor 1977.
75. Marmor 1973, p. 7.
76. For a detailed account of the pre-World War II activities of the AMA, see Garceau 1941; for the postwar period through the passage of the 1965 legislation, see Marmor 1973, *passim*.

77. LeClair 1975, p. 19.
78. Bowler, Kudrle, and Marmor 1977, p. 164.
79. For a review of these developments, see LeClair 1975, pp. 11-18.
80. For a discussion of the generally unsatisfactory results of attempting to use flat-rate copayments in the provincial schemes, see Evans in Andreopoulos 1975, pp. 130-132.
81. Thus, both Medicare and Medicaid as well as much of the Great Society legislation could be seen to confirm the "hypothesis."
82. In light of the investigation presented here, Lipset's recent conclusion that Canada's adoption of the "welfare state policies designed to further egalitarian ideals" were "later than their Southern neighbor in most cases" does not appear useful. Lipset 1976, p. 22. The generalization is particularly inappropriate as it appears in the absence of a discussion of constitutional problems.
83. Lipset 1976, especially pp. 40-46.
84. Lipset 1968.
85. Lipset 1968, p. 52.
86. Lipset 1968, p. 28.
87. Economic Council of Canada 1975, pp. 12, 18; and Congressional Budget Office 1975.
88. Council of Economic Advisers, 1976; Statistics Canada 1976.

References

Bowler, M. Kenneth, Kudrle, Robert T. and Marmor, Theodore. 1977. "The Political Economy of National Health Insurance: Policy Analysis and Political Evaluation." In *Toward A National Health Policy*, ed. Kenneth M. Friedman and Stuart H. Rakoff, pp. 158-188. Lexington, Mass.: D. C. Heath and Company.

Bryden, Kenneth. 1974. *Old Age Pensions and Policy-Making in Canada*. Montreal: McGill-Queen's University Press.

Congressional Budget Office. 1975. *Budget Options for Fiscal Year 1977: A Report to the Senate and House Committees on the Budget*. Washington, D. C.: U. S. Government Printing Office.

Council of Economic Advisers. 1976. *Economic Report to the President*. Washington, D. C.: U. S. Government Printing Office.

Economic Council of Canada. 1975. *Options for Growth, Twelfth Annual Review*. Ottawa: Minister of Supply and Services Canada.

Evans, Robert G. 1975. "Beyond the Medical Marketplace: Expenditure, Utilization and Pricing of Insured Health Care in Canada." In *National Health Insurance*, ed. Spyros Andreopoulos, pp. 127-203. New York: John Wiley & Sons.

Feldstein, Martin. 1975. "Unemployment Insurance: Time for Reform." *Harvard Business Review*, March-April, pp. 51-61.

Feldstein, Martin. 1977. "Social Insurance." In *Income Redistribution*, ed. Colin D. Campbell, pp. 71-97. Washington, D. C.: American Enterprise Institute for Public Policy Research.

Flora, Peter, with Alber, Jens, and Kohl, Jürgen. 1976. "On the Development of the Western European Welfare State." Paper prepared for the 1976 Congress of the International Political Science Association.

Garceau, Oliver. 1941. *Political Life of the AMA*. Cambridge, Mass.: Harvard University Press.

Glaser, William. 1969. "Making Decisions in the Canadian Federal System: Dilemma for Public Participation." Paper prepared for Conference on Participation and Policy Making, Akademie Tutzing, Federal Republic of Germany, June.

Hockin, Thomas A. 1975. *Government in Canada.* New York: W. W. Norton & Company, Inc.

Horowitz, Gad. 1968. "Conservatism, Liberalism, and Socialism in Canada: An Interpretation." In *Canadian Labour in Politics.* Toronto: University of Toronto Press.

LeClair, Maurice. 1975. "The Canadian Health Care System." In *National Health Insurance: Can We Learn From Canada?,* ed. Spyros Andreopoulos. New York: John Wiley & Sons.

Leman, Christopher. 1977. "Patterns of Policy Development: Social Security in the United States and Canada." *Public Policy,* 25: 261-291. (Spring).

Leman, Christopher, 1980. *The Collapse of Welfare Reform: Political Institutions, Policy, and the Poor in Canada and the United States.* Cambridge, Mass.: MIT Press.

Lipset, Seymour Martin. 1968. *Agrarian Socialism: The Cooperative Commonwealth Federation in Saskatchewan.* Garden City, N. Y.: Anchor Books.

Lipset, Seymour Martin. 1976. "Radicalism in North America: A Comparative View of the Party Systems in Canada and the United States." *Transactions of the Royal Society of Canada,* Series 4, Volume 14.

Marmor, T. R. 1973. *The Politics of Medicare.* Chicago: Aldine.

Marmor, T. R. 1977. "The Politics of National Health Insurance." *Policy Analysis,* 3, no. 1 (Winter).

Marmor, T. R. and Rein, Martin, with the assistance of Sally Van Til. 1969. *Postwar European Experience with Cash Transfers: Pensions, Child Allowances, and Public Assistance,* Technical Study of the President's Commission of Income Maintenance Programs. Washington, D. C.: U. S. Government Printing Office.

Morgan, John S. 1969. "An Emerging System of Income Maintenance: Canada in Transition." In *Social Security in International Perspective: Essays in Honor of Eveline M. Burns,* ed. Shirley Jenkins. New York: Columbia University Press.

Moynihan, Daniel P. 1973. *The Politics of a Guaranteed Income: The Nixon Administration and the Family Assistance Plan.* New York: Vintage Books.

Rathbone, Eleanor. 1949. *Family Allowances.* London: George Allen and Unwin.

Reede, Arthur H. 1947. *Adequacy of Workmen's Compensation.* Cambridge, Mass.: Harvard University Press.

Rimlinger, Gaston V. 1971. *Welfare Policy and Industrialization In Europe and America.* New York: John Wiley & Sons, Inc.

Simeon, Richard. 1972. *Federal-Provincial Diplomacy.* Toronto: University of Toronto Press.

Skolnik, Alfred M. and Dales, Sophie R. 1976. "Social Welfare Expenditures, 1950-75." *Social Security Bulletin.* (January).

Somers, Herman Miles and Somers, Anne Ramsay. 1954. *Workmen's Compensation.* New York: John Wiley & Sons.

Statistics Canada. 1976. *Social Security: National Programs.* Ottawa: Statistics Canada.

Turnbull, John G., Williams, C. Arthur, Jr., and Cheit, Earl F. 1967. *Economic and Social Security,* 3rd ed. New York: The Ronald Press Company.

Unemployment Insurance Commission. 1977. *Report on the Comprehensive Review of the Unemployment Insurance Program in Canada.* Ottawa: mimeographed.

Van Loon, Richard J. and Whittington, Michael S. 1971. *The Canadian Political System: Environment, Structure, and Process.* Toronto: McGraw-Hill Company of Canada, Ltd.

Wilensky, Harold L. 1975. *The Welfare State and Equality*. Berkeley, Calif.: University of California Press.

Willard, Joseph W. 1968. "Family Allowances in Canada." In *Children's Allowances and the Economic Welfare of Children: The Report of a Conference*, ed. Eveline M. Burns. New York: Citizens' Committee for Children of New York, Inc.

Zakuta, Leo. 1964. *A Protest Movement Becalmed: A Study of Change in the CCF*. Toronto: University of Toronto Press.

Part Three

Social Security: The Importance of Socioeconomic and Political Variables

Chapter 4

The Growth of Social Insurance Programs in Scandinavia: Outside Influences and Internal Forces

Stein Kuhnle

Introduction

The purpose of this chapter is to compare the responses of Denmark, Finland, Norway, and Sweden to the challenge of the new ideas about the role of the state in the protection and development of the social rights of citizens in the early phase of the creation of the modern welfare state. The Nordic countries share a basic cultural unity and are often, and not completely without foundation, looked upon as one single entity. The Nordic countries have traditionally had an eye on each other, learned from each others' experiences, and used one or several of the other countries as justifying references for the implementation of specific policies or for the introduction and refusal of new ideas. After World War II, closer formal cooperation was instituted at the top political and administrative levels. Ties were established that not only furthered the coordination of public policies on a number of topics, but which contributed, and still contribute, to the development of similar policies within each of the national territories.[1] But not since the period from 1389 to 1520 have the Nordic countries been one political-administrative unit. The area is split into five different national units—each of which has had, to a large but varying extent, its own unique history. With the exception of Iceland, each of the countries has since 1815 been independent in domestic affairs. For the last ten years considerable attention has been devoted to comparisons of social security expenditures and the development of social security programs among nations. Scholars have attempted to isolate the effects of diffusion patterns from innovative nations, political learning and problem solving by elites, and macrocharacteristics (political, economic, and organizational) of individual nations in the initiation and development of various welfare state activities. The following pages will apply and test these propositions for the four Scandinavian[2] nations. Was the influence of Bismarck's Germany upon early welfare legislation so great as to override the importance of domestic characteristics in the Nordic countries? Why was the principle of compulsory social insurance accepted early in some nations but not in other nations? Can differences in levels of economic development or differences of stages in the development of mass democracy account for variations in the timing of government legislation on social insurance?

In the first part of this chapter, I shall discuss the impact of diffusion on early social insurance legislation in Scandinavia. This part will provide only a limited explanation of the timing and actual contents of the first laws passed. In the second part a presentation of data on levels of internal socioeconomic and political development is made as a background for our search for alternative, or supplemental, factors of explanation. In the third part I try to interpret the effect certain differences in macrocharacteristics may have had on the timing of first laws as well as the effect on the likelihood of the introduction of compulsory insurance.

I. The Mixed Impact of Diffusion

Most writers trace the initiation of the welfare state, or at least the beginning of the present stage of development, to Bismarck's large-scale social insurance schemes of the last quarter of the nineteenth century.[3] On 15 June 1883, Bismarck and his government obtained the *Reichstag* approval of their proposal to establish a national, compulsory sickness insurance scheme for all industrial workers. This event marked the first of a series of German social insurance enactments during the 1880s, the other most important dates being 1884 (accident insurance) and 1889 (old age and invalidity pensions insurance). Bismarck had the state sponsor social legislation on a scale unprecedented in terms of population covered by insurance and in terms of risks met. The German program can be truly described as an agenda-building event. Its impact was immediate in the international environment. Governments established investigatory committees to draft legislative proposals. International congresses were convened to discuss insurance principles: the first congress on accident insurance was held in Paris in 1889. For better or worse, the German legislative actions provided the international community of legislators, administrators, employers, workers, and academics with a model. The historian Asa Briggs was most emphatic in attributing future welfare legislation to the German initiative: "German social insurance stimulated foreign imitation. Denmark, for example, copied all three German pension schemes between 1891 and 1898."[4] Many scholars, however, question this interpretation. For example, a contrasting view is evident in the following assessment of the same nation: "It has occurred that the modern social policy has been credited to Bismarck's policies in Germany. . . . Maybe one or two socialist-stricken Danes have thought 'So ein Ding müssen wir auch haben'. . . .But there is no sign that Bismarck's policies have had any significant influence on Danish social policy of 1891-1892. . . . None of Bismarck's ideas were at the time taken over by Denmark."[5]

How can two competent scholars reach such divergent conclusions concerning the same phenomenon? The answer lies partially in the degree to which the authors move from a broad historical overview like Briggs to historically specific conditions like Philip. This distinction can be illustrated best in reference to the most complete study of the diffusion of social security legislation.

Collier and Messick conclude that internal socioeconomic conditions (prerequisites in their terminology) had little effect upon (indeed were negatively correlated with) the initial adoption of social security legislation (in almost all cases insurance against work injury) in Western Europe.[6] The authors treat the enactment of such programs from 1883 to 1907 as a diffusion process "up a hierarchy" from the less to the most developed nations and spatially from Germany outward through Europe and the rest of the world. Collier and Messick make no reference to political or constitutional variables, to the previous history of social legislation and institutions, or to the specific content of the social security legislation. The two authors acknowledge that the dominant social classes and their ideology influenced the development of social security in Europe.

The challenge to the diffusion explanation, then, becomes less a refutation of its content than an elaboration of its limitations. These include the failure to consider welfare developments prior to Bismarck's initiative, the substantive content of subsequent legislation, and internal macrocharacteristics (especially differences associated with the political system and previous welfare policy).

The challenge to the diffusion explanation takes two forms. First, Bismarck himself did not invent state-organized social insurance. The following antecedents to Bismarck's historic actions formed an important prehistory of "modern" welfare state development:

1. legislation to protect individual welfare and morality of city dwellers in the later Middle Ages (late fifteenth and early sixteenth centuries);[7]
2. the insurance principles and functions of Medieval guilds;[8]

3. the "poor law" period stretching from the sixteenth until the eighteenth and nineteenth centuries and the "liberal break" of the nineteenth century;[9]
4. earlier national legislation on social insurance either establishing compulsory insurance for limited groups (miners, seamen) or extending state subsidies to mutual benefit societies and insurance funds;[10]
5. the advocacy of compulsory state insurance by German academic socialists.[11]

All of these actions predated Bismarck's initiatives and conceivably had some impact upon Bismarck and subsequent welfare state development.

Thus it is reasonable to conclude that, had Bismarck not catalyzed international action toward wide-ranging, compulsory, national social insurance, some other nation or leader would have so acted upon these precedents within a reasonably short period of time. By implication, much subsequent legislation can be reasonably attributed to the historical antecedents, to Bismarck's initiatives or to the contemporary economic, social, and political variables within the specific country.

The second challenge to the diffusion perspective points to the unique characteristics of the policies adopted within each nation that could not possibly be said to emanate from Germany.

Let us consider one interpretation of the diffusion concept, and the extent to which the first laws on social insurance in Scandinavia can be said to have been objects of diffusion from Germany. The diffusion concept is problematic when applied to highly complex legislation. Various operationalizations have been suggested and used.[12] The operationalization chosen here goes like this: to talk about diffusion from Germany, countries passing legislation at a later date must at least have adopted the principle of compulsion in their first laws of accident, sickness, and old age pension insurance and must also have adopted their first laws within a reasonable span of time after the first German laws, before the outbreak of World War I, for example. Let us review legislative initiatives and the first Nordic laws following the German legislation.[13]

Sweden was first out of the four Nordic countries: A proposal referring to the German legislation of 1883 in the 2nd Chamber of May 1884 led the king to set up an investigatory committee in October 1884. The committee was asked to study the German programs and to propose legislation. A proposal for accident insurance was presented in July 1888, for old age insurance in May 1889, and for sickness insurance in October 1889. Accident and old age insurance proposals were both based on the German principle of compulsion, but none were accepted by parliament. The proposal on sickness insurance was similar to a Danish proposal to subsidize voluntary sickness funds—a different solution from the German—and was passed in May 1891. Swedish participation at the International Congress on Accident Insurance in Bern in September 1891 led the government a month later to appoint a new commission to outline proposals for accident insurance and old age pension insurance. An employers' liability act based not on the German model, but rather on the English Workmen's Compensation Act of 1897 and a similar Danish law from 1898, was finally passed in 1901. The old age pension law passed in 1913 went further than any existing national law in the world: insurance was made universal so that with minor exceptions, the entire population was covered.

The first legislative initiatives in Sweden were clearly triggered by the German legislation, but the first two laws implemented did not follow the German model, and it is doubtful to call the 1913 law diffusion from Germany. The law was based on the proposal from 1889 that appeared before the enactment of the German old age pension law. The principle of universal coverage, which was a far more radical idea than proposed in the German law, was included in the first proposal that guided later legislation.[14] So, in fact, it is hardly correct to state that any of the first laws in Sweden were the objects of diffusion from Germany.

Denmark had had official commissions working on sickness insurance proposals before Bismarck's laws were introduced or even proposed in 1862, 1866, and 1875. The efforts did not lead to legislation right away. A new commission was appointed on 4 July 1885, after the passage of the first law in Germany and after the appointment of the Swedish committee. The commission's proposal of December 1887 differed from the German law by ordaining state subsidies to established sickness funds, based on voluntary insurance—and the (more rapid) work of the Danish commission influenced the Swedish proposal that came later. The proposal became law in April 1892. The 1885 commission also drew up plans for accident insurance mainly based on the German law, but, as in Sweden, the proposal, submitted in 1888, failed in parliament. A new commission, established in 1895, came up with a different proposal for accident insurance then and again in 1896, in which the principle of compulsion was rejected and reference made to German and Austrian experiences: the rapidly growing number of accidents in Germany and Austria was thought to be the result of compulsory insurance. The proposal was modified during 1897, and a law more in line with the English act of 1897 was finally passed in January 1898—without the principle of compulsion. As in Sweden, accident insurance was made obligatory on the employers first in 1916. Whereas the initiatives on sickness and accident insurance were related to external influences, the law on old age pensions of April 1891 was more one of Danish invention. It was a noncontributory pension scheme intended to support old people without means, but who at the same time had not received poor relief over the previous ten years. The first initiatives for old age support originated with the 1875 commission, and various proposals were discussed in the parliament each year during the period from 1880 to 1885. The law was to be administered by the communes, but the state would carry half the cost.

As in the case of Sweden, it is tempting to conclude that none of the first four laws in Denmark were products of diffusion from Germany. Legislative activity on social insurance problems may be said to have accelerated as a result of the German example, but the contents of the laws passed were either influenced by developments in countries other than Germany or represented novel ideas.

Referring to German and Swedish[15] initiatives, the Norwegian government appointed a committee to study workers' insurance on 19 August 1885. Proposals for accident insurance and sickness insurance were presented in February 1890, and a proposal for old age insurance was made in 1892. The Norwegian proposals were more in accordance with the German models than with the Danish and Swedish ones. Quite remarkably, the committee was unanimously in favor of compulsory accident insurance. The proposal was approved, with minor modifications, in July 1894. In one respect, the law was innovative: employers had to insure their workers in a centralized government-created insurance institution. The government submitted the proposal on sickness insurance, which was to be compulsory for large groups of workers[16] in 1893, but it was rejected. The same happened in 1894, 1895, and 1896 (to a somewhat more comprehensive proposal). A parliamentary commission, appointed in 1900, came up with another proposal in 1902, but there was still no agreement on legislation. Not until 1909 was a sickness insurance law passed.

When the proposal for an old age pension scheme was discussed in the parliament in 1892, one representative proposed a law following the principles of the Danish 1891 law instead. Nothing came of this, and in spite of work by new committees, a law was not agreed upon until 1923 and then was not implemented because of alleged financial problems.[17] An almost identical law was passed in 1936 and implemented in 1937.

In the Norwegian case, we can, to some extent, clearly justify the notion of diffusion from Germany. Both the accident insurance law and the sickness insurance law were modelled after German efforts.

Referring to German developments, the Finnish *Landtag* petitioned the government in 1888 to appoint a commission to draft proposals for worker insurance. A committee was appointed on 11 October 1889, and was instructed to study the need for accident and sickness insurance legislation.[18] Only a minority of the committee favored a compulsory sickness insurance in the proposal submitted in February 1892. The majority suggested governmental control with private funds based on voluntary insurance, and that these funds might qualify for public subsidies. The statute of October 1897 stopped short of offering public subsidies: it only required that private sickness and pension funds be audited by a governmental agency. Since the statute only meant government control and did not entail public outlays for insurance, it can hardly be listed along with the laws of

Finland's Scandinavian neighbors as an example of insurance laws. A law on accident insurance was approved by the government and the czar in December 1895. Insurance was made semicompulsory: full compulsory insurance was enacted in 1917.

The accident insurance law of 1895 was the only social insurance law passed in Finland before World War I or within what can be defined as a "reasonable span of time." The main principle of the law was not fully similar to the German text, but compared to the relation of the Danish and Swedish laws to the German law, the deviation was less. It will probably become more obvious after reading the next part of the chapter why Finland was slower in responding to the ideas spread from Germany. In Table 4.1 we have summarized the above discussion and findings on the various countries. It convincingly documents that while all of the Nordic legislative initiatives on social insurance in the 1880s were spurred by the German legislation to a large extent, only a few of the subsequent laws that went into effect bore significant resemblance to the German laws. The several instances of "nonlegislation," as shown in the table, further reduce the importance of the diffusion theory in trying to understand when and how and with what results, legislation came about. If additional dimensions of first laws had been taken into consideration, the diffusion concept might have been found even less appropriate.

Both in order to account for the timing of extensive social insurance legislation and to get a better understanding of the fate of the principle of compulsory insurance for some risks, we shall look into data on various macrocharacteristics of the four countries. We shall suggest that while aspects of political development, levels of socioeconomic development, and degree of continuity of social legislation may affect the timing of new social insurance laws, the spread and strength of voluntary insurance organizations combined with the ideological setting will influence the likelihood of the introduction of compulsory insurance.

II. Macrocharacteristics of the Nordic Countries in the 1880s

Before turning to the discussion of how we think various macrocharacteristics[19] affect legislative outcomes, let us present data illustrating some important similarities and differences among the four countries. We want to find out how the Nordic countries were characterized in a number of dimensions at the time of the emergence or breakthrough of the idea of state-organized social insurance.

We have chosen to distinguish among four major types of macrocharacteristics or macrosettings: the political, socioeconomic, ideological, and the institutional or organizational. We shall briefly outline and discuss the national ratings for each of these types of characteristics.

Table 4.1
Summary of Diffusion Evidence

First laws passed by World War I - or within c. 30 years of the German legislation and to what extent they can be said to have complied with the German principle of compulsion. "Yes" means that the law can be regarded an object of diffusion from Germany; "No" means that the diffusion concept is not very meaningful.

Type of law	Denmark	Finland	Norway	Sweden
Accident insurance	1898: No	1895: Yes and No	1894: Yes	1901: NO
Sickness insurance	1892: No	-	1909: Yes	1891: No
Old age pensions	1891: No	-	-	1913: Yes and No [a]
Unemployment insurance[b]	1907: No	-	1906: No	-

A. Political Macrocharacteristics

As shown in Table 4.2 below, all four countries were in their early phases
of development toward participatory mass democracy by the time Bismarck gained support for state-organized social insurance. All four had
restrictions on suffrage, and with the exception of Finland, mass party
organizations had been, or were in the process of being, established everywhere by the late 1880s and what we, for lack of better terms, may call
"modern systems of representation" had been created in Denmark, Norway, and Sweden.

But Table 4.2 also provides information on some significant differences.
Denmark, for example, had the widest enfranchisement, was close to
manhood suffrage and had reached the highest levels of electoral participation of the four nations. It had the most established mass party organizations and was the only country in which the social democratic party had
gained parliamentary representation. Norway was not far behind Denmark in terms of enfranchisement and levels of electoral participation.[20] It
was the only country to introduce the principle of parliamentarism in this

Table 4.2
Political Macrocharacteristics

Political macro-characteristics of the Nordic countries at the time of Bismarck's social insurance legislation in Germany (1883–1889)

	Denmark	Finland	Norway	Sweden
Sovereignty	Full sovereignty	A Grand Duchy of Russia. Large degree of national autonomy. From mid-1890s: "russification" - legislation under Russian surveillance [a]	Domestic self-government. Foreign affairs directed by Sweden	Full sovereignty
Systems of represent- ation	Two-chamber parliament: Landstinget (upper house) Folketinget (lower house)	Diet of four estates: nobility, clergy, burghers, peasants [b]	One-chamber parliament: Stortinget	Two-chamber parliament: 1st chamber (upper house) 2nd chamber (lower house)
Character- ization of government [c]	1875–94: conservative	conservative officials; in 1882: liberal leaders appointed	Until 1894: conservative officials; 1884–1889: liberal government	conservative officials/ politicians; 1888–89 Free Traders members of government
Principle of parliament'arism established	No	No	Yes: 1884	No
Existence of mass party or- ganizations [d]	Conservative, Liberal, So- cial Democra- tic parties from 1870s	No mass party organizations	Conservatives and Liberals from 1882–84; Social Demo- crats 1887	First mass party mobili- zation 1887: "free traders" "protectionists" Social Demo- crats 1889
Suffrage extension [e]	1885: 80 % of males 30 years+	c. 20 % of males 25 years+	1885: 42 % of males 25 years+	1885: 23 % of males 21 years+
Electoral turnout [f]	1880s: varying between 50–72 %	-	1880: varying between 48–50 %	1880s: varying between 25–47 %
Social Demo- cratic repre- sentation in parliament [g]	Since 1884	-	-	-

early period (Denmark: 1901; Finland: 1917; Sweden: 1917) and the only country with an all-liberal ("left") government. Sweden, on the other hand, witnessed a much slower and gradual transition toward mass democracy than Denmark and Norway; whereas Finland was the only one of the four countries not enjoying full domestic self-government and not having a modern system of representation.

B. Socioeconomic Macrocharacteristics

None of the Nordic countries were among the leading industrial nations in Europe by the latter decades of the nineteenth century. But even within this group of moderately industrialized countries some striking differences stand out. Table 4.3 demonstrates that Denmark definitely was the most urbanized of the four nations and had the largest share of the labor force employed in the nonprimary sector of the economy. Denmark also witnessed the most marked overall economic growth during the 1880s. Norway clearly lagged behind Denmark in terms of levels of urbanization and industrialization, but was more developed socioeconomically than Sweden, which experienced its major change from an agrarian to an industrial and service-oriented economy during the period from 1890 to 1910, but at a more rapid tempo.

Table 4.3
Socioeconomic Macrocharacteristics

Socio-economic characteristics of the Nordic countries at the time of Bismarck's social insurance legislation in Germany (1883–1889)

		Denmark	Finland	Norway	Sweden
Total population[a] (in 1000s)	1880	1969	2061	1919	4566
Proportion of population living in towns[b]	1880	28.1	8.4	20.0	15.1
	1890	33.3	9.9	23.7	18.8
Proportion of labor force employed in the non-primary sectors[c]	1880	49.6	21.0	40.7 (1875)	29.8
	1890	53.1	24.0	44.7	32.8
Economic growth in the decade 1880–1890[d]		moderate, but rel. most marked	rel. slow	stagnant in early 80s; recuperation in 2nd half	moderate, but slower than in Denmark

C. Ideological Setting

The *ideological setting* is a phenomenon that is more or less linked to characteristics of the sociostructural development. While we shall argue that characteristics of political and socioeconomic development have an impact upon the timing of state action on social insurance, it is our contention that an ideological setting may influence the type of state action. Ideological setting is a variable that is hardly measurable at all. It may seem dubious to introduce such a problematic variable, but we think an ideological setting may exert a strong, independent influence on the perception of workable or acceptable policy options.

An ideological setting may represent a barrier to the range of potential political actions that could, objectively, be resorted to. An ideological setting may define the premises for political debate. Specific settings are conducive to some kinds of ideas, but not to others.

Now, given that ideological setting is justifiably brought in as a variable accounting for differences in types of state action, what was the predominant ideological setting in Scandinavia at the time of the German social legislation? The theories of economic liberalism were influential in all of the Nordic countries in the nineteenth century, but probably gained its strongest foothold in Denmark, or rather the impact came to be more pronounced there because Denmark was the most urbanized and commercialized and had started industrialization earlier. The ideology of individual self-reliance and resistance to state intervention gained a foothold during the same decade as Denmark finally put an end to royal absolutism and introduced a system of representative democracy (1849).[21] A movement stressing the principle of self-reliance grew rapidly from the mid-1850s and nowhere else in Europe was the principle pushed more energetically and successfully, according to one source.[22] The guild system which was more firmly established and significant than in any of the other countries, was dissolved through the passage of the Trade Act in 1857 (implemented 1862).[23] A strong organizational basis for the formation of mutual benefit societies, from that date to be based on voluntary membership, thus existed. The first sickness funds were organized in the 1820s, but the number multiplied during the period from 1865 to 1875,[24] more or less as a direct result of the downplaying of the role of the state during the most viable years of liberalism. The dismal fate of some proposals for state-organized social insurance in the latter half of the 1870s could probably to some extent be attributed to the overall strength of the liberal ideology, as can the sudden deaths of early proposals for the old age pension scheme in Norway.

The order of the day was radically changed, however, when Bismarck demonstrated that the state could in fact take an active role in social insurance. A successful adoption of an alternative interpretation of the role of the state in an industrializing nation gave the liberal ideology a serious and fateful blow, though the effect was not, and could not be expected to be, instantaneous in countries with strong liberal traditions because of slow changes in political representation. What made the blow particularly powerful was the fact that the man who inexorably discarded liberalism was considered a conservative and certainly not a socialist. Proposals for government intervention in the market could not so easily be argued against by other conservative and/or liberal governments and legislatures.

D. Institutional or Organizational Macrocharacteristics.

Table 4.4 below indicates some fundamental similarities between the Nordic countries. Voluntary sickness, and burial, funds or societies existed in all countries. All countries had poor law legislation, with administrative responsibilities laid on the communes and with developments almost identical in Finland, Norway, and Sweden.

But differences between the nations should be more conspicuous. If we control for total population (figures included in Table 4.3), it is evident that Denmark had the most extensive network of voluntary sickness funds or societies and with the highest membership ratios, whereas Finland just as clearly occupied the bottom ranking. Denmark also had the most developed trade union organizations, although even in Denmark trade unionism found itself in an embryonic stage. Similarly, Denmark could boast the best record of previous parliamentary initiatives to establish some kind of social insurance legislation on a broad scale, although no proposals resulted in legislation. Norway had special enactments for miners (not applicable in Denmark with no miners) and seamen, but the practical significance of these laws is difficult to assess. Interestingly enough, Sweden was ahead of Norway in terms of spread and strength of sickness fund organizations, in spite of the fact that Sweden lagged behind Norway in terms of levels of urbanization and industrialization.

The comparison of various macrocharacteristics has provided us with the following profiles. During the 1880s, Denmark ranked as number one in terms of socioeconomic and political (democratic) development, Norway ranked second, Sweden third, and Finland fourth on the same indicators.

Table 4.4 indicates that Denmark made more frequent initiatives and efforts in the field of social legislation prior to Bismarck's first laws and that Norway might be ranked second, Finland possibly as number three, and Sweden either ranked equal to Finland or as number four. Economic liberalism is found to be the predominant ideological setting in all countries, but is considered to uphold a relatively stronger position in Denmark. Voluntary sickness funds are found to be in the strongest position in Denmark, in a weaker position in Sweden, and markedly weaker in Nor-

Table 4.4
Organizational Characteristics and Legislative Records

Organizational characteristics of the Nordic countries at the time of Bismarck's social insurance legislation in Germany (1883-1889), and records of previous legislation or legislative efforts.

	Denmark	Finland	Norway	Sweden
No. of voluntary sickness funds[a]	1885: c. 1000	1888: 78	1885: c. 225	1884: 956
Total no. of members in voluntary sickness funds[a]	1885: 164.000	1888: 15.400	1885: 30-35.000	1884: 121.000
No. of members in pension funds[b]	?	(1899: 7519)	?	1891: 18.708
Emergence of trade unions	from the early 1870s	from the 1880s	from the early 1870s	from the early 1870s
Total trade union membership[c]	1885: 20.000	(1900: 5-6.000)	1889: 3-4.000	1886: 8-9.000
Poor law legislation[d]	1803; 1849 (constitution) (1856) (1863-67)	1852; 1879 (restriction)	1845; 1863 (restriction)	1847; 1871 (restriction)
Parliamentary initiatives/ laws on social insurance prior to Bismarck's legislation of 1883[e]	1862,1866,1875: investigatory committees set down to define relationships between the state and voluntary sickness funds. Many proposals, but no legislation. 1881-1883: proposals on old age pensions.	1873: Sea Statute: seamen to receive medical care and treatment in case of sickness/accidents. Seamen must belong to pension funds. 1882: Diet of Four Estates sets down committee to study worker questions and need for accident insurance.	1842: Mining Law compensation for miners in case of accidents. 1844: first proposal for old age pensions (comp.); 1852,1869: new proposals voted down in parliament. 1860: Maritime Law compensation for seamen in case of accidents, medical care in case of sickness.	1850-1880: frequent parliamentary discussions of die Arbeiterfrage, but no proposals.

way and Finland. Voluntary old age pension funds were poorly developed in Finland and Sweden, and we suspect the same to be true for Denmark and Norway though (or maybe because) we lack data on this.

In the next part we shall propose some hypotheses on the relationship between macrocharacteristics and the timing of the first laws, as well as the likelihood of the adoption of compulsory insurance in the first social insurance laws in Scandinavia.

III. The Timing of the First Laws and the Likelihood of Compulsory Insurance: Some Explanatory Attempts

We shall formulate three general propositions and test them with respect to the Nordic countries. The first two refer to the timing and scope of governmental legislation, the third concerns the compulsory character of this legislation.

A. Timing and Scope of Social Insurance Legislation

Proposition 1. Social insurance legislation tended to develop earlier and with a larger degree of public investment in countries that had attained relatively higher levels of socioeconomic development and political mobilization at the time of the breakthrough of the idea of state-organized social insurance.

Proposition 2. The more continuity of legislation or legislative initiatives within the social policy area, the greater the likelihood of an early timing and relatively more extensive scope of government efforts in social insurance legislation once the idea of state-organized social insurance was born.

It seems reasonable to assume that characteristics of the macrosetting in the 1880s could influence early legislative initiatives not only for a few years, but for a somewhat longer period until around the outbreak of World War I. To understand developments after that date, the dynamic changes of the macrosetting as well as of the international context would have to be taken into consideration. The outbreak of World War I may seem to be arbitrarily set, but we think it marks the end of one era of political development and the beginning of another. In terms of social legislation development, a more specific crucial date might possibly be set: the year 1911 when Britain, the cradle of liberalism, introduced compulsory sickness and unemployment insurance[25] may be said to mark the beginning of a new era of social legislation.

Propositions 1 and 2 differ from propositions set forth in the studies by Heclo, Collier and Messick, and Flora and Alber because the focus is on a set of conditions at the start of the diffusion of the idea of broadly based social insurance and because not only the dates of legislation, but also the scope of governmental effort is considered.

The factor *continuity of legislation* is important because it indicates the degree of attention a government has given to problems of social insurance. The more continuous this attention, the greater the likelihood of a spurt of legislative action following successful legislation in a nearby country.

On the basis of the above propositions, one should expect Denmark to take the lead in social insurance in the Nordic countries. The tabular information presented in Part II suggests that only Denmark had had investigatory committees at work prior to the German legislation and Denmark was clearly the most developed economically, and had proportionally the largest and most mobilized electorate. Norwegian legislation should, considering the same variables, develop later than in Denmark, but would appear earlier than in Sweden. Finland should come out last according to our propositions.

In Table 4.5, I present the dates of the first laws on each of the four risks, the extent of public contributions or support for the various insurance programs, plus information on the number of persons covered by the laws, and in the case of old age insurance programs, the number of persons receiving pensions. These were based on means-tests in all of the first national laws; age was not a sufficient qualification for pension.

Table 4.5 demonstrates that Denmark had passed legislation implying governmental participation and concern for all four risks by 1907. Norway and Sweden had passed three important laws by the outbreak of World War I, but the third Swedish law came some years later than the third Norwegian law. Finland had only passed one law during the period that we consider a reasonable span of time for the measurable impact of the macrosettings of the 1880s.

The Danish state (and communes) started earlier and spent more on sickness and old age pensions than any of the other nations. The Norwegian efforts were more pronounced than the Swedish until 1910. The Swedish public support for voluntary sickness funds in the 1891 law was almost merely symbolic. Swedish efforts became more equal to the Norwegian ones after 1910 when state contributions to sickness funds were somewhat increased and after 1913 when Sweden introduced its comprehensive old age pension program.

Although the pattern of timing and scope of governmental efforts fits well into our Propositions 1 and 2, a general problem and two more specific questions remain. Since the ranking of the Nordic countries with respect to the levels of socioeconomic and political development as well as to the continuity of legislation is almost identical, we cannot point to the decisive factor or the decisive combination of factors explaining the timing and scope of governmental effort. But we also cannot simply exclude one or several of the independent variables, since we know from Chapter 2 that their relationships are different for other European countries and that no single variable provides a sufficient explanation.

The two more specific questions refer to the differences in the timing and scope of governmental effort between Norway and Sweden on the one hand and between Sweden and Finland on the other. The differences between Norway and Sweden with respect to social insurance legislation

Table 4.5
First Social Insurance Laws Passed

First laws passed: Year; proportional size of public contributions; number of persons covered. Laws passed before 1910 are of interest for the propositions set forth in the text.

Type of Insurance	Denmark	Finland	Norway	Sweden
Accident Ins.[a]				
Year	1898	1895	1894	1901
Public contributions	Insurance paid by employer	Insurance paid by employer	Insurance paid by employer	Insurance paid by employer
No. of persons covered		1898: 70288	1896: 127000	1905: 361000
Sickness Ins.[b]				
Year	1892	1963	1909	1891
Public contributions	1894: 26 % of total revenues	Shared between ind.premiums/ employers/state/ communes	State: 15 %, communes: 10 % of revenues (ind. prem.: 75 %)	1892: 3.2 % of benefits
No. of persons covered	1893: 116763 in recognized funds	1963: 3274000	1912: 361000 compulsory insured	1892: 25000 in recognized funds
Old Age Ins.[c]				
Year	1891	1937	1936	1913
Public contributions	1892: State 28.4%, communes 71.6%	State/communes paid supplementary pensions to needy persons	State/communes 50 % of pension expenditures	Public subsidies: 1914: 11%, 1919: 47%
No. of persons covered/receiving pensions:	1892: 19.5% of pop. 60 years+ = 43026 pers.	1942: 1900000 covered; 200 recipients	1940: 107297 recipients	1914: 3240000 covered; 73216 recipients
Unemployment Ins.[d]				
Year	1907	1917	1906	1934
Public contributions	State: 1/3, communes: 1/6 of total contributions	State: 2/3 or 1/2 of benefits paid (according to whether worker has dependants or not)	25% of total contributions 1908: 1/3; 1915: 1/2	State: 40% of total contributions
No. of persons	1908: 75000	?	1909: 13000	1941: 291139

are clearly less than one would expect from the marked differences in levels of socioeconomic and political development. Conversely, the differences in legislation between Finland and Sweden are much greater than the differences in levels of socioeconomic and political development would suggest. To account for these smaller inconsistencies one would have to introduce new variables. For example, the marked differences between Finland and the rest of the countries may be explained by the variable of national independence included in Table 4.2. Countries that have not reached national independence and at the same time have not developed a modern system of representation with widespread suffrage face higher barriers to effectuate social legislation. An assumption would be that countries that have passed these phases toward national independence and mass democracy more easily can turn their attention toward existing and emerging social problems.

Despite these questions, the pattern of timing and scope of governmental efforts on the whole correspond with our first two propositions. Thus, we can turn to the next hypothesis referring to the question of which nations have a better chance of approving the principle of compulsory insurance.

B. The Principle of Compulsory Insurance

Proposition 3. The introduction of a compulsory insurance is likely when the ideological setting of liberalism is weak and/or when voluntary insurance funds are relatively weakly developed; state subsidies to voluntary insurance funds are likely when both economic liberalism is strong and voluntary insurance funds are relatively strongly developed (as measured by number of members as a proportion of total population).

The assumption is that where voluntary funds can claim substantial membership support, strong organizational interests to preserve and expand the system of voluntary insurance would prevail. In such a context, state subsidies to voluntary funds should be a more likely immediate development than the introduction of a compulsory system run by the state. This proposition applies to sickness insurance in the Nordic context. All of the Nordic countries had private funds operating; however, the national differences in numbers and membership strength were large.

Generally, the proposition should also apply to old age pension insurance, but our assumption is that since statistics on the existence and scope of voluntary pension funds or private pension insurance in the 1880s seem lacking, indicating that no movement similar to the sickness insurance movement existed, state subsidies to voluntary pension funds was not a relevant legislative option for the Scandinavian governments. Old people, who could not make provisions for themselves or be taken care of by families, presumably had to rely on municipal poor relief. If we are correct in assuming that private old age pension insurance was negligible (and data for the 1890s from Finland and Sweden support the assumption), a precondition for an early breakthrough of the principle of compulsory old age pension insurance should be present. The proposition about the strength of the organization of voluntary insurance funds applies to the immediate time period following the German legislation.

However, as our proposition indicates, the dominant existence of voluntary insurance organizations would not be a sufficient condition to explain the fate of the principle of compulsion. The German law of 1883 instituted compulsory insurance based on the existing network of sickness funds. But a major difference between Germany and all of the Nordic countries was the impact of liberalism. Though the predominance of an ideology in a society is hard to measure, few would contest this assumption. Many German philosophers developing a paternal view of the state as opposed to *laissez-faire* liberalism exerted a marked influence in the nineteenth century. And Prussia is known to have had a long tradition of state paternalism. Denmark was in a similar position to Germany, with respect to the spread of voluntary sickness funds, but a long-lasting exposure to the ideas of liberalism would make state compulsion a less likely development at this time. Compulsory sickness insurance would most likely develop either in nations where the network of private sickness funds was poorly developed and/or where liberalism was weak; the same reasons apply to compulsory old age pension insurance. Wherever liberalism is weak, compulsory insurance is likely, but an organizational solution is dependent upon the existence and strength of voluntary insurance organizations, and where liberalism is strong, the principle of voluntary insurance will survive (at least for a while) only where an extensive network of private organizations exist, while compulsory insurance is more likely if such a network is missing.[26]

According to this hypothesis, Denmark and Sweden would, given the legislative options, be likely to implement a sickness insurance law providing subsidies to voluntary funds, while Norway might be expected to introduce compulsory insurance. All three countries should be likely candidates for introducing compulsory old age pension schemes. According to our hypotheses about the timing of legislation, Finland would be, and was shown to be, a latecomer, and thus our hypothesis on the principle of insurance does not really pertain to Finland. But if a governmental action had been likely at all, Finland would, as judged by the data on voluntary funds, be expected to introduce compulsory insurance.

Our third proposition was, as the other two, elaborated for legislation prior to World War I. Both the Finnish laws and Norwegian laws on old age insurance were passed a long time afterwards, and even though the principle of compulsion was approved of in all instances, we do not ascribe this fact to macrocharacteristics of the 1880s. For the explanation of the

Table 4.6
Principles of First Laws Passed

First laws passed on sickness insurance and old age pension schemes, and the principles of insurance applied.

	Denmark	Finland	Norway	Sweden
Sickness Ins.				
Year	1892	1963	1909	1891
Principle	state subsidies to voluntary funds	compulsory/ universal	compulsory for wage earners below income-limit	state subsidies to voluntary insurance funds
Old Age Ins.				
Year	1891	1937	1936	1913
Principle	non-contributory; pensions based on means test and moral test	compulsory/universal for contributions; pensions based on means test	compulsory/universal for contributions; pensions based on means test	compulsory/universal for contributions; pensions based on means test

Swedish laws and the sickness insurance laws of Denmark and Norway, our proposition gains support. The only case that might be disputed is the Danish old age pension program of 1891 which neither represented state-subsidized voluntary insurance nor compulsory insurance in the normal sense of the concept. But one might argue that the principle of a non-contributory pension scheme is closer to the principle of compulsion than the principle of voluntary insurance: the scheme is financed by general public revenues and all taxpayers are automatically obliged to contribute. Thus, even the Danish old age pension program may be said to support our proposition that in the (assumed) absence of widely spread voluntary pension insurance, compulsory state insurance would be likely. Norway did pass a law on sickness insurance for all wage earners in 1909, which in principle was compulsory; Denmark and Sweden chose a system of subsidies to voluntary funds (that had to be recognized by the state); and Sweden introduced compulsory old age pension insurance in 1913.

The principles of all these laws are in agreement with our proposition. In the Nordic context, the existence or nonexistence of strongly developed voluntary insurance funds would be a sufficient explanatory variable, since all countries were relatively strongly influenced by a common ideological setting: economic liberalism. The ideological setting was incorporated in order to explain the German case with a compulsory insurance based on an existing relatively strong network of insurance organizations. In addition, there might also be a threshold value: when voluntary insurance is close to encompassing the entire population, the step toward transforming the system into a universal, compulsory one is smaller and less drastic, and should not stir the same ideological fervor. Thus, our third proposition might perhaps be refined in the following way: compulsory insurance is likely whenever either very few or very many are voluntarily insured. Figure 4.1 gives a graphic presentation of this hypothesis.

Figure 4.1
Strength of Voluntary Insurance and State Involvement

Hypothetical correspondence between the strength of voluntary insurance funds and the principle of state involvement likely to be adopted

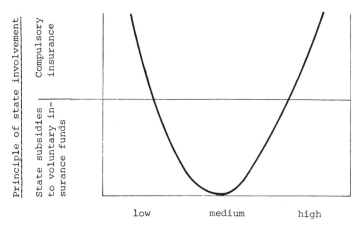

Of course, several factors would combine to make compulsory insurance a more acceptable legislative option over time. In addition to the threshold argument, one might think that a long experience with voluntary insurance, and the influence of changing ideologies, might reveal that those most in need of insurance are not insured, thus proving the system both ineffective and unfair.

Conclusion

We have indicated that a variety of characteristics of the macrosetting in the 1880s made Denmark a likely candidate to head the development of the modern welfare state in the Scandinavian context. According to the same characteristics, Finland was just as likely to become a laggard and it did. In terms of principles of sickness and old age pension insurance, we have gained suport for the hypothesis that the strength of voluntary insurance funds influenced what kind of legislative action was taken: poorly developed organizations in Norway lead to compulsory sickness insurance; relatively strong sickness funds in Denmark and Sweden lead to state subsidies to such funds.

For an analysis of later developments following World War I until today, one would, of course, have to study the changes of the macroconfigurations, the changes of the problem pressure, and the constraints within which legislators and administrators must act. In addition, one would have to consider international trends as well as the impact of the accumulating knowledge and experience on the operation of foreign laws. Above all, however, we should be aware that any analysis at the macrolevel can only take us a certain distance on the way to a full understanding of how legislative developments came about. For such an understanding we would have to study the processes of actual decision making, the divergent perceptions and motivations, interests and arguments involved. This is a particularly enormous task when comparisons are made not only across time and among nations, but also among different types of social insurance laws. Thus, in the following chapter, Alber studies and compares longterm changes from the First World War until today by focusing on only one system of social security that was usually the latest to be established (and therefore not studied by Kuhnle) and that can claim a special place in social legislation history: unemployment protection.

Notes

1. For an account of Nordic unity and disunity through history, consult Nielsen 1938, and for a recent evaluation of integration efforts at different levels after World War II, see Solem 1977.
2. *Scandinavia* encompasses Denmark, Norway, and Sweden, but it has become more and more common to include Finland under the same heading. *Scandinavian* and *Nordic* will be used interchangeable as synonyms in this text.
3. See, for example, Flora and Alber in Chapter 2; Dorwart 1971; Perrin 1969; Heclo 1974; Rimlinger 1971; and such general historical works as Achorn 1934 and Eyre 1937.
4. Briggs 1961, p. 147.
5. Philip 1947, p. 71. The quotation is a translation from the Danish text.
6. Collier and Messick 1975.
7. See Dorwart 1971.

8. See, for example, ILO, *Studies and Reports,* Ser. M, No. 4, 1925; and U. S. Department of Labor, *Fourth Special Report of the Commissioner of Labor,* 1895.
9. Rimlinger 1971.
10. See, for example, Alber 1976; Frankel and Dawson 1910; International Labor Office, *Studies and Reports,* Ser. M., No. 1, 1933; and *Social Security Legislation Throughout the World* 1949.
11. But the legislation proposed by Bismarck was opposed by the German Social Democrats. For a thorough discussion of the role of the German socialists, see Rimlinger 1971.
12. See Collier and Messick 1975; Flora and Alber in Chapter 2.
13. Developments before 1910 are for the most part based upon: Zacher 1898a, 1898b, 1899, and 1900; and Handwörterbuch der Staatswissenschaften 1909.
14. Cf. Heclo 1974, p. 182.
15. Berner 1894 suggests that the Swedish commission in work was the model for the Norwegian committee established.
16. Note that no country had at this time proposed the radical idea that the entire population should be covered by a sickness insurance law.
17. See Ormestad 1948.
18. The question of worker protection was raised, and statistics on accidents collected, by a committee appointed as early as 1883 (Zacher 1899).
19. The term "macro"-characteristic may not seem entirely accurate for all of the characteristics listed in Tables 4.2-4.5. It is used here as a short-hand term for characteristics that characterize the nation as a whole. The characteristics are thought to make up settings or contexts within which governments and legislatures must act.
20. Note that the figures in Table 4.2 refer to number of votes as a percentage of qualified voters, not as a percentage of registered voters. The figures given here are therefore lower than the ones published in Rokkan and Meyriat 1969, and in Mackie and Rose 1974, who used registered voters as the basis of calculation. The figures in Table 4.2 are, in our opinion, more comparable to the figures for the other nations.
21. The strong influence of liberalism in Denmark and its effect upon the development of a self-reliance movement is stressed in Berner 1894.
22. U. S. Department of Labor, *Fourth Special Report to the Commissioner of Labor,* 1895.
23. Cf. Galenson 1952 for a comparative account of the significance of the guild system in Denmark, Norway, and Sweden.
24. Philip 1947.
25. Cf., for example, Heclo 1974.
26. At this stage, at least, the variables cannot be differentiated into more than *relatively weak or strong* (i.e., voluntary funds; liberalism). With more cases one might consider it necessary to produce an indicator of the proportion of the adult population that are members of private insurance organizations, plus a stricter operationalization of the strength of liberal ideology.

Notes to Tables 4.1-4.5

Table 4.1

a. Cf. the text for an explanation.
b. Germany did not introduce unemployment insurance until 1927. The first unemployment insurance fund on a territorial basis was established in Bern in 1893, and the first national law came in 1905 in France. Cf. Perrin 1969.

Table 4.2
a. Examples of "russification" from the 1890s, see Puntila 1975.
b. Until 1886 the Diet could only petition the czar to propose bills. From that date the Diet could introduce its own legislation (but note information about later "russification"). See Puntila 1975.
c. Sources: De: Winding 1967; Fi: Puntila 1975; No: Rokkan 1966; Sw: Andren 1966.
d. "Mass party organizations" as distinguished from strictly parliamentary party groups (which had long existed in Sweden). The Swedish elections of 1887 - two in that year - have been described as the first mass party mobilizations in Lewin 1972 and in Stjernquist 1966. Generally on party developments, see *Problemer i Nordisk historieforskning* 1967.
e. Sources: De: Falbe-Hansen & Scharling 1891; Fi: Pesonen 1969; No: Rokkan 1967; Sw: *Statistisk Centralbyråns Underdaniga Berättelse rørande Riksdagsmannavalen 1885-1910*.
f. Since Denmark had a mixture of written and oral elections in this period, turnout has been estimated on the basis of data given in Warming 1913 and Falbe-Hansen & Scharling 1981. The estimation procedure is explained in Kuhnle 1973, where also sources for No. and Sw. are listed.
g. Social Democrats were first represented in the (new) Finnish parliament in 1907; in the Norwegian in 1903; and in the Swedish in 1896. For a comparative overview of the development of party representation, see Mackie & Rose 1974.

Table 4.3
a. Sources: De: *Danmark, Précis de statistique* 1907; Fi: *Statistical Yearbook* 1972; No: *Historical Statistics 1968* 1969; Sw: *Historisk Statistik for Sverige* 1969.
b. Sources: same as for total population.
c. Sources: De: Bjerke & Ussing 1958; Fi: Clark 1951; No: *Economic Survey 1900-1950* 1955; Sw: Jungenfelt 1966.
d. For a Nordic comparative overview, see Jorberg 1970. The characteristic applies to the economy as a whole, *not* to developments within various sectors. If Gross Domestic Product per capita (in fixed prices) is set to 100 in 1880, the scores would be in 1890: De: 124; No: 113; Sw: 117. Sources: De: Bjerke & Ussing 1958; No: *Historical Statistics 1968* 1969; Sw: Johanson 1967. The Danish figures and index are based on Net National Product.

Table 4.4
a. Sources: De: Zacher 1900; Fi: Zacher 1899; No: Zacher 1898a; Sw: Zacher 1898b. Note that Westergaard 1922 gives the Danish membership figure 120,000.
b. Sources: Fi: *Statistical Yearbook* 1912. Sw: *24th Annual Report to the Commissioner of Labor 1909*, U.S. Dept. of Labor 1911.
c. Sources: De: Westergaard 1922; Fi: Wuorinen 1965; No: Galenson 1970; Sw: Westerståhl 1945. Guinchard 1914 gives the figure 8392 in 1890 in Sweden.
d. Sources: De: Philip 1947, *Socialt Tidsskrift* 1941; Fi: *Social Legislation and Work in Finland* 1946; No: Kluge 1973; Sw: Højer 1965.
e. Sources: De: Philip 1947, Westergaard 1922; Fi: Zacher 1899; No: Ormestad 1948, mining law: *Nya arbetareforsakringskomitens betankande* 1892, maritime law: *Arbetareforskringskomitens betankande* 1889; Sw: Heclo 1974. According to Liedstrand 1924, the question of social insurance in Sweden was first raised in the *Riksdag* in 1884.

Table 4.5
a. Sources: De: Zacher 1900; Fi: *Statistical Yearbook* 1912 (note that additional

7,942 workers were covered by voluntary insurance); No: (coverage), Alber
1976; Sw: *Historical Statistics* 1960.

b. Sources: De: *Danemark, Précis de statistique* 1907; Fi: (contributions), *Social
Legislation and Work in Finland* 1946; (coverage), Alber 1976; No: *Historical
Statistics* 1968 1969, Ormestad 1948; Sw: *Historical Statistics* 1960 (note that
share of state contributions increased to 12.7% through a new law in 1910).

c. Sources: De: *Danemark, Précis de statistique* 1907 (note: not insurance law in
strict sense; one considered payment of taxes through life to be equivalent to
the payment of premiums); Fi: *Statistical Yearbook* 1952; (contributions),
Social Services in Finland 1969 (note the first disability pensions were paid in
1942, and the first old age pensions in 1947); No: (contributions), Ormestad
1948, (recipients), *Historical Statistics 1968* 1969; Sw: (coverage), *Historical
Statistics* 1960; (subsidies), ILO, *Studies & Reports, Ser.M.,* No. 10, 1933.

d. Sources: De: Westergaard 1909; Fi: *Social Legislation and Work in Finland*
1946, (subsidies), *International Labour Review*, Vol. XXIII 1931; No:
Ormestad 1948 (note that by 1977, Norway is the only of the four countries to
have compulsory insurance, introduced (for industrial workers) already in
1938); Sw: *Historical Statistics* 1960 (note that Sweden introduced an
unemployment assistance program in 1914 through which the state and
communes paid cash benefits (*Arbets-löshetsforsäkringen* 1963.

References

Achorn, E. 1934. *European Civilization and Politics Since 1815*. New York: Har-
court, Brace and Company.
Alber, Jens. 1976. "Social Security I: Participants of Social Insurance Systems in
Western Europe." HIWED Report No. 4. Cologne: Forschungsinstitut für
Soziologie, University of Cologne.
Andrén, Nils. 1966. *Från Kungavelde till folkstyre*. Stockholm: Liber.
Arbetareförsäkringskomitens betänkande. 1888. II. *Öfversigt af lagstiftningen
rörande arbetareförsäkringen i åtskilliga främmande länder*. Stockholm:
Beckman.
Arbetslöshetsförsäkringen. 1963. *SOU: 40*. Stockholm.
Berner, H. E. 1894. "Arbeiderforsikringen i de nordiske lande." *Statsökonomisk
tidsskrift* (Norway).
Bjerke, Kjeld and Ussing, Niels. 1958. *Studier over Danmarks nationalprodukt
1870-1950*. Copenhagen: G.E.C. Gads Forlag.
Briggs, Asa. 1961. "The Welfare State in Historical Perspective." *Archives Euro-
péennes de Sociologie*. 2: 221-258.
Central Bureau of Statistics, 1955. *Economic Survey 1900-1950. Samfunnsokono-
miske studier, 3*. Oslo: Central Bureau of Statistics.
Central Bureau of Statistics, 1968, 1969. *Historical Statistic*. Oslo: Central Bureau
of Statistics.
Central Bureau of Statistics. n.d. *Statistiska Centralbyråns underdåniga berättelse
rörande Riksdagsmannavalen 1885-1910*. Stockholm: Central Bureau of
Statistics.
Central Bureau of Statistics. 1960. *Historical Statistics*. Stockholm: Central
Bureau of Statistics.
Central Bureau of Statistics. 1969. *Historical Statistics: Part 1, Population, 1720-
1967*. 2nd ed. Stockholm: Central Bureau of Statistics.
Clark, Colin. 1951. *Conditions of Economic Progress*. 2nd ed. London: Macmillan
and Co.
Collier, David and Messick, Richard. 1975. "Prerequisites Versus Diffusion: Test-

ing Alternative Explanations of Social Security Adoption." *American Political Science Review* 69: 1299-1315.
Danemark: Précis de statistique. 1907. Copenhagen.
Dorwart, Reinhold A. 1971. *The Prussian Welfare State before 1740.* Cambridge, Mass.: Harvard University Press.
Eyre, E. 1937. *European Civilization: Its Origins and Development.* New York: Oxford University Press.
Falbe-Hansen, V. and Scharling, Will. 1891. *Danmark i 1890: Statistisk Haandbog. Supplementsbind til Danmarks Statistik I-V.* Copenhagen.
Federal Security Agency, U. S. Social Security Administration. 1949. *Social Security Legislation Throughout the World.* Washington, D. C.: U. S. Government Printing Office.
Frankel, Lee K. and Dawson, Miles M. 1910. *Workingmen's Insurance in Europe.* New York: Russell Sage Foundation, Charities Publication.
Galenson, Walter. 1952. "Scandinavia." In *Comparative Labor Movements,* ed. Walter Galenson. New York: Prentice-Hall, Inc.
Galenson, Walter. 1970. *Labor in Norway.* New York: Russell & Russell.
Guinchard, J. 1914. *Sweden: Historical and Statistical Handbook.* 2nd ed. First Part. Stockholm: Government Printing Office.
Heclo, Hugh. 1974. *Modern Social Politics in Britain and Sweden.* New Haven, Conn.: Yale University Press.
Höjer, Karl J. 1965. *Den svenska socialpolitiken.* Stockholm: P. A. Norstedt & Söner.
International Labour Office. 1925. "Sickness Insurance." Studies and Reports. Series M, No. 4. Geneva.
International Labour Office. 1931. "Unemployment Insurance: Tabular Analysis of the Legislation in Force." *International Labour Review* 23, No. 1, 48-66.
International Labour Office. 1933. "Compulsory Pension Insurance." Studies and Reports. Series M, No. 10. Geneva.
Johansson, Östen. 1967. *The Gross Domestic Product of Sweden and Its Composition 1861-1955.* Stockholm: Almqvist & Wiksell.
Jörberg, Lennart. 1970. "The Industrial Revolution in Scandinavia 1850-1914." In *Fontana Economic History of Europe,* ed. Carlo M. Cipolla, vol. 4. London: Collins.
Jungenfelt, Karl G. 1966. *Löneandelen och den ekonomiska utvecklingen.* Uppsala: Almqvist & Wiksell.
Kluge, Liv. 1973. *Sosialhjelp för og nå.* Oslo: Sosialdepartementet, Fabritius.
Kuhnle, Stein. 1973. Social Mobilization and Political Participation: The Nordic Countries c. 1850-1970. Dissertation. University of Bergen.
Lewin, Leif. 1972. *The Swedish Electorate 1887-1968.* Stockholm: Almqvist & Wiksell.
Liedstrand, Emil. 1924. "Social Insurance in Sweden." *International Labour Review* 9, No. 2. 177-195.
Mackie, Tom and Rose, Richard. 1974. *The International Almanac of Electoral History.* London: MacMillan Press.
Ministry of Social Affairs. 1946. *Social Legislation and Work in Finland.* Helsinki: Ministry of Social Affairs.
Ministry of Social Affairs. 1963. *Social Services in Finland.* Helsinki: Ministry of Social Affairs.
National Industrial Conference Board. 1949. *The Social Security Almanac.* New York: National Industrial Conference Board.
Nielsen, H. 1938. *Nordens Enhed gennem Tiderne I-III.* Copenhagen: Nyt Nordisk Forlag.
Nya arbetareförsäkringskomitens betänkande. 1892. *III. Översigt af lagstift-*

ningen rörande arbetareförsäkringen i åtskilliga främmande länder. Stockholm: Beckman.

Ormestad, M. 1948. *De sosiale trygder: historikk og grunnprinsipper.* Oslo: Sem og Stenersen.

Perrin, Guy. 1969. "Reflections on fifty years of social security." *International Labour Review* 99, no. 3: 249-292.

Pesonen, Pertti. 1969. "Political Parties and the Finnish Eduskunta: Voters' Perspectives, Party Nominations, and Legislative Behavior." University of Tampere and University of Iowa: mimeographed.

Philip, Kjeld. 1947. *Staten og fattigdommen.* Copenhagen: Jul Gellerups Forlag.

Problemer i Nordisk historieforskning. 1967. Bergen: Universitets-forlaget.

Puntila, L. A. 1975. *The Political History of Finland 1809-1966.* Helsinki: The Otava Publishing Co.

Rimlinger, Gaston V. 1971. *Welfare Policy and Industrialization in Europe, America, and Russia.* New York: Wiley & Sons.

Rokkan, Stein. 1966. "Numerical Democracy and Corporate Pluralism." In *Political Oppositions in Western Democracies,* ed. Robert A. Dahl. New Haven, Conn.: Yale University Press.

Rokkan, Stein. 1967. "Geography, Religion, and Social Class: Crosscutting Cleavages in Norwegian Politics." In *Party Systems and Voter Alignments,* eds. Seymour Martin Lipset and Stein Rokkan. New York: Free Press.

Rokkan, Stein and Meyriat, Jean. ed. 1969. *International Guide to Electoral Statistics.* The Hague: Mouton.

Socialt Tidsskrift. 1941. "Danmarks sociale lovgivning 1891-1941." Copenhagen.

Solem, Erik. 1977. *The Nordic Council and Scandinavian Integration,* New York: Praeger Publ.

Statistical Yearbook Finland. 1912. 1952. 1972. Helsinki.

Stjernquist, Nils. 1966. "Sweden: Stability or Deadlock?" In *Political Oppositions in Western Democracies,* ed. Robert A. Dahl. New Haven, Conn.: Yale University Press.

U. S. Department of Labor. 1895. *Fourth Special Report to the Commissioner of Labor: Compulsory Insurance in Germany.* Washington: U. S. Government Printing Office.

U. S. Department of Labor. 1911. *Twenty-fourth Annual Report of the Commissioner of Labor 1909: Workmen's Insurance and Compensation Systems in Europe.* Washington, D. C.: U. S. Government Printing Office.

Warming, Jens. 1913. *Haandbog i Danmarks Statistik.* Copenhagen.

Westergaard, Harald. 1922. *Economic Development in Denmark.* Oxford: Clarendon Press.

Westergaard, Harald. 1909. "Die Arbeiterversicherung in den einzelnen Staaten." In *Handwörterbuch der Staatswissenschaften.* 3rd ed., vols. 1, 2.

Westerståhl, Jörgen. 1945. *Svensk fackföreningsrörelse.* Stockholm: Tidens Förlag.

Winding, Kjeld. 1958. *Danmarks Historie.* Copenhagen: Fremads Fokusböger.

Wuorinen, J. H. 1965. *A History of Finland.* New York: Columbia University Press.

Zacher, Dr. 1898a. *Die Arbeiterversicherung im Auslande: Vol. 3, Die Arbeiterversicherung in Norwegen.* Berlin: Verlag der Arbeiter-Versorgung.

Zacher, Dr. 1898b. *Die Arbeiterversicherung im Auslande: Vol 2, Die Arbeiterversicherung in Schweden.* Berlin: Verlag der Arbeiter-Versorgung.

Zacher, Dr. 1899. *Die Arbeiterversicherung im Auslande: Vol 10, Die Arbeiterversicherung in Finland.* Berlin: Verlag der Arbeiter-Versorgung.

Zacher, Dr. 1900. *Die Arbeiterversicherung im Auslande: No. 1, Die Arbeiterversicherung in Danemark.* Berlin: Verlag der Arbeiter-Versorgung.

Chapter 5

Government Responses to the Challenge of Unemployment: The Development of Unemployment Insurance in Western Europe

Jens Alber

I. Origins of Modern Unemployment Provisions

A. Unemployment and its Historical Solutions

The historical roots of unemployment in Western Europe can be traced back to the sixteenth century when the commercialization of agriculture displaced peasants from the countryside and began to dissolve traditional feudal systems of protection and obligation. As market expansion and accelerated industrialization induced cyclical fluctuations in labor demand, the modern worker increasingly faced unemployment and with it destitution. The public unemployment protection schemes that emerged may be classified into two categories: the payment of cash benefits to replace lost earnings and the development of new employment opportunities through the provision of work. The compensation of lost earnings can occur through insurance programs where the receipt of benefits is contingent upon contributions or through assistance programs that provide benefits subject to a means test. Elementary assistance in finding employment can be attained through the institution of labor exchanges. Finally, while support sometimes takes the form of a public subsidy of labor, a more direct and effective way lies in public work programs. Among these modern forms of protection, cash benefit schemes and especially the insurance method have so far been dominant.

Unemployment insurance generally tended to be introduced as the last of the four major social insurance schemes. The first national programs were only instituted after the turn of the twentieth century. This relatively late introduction may be attributed to various factors. The cataclysmic effects and relative unpredictability of massive unemployment rendered the application of insurance techniques difficult, as increasing numbers of beneficiaries and decreasing contributors threatened the solvency of the systems. Income maintenance programs for the unemployed are "inherently the most controversial"[1] of any social security provisions, because they always involve the question of the causes of unemployment: individual idleness, collective labor disputes, or the general economic situation.

Despite such problems, unemployment insurance did not entirely start from scratch, but built on the experience assembled in the administration of other public protection schemes. After unemployment had for a long time been interpreted as a problem of work-shy malingerers who should be supported only within "the frame-work of repression" in the "well-regulated workhouse,"[2] assistance to the unemployed was divested of its stigmatizing and repressive characteristics by the growing trade union movement. The unions could build on the tradition of mutual aid reaching back to the medieval guilds that had supported their unemployed members with the so-called gift or travel benefit. After the first union fund for the unemployed was established by the English foundrymen's union in 1831, union-organized unemployment programs slowly diffused to all countries of Western Europe. The unions were not only motivated to alleviate poverty among their fellows and attract new members, but also to ensure a minimum wage against competition from the "industrial reserve army."[3]

The second source of modern programs, local government schemes without stigma, did not emerge until extensive unemployment had wracked Europe in the mid-1880s and early 1890s. Here, Switzerland was the pioneer. After a social democratic party convention in 1891 had demanded public support for the unemployed, a limited voluntary insurance fund was instituted in Bern (1893) and soon copied by other European cities (e.g. Cologne 1896). These early attempts soon inspired bolder moves: After a bill to introduce compulsory unemployment insurance in Basel had only failed in a referendum, a similar initiative in the canton of St. Gallen achieved implementation in 1895. Without sufficient safeguards against abuse, this first compulsory unemployment insurance program soon went bankrupt and was discontinued in 1897.[4] Other communes started to subsidize voluntary funds, set up by friendly societies or trade unions. In 1901, the Belgian city of Ghent established a program that soon became a model for much of Europe. The Ghent system consisted of public supplements to unemployed trade union members equaling 50 to 75 percent of voluntary fund benefits.[5]

B. The Modern Approaches

The administrative experience gained from the regionally limited schemes paved the way for more extensive protection programs. State-sponsored insurance schemes on a national scale were instituted in all European countries during the first third of the twentieth century. Two basic approaches were followed: subsidized voluntary and compulsory insurance. Both were variants of the social insurance technique insofar as financing came not only through uniform contributions independent of individual risk, but also through varying degrees of state participation. Which of the two alternative approaches was followed depended on country specific traditions that cannot be pursued here in any detail. It appears that the early institutionalization of communal schemes in Switzerland, France, and Belgium might have hampered the national development of compulsory insurance, because it provided the basis for functional substitutes such as subsidized voluntary insurance or centrally coordinated municipal assistance schemes.

Voluntary insurance was first adopted by most countries. In 1905 France pioneered as the first country to introduce a subsidized voluntary unemployment insurance scheme on the national level. Government subsidies were made to voluntary funds satisfying certain administrative requirements as a proportion of the benefits paid by the funds. Organizational specifics were left to the funds' administration. Within two years, Norway (1906) and Denmark (1907) followed the French example with five more countries adopting subsidized voluntary insurance systems somewhat later: the Netherlands 1916, Finland 1917, Belgium 1920, Switzerland 1924, and Sweden 1934. These initial schemes were later replaced by compulsory systems in all countries except Denmark, Finland, and Sweden.

The take-off of public unemployment protection schemes cannot easily be related to general patterns of social and political development. It is true that the early Swiss and French communal schemes of the 1890s followed not only major economic depressions but also the organizational consolidation of labor parties while trade union funds as potential substitutes for public provision were not as developed as in England or Germany. However, the impact of such background variables has not been the same in all countries. Whereas the social democratic party of Denmark had pressed for the 1907 law that was favorably received by the unions, Norwegian union leaders opposed their new insurance system and boycotted its implementation.[6] The same was true in France where the reluctance of the unions virtually left the law a dead letter. Some union leaders resisted state-sponsored schemes for fear that state participation would threaten union autonomy. In addition, the unions opposed the new provisions for the admittance of unskilled nonunionists who drew the most benefits, but paid only small contributions. Thus, trade unions pursued very different policies in different national and chronological contexts.

When in the United Kingdom deliberations on the world's first national compulsory insurance scheme began, much attention was given to integrating union leaders into consultations. The 1911 law provided for tripartite financing by workers, employers, and the state and for flat contributions to ensure that better-paid workers would not foot the bill for their high-risk colleagues.[7] Rather low flat benefits were introduced to give the unions the opportunity to organize supplementary schemes, and voluntary systems for workers not under compulsory insurance were subsidized. Although benefits were held to minimum subsistence levels, the law represented a complete reversal of the principles of the old English poor law. Whereas the latter had confined public relief outside the workhouse to the impotent, the insurance scheme strictly limited the benefit payments to the able-bodied. In sharp contrast to their former characterization as "work-shy malingerers," they were now referred to as the "respectable poor." To receive benefits, the unemployed were not obliged to accept any available employment opportunity, but only those vacancies considered suitable in light of their previous occupation, the level of wages, and the locality.

Nevertheless, the idea of regulating the poor had not entirely vanished and prevailed in the political motives for introducing the scheme, as well as in some of its legal provisions. Various accounts of the development of British unemployment policy agree that the attempts to separate the able-bodied unemployed from the socially declassed poor through differentiated protection schemes were motivated by the fear that the "respectable poor would be infected by contact with the residuum during periods of social distress . . . and might be tempted to throw in their lot with social agitators and elements among the residuum in a struggle for the redistribution of wealth."[8] Several qualifying conditions ensured that applicants had not lost employment through their own fault and had paid sufficient contributions. To prevent abuse in the form of simulated unemployment for a short vacation, the payment of benefits would only begin after a waiting period, with the duration of benefits limited so as to stimulate the search for a new job.

With some modifications, provisions of this sort were to be contained in all national insurance laws adopted thereafter. Italy was first to follow the British example with a compulsory insurance scheme in 1919. By the outbreak of World War II Austria (1920), Ireland (taking over the British scheme in 1923), Germany (1927), and Norway (1938) had also adopted the compulsory insurance approach. When Belgium (1944), the Netherlands

(1949), and, with some time-lag, France (1967) and Switzerland (1976) had provided for compulsory schemes, the Scandinavian countries were the only ones left with voluntary systems. This trend toward the adoption of compulsory insurance systems was supported by international influences, such as recommendations of the International Labor Organization (ILO). Already in 1919 the ILO adopted an Unemployment Recommendation urging all countries to introduce effective systems of unemployment insurance. After a series of other recommendations, the Social Security (Minimum Standards) Convention of 1952 set forth specific standards concerning the definition of contingency and qualifying conditions, the scope of the schemes, and the minimum level and duration of benefits.

To meet modern standards of adequate protection, the initial schemes—especially those of the early adopters—had to be considerably expanded. Three consolidating steps were of particular significance: (1) the limited scope of the schemes had to be widened to cover the majority of all employees, including agricultural workers who had frequently been excluded at the outset; (2) dependants' benefits had to be introduced to ensure the adequacy of payments to heads of families; (3) the duration of benefits had to be extended to provide for long-term unemployment. Table 5.1 illustrates that today most countries have taken these consolidating steps.

Providing for long-term unemployment, however, could not be satisfactorily managed within the framework of insurance systems. Often introduced as a provisional measure during economic depression, the payment of extended benefits independent of a contribution test brought several schemes near bankruptcy in the years between the two world wars and led to heated political controversies. To relieve the strain on insurance systems, most countries differentiated the provisions for long-term benefits from insurance, and instituted special unemployment assistance schemes that paid lower rates only after a means test. The institutional predecessors of these assistance schemes go back to the economic depression at the end of World War I, when special emergency relief programs were introduced by several nations. Today, insurance and assistance schemes coexist in most countries, thus furnishing a double net of income security.

Assessing the adequacy of national unemployment protection efforts would require a detailed consideration of assistance schemes and other policy measures to combat unemployment that are of more recent origin. Some countries (e.g. Italy 1968 and France 1969) have established special programs providing for an almost complete wage substitution for workers collectively dismissed. Others, such as the United Kingdom (1965), Ireland (1967), and Finland (1970) have introduced redundancy payment schemes where compensations for job loss due to economic change are paid even if the beneficiary immediately secures new employment. In addition to these

Table 5.1
Major Steps in the Development of Unemployment Insurance Schemes

Country	Voluntary insurance	Compulsory insurance	Dependants' benefits	Extension to agriculture	Other core insurance laws	Extended benefits/ Assistance
Austria (AU)	-	1920	1920	1949	?	1926 (1918, 1922)
Belgium (BE)	1920 (1907)	1944	1944	1944	1933, 1938, 1952, 1971	-
Denmark (DE)	1907	-	1919	1907	1933, 1967	1921
Finland (FI)	1917	-	1917	1917	1934, 1960	1960
France (FR)	1905	1967	1967	-	1939, 1959	1914, 1951
Germany (GE)	-	1927	1927	1927	1956, 1969	1918
Ireland (IR)	-	1923	1923	1953	1948, 1952, 1973	1933
Italy (IT)	-	1919	1937	1949	1923, 1935, 1939, 1952	1946 (1917-1919)
Netherlands (NE)	1916	1949	1921	1949	1964 (1948)	1964
Norway (NO)	1906	1938	1938	1949	1959	-
Sweden (SW)	1934	-	1934	1934	1941, 1944, 1953, 1974	1916, 1973
Switzerland (SZ)	1924	1976	1924	?	1951	(1917, 1924, 1942)
United Kingdom (UK)	-	1911	1921	1936	1920, 1946, 1966, 1975	1934 (1921)

( ) Temporary measures.

Underlined laws are included in the analyses of part III.

programs, policies to provide work were also established, so that most countries now rely on all of these approaches in varying combinations. Already by 1930, all Western European countries had taken steps to provide state-controlled labor exchanges.[9] Direct attempts to provide employment through public work programs were sponsored by several national governments after World War I. In Sweden, this so-called work-approach even became the foundation of Swedish unemployment policy.[10] The fact that Sweden as the unemployment insurance laggard had developed other effective means to alleviate unemployment should caution any attempt to draw broader conclusions about a nation's unemployment policy effort simply on the basis of its unemployment insurance programs.

Judgments about the adequacy of national unemployment protection schemes, however, are beyond the intention of this chapter. Unemployment insurance is studied here, not because it provides the backbone of national unemployment protection efforts, but because it represents a crucial area of welfare policy that is particularly suited to an examination of the interrelationship of politics and policies. First, unemployment is politically relevant because it affects great numbers of people who may be easily mobilized to challenge governments. Second, unemployment may be considered the only area where an involuntary loss of earnings can be affected directly by government action.[11] Finally, ideological controversies over the extent of income maintenance and welfare state measures in general are revealed in particularly sharp form in the determination of unemployment schemes. In most countries, especially Austria, Germany, and Italy, unemployment compensations are still decidedly less than sickness payments, perhaps reflecting the traditional conception of unemployment as a problem of individual idleness. Even if unemployment is perceived as a general decline in the demand for labor, lower benefit levels are often considered as necessary to maintain work incentives. Some contemporary programs still make the receipt of benefits conditional upon a decent life style (as in Belgium) or upon sufficient efforts to find work (as in the Netherlands). Questions about the adequate strength of such controls and the desirable level of benefits lay at the heart of the political controversies that accompanied the development of unemployment programs in Western Europe. Analyzing the provisions of the unemployment insurance laws, the following section examines these characteristics in more detail.

II.   Characteristics, Changes and Trends in Modern Unemployment Insurance

A. Crucial Characteristics

At least four characteristics of unemployment insurance, their interrelations, and changes are important in tracing the development of modern programs. These are the following:

1. *Generosity.* To what extent do the schemes provide effective income maintenance; how generous are the benefits?
2. *Control.* Do the modern systems still contain traditional elements of "regulating the poor"; how strong are the checks against possible abuses?

3. *Penetration.* What is the extent of state intervention and participation in the schemes?
4. *Redistribution.* Do the provisions involve a vertical redistribution of incomes?

The level and duration of benefits reflects the generosity of the programs: the higher the earnings-replacement ratios and the longer the period of indemnification, the more generous the system. Among the statutory conditions for the receipt of benefits, the length of the waiting and disqualification periods may be used as quantitative indicators of controls against possible abuses. The degree of state penetration is directly expressed by the administrative type of the schemes: compulsory systems reflect a stronger intervention than subsidized voluntary programs. The state share of financing is additionally used to indicate the degree of penetration within each type of system. Table 5.2 summarizes the crucial provisions of unemployment insurance laws with respect to these characteristics.

The redistributive capacity of the programs is more difficult to measure. Some information about the degree of redistribution may be gained by cross-classifying the principles underlying the calculation of benefits and contributions as follows:

Contributions

Benefits	Earnings-related (Fixed percentages)	Flat rate	Inversely earnings-related
Earnings-related (Fixed percentages)	nonredistributive	(nonexistent)	(nonexistent)
Flat rate	redistributive	non-redistributive	(nonexistent)
Inversely earnings-related	redistributive	non-redistributive	non-redistributive

Although this classification cannot capture the redistributive effects of the specific laws, it provides a simple guide to their redistributive intentions. Systems providing for earnings-related contributions, but for flat rate or inversely related benefits that lead to lower earnings-replacement ratios for the higher income groups, are classified as redistributive. Systems with contributions and benefits as fixed percentages of earnings imply a preservation of social status and are classified as nonredistributive, together with systems providing both contributions and benefits inversely related to earnings. Finally, programs with flat rate benefits and contributions, which presumably stress equal citizenship rather than redistribution are classified as nonredistributive although an assessment of their implications is more difficult.

Table 5.2
Basic Characteristics of Unemployment Insurance Laws

Dimension	Subdimension	Typical legislative provisions
I. Administr. type	Type of scheme +)	Subsidized voluntary or compulsory insurance
	Administration	By public authorities or by autonomous associations, or by various combinations of both
II. Benefits	Principle of calculation	Flat rate or earnings-related. Under the flat rate principle every person receives the same amount of benefit. Under earnings-related schemes, benefits are either expressed as a constant percentage of earnings (so that every beneficiary gets the same replacement of earnings), or as sliding percentages varying inversely with earnings (so that earnings replacement ratios for persons with higher earnings are lower).
	Level	The level of benefits may be expressed as a ratio of lost earnings. Where percentages are not directly stated in the legal texts, the earnings-replacement ratio attained by a single male beneficiary previously earning the average wage of an industrial earner has been calculated.
	Family supplements	Existent or non-existent; flat rate or earnings-related.
	Duration	The period during which benefits may be continuously drawn is usually limited. A maximum number of weeks is either stated as a general standard, or as a variable limit dependent upon the number of paid contributions.
III. Statutory conditions	Waiting period	A waiting period of several days must usually be served before benefits become payable. The number of days is either explicitly stated, or expressed as a variable period within lower and upper limits.
	Qualification period	The granting of benefits is usually made contingent upon the previous payment of a certain number of contributions or a certain period of membership.
	Qualifying conditions	Benefits are only paid if certain conditions are met, the number and content of which vary. Most laws list some standard prerequisites (capability of and availability for work, registration with labour exchange etc.), but some specify additional conditions such as sufficient efforts to find employment, decent behavior, or personal need.
	Criteria of suitability	The receipt of benefit is usually made contingent upon the claimant's readiness to accept suitable employment, but the definition of what constitutes suitability varies. The laws usually specify a number of criteria that a vacancy must meet (such as level of wages, distance of locality etc.).
	Disqualifications	Benefits are usually denied if unemployment results from specific causes such as labor disputes, dismissal for misconduct, or voluntary leaving. Other disqualifications include the rejection of suitable employment, the refusal to undergo training, or personal misbehavior.
	Disqualification period	In most cases, disqualification for benefit is not absolute, but limited to a certain number of weeks which may vary with the different reasons for disqualification. The duration of the disqualification is either explicity stated, defined within lower and upper limits, or left to administrative discretion.
IV. Financing	Source of funds	The systems may be financed by the insured persons, the employers, the state, or through various combinations of these sources of income. The share borne by each source is either explicitly stated in the legal texts, or may be calculated on the basis of the legislative provisions.
	Principle of calculation	Flat rate, earnings-related with constant percentages, or inversely earnings-related (cf. benefits above).

+) Characteristics in frames are analyzed in more detail.

For the empirical analysis of the four general characteristics of unemployment insurance in our thirteen Western European countries, two sets of laws on subsidized voluntary or compulsory insurance have been selected: the introductory laws and the laws existing in 1975.[12] Tables 5.3 through 5.6 contain the information about the eighteen laws on compul-

Table 5.3
A Comparison of Dimensions of the Introductory Laws
on Compulsory Unemployment Insurance

Country	BENEFITS Level	BENEFITS Duration	BENEFITS Principle of Calculation	CONTRIBUTIONS Principle of Calculation	Source of income Ins.pers. %	Source of income Empl. %	Source of income State %	DISQUALIFICATIONS Waiting Period (days)	Disqual. Period (weeks)	Qualif. Period (weeks)
UK (1911)	(20 %) c)	15	Flat-rate	Flat-rate	37.5	37.5	25	6	1-6 (3)	26
IT (1919)	36 % b)	20	Earnings-related with inverse percentages in wage classes	Earnings-related with inverse rates in wage class.	50	50	(low: Deficit)	7	Compl. (20)	48
AU (1920)	(36 %) a)	12	Earnings-related with const. percentages in wage classes	Earnings-related and risk-related with const. percentages in wage class.	33	33	33	7	4	20
IR (1923)	(25 %) c)	15	Flat-rate	Flat-rate	35	39	26	6	1-6 (3)	20
GE (1927)	35 % c)	26	Earnings-related with inverse percentages in wage classes	Earnings-related with const. percentages in wage classes	50	50	(Low: Deficit)	7	4	26
NO (1938)	28 % b)	15	Earnings-related with slightly inverse percentages in wage classes	Earnings-related with slightly inverse rates in wage classes	40	40	20 comm. (State: Low: Deficit)	6	4 (+)	45
BE (1944)	33 % b)	(52)	Flat-rate	Earnings-related with const. percentage	(25)	(25)	High (50)	4	1-13 (7)	1 day
NE (1949)	70 % a)	21	Earnings-related with fixed percentage	Earnings-related with const. percentage	(38)	(38) Both systems	(24)	3	(at dis-cret.)	13
FR (1967)	56 % b)	52	Earnings-related component with const. percentage + flat-rate component (inverse effect)	Earnings-related with const. percentage	(14)	(58) Both systems	(28)	0	6	12

a) percentage in legal text   b) daily benefit as % of average daily earnings
c) weekly benefit as % of average weekly earnings   d) monthly benefits as % of average monthly earnings
e) benefits taxable

Table 5.4
A Comparison of Dimensions of the Introductory Laws on Voluntary Unemployment Insurance

Country	BENEFITS			CONTRIBUTIONS				DISQUALIFICATIONS		
	Level	Duration (weeks)	Principle of Calculation	Principle of Calculation	Source of Income — Ins. pers. %	Empl. %	State %	Waiting Period (days)	Disqual. Period (weeks)	Qualif. Period (weeks)
FR (1905)		10	Variable, with upper limit for subsidies	not specified			about 20 (varying with type of fund)	not sp.	variable	26
NO (1906)		15	Earnings-related; statut. maximum with const. percentage	not specified	75		25	3	not sp.	26
DE (1907)		12	Earnings-related; statut. maximum with const. percentage	not specified	75		25	6–15 (10)	Complete	52
NE (1916)		10	Earnings-related; statut. maximum with const. percentage	not specified			50 (max., with comm.)	not sp.	not sp.	not sp.
FI (1917)		15	Variable, within statut. limits	not specified			about 60 (with comm.) (varying with type of benefit)	6–15 (10)	Complete	26
BE (1920)		(8)	Earnings-related; statut. maximum with const. percentage	not specified	66.6		33.3	2	4	52
SZ (1924)		15	Earnings-related; statut. maximum with const. percentage	not specified			about 35 (varying with type of fund)	3	Complete	30
SW (1934)		20	Earnings-related; statut. maximum with const. percentage	not specified			about 30 (varying with level of benefit)	6	4 (or more)	52

Table 5.5
A Comparison of Dimensions of the Present Laws on Compulsory Unemployment Insurance (1975)

Country	BENEFITS Level	BENEFITS Duration	BENEFITS Principle of Calculation	CONTRIBUTIONS Principle of Calculation	Source of Income Ins.pers. %	Source of Income Empl. %	Source of Income State %	DISQUALIFICATIONS Waiting Period (days)	DISQUALIFICATIONS Disqual. Period (weeks)	DISQUALIFICATIONS Qualif. Period (weeks)
UK 1911	34 % c)	52	Flat-rate with earnings-related supplement	Earnings-related with const. percentage	(32) (for comprehensive system)	(50)	(18)	3	1–6 (3)	26
IT 1919	5 % b)	26	Flat-rate	Employer's contr. only. Percentage of pay-roll		(100)	(Low: Ad-ministrat. cost)	7	5	104
AU 1920	33 % d)	30	Earnings-related with inverse rates in wage classes	Earnings-related with const. percentage	50	50	(Low: Deficit)	3	4	52
IR 1923	45 % c)	26	Flat-rate	Flat-rate	(33) (for comprehens.insur.system)	(46)	(20)	3	1–6 (3)	26
GE 1927	46 % c)	52	Earnings-related with const. rate (of net earnings)	Earnings-related with const. percentage	50	50	(Low: Deficit)	0	2–4 (3)	26
NO 1938	28 % b)	21	Flat-rate plus earnings-related component	Earnings-related with const. percentage			(Low: Deficit) (~15)	3	4	30
BE 1944	60 % a), e)	(52)	Earnings-related with const. percentage	Earnings-related with const. percentage	21	29	50 + Deficit	1	4–13 (7)	15 rising with age of claimant
NE 1949	80 % a), e)	26	Earnings-related with const. percentage	Earnings-related with const. percentage	(36)	(36) Both systems	(28)	0	?	13
FR 1967	53 % b)	52	Earnings-related with const. percentage + flat-rate component	Earnings-related with const. percentage	(15)	(61) Both systems	(24)	0	?	12

a) percentage in legal text
b) daily benefit as % of average daily earnings
c) weekly benefit as % of average weekly earnings
d) monthly benefits as % of average monthly earnings
e) benefits taxable

Table 5.6
A Comparison of Dimensions of the Present Laws on Voluntary Unemployment Insurance (1975)

Country	BENEFITS			CONTRIBUTIONS					DISQUALIFICATIONS		
	Level	Duration (weeks)	Principle of Calculation	Principle of Calculation	Source of Income Ins. pers. %	Empl. %	State %		Waiting Period (days)	Disqual. Period	Qualif. Period (weeks)
DE 1907	about 60 % c), e)	130	Earnings-related with constant percentages (inverse effect due to low ceiling)	Earnings-related with constant rates (inverse in effect)			High (about 60 %)		0	?	52
FI 1917	about 35 % c)	25			(7)	(43)	(50)		5	?	26
SZ 1924	55 % b)	18	Earnings-related with constant percentages (inverse effect due to low ceiling)				Low (about 5 % in aggregate)		1	up to 10	30
SW 1934	about 60–70 % b), e)	60					(75)		5	4	52

a) percentage in legal text   b) daily benefit as % of average daily earnings
c) weekly benefit as % of average weekly earnings   d) monthly benefits as % of average monthly earnings
e) benefits taxable

sory insurance (nine at its introduction, nine in 1975) and the twelve laws on subsidized voluntary insurance (eight at its introduction, four in 1975) used in this analysis. Since the statutory provisions for subsidized voluntary schemes are frequently vague and leave much to administrative discretion, the following discussion is largely limited to the more specific compulsory programs. First, relationships between the four basic characteristics are examined through a joint analysis of the introductory and present laws; then, some trends and changes between the time of introduction and the present will be studied.

B. Relationships between Program Characteristics

The level and duration of benefits probably are the most important aspects of any insurance scheme besides its scope. Both reflect the generosity of the systems, though one may substitute for the other (i. e., systems providing high earnings-replacement ratios may grant benefits only for short periods and vice versa). Correlation analysis reveals that substitution does not occur in practice. There is a modest positive correlation between these two dimensions for the nine introductory compulsory laws ($r = .34$) as well as for the thirteen laws in 1975 ($r = 0.30$, for all twenty-two laws $r = .36$).

The national variations in the level of benefits are marked, ranging from 20 percent in the United Kingdom to 70 percent in the Netherlands among the introductory laws, and from 5 percent in Italy to 80 percent in the Netherlands among the 1975 laws. Variations in the level of benefits of social insurance schemes have frequently been related to differences in the method of financing.[13] In this context, we can examine two questions: (1) Are redistributive systems more generous, by providing relatively high earnings-replacement ratios? (2) Are high state shares in financing associated with low benefit levels since, as often is argued, they have to compete with other social programs for shares in the budget?

The first question can only be examined with respect to the compulsory systems. As the cross-classification of schemes shows below, eight (enframed) of the eighteen laws are redistributive according to our earlier criteria, but these systems do not provide higher benefits. The average earnings-replacement ratio of the redistributive systems is even lower (35 percent in eight cases) than that of the non-redistributive programs (45 percent in ten cases).[14]

The hypothesis that high levels of state financing depress benefits— usually based on aggregate analyses of social security receipts and expenditures[15]—is also contradicted by a more detailed analysis of the legislative provisions. For the eleven cases (nine compulsory and two voluntary schemes) where enough information for a quantitative analysis is available, there is a low positive correlation $(r = 0.21)$ between state shares and benefit levels. If we simply distinguish between low, medium, and high state shares,

Contributions

Benefits	Earnings-related (Fixed percentages)	Flat rate	Inversely earnings-related
Earnings-related (Fixed percentage)	Introd.: AU, NE 1975: BE, GE, NE	—	—
Flat rate	Introd.: BE 1975: -	Introd: UK, IR	—
Inversely earnings-related	Introd.: FR, GE 1975: AU, FR, NO, UK, IT	Introd.: - 1975: IR	Introd.: IT, NO 1975: -

ten additional laws can be included in the analysis. In clear contradiction to the hypothesis, the average earnings-replacement ratio consistently rises with the level of state financing from 35 percent in the low category (n = 6) to 43 percent in the medium group (n = 11) and 50 percent in the high category (n = 5). This pattern is also confirmed by separate dichotomized analyses of the nine introductory laws on compulsory insurance and the thirteen laws of 1975.

A high level of state financing is frequently interpreted as indicative of redistributive social insurance schemes.[16] If we cross-classify the redistributive capacity of the systems with the level of state shares, however, we find that the nonredistributive programs are overrepresented in the categories of medium and high state shares. A high state participation in financing, therefore, does not seem to imply a redistributive effort and is perhaps simply an attempt to control the financial solvency of the schemes.

Finally, the extent to which systems maintain controls may be analyzed through the length of the waiting and disqualification periods. The average waiting period is four days for the compulsory and about six days for the voluntary systems, with the average disqualification period about five weeks and eight weeks respectively.[17] Surprisingly the association between the lengths of the waiting and disqualification periods is only modest (r = .52 for the subsidized voluntary programs, r = .21 for the compulsory systems, and r = .38 for both combined). To some extent, this may also be the result of the special difficulties in quantifying the provisions of the disqualification period, which are seldom stated precisely in the legislative texts. In analyzing the relationship between control and generosity therefore, we rely on the more precise information regarding the length of the waiting period.

In this case, the obvious expectation that control and generosity are inimical twins is confirmed. An analysis of the length of the waiting period and the level and duration of benefits consistently reveals a negative relationship between these control and generosity elements of the schemes. The correlation between the length of the waiting period and the duration of benefits is r= -.49 for all laws (r = -.68 for the compulsory schemes, and r = -.42 for the subsidized voluntary programs). The association between the length of the waiting period and the level of benefits is even stronger: r = -.70 for all systems (eighteen compulsory programs and the four voluntary schemes of 1975), and r = -.72 for the compulsory schemes alone.

We have seen that schemes with a higher state share of financing tend to be slightly more generous. Does this then imply that state penetration means less control through shorter waiting and disqualification periods? Although we could show that both periods average less in the compulsory schemes than in voluntary systems, there seems to be no relationship between the extent of state financing and the stringency of these controls: correlation coefficients are consistently near zero or negative regardless of whether the compulsory and voluntary schemes are analyzed separately or jointly, at the time of introduction or for 1975.

Summarizing the empirical evidence, we may draw the following conclusions about the interrelations of the basic characteristics of unemployment insurance systems in Western Europe:

1. More generous systems also tend to be more lenient, characterized by weaker controls.
2. Within the dimensions of generosity and control, however, the various provisions (waiting and disqualification period; level and duration of benefits) are only modestly associated, and do not reflect consistent policies.
3. Redistributive systems are not more generous than nonredistributive programs
4. A strong state penetration does not have marked effects on any of the other three characteristics. Largely state financed schemes provide for only slightly higher benefits, but not for more redistribution or for more lenient controls.

If unemployment insurance programs were the product of straightforward policy designs, we could expect them to have a systematic character. As our investigation points out, they are obviously much more complex. The virtual lack of "systemness" in the schemes suggests that they have primarily been the outcome of a series of compromises that blurred any coherent conception that might have existed at the outset. Historical accounts of the development of other insurance systems concur with such an interpretation. Thus, in his study of British health insurance legislation, Gilbert describes the evolution of the first scheme as a "story of lobby influence and pressure groups," and comes to the conclusion that "the scheme that became law in mid-December 1911, bore practically no resemblance to the plan originally conceived."[18] Before we address the question of whether the evolution of the schemes can only be seen as a "random walk,"[19] we must examine some of their basic changes from the time of introduction to 1975.

C. Program Changes and Trends

There clearly is a trend toward more generous levels and durations of benefits. Among the nine introductory laws on compulsory insurance, the average earnings-replacement ratio was 38 percent. This average rose to 43 percent among the compulsory and 46 percent among all systems in 1975, despite the fact that Italy lowered the ratio to the derisory level of 5 percent. The average duration of benefits increased more drastically from 20 weeks among all introductory laws to 44 weeks in 1975. For the compulsory systems, however, the increase (from 25 to 37 weeks) was less pronounced than for the four still existing voluntary programs (from 16 to 58 weeks). At the same time, the controls of the systems have become considerably more lenient. Among the compulsory schemes the average length of the waiting period decreased from 5 to 2.2 days and the length of the disqualification period was almost halved (from 6.4 to 3.6 weeks).[20]

Thus, in general, the programs have become both more generous and more lenient. This does not imply, however, that they have become more similar. In fact, national variations in the level of benefits and the length of the waiting period have even increased, as shown by the coefficients of variability for the introductory and the 1975 laws (level of benefits at introduction: $V = .39$, in 1975: $V = .48$;[21] waiting period at introduction: $V = .44$, in 1975: $V = .97$). Only the duration of benefits among the compulsory systems has become more similar (at introduction: $V = .58$, in 1975: $V = .35$).

No clear trend is discernible with respect to the redistributive character of the programs. Although the number of redistributive systems increased among the compulsory schemes from three at introduction (Belgium, France, Germany) to five in 1975 (Austria, France, Italy, Norway, the United Kingdom), two of the three countries that started with a redistributive orientation later moved away from it (Belgium, Germany). If we examine the benefit and contribution calculations underlying these classifications, a trend appears toward fixing contributions as a constant percentage of earnings. This approach was followed by five systems at introduction, but by eight in 1975.[22] None of the programs abandoned the principle of earnings-related contributions, while the calculation of benefits did change, however, without a clear pattern. Today most programs provide for benefits inversely related to earnings.

An examination of the procedure leading to benefits inversely related to earnings reveals an interesting development. In recent years, several countries have introduced (France) or moved toward (Ireland, Norway, the United Kingdom) a combination of flat rate benefits and earnings-related supplements at constant percentages. Similar changes have recently occurred among the European pension insurance schemes.[23] It could be that these contemporary reforms reflect a general attempt to combine two competing social policy goals: the preservation of status differentials on the one hand and the equality of citizenship on the other.

The most obvious trend with respect to state penetration of the insurance schemes consists in the replacement of subsidized voluntary programs by compulsory ones. However, this development was not accompanied by increased state financing of the schemes. A comparison of the state shares, neglecting the problems of comparability, among the introductory and the 1975 laws shows that the average share has remained the same (29 percent) and even decreased for the compulsory systems (from 25 percent to 21 percent).[24]

More generosity and less control, but not greater similarity; no consistent change in the redistributive character, but a trend towards earnings-related contributions; more compulsory schemes, but no increase in state financing—these are the results with respect to single characteristics of unemployment insurance schemes. But what about their interrelations: has the "systemness" of the programs increased? Given the small number of cases, this question can only be analyzed with respect to quantitative characteristics.

Apparently, the reverse of what we would have expected has happened: the complexity of the schemes increased reducing their systematic quality even further. A comparison of the correlation coefficients between single characteristics of the programs at the time of introduction and in 1975 shows that their relationships have become weaker: there is less correspondence between the "generosity" elements of level and duration of benefits (r = .34 at introduction; r = .19 in 1975). There is an equally weak correspondence between the length of the waiting and disqualification periods (r = .19 and r = .13 for the compulsory systems), the elements of "control." With respect to the relationship between generosity and control, the results are inconclusive. The association between the duration of benefits and the length of the waiting period decreased (from r = -.70 to r = -.50 for the compulsory schemes and from r = -.61 to r = -.36 including the four countries with voluntary programs in 1975). On the other hand, the level of benefits and the length of the waiting period have become more closely related (r = -.68 at the introduction, r = -.87 in 1975).

The persistently low and even decreasing systemness of the programs might be explained by the opposition of powerful vested interests that prevented comprehensive and systematic reforms, allowing only piecemeal modification of single provisions. If this explanation were true, the institutional heritage and the origin and age of the systems should have a marked impact on contemporary program characteristics. These relationships shall now be examined.

D. The Importance of Program Timing

The fact that relative standards of modernity, ideological climates, and theoretical concepts change over time would suggest that the historical point when programs were introduced influenced their formation.[25] Since the systems have become more generous and more lenient over time, it is reasonable to expect that late adopters started with relatively more generosity and less control. This is indeed supported by the correlation coefficients between the year of introduction on the one hand and the level of benefits ($r = .72$ for the nine compulsory systems) and the duration of benefits ($r = .74$ for the compulsory and $r = .54$ for the eight voluntary systems) on the other. To determine control elements, we can analyze only the association between the length of the waiting period and the time of introduction. Among the compulsory schemes, there is a marked tendency for late adopters to institute shorter waiting periods ($r = -.91$), while this relationship is less strong among the voluntary programs ($r = -.20$). Since most of the voluntary systems were established before World War I already, this difference suggests that decisive changes of the ideological evaluation of unemployment occurred only after the war.

The above results demonstrate that the time when systems were established clearly influenced their characteristics. Is this also true for the age of the systems? Is there a tendency for social programs to mature over time and for benefits to increase? Some studies have shown that present benefit levels as a percentage of aggregate social expenditures are closely related to the age of the systems.[26] This has been interpreted as a tendency for expenditures to grow incrementally on the basis of previous budget shares and under the bureaucratic expansionary pressures.[27] In sharp contrast to these studies on aggregate expenditures, our analysis of institutional provisions shows that older systems tend to have lower benefit levels ($r = -.62$ for the compulsory programs, $r = -.42$ for all 1975 schemes). They also tend to provide for more stringent controls through longer waiting periods ($r = .64$ for compulsory schemes, $r = .38$ for all schemes).

This alone does not yet imply that the incrementalist hypothesis should be rejected, since it is still possible that while older systems have exhibited higher growth rates in the level of generosity, this rate has been insufficient to compensate for their start at lower levels. Examining the changes of the schemes between the time of introduction and 1975, we find that the age of the systems is indeed moderately related to the increase in the duration of benefits ($r = .49$ for all, $r = .43$ for the compulsory programs), as well as to the decrease in the length of the waiting period ($r = .51$ for all, $r = .33$ for the compulsory schemes). Changes in the level of benefits do not seem to be associated with system age ($r = -.07$), but this result is heavily affected by the deviant Italian scheme with its sharp decrease in benefit levels. Thus, these findings suggest that while all systems may grow incrementally, the older systems do not catch up on the more recent schemes. The level at which the national systems started clearly affects contemporary provisions, indicating a strong persistence of the original institutions. Apparently, it is easier to establish a new system at high levels of generosity than to bring an existing scheme into parity with modern standards.

The degree to which programs have been historically determined can be directly examined if the contemporary provisions are correlated with those of the introductory laws. To a considerable extent, the present benefit levels of the compulsory schemes still reflect the benefit levels at introduction (r = .62). Similarly, original provisions have a marked impact on the duration of benefits (r = .65),[28] and on the length of the waiting period (r = .42 for all, r = .60 for the compulsory programs). These results lend support to the conclusion drawn by Taira and Kilby that "history" is one of the chief determinants of the modern social insurance schemes.[29] However, the institutional legacy can only explain the persistence of national differences, but not the dynamics of the general evolution of programs. At least two factors should be considered in this respect: first, whether a nation's experience with unemployment has affected its unemployment insurance systems and second, whether different governments have influenced the shape of programs. We shall first analyze under which governments the introductory laws were adopted and then examine the responses of different party governments to varying conditions of unemployment.

III. The Role of Governments in the Development of Unemployment Protection

A. The Parties Behind Program Introduction

If governments significantly shape social policy, an examination of the legislative activity of different ruling parties should reveal some variations in the unemployment protection laws passed under their authority. Three types of party governments are distinguished: Labor, Liberal, and Conservative,[30] with the number and type of the introductory laws adopted by each of them summarized in Table 5.7.

Table 5.7
Introductory Laws on Unemployment Insurance by Type of Government

	Labour	Liberal	Conservative	not classified
All schemes (compulsory and voluntary)	4	6	5	2
Compulsory schemes	3 (AU, NE, NO)	2 (IT, UK)	3 (BE, FR, GE)	1 (IR)
Subsidized voluntary schemes	1 (SW)	4 (DE, FR, NE, SZ)	2 (BE, FI)	1 (NO)
First national schemes (compulsory or voluntary)	2 (AU, SW)	6 (DE, FR, IT, NE, SZ, UK)	3 (BE, FI, GE)	2 (IR, NO)

At first glance, no significant differences appear with respect to the total number of introductory laws. The administrative type of the systems, however, reveals an interesting difference: liberal governments strongly tended to introduce subsidized voluntary programs (four to two compulsory schemes), whereas labor and conservative governments were more inclined to establish compulsory systems (six compulsory versus three subsidized voluntary programs for both types together). If we examine which parties established the first national schemes (regardless of type), the data seem to underscore the results of several historical studies that "the successful first efforts have come from Liberals rather than the Socialist Left."[31] Indeed, in six of the eleven countries included in the analysis, the first schemes were established under liberal governments, while conservatives established three and labor governments only two.

It is important to note, however, that Table 5.7 does not provide enough information about the relative propensity of different party governments to establish unemployment insurance schemes. Instead the capacity of each party to pass an introductory law must be considered, for if a particular party was never in power before the first laws were established, the opportunity to introduce a system did not exist. In Table 5.8 therefore, a "ratio of unemployment insurance realization" is calculated for each type of party government. This ratio is constructed in two steps. First, the number of systems actually introduced is related to the number of potential first schemes, which is derived from the number of countries in which the respective party was in power before the first programs were established. Second, this fraction is then divided by the number of years that each party was in power in order to standardize for the length of time that each party government had to pass laws. This procedure yields an "average annual realization score of unemployment insurance." The time period considered extends from 1905, the year when the first national unemployment insurance scheme was introduced, to the respective years of introduction in any one country. Table 5.8 summarizes the information.

If we look at the unadjusted realization scores, liberal governments show the highest propensity to first establish national schemes (75 percent, as compared to 66.6 percent of labor, and 50 percent of conservative governments). They also have the highest activity score with respect to the introduction of subsidized voluntary insurance schemes (50 percent; 33 percent for labor and conservative governments), but they appear relatively reluctant to introduce compulsory schems (20 percent, as compared to 37.4 percent for conservative, and 33.3 percent for labor governments). Once the unequal chances for legislation are taken into account, however, labor, rather than liberal, governments appear most prone to establish unemployment insurance systems.[32] Although they were only in power in three countries for a total of eight years, labor parties introduced two of the first national unemployment insurance systems (average realization score

Table 5.8
The Propensity of Different Parties to Introduce
Unemployment Insurance

	First national schemes (regardless of type)			Compulsory Schemes			Subs. voluntary schemes		
	Labour	Liberal	Conservative	Labour	Liberal	Conservative	Labour	Liberal	Conservative
Actual no. of laws introduced	2	6	3	3	2	3	1	4	2
Potential no. of laws	3	8	6	9	10	8	3	8	6
Realization score	66.6	75.0	50.0	33.3	20.0	37.4	33.3	50.0	33.3
Years in power	8	34	68	105	118	137	8	34	68
Average realization score	8.33	2.21	0.74	0.32	0.17	0.27	4.17	1.47	0.49

= 8.33 percent). Liberal governments introduced six of the first systems, but they were in office in eight countries for a period of thirty-four years. Their average realization score (2.21 percent), therefore, is much lower than that of labor governments, but still distinctly higher than that of conservative parties (0.74 percent), which were in power in six countries for a total of sixty-eight years.

Even if the administrative types of systems are considered, labor governments still have the highest propensity to enact introductory laws. In compulsory schemes, they have a distinctly higher score than liberal governments (0.32 to 0.27 percent) and a slightly higher propensity than conservatives (0.27 percent). In subsidized voluntary systems, labor governments (0.32 to 0.17 percent) and a slightly higher propensity than conservatives (0.27 percent). In subsidized voluntary systems, labor governments appear more inclined to adoption than liberals (4.17 to 1.97 onstrate why this small number of cases should not lead to too far-reaching conclusions, since the high realization score of labor governments is attributable to the establishment of a single system, the Swedish scheme of 1934.[33]

In order to understand further the propensity of different governments to enact unemployment benefit programs, we must include the later development of the systems in the analysis, and examine which governments passed the "core laws" (cf. Table 5.1) marking the most important steps in program evolution. Due to missing data for the most recent period, only the developments up to 1969 could be analyzed. Of the 63 core laws in this period, 51 could be classified according to the party in power at the time of

Table 5.9
Core Unemployment Benefit Laws by Type of Government

Party	Labour	Liberal	Conservative
No. of core laws passed	16	14	21
No. of years in power	167	128	288
Activity score (laws per year)	9.6	10.9	7.3

passage. The "legislative activity scores" of each party government (number of laws divided by the number of years in power) are shown in Table 5.9.

These data now seem to emphasize the active role of liberal parties in the development of social policy that historical studies have traditionally assigned to them. However, the difference between labor and liberal governments should not be overstated, since an inclusion of the years that could not be classified with respect to the party in power would presumably lower the liberal activity score.[34] Nevertheless, liberal and labor governments have distinctly higher scores than conservative governments. Now the issue is how to interpret these differences between party governments: do they reflect different ideological traditions and levels of responsiveness to working-class demands or are they produced simply by differences in the intensity of social problems, specifically different levels of unemployment? In order to approach this question, we first examine at what levels of unemployment the laws were passed and then try to discover whether the differences between governments persist when the level of unemployment is held constant.

B. Variations in Party Responses to the Challenge of Unemployment

Of the 63 core laws in the period under analysis, 58 could be classified according to the level of unemployment at the time of passage. To assess the impact of unemployment levels on legislative activities, we must again take into account the number of years in which the respective levels prevailed. Table 5.10 shows the result if simply "moderate" and "high" levels of unemployment are distinguished.[35]

The data show that higher unemployment levels seem to induce the

Table 5.10
Core Laws on Unemployment Benefit Programs
by Level of Unemployment

Level of unemployment	Moderate	High
No. of care laws passed	30	28
No. of years with respective level of unemployment	422	257
Legislative activity score (laws per year in resp. category)	7.1	10.9

enactment of unemployment benefit programs. This concurs with Heclo's earlier observation for Britain and Sweden that economic downturns "occasioned far more concentrated attention to social policy alternatives than occurred in more normal times."[36] Does this imply that unemployment protection policy is reflexive rather than preventive, a response to needs rather than to the availability of resources? An attempt to answer this question requires a further differentiation of the levels of unemployment. Table 5.11 subdivides the two general categories of moderate and high unemployment into two more specific levels.[37]

Table 5.11 shows that legislative activity increased with the level of unemployment only up to a certain limit. During high unemployment, the propensity to legislate core laws decreased, but the score is still higher than

Table 5.11
Core Laws on Unemployment Benefit Programs
by Four Levels of Unemployment

Level of unemployment	Low	Medium	High	Very high
No. of core laws passed	16	14	14	14
No. of years with respective level of unemployment	236	186	101	156
Legislative activity score (laws per year in resp. category)	6.8	7.5	13.9	9.0

during low and medium unemployment periods. As financial resources (governmental revenues) are abundant during periods of full employment but decline with higher levels of unemployment, these findings suggest need rather than resource availability as the prime determinant of government action. Only a severe decline of resources during very high unemployment seems to limit the governments' responsiveness.

Different governments may respond differently to similar levels of social distress, however. Table 5.12 analyzes the legislative activity of the three party governments on the same level of unemployment. Forty-seven of the 63 core laws could be classified.

Table 5.12
Core Laws by Type of Government and Level of Unemployment
(activity scores in %)*

| Unemployment | Governments | | | Total |
	Labour	Liberal	Conservative	
Moderate	10.4 (11/106)	10.1 (7/69)	5.2 (8/153)	7.9 (26/328)
High	9.3 (5/54)	13.3 (6/45)	10.4 (10/96)	10.8 (21/195)
Total	10.0 (16/160)	11.4 (13/114)	7.2 (18/249)	9.0 (47/523)

*) in brackets: No. of laws/no. of years

The data once again demonstrate that the propensity to enact unemployment benefit programs is greater in periods of high unemployment, but also reveal an interesting difference in party responses. Liberal and conservative governments have higher activity scores during high unemployment periods. For the conservative governments, the propensity to legislate is actually twice as great during high levels than during moderate levels of unemployment. In marked contrast, labor governments show the highest activity during moderate levels of unemployment. The previous finding of liberal governments as most active is now confirmed only for high levels of unemployment. During moderate unemployment periods, labor governments have a slightly higher propensity to legislate (10.4 percent, compared to 10.1 percent for liberals). Both types of governments are distinctly more active during moderate unemployment than conservative governments (5.2 percent). In marked contrast to their outstanding propensity to legislate in periods of modest unemployment, labor governments show the lowest activity score of all governments when unemployment is high (9.3 percent as compared to 13.3 percent for liberal and 10.4 percent for conservative parties).

How can such differences be explained? In this context, we can only suggest a tentative answer. Perhaps labor parties are generally the most responsive to the political demands of the working class, reflected here by their relatively high activity during moderate levels of unemployment. But compared to liberals and conservatives, labor parties might run a reduced risk of losing the political loyalty of workers and trade unions if alleviating measures under conditions of high unemployment are not enacted, because their identification as the "party of the working class" provides greater leeway to pursue austerity measures when resources are strained.

Of course, our data on core laws do not allow the testing of such hypotheses, since they only capture the time of legislation and some cursory characteristics of the laws but not their specific contents. Even if liberal and conservative governments are more active during high levels of unemployment, it is still possible that they increase the controls rather than the generosity of the schemes. To come closer to understanding the substance of the core laws, Table 5.13 distinguishes between insurance and assistance laws to determine what governments established which type of schemes.

Table 5.13
Core Laws on Unemployment Insurance and Assistance
by Type of Government
(activity scores in %)*

	Labour	Governments Liberal	Conservative	Total
Insurance	9.0 (15/167)	8.6 (11/128)	5.6 (16/288	7.2 (42/583)
Assistance	0.6 (1/167)	2.3 (3/128)	1.7 (5/288)	1.5 (9/583)
Total	9.6 (16/167)	10.9· (14/128)	7.3 (21/288)	8.8 (51/583)

*) in brackets: No. of laws/no. of years

With respect to the insurance systems, the data confirm the results found earlier on the introduction of the systems: labor governments have the highest propensity to adopt unemployment insurance systems (9.0 percent), with the propensity of liberal governments only slightly smaller (8.6 percent). The pattern characterizing assistance schemes is different: here liberal governments have the highest activity score (2.3 percent), surpassing even conservative governments (1.7 percent) which have established the most assistance schemes (5) in absolute terms. Labor governments have by far the lowest propensity to adopt unemployment assistance schemes (0.6 percent). The only assistance system introduced by a labor government was in Germany during the revolutionary turmoil after World War I.

Perhaps this apparent reluctance of labor governments to legislate assistance measures can be seen as a reflection of the resistance to the "hated means-test" that has been attributed to labor parties in various national monographs. Thus, Bruce concludes his description of unemployment scheme development in Britain by noting that "eventually, and under Labour pressure, the means test was swept away by the wartime coalition."[38] Presently, traditional party attitudes toward means-tested programs are being revived in the debate over the selectivity versus the universality of social services. An attempt to grasp such differences in the social policies of various parties would require a much more detailed analysis of specific legislation. But such a task would go far beyond the scope of this chapter.

Summary and Conclusions

What, then, are some of the more general implications of this study and how do the findings relate to the results of conventional analyses of aggregate social spending? First, the general tendency toward growth and extension of the schemes exhibited by rising social expenditure ratios is also revealed in the legislative provisions: over time, benefits have become more generous and controls have been loosened. Aggregate expenditure analyses always beg the question of the underlying causes of growth: an increase in the contingency (rising numbers of unemployed), built-in growth mechanisms (an automatic increase of earnings-related benefits as wages rise), maturing processes (increases of the covered population due to demographic changes or changes of the wage structure), or changing policy efforts modifying legal regulations. Following this study, we feel safe in concluding that rising total outlays are indeed related to more generous legislative provisions signifying greater welfare efforts of those in power.

Second, we have seen that although the systems do grow more generous over time, older programs do not provide for higher benefit ratios or less stringent controls. As the study of legislative provisions reveals, the original regulations of introductory laws tend to persist. Since older systems have started at less generous levels, they also tend to be less generous than younger systems in the present. The frequent finding of aggregate expenditure analyses that older systems have higher outlays can thus not be related to higher welfare efforts of old established bureaucracies. Perhaps it may be explained by such factors as the affluence and the demographic structure of countries with older social security systems. Third, international efforts toward standardization or harmonization could not successfully counteract the historical determination of national schemes. The legislative provisions of the Western European unemployment insurance systems have not become more alike over time. The only converging trend consists in the replacement of voluntary programs by compulsory schemes.

Since the present schemes largely reflect initial regulations, the question of who established the institutional core of the systems becomes of particular relevance. Our attempt to answer this question led to the most marked deviations from the conclusions of traditional social policy analyses. Although the programs proved too complex to be understood as systems that reflect coherent policy approaches, the notion explicitly or implicitly contained in many quantitative policy studies, that the role of parties and governments is secondary or even negligible vis-à-vis the imperatives of economic growth or various "system needs,"[39] did not receive any convincing support by an analysis of institutional developments. Economic circumstances do not inevitably prescribe governmental action. Some parties may be more responsive to need than others, and the programs they establish may vary. Apparently governments are more than the executing arm of an historical logic embedded in the process of industrialization, economic growth, and business cycles. Within the boundaries set by changing socioeconomic contexts they dispose of a margin for purposive action that allows them actively to shape social reality. To determine the extent of this margin more exactly, we need more systematic records of the legislative activity of different parties in power. The present chapter can only serve as the first step in such a larger research effort.

Notes

1. Kaim-Caudle 1973, p. 204.
2. Rimlinger 1971.
3. Bogs 1956.
4. Gilbert 1973, pp. 265 ff.
5. Kumpmann 1923, p. 814.
6. Frankel and Dawson 1911, pp. 375-380.
7. Heclo 1974, pp. 86-87.
8. Hay 1975, p. 34.
9. International Labour Office 1933a.
10. Huss 1932.
11. Kaim-Caudle 1973, p. 202.
12. Information on the introductory laws was compiled from the International Labour Office Legislative Series; the data on the 1975 laws were collected from U. S. Department of Health, Education, and Welfare 1975.
13. Aaron 1967; Kincaid 1973.
14. If the debatable classification of the Italian law of 1975 which has extremely low benefits is left out, the average replacement ratio still is only 39 percent.
15. Aaron 1967 and 1968.
16. Paukert 1968, pp. 121 ff.
17. Comparisons between the two types of systems are disturbed by the effects of time. Since voluntary programs came not only earlier, but were also replaced by compulsory schemes in all but four cases, "modern" provisions are underrepresented among voluntary programs.
18. Gilbert 1973, p. 290.

19. This term is from Heclo who sees public policy as a "process of social learning" that "finds its sources not only in power but also in uncertainty"; see Heclo 1974, pp. 305 and 308.
20. The information on the disqualification period excludes the Dutch system, for which no quantifiable data on the length of the period could be obtained.
21. Even if the outlier Italy were disregarded, the 1975 coefficient of variability (V = .34) would still be about the same as that for the introductory laws.
22. This includes the debatable classification of the Italian scheme that is exclusively financed by employers' contributions.
23. See Chapter 2 by Flora and Alber.
24. For countries with unified national insurance schemes the proportion of state funding for the entire system has been used. Systems with "low" state shares were given the value 10 percent.
25. Marshall 1964; Rimlinger 1971; and Blume 1976. Marshall relates the development of social security to the spirit of social solidarity during or immediately after wars; Rimlinger distinguishes an era of "the liberal break"; Blume describes the evolution of social policy as a series of competing concepts or "paradigms" comparable to the development of science.
26. Aaron 1967 and 1968; Pryor 1968.
27. Wilensky 1975, pp. 10-11.
28. If the voluntary systems are included in the analysis, this relationship vanished (r = .07). But this is largely due to the extreme extension of the indemnification period in Denmark. If the Danish case is excluded, the correlation for all systems is r = .56.
29. Taira and Kilby 1969, pp. 150 and 153.
30. Governments were classified following von Beyme 1970; Spuler 1964; de Swaan 1973. In general, coalition cabinets were classified according to the party identification of the prime minister, with additional consideration of the strongest party represented in the cabinet. Where several parties of similar strength formed the coalition or where the prime minister belonged to a minority party, the cabinets were not classified. It is obvious that the crude classification cannot capture important national variations in the political character of parties that are equally labelled. Because of the small number of cases, further differentiation of the types of governments did not seem advisable.
31. Heclo 1974, p. 296.
32. Thirty percent of all years in the considered period could not be classified with respect to the party in power. If these missing years were included, the realization scores of liberal and conservative governments would presumably be still lower, because in most cases the unclassified governments were clearly not labor, but doubtful with respect to their assessment as liberal or conservative.
33. The small number of cases also prohibits a further analysis of the political determinants of the specific provisions of the laws.
34. Seventy-five percent of all years could be classified according to the party in power. For about half of the remaining 25 percent, the type of government was known, but did not fit into one of the three categories (e. g., Fascists). For the other half, the party composition of the government could either not be obtained or remained doubtful with respect to the proper classification. Again, most of the doubtful cases were either liberal or conservative but clearly not labor. Ireland was excluded from the analysis due to the peculiarities of its party system.

35. The data on unemployment were mostly taken from Mitchell 1975. For comparative purposes the data are usually expressed as a percentage of the dependent labor force and a ratio of 3 percent is frequently referred to as the upper limit of "full employment." Ten percent, on the other hand, may be considered a threshold indicating very high unemployment that was only surpassed during severe economic crises. Given these two limits, the data were grouped into four categories using the following standard classification: 0-3.3 percent (low), 3.4-6.6 percent (medium), 6.7-9.9 percent (high), 10 percent and more (very high). Combination of the two first and last categories led to the classification of *moderate* and *high* unemployment. Since not all data are given as percentages of the labor force, the standard classification could not always be applied. A closer description of the classification procedures together with a list of sources consulted in addition to Mitchell may be found in Alber 1978.
36. Heclo 1974, p. 286.
37. For a description of the classification procedure see note 35.
38. Bruce 1968, p. 274.
39. Cutright 1965.

References

Aaron, Henry J. 1967. "Social Security: International Comparison." In *Studies in the Economics of Income Maintenance*, ed. Otto Eckstein, pp. 13-48. Washington, D. C.: The Brookings Institution.
Aaron, Henry J. 1968. "International Comparisons." In *Social Security Perspectives for Reform*, ed. Joseph A. Pechman, Henry J. Aaron, Michael K. Taussig, pp. 294-304. Washington, D. C.: The Brookings Institution.
Alber, Jens. 1978. "On the Development of Unemployment Insurance in Western Europe." HIWED Report No. 7. Cologne: mimeographed.
Beyme, Klaus von. 1970. *Die parlamentarischen Regierungssysteme in Europa*. Munich: Piper.
Blume, Stuart S. 1976. "Policy as Theory." Paper presented at a seminar of the European Centre for Social Welfare Training and Research on "Use of Social Research." Strobl: mimeographed.
Bogs, Walter. 1956. "Arbeitslosenfürsorge und Arbeitslosenversicherung." In *Handwörterbuch der Sozialwissenschaften*, vol. 1, pp. 312-321. Stuttgart: Vandenhoeck and Ruprecht.
Bonizzi, Cesare. 1944. *Die Sozialversicherung Italiens*. Zürich: Kommerzdruck.
Bruce, Maurice. 1968. *The Coming of the Welfare State*. London: Batsford.
Bundesministerium für Arbeit und Sozialordnung. 1974. *Übersicht über die soziale Sicherung*. Bonn: Bundesministerium für Arbeit und Sozialordnung.
Bundesministerium für soziale Verwaltung. 1968. *Fünfzig Jahre Bundesministerium für soziale Verwaltung 1918-1968. Festschrift*. Vienna: Bundesministerium für soziale Verwaltung.
Burton Skardal, Dorothy. 1955. *Social Insurance in Norway*. Oslo: The Norwegian Joint Committee on International Social Policy.
Calman, John, ed. 1967. *Western Europe. A Handbook*. London: Anthony Blond.
Creutz, H. 1966. "Social Security in Austria." *Bulletin of the International Social Security Association* 19: 3-60.
Cutright, Phillips. 1966. "Political Structure, Economic Development, and National Security Programs." *American Journal of Sociology* 70: 537-550.

Dupeyroux, Jean-Jacques. 1966. *Entwicklung und Tendenzen der sozialen Sicherheit in den Mitgliedstaaten der Europäischen Gemeinschaften und in Großbritannien.* Luxemburg: Europäische Gemeinschaft für Kohle und Stahl. Hohe Behörde.

Dupeyroux, Jean-Jacques. 1971. *Sécurité sociale.* Paris: Dalloz.

Eidgenössisches Volkswirtschaftsdepartement. 1925. *Volkswirtschaft, Arbeitsrecht und Sozialversicherung der Schweiz.* Erster darstellender Teil. Einsiedeln: Benzinger.

Europäische Wirtschaftsgemeinschaft. 1962. Studien, Reihe Sozialpolitik Nr. 4, Vergleich der Leistungen der sozialen Sicherheit in den Ländern der EWG. Brussels.

Farley, Desmond. 1964. *Social Insurance and Social Assistance in Ireland.* Dublin: Institute of Public Administration.

Frankel, Lee K. and Dawson, Miles M. 1911. *Workingmen's Insurance in Europe.* New York: Charities Publication Committee.

Gilbert, Bentley B. 1973. *The Evolution of National Insurance in Great Britain.* London: Michael Joseph.

Harris, José. 1972. *Unemployment and Politics.* Oxford: At the Clarendon Press.

Hay, J. R. 1975. *The Origins of the Liberal Welfare Reforms 1906-1914.* London: Macmillan.

Heclo, Hugh. 1974. *Modern Social Politics in Britain and Sweden.* New Haven, Conn.: Yale University Press.

Heclo, Hugh. 1975. "Income Maintenance: Patterns and Priorities." In *Comparative Public Policy. The Politics of Social Choice in Europe and America,* ed. Arnold J. Heidenheimer, Hugh Heclo, Carolyn Teich Adams, pp. 187-226. New York: St. Martins Press.

Huss, E. G. 1932. "The Organisation of Public Works and other Measures for the Relief of Unemployment in Sweden." *International Labour Review.* 26: 26-50.

International Labour Office. 1920-1975. Legislative Series. Geneva: International Labour Office.

International Labour Office. 1922. "Unemployment Insurance. An International Survey." *International Labour Review* 6: 365-374.

International Labour Office. 1925. "Unemployment Insurance. Study of Comparative Legislation." Studies and Reports, Series C (Employment and Unemployment), No. 10. Geneva: International Labour Office.

International Labour Office. 1931. "Unemployment Insurance: Tabular Analysis of the Legislation in Force." *International Labour Review* 22: 48-66.

International Labour Office. 1933a. "Employment Exchanges. An International Survey of Placing Activities." Studies and Reports, Series C (Employment and Unemployment), No. 18. Geneva: International Labour Office.

International Labour Office. 1933b. "International Survey of Social Services." Studies and Reports, Series M (Social Insurance), No. 11. Geneva: International Labour Office.

International Labour Office. 1936. "International Survey of Social Services, 1933." Studies and Reports Series M (Social Insurance), No. 13, 2 vols. Geneva: International Labour Office.

International Labour Office. 1955. "Unemployment Insurance Schemes." Studies and Reports, New Series, No. 42. Geneva: International Labour Office.

International Labour Office. 1976. *Social Security for the Unemployed.* Geneva: International Labour Office.

Internationales Arbeitsamt. 1902-1919. *Bulletin des Internationalen Arbeitsamtes.* Jena: Gustav Fischer.

Internationale Vereinigung für soziale Sicherheit. 1959a. *Entwicklung und Tendenzen der sozialen Sicherheit: Vol. 1, Belgien.* Genf: Internationale Vereinigung für soziale Sicherheit.
Internationale Vereinigung für soziale Sicherheit. 1959b. *Entwicklung und Tendenzen der sozialen Sicherheit: Vol. 2, Bundesrepublik Deutschland.* Genf: Internationale Vereinigung für soziale Sicherheit.
Internationale Vereinigung für soziale Sicherheit. 1959c. *Entwicklung und Tendenzen der sozialen Sicherheit: Vol. 3, Frankreich.* Genf: Internationale Vereinigung für soziale Sicherheit.
Internationale Vereinigung für soziale Sicherheit. 1959d. *Entwicklung und Tendenzen der sozialen Sicherheit: Vol. 4, Italien.* Genf: Internationale Vereinigung für soziale Sicherheit.
Internationale Vereinigung für soziale Sicherheit. 1959e. *Entwicklung und Tendenzen der sozialen Sicherheit: Vol. 6, Niederlande.* Genf: Internationale Vereinigung für soziale Sicherheit.
Jackman, Robert W. 1974. "Political Democracy and Social Equality: A Comparative Analysis." *American Sociological Review* 39: 29-45.
Jackman, Robert W. 1975. *Politics and Social Equality: A Comparative Analysis.* New York: John Wiley & Sons.
Jensen, Orla. 1961. *Social Welfare in Denmark.* Copenhagen: Det Berlingske Bogtrykkeri.
Kaim-Caudle, P.R. 1968. *Social Policy in the Irish Republic.* London: Routledge & Kegan.
Kaim-Caudle, P .R. 1973. *Comparative Social Policy and Social Security. A Ten Country Study.* London: Martin Robertson.
Kelders, Freddy. 1955. *L'organisation administrative de la sécurité sociale en Belgique.* Liège: Faculté de Droit de Liège.
Kincaid, J. C. 1973. *Poverty and Equality in Britain.* Harmondsworth: Pelican.
Klein, Otto. 1954. "Die Sozialversicherungen Deutschlands, Frankreichs und Großbritanniens. Ein zwischenstaatlicher Vergleich." Dissertation. University of Mannheim.
Kumpmann, K. 1923. "Arbeitslosigkeit und Arbeitslosenversicherung." In *Handwörterbuch der Staatswissenschaften, 4th ed.* Vol. 1, pp. 791-824. Jena: Gustav Fischer.
Laati, Iisakki. 1940. *Soziale Gesetzgebung und Wirksamkeit in Finnland.* Helsinki: Tilgmann.
Mackie, Thomas T. and Rose, Richard. 1974. *The International Almanac of Electoral History.* London: Macmillan.
Marshall, T. H. 1964. *Class, Citizenship and Social Development.* New York: Doubleday.
Metropolitan Life Insurance Company. 1932. *Social Insurance Legislation.* Monograph Four. New York: Metropolitan Life Insurance Company.
Ministry of Social Affairs and Health. 1969. *Social Services in Finland: Vol 3, Social Insurance.* Helsinki: Government Printing Centre.
Mitchell, B. R. 1975. *European Historical Statistics 1750-1970.* London: Macmillan.
Mittelstädt, Axel. 1975. "Unemployment Benefits and Related Payments in Seven Major Countries." In OECD *Economic Survey: Occasional Papers,* pp. 3-22. Paris: Organization for Economic and Cultural Development.
National Insurance Institution. 1966. *The Norwegian System of Social Insurance. A Survey.* Oslo: The National Insurance Institution.
Paukert, Felix. 1968. "Social Security and Income Redistribution: Comparative Experience." In *The Role of Social Security in Economic Development,* ed.

Everett M. Kassalow, pp. 101-127. Washington, D. C.: U. S. Department of Health, Education and Welfare.

Peters, Guy. 1972. "Economic and Political Effects on the Development of Social Expenditures in France, Sweden, and the United Kingdom." *Midwest Journal of Political Science* 16: 225-238.

Peters, Horst. 1959. *Die Geschichte der Sozialversicherung.* Bad Godesberg: Asgard.

Pryor, Frederick L. 1968. *Public Expenditures in Communist and Capitalist Nations.* Homewood: Irwin.

Raynes, Harold E. 1957. *Social Security in Britain. A History.* London: Pitman.

Rimlinger, Gaston V. 1971. *Welfare Policy and Industrialization in Europe, America and Russia.* New York: John Wiley & Sons.

Saxer, Arnold. 1970. *Die soziale Sicherheit in der Schweiz.* Bern: Haupt.

Spitaels, G., Klaric, D., Lambert, S., and Lefevere, G. 1971. *Le salaire indirect et la couverture des besoins sociaux. Vol. III: La comparaison internationale.* Brussels: L'Institut de Sociologie de l'Université Libre de Bruxelles.

Spuler, Berthold. 1962-1972. *Regenten und Regierungen der Welt,* vols. 3-5. Würzburg: Ploetz.

Swaan, Abram de. 1973. *Coalition Theories and Cabinet Formation.* Amsterdam: Elsevier.

Taira, Koji and Kilby, Peter. 1969. "Differences in Social Security Development in Selected Countries." *International Social Security Review* 2: 139-153.

Tillyard, Frank and Ball, F. N. 1949. *Unemployment Insurance in Great Britain 1911-1948.* Leigh-on-Sea: Thames Bank.

Uhr, Carl G. 1966. "Sweden's Social Security System." Social Security Administration, Research Report No. 14. Washington, D. C.: U. S. Department of Health, Education, and Welfare.

U. S. Commissioner of Labor. 1911. *Twenty-Fourth Annual Report of the Commissioner of Labor 1909: Workmen's Insurance and Compensation Systems in Europe.* Washington, D. C.: U. S. Government Printing Office.

U. S. Department of Health, Education and Welfare. 1975. *Social Security Programs Throughout the World, 1975.* Washington, D. C.: U. S. Government Printing Office.

Wechselmann, Sigurd. 1936. *The Danish National Insurance Act.* Copenhagen: Schultz.

Wilensky, Harold L. 1975. *The Welfare State and Equality.* Berkeley: University of California Press.

Zöllner, Detlev. 1963. *Öffentliche Sozialleistungen und wirtschaftliche Entwicklung.* Berlin: Duncker & Humblot.

Part Four

Economic Equality: The Distribution of Incomes

Chapter 6

The Historical Development of Income Inequality in Western Europe and the United States

Franz Kraus

I. Problems in Examining Income Inequality

A. Defining Income Distribution

Today material welfare is much less dependent on market incomes or rewards for labor and property in the production process than in earlier times. Direct and indirect taxes, transfer payments, and the provision of public services—all consequences of the growth of the welfare state—have clearly weakened the importance of wages and assets in determining economic status. To analyze income inequality with respect to the development of the welfare state, we must distinguish between a *producer inequality* that simply refers to market incomes, and a *consumer inequality* that reflects the final distribution of income after taxes, transfer payments and the consumption of public goods have been taken into account.

To assess income inequality from a comparative and historical perspective, we must ask how these two fundamental aspects of economic inequality differ from each other, how they vary between countries, and how they have changed over time. Furthermore, we want to examine the relationships between producer inequality and consumer inequality: who finances, and to what extent, public expenditures, and who benefits, and to what extent, from transfer payments and public goods?

187

Because of the shortcomings of available sources, particularly for previous periods, quantitative assessment of the extent men benefit from
public goods is most difficult.[1] Similarly it is difficult to estimate the impact
of public expenditures on income inequality through changes in factor
demand and supply, such as the extension of public education or the civil
service. However, if we leave aside these more qualitative questions, we can
still learn much from analyzing the successive steps by which producer
inequality is transformed into consumer inequality. Figure 6.1[2] provides a
simplified overview[3] of the different stages comprising the circular flow of
money (primary, secondary, tertiary, and final distribution), the major
types of exchanges and transactions (market exchanges and government
transfers), and the main economic agents involved (private households,
public institutions, private and public enterprises).

Income inequality broadly refers to inequality among private households. At the stage of production, this inequality is the result of differing
access to productive factors, differing amounts of available factors offered
in the market for productive services, and unequal distribution of factor
remuneration (*primary distribution*). These rewards are supplemented by
public transfer payments and reduced by direct taxes and contributions to
social security schemes. The inequality of market incomes is thereby transformed into an inequality of disposable incomes (*secondary distribution*).
At the stage of consumption, the inequality of disposable incomes is further
altered by the effects of indirect taxation, fees, and subsidized market
prices shown in Figure 6.1 (*tertiary distribution*). In addition to the differential access to private goods and resources, differential access to public
goods or free meritorious goods (*final distribution*) must be taken into
account. This final distribution represents the most comprehensive meaning of consumer inequality.

Redistribution refers to the process by which the primary distribution,
measuring the producer inequality, is transformed gradually into the consumer inequality of the final distribution. In correspondence with the four
kinds of income distributions, three types of redistributions can be distinguished. As commonly understood *primary redistribution* refers to
changes in income distribution by direct taxes and transfer payments: both
a vertical redistribution between income groups and a horizontal redistribution between equal income groups to compensate for different characteristics such as number of children or civil status. Next, total *monetary
redistribution* embraces the effects of indirect taxes. This level must be
distinguished from primary redistribution not only for statistical reasons,
but because direct and indirect taxation have historically represented
different methods and approaches to income redistribution. Because the
provision of public goods may represent to some extent an alternative to
transfer payments (see Chapter 9), it must be included at the stage of *total*

Figure 6.1
Production, Consumption and Income Inequality

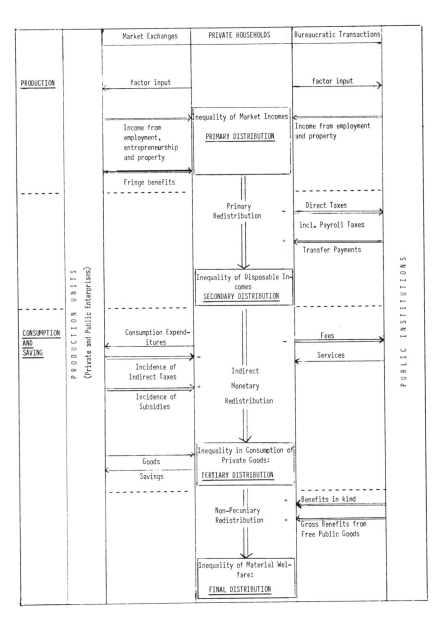

redistribution that reflects the redistributive impact of all transactions, including differential access to these public goods.

For an empirical assessment of the tertiary and final distribution, one has to know the consumption behaviour of income groups. Such information is only provided by sample surveys and therefore is limited to the period after World War II. Prior to this time, we can only approximate the importance and direction of total monetary redistribution by evaluating the total amount and the structure of indirect taxes and public goods.[4] Such indirect evaluations may justify some tentative conclusions about redistributive efforts and effects, but a more direct and quantitative study of long-term changes in economic inequality must be restricted to primary distribution—and to some aspects of secondary distribution.

B. Sources on Income Inequality

Studies on the total distribution of income by size have two main sources: tax statistics and sample surveys. Since the surveys are generally[5] of more recent origin, any long-term analysis must rely primarily on tax statistics.[6] The modern European income tax systems developed historically from two types: scheduled taxes and lump-sum taxes.[7] The *scheduled income tax* is a set of taxes on different types of income that are not added to form a person's total income. Very often only certain types of incomes have been taxed (partial scheduled income tax). Thus, at best the number of income units and their incomes for each separate schedule are known. Pure scheduled taxes no longer exist; they have either been supplemented by a personal income tax (*supplementary personal income tax*) or replaced by a general personal income tax.[8] The *lump-sum income tax*, on the other hand, levies taxes on an individual's income, so that data on both the number of income units and the amount of total taxable income are recorded. Formerly, this tax was very often confined to earned income only (*partial income tax*). Today, partial personal income taxes have been transformed into the general (or comprehensive) personal income tax that covers earned as well as unearned income.

Table 6.1 shows in which years various income tax systems were introduced in Western Europe and the United States. The systems are ranked according to their appropriateness to the study of income distribution. Only supplementary income taxes and general personal income taxes (last two columns) cover the incomes from all sources and thus provide sufficient information on the size distribution of income. The years in which they were introduced mark a watershed in the historical study of income inequality. For earlier periods, data are available for only certain types of income.

Income tax statistics usually give the following figures for the various nominal income classes: the number of income units, the taxable income, and the assessed taxes (or class-specific tax rates). The longest time series on income distribution available is confined to these data. Much less

Table 6.1
The Introduction of Income Tax Systems[9]

Country	SCHEDULE TAXES		LUMP-SUM TAXES		
	Partial Schedule Tax	Schedule Tax	Partial Personal	Supplementary Personal Income Tax	General Personal Income Tax
AUSTRIA	1849-1896				1896/98 -
BELGIUM		1919/20-1962		1919/20-1962	1963 -
DENMARK					1810-1844 1870-1872 1903 -
FINLAND					1865-1881
FRANCE	1872-1917	1918-1959		1917-1959	1960 -
GERMANY					1920 -
PRUSSIA			1812-1814 1851-1872		1873-1919
SAXONY					1877-1919
IRELAND		1923/24 -		1923/24 -	
ITALY	(1864) 1877-1923			1918-1923	1923 -
NETHERLANDS			1892/93-1914		1914-1918 1918
NORWAY					1892 -
SWEDEN			1861-1928		1810-1811 1903
SWITZERLAND			1916-1932		1933-[10)
UNITED KINGDOM		1803-1816 1842-1918		1910-1918 1952 -	1799-1802 1918 -
UNITED STATES					1863-1872 1894-1895 1913

information can be found in tax statistics on the distribution of income with respect to profession, region, economic sector, age and sex, and there is no consistency or uniformity in data sources between periods or countries.

Data on income distribution derived from tax statistics cannot be compared and analyzed until we know whether the *income units* and *income* have been appropriately defined and how many income recipients and what income shares covered in the tax statistics.

In tax statistics *income units* are defined as individuals, households, or income cases.[11] The older, broad concept of the household[12] is no longer used, but great differences in the treatment of the earnings of married couples still exist.

It cannot be determined exactly how much they affect the comparability of the data on income distribution over time and between countries.[13] The varying coverage of income units, however, poses still greater problems. The figures in Table 6.2[14] show that before World War II a high coverage of income units was the exception rather than the rule. For the interwar period, income distribution can be compared cross-nationally for the upper 50% of income recipients at most, while prior to World War I only the upper 10% (or even less) can be compared.

Data on *incomes* suffer from a number of shortcomings. As defined by tax laws, (gross) income includes not just market income but often some transfer payments as well.[15] Some kinds of market income are virtually not taken into account: undistributed profits usually are excluded, while capital gains and fringe benefits are only partially treated as incomes.[16] Moreover, at earlier times, not gross income but net taxable income is provided in tax statistics. In fact, the main problem of comparability arises at least until World War II, from variations in tax exemptions and credits both over time and across countries. Differences in tax exemption levels, deductible items, allowances and even tax evasion lead to varying coverage of incomes. In general, the coverage of true market income can be estimated only for more recent periods.[17] In 1968, for instance, the ratio of incomes in tax statistics to total private incomes in national account statistics varied between 51% for Germany and 90% for the Netherlands.[18]

Three periods can be distinguished with respect to the data basis for income distribution studies:

- Prior to World War I tax statistics on income distribution are available for the following countries only: Austria, several German Länder (above all Prussia and Saxony), Denmark, Finland, Norway, and Sweden. Coverage tends to be low. The data refer to the pretax income distribution,[19] but in some countries the posttax distribution can also be estimated.

- In the interwar period income tax results were published far less frequently, but statistics are now also available for Belgium, France, Luxembourg, the

Table 6.2
Coverage of Tax Statistics: Tax Units as Percentage
of Economically Active Population

Year	AU	BE	DE	FI	FR	GE	IR	NE	NO	SW	SZ	UK
1870			8	$5^{a)}$								
1875				$7^{a)}$								
1880				28								
1885										9		
1890												
1895	$7^{a)}$					$22^{b)}$			8	13		
1900	$9^{a)}$					$27^{b)}$		14	11	17		
1905	$11^{a)}$		94			$32^{b)}$		16	12	33		
1910	$14^{a)}$		96			$43^{b)}$		20	15	41		
1915	$18^{a)}$					82		27	31			
1920				40	2	83		50	47	80		40
1925				40	7	94		56	37			23
1930	68			40	8	97		60	28	91	15	24
1935	53		94	19	8	98		40	27		15	37
1940			94	36	10	97	0.3	43	40		21	45
1945			98		13		0.4	95	57	125	19	83
1950	65	22	101	81	16	53	0.5	101	73	120	45	89
1955	65	33	101	108	15	75	0.9	106	98	123	55	84
1960	74	42	106	108	26	84	0.8	115	102	125	41	84
1965	78	80	104	120	39	82	0.7	128	102	122	40	83
1970	81	79	112	130	49	80	0.6	135	112	126	52	83

a) Population represented by tax returns as % of total population.

b) Refers to Prussia only.

Netherlands, the United Kingdom, and the United States. The coverage of incomes slightly increased, and the data refer often to pretax as well as posttax incomes.

After World War II data on the size distribution of incomes are available for all West European countries.[20] In general the coverage of income recipients in tax statistics is high and the problems of comparability relatively smaller. The data usually refer to pretax and posttax incomes.

C. Improvement of Comparability

For all these reasons, then, the construction of long-term time series raises numerous problems. With respect to historical sources, conceptual incomparabilities are most difficult to overcome. Virtually no adjustment can be made for differing definitions of the income unit and the separation of transfer payments from market incomes. But comparability seems less impaired by conceptual discrepancies than by variations in the coverage of income units. Two quite distinct procedures are available that make a rough comparison at least feasible: adjustment for incomplete coverage of income units only or adjustment for unreported recipients *and* their presumed incomes. The first procedure requires definition and subsequent references to a constant fraction of the total (estimated) number of income units.[21] Historical description then is limited to the distribution of incomes within a tentatively small group only.[22] The second procedure additionally requires an estimate of those incomes not reported in tax statistics, a calculation that raises significant but not insurmountable conceptual and empirical problems.[23] But analytical restrictions are markedly reduced when inequality is expressed not as inequality among a group of top income recipients, but as the comparable group's share of total private income.[24] Hence, the latter procedure should be adopted.

II. The Development of Income Inequality in Western Europe and the United States

Quantitative descriptions of income inequality are by no means only recent. In the late seventeenth century Gregory King made the first attempt to estimate the size and average income of major social classes in England. This famous study was, however, rather an aberration in the history of income distribution analysis, since official statistics themselves had not been sufficiently developed. It was only in the last third of the nineteenth century that so-called social statisticians started to produce numerous studies of income distribution, and that the first decisive steps to improve the historical depth (Schmoller),[25] comparative perspective (Kiaer),[26] and theoretical analysis (Pareto)[27] of income distribution were taken. This progress ceased with World War I, and the achievements of the interwar period cannot be compared to the earlier advances.

After World War II students viewed the question of whether and to what extent income inequality had changed over time with new and strengthened interest. More appropriate attempts were then made to improve longitudinal and cross-national comparability of income distribution data. In 1957 a research group of the United Nations' Economic Commission for Europe[28] provided detailed and well-documented data on changes in income inequality for several Western countries since the eve of World War II. Simon Kuznets[29] incorporated these data into his famous collection on long-term changes in income inequality, adding data for other countries and earlier years and using various national studies with differing concepts and degrees of reliability. In 1967 the ECE/UN[30] supplied additional data, comparing the early 1950s with the early 1960s. The most important updated collections and studies published in the 1970s are Roberti's,[31] which contain a roughly comparable set of data for most West European countries and the United States for the two decades after the war; Sawyer's 1976 study of income inequality in countries of the Organization for Economic Cooperation and Development (OECD);[32] and Stark's,[33] which provides a very careful and comprehensive comparison of the level and structure of income inequality for nine countries. These collections, along with several national studies, can be used to examine the change of pretax income inequality over time.

The following discussion focuses on a cross-national comparison of trends and patterns of development.[34] Three broad income strata are distinguished: a top income stratum (top 5%, top 10%), a middle income stratum (deciles 9-7), and a lower income stratum (deciles 6-1).

The selection of a top income stratum of 10% or 5% is clear,[35] but why distinguish between the income deciles 1-6 and 7-9? In almost all countries examined, the income share of the sixth decile is smaller than 10% while that of the seventh decile is greater, at least since World War II.[36] The two income strata are thus divided by a hypothetical equality line, defined by this proportionate income share of 10%. This division facilitates an interpretation of changes in the income shares of the bottom 60% and the other two groups.[37]

Figure 6.2 shows the long-term trends since the late nineteenth century of the upper 5% (10%) in total private income for four countries (Denmark, Germany, the United Kingdom, and the United States). Figures 6.3 and 6.4 present a more detailed picture of the trends of all three income strata: Figure 6.3 covers the period from the turn of the century up to World War II for Denmark, Germany, and the United States, while Figure 6.4 shows the shares for nine countries (Denmark, Finland, Germany, the Netherlands, Norway, Sweden, Switzerland, the United Kingdom, and the United States), starting around the beginning of World War II. Data on the overall level of inequality[38] (Gini-Indices)[39] for these countries and periods are also tabulated in the appendix.

The data used here are only rough estimates, especially with respect to the period before World War II. They are not strictly comparable, even for more recent periods. To give a limited but rough idea of the crudeness of the data, alternative (deviating) series are shown wherever available. It turns out that differences among these estimates are generally small with respect to trends,[40] although differences in levels are more significant.[41] As a result, we can reach only tentative interpretations rather than conclusions about cross-country comparisions. These are based only on the very marked changes which occur.

Figure 6.2
Long-Term Trends: Income Shares of Top Income Recipients

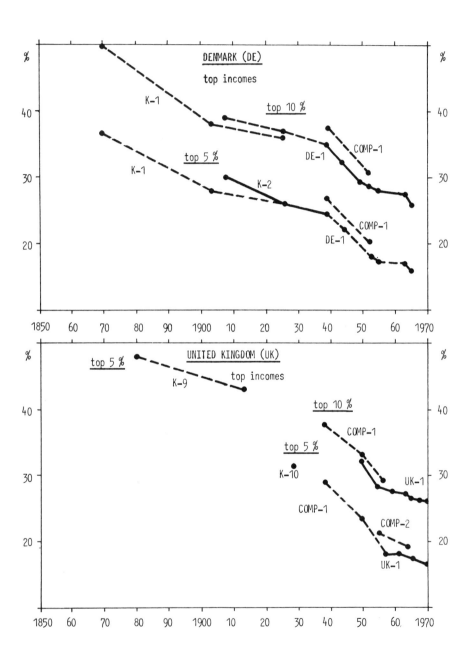

**Figure 6.2
(Continued)**

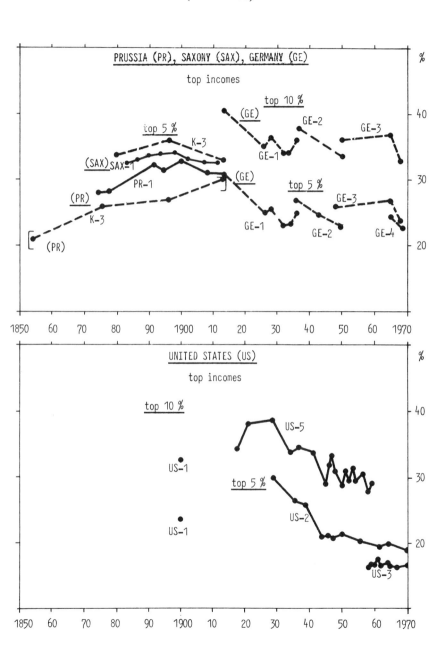

Figure 6.3
Patterns of Change in Inequality, 1900-1940

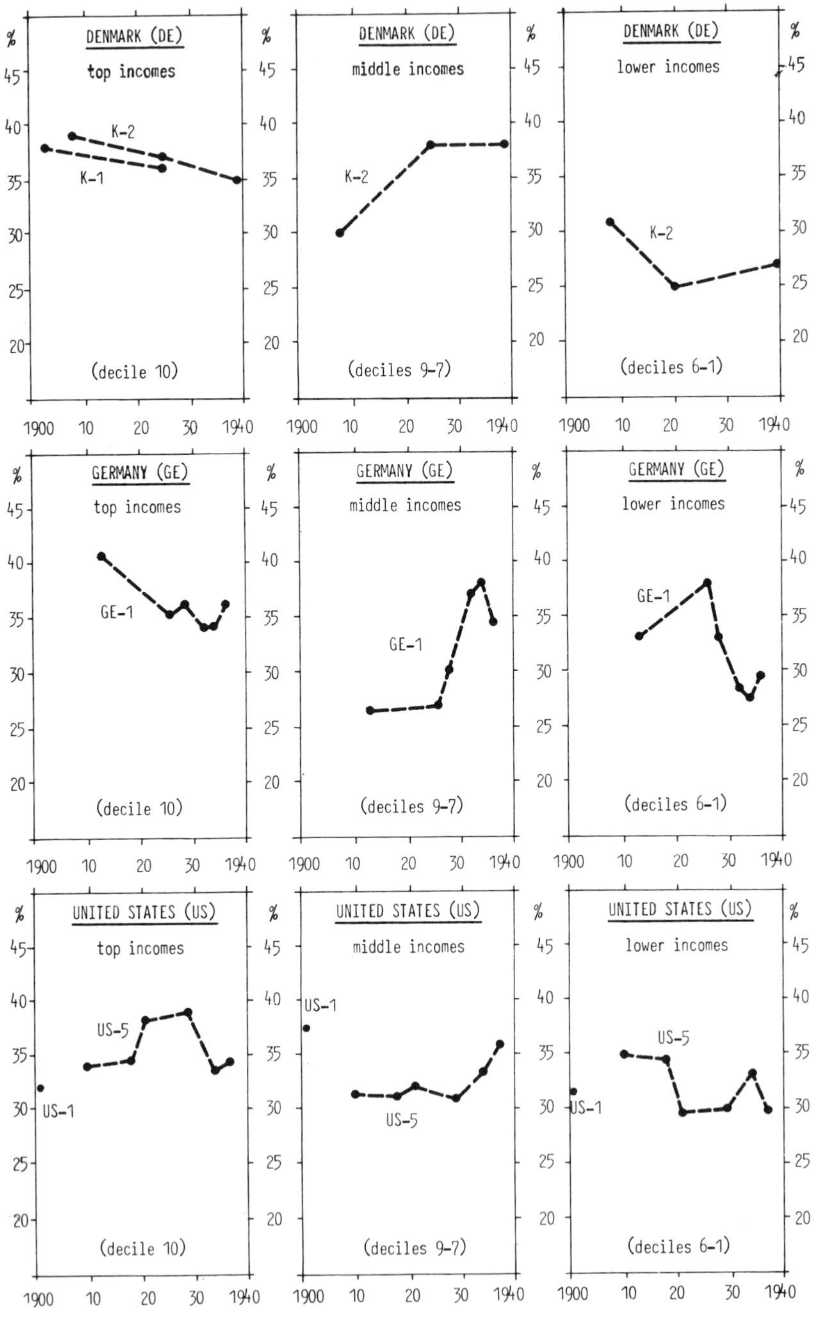
DENMARK (DE)
top incomes
K-1
K-2
(decile 10)
DENMARK (DE)
middle incomes
K-2
(deciles 9-7)
DENMARK (DE)
lower incomes
K-2
(deciles 6-1)
GERMANY (GE)
top incomes
GE-1
(decile 10)
GERMANY (GE)
middle incomes
GE-1
(deciles 9-7)
GERMANY (GE)
lower incomes
GE-1
(deciles 6-1)
UNITED STATES (US)
top incomes
US-5
US-1
(decile 10)
UNITED STATES (US)
middle incomes
US-1
US-5
(deciles 9-7)
UNITED STATES (US)
lower incomes
US-5
US-1
(deciles 6-1)
%
45
40
35
30
25
20
1900 10 20 30 1940

Figure 6.4
Patterns of Change in Inequality, 1935-1970

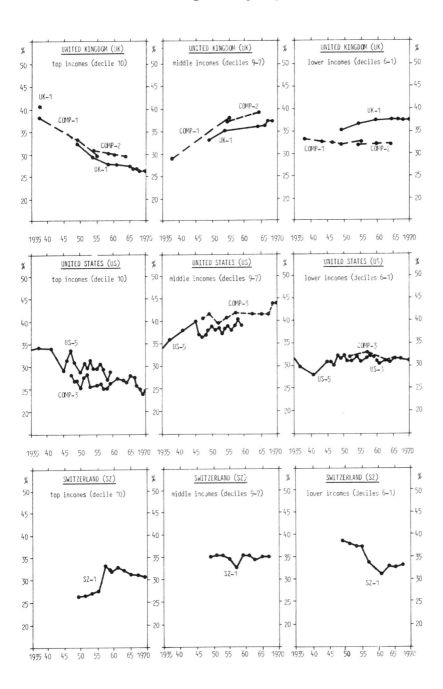

Figure 6.4
(Continued)

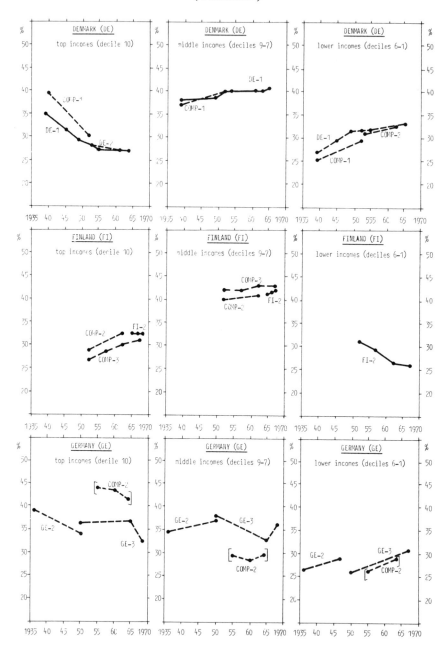

Figure 6.4
(Continued)

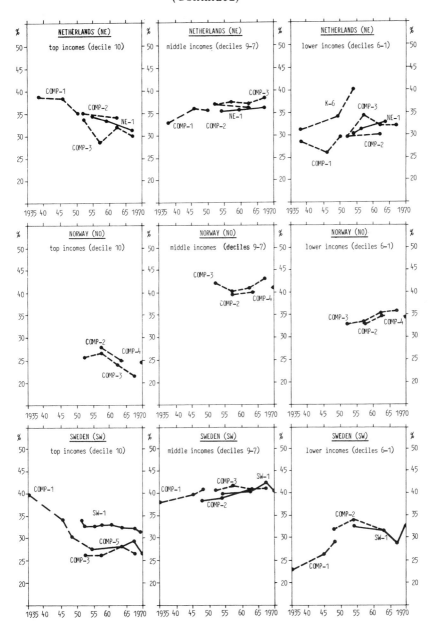

A. Trends in the Top Income Stratum

With few exceptions, all countries demonstrate an overall decline in the top 5 and 10% income shares, although initial levels and patterns of change vary. The long-run decline is most obvious for the top 5%, and is very sharp in Denmark and the United Kingdom. Here, the income shares of the top 5% in the late 1960s are only about half the level observed in the late nineteenth century.[42] In Germany and the United States, however, the decline is much less marked: the income shares of the top 5% in Prussia in 1875 appear to be only slightly higher than those of West Germany in 1968, while a similarly slight decline seems to have occurred in the United States between 1900 and 1970.[43]

There is also a convergence between countries in the income shares of the top 5%. In the late nineteenth century, these shares varied from about 30% in various German Länder to 34% in Denmark and more than 45% in the United Kingdom. In some German Länder they increased until the turn of the century (or even until World War I), whereas in Denmark and the United Kingdom they seem to have declined slightly. In the United States the respective income share of 23 to 25% at the turn of the century was comparatively low, but presumably rose afterwards to a more similar level.[44] [45]

Compared to prewar levels, the income shares of the top 5% are clearly lower and more similar at the onset of World War II. Including the United States, the levels vary only between 25 and slightly more than 30%. Around 1950 the income shares drop about 5 percentage points to fall between 20 and 25% in all nine countries for which data are available. Throughout the 1950s the decline slackens and during the 1960s tends to level off, or even to reverse. In 1970 the income shares are only slightly lower than in the early 1950s.

The development of the income shares of the top 10% largely corresponds with the top 5%. This appears true at least for the three countries for which data are available prior to World War I (see Figure 6.2). Whereas in Denmark and Germany the shares steadily declined from about 39% until World War II, the shares in the United States seem to have risen up to 1929 and declined only afterwards.[46]

In the late 1930s the income shares of the top 10% varied between 35 and 40% in these three countries as well as in the Netherlands, Sweden, and the United Kingdom. During World War II, the shares of the top 10% again decline. By the early 1950s, the shares averaged 5% less, ranging from 30 to 35%. In Finland, Norway, and Switzerland, the shares were even lower, falling below 30%.

Developments are less uniform from the mid-1950s to 1970. In all countries changes are much less significant. Clearly rising shares are reported for Finland for the whole period, for Switzerland up to the early

1960s and for Sweden starting in the 1960s. In the remaining countries, income shares changed little with no clear pattern over time or between countries. Around 1970 in all nine countries the top 10% bracket varied between 24 and 31%.

Most of the change in income shares of the top 10% actually occurred in the upper half of the decile,[47] or the top 5% stratum. In contrast, the lower half of the top 10% generally suffered only a minor deterioration of income position or even maintained their shares.

B. Trends in Middle and Lower Strata

Three periods are distinguished in Figures 6.3 and 6.4 for our analysis: 1900 to 1940, 1935 to the early 1950s, and the mid 1950s to the late 1960s. The development of the income shares of deciles 1-6 and 7-9 for the first period from 1900 to 1940 are shown in Figure 6.3. Although data are scanty and extremely unreliable for these strata prior to World War II, the uniformity of the development patterns is striking. In all three countries (Denmark, Germany, the United States) the bottom 60% lost ground. Their income shares declined considerably up to the late 1930s, causing the middle income strata to become the main winners.

Around 1910, the middle strata received between 26 and 32% of the income shares, and by the late 1930s the shares in Denmark and Germany had increased about 8%. In Denmark most of the change had taken place by the mid 1920s, whereas in Germany the increases only began at this time. In the United States the increase appeared to be somewhat smaller and did not occur until the early 1930s.

Figure 6.4 includes the additional data available for the United Kingdom, the Netherlands, and Sweden from the late 1930s to the early 1950s. In all countries the income shares of the middle strata continued to rise. Compared to the previous period, the increase is smaller, averaging about 3% to bring shares between the 35 and 40% level. Remarkably, during this same period the bottom 60% also improved or at least maintained their shares at the expense of the top 10%. The pattern of change differs with each country; a considerable increase of about 7% is reported for Sweden, although it started at the comparatively low level of about 23%. Changes in Denmark, Germany, and the Netherlands were moderate. Shares probably remained constant in the United Kingdom[48] and the United States, with the bottom 60% receiving comparatively high initial shares in both countries. By the early 1950s income shares vary only between about 30 and 34% compared to 23 to about 35% in the late 1930s.

After the mid-1950s income shares have been fairly stable in most of the countries studied. In Denmark, Norway, the United Kingdom, and the United States income shares of both the bottom 60% and the middle strata have remained virtually unchanged. In Finland, Sweden, and Switzerland stability is reported for the middle strata only; the lower strata apparently experienced marked reductions of about 5% to the advantage of the top 10%. Germany fits least into this general pattern: the bottom 60% seems to have gained, mostly at the expense of deciles 7-9.[49] By the late 1960s income shares of the lower strata vary between 32 and 35% for all countries except Finland with roughly 26%. The shares of the middle strata vary between 38 and 42% except in Switzerland where the level amounts to only about 35%.

C. Income Shares and Social Inequality

How have these changes in income shares affected the overall level of inequality and how can they be explained? Rising shares of the bottom 60% (and prior to World War II of the lowest 70%) very likely indicate a reduction in the overall level of inequality, while increased shares for the remaining strata certainly reflect an overall increase in inequality.[50] Before World War II, the overall level of inequality probably was most affected by changing shares of the top income recipients. Data on the behavior of the income shares of the remaining strata, so far as they are available, suggest an increasing, though lesser influence. The extent of the changes cannot be calculated reliably because of the lack of properly detailed size distributions.[51]

Between the late 1930s and early 1950s the decreasing shares of the 5% and increasing shares of the bottom 60% exert a leveling effect on the overall level of inequality. Countervailing effects stem from the rise of the upper strata's income shares with an increasing divergence from the equality line. According to Gini-Indices, overall inequality probably has declined most in Sweden (about 10 percentage points). Of course, we must take into account that the prewar level was certainly well above the average. The reduction seems to have been remarkable also in Denmark, averaging at least 6 percentage points, but the prewar level of inequality was again slightly above average. In Germany and the Netherlands declines have been comparatively small—about 3 percentage points. In the United Kingdom, the prewar level seems to have been well below average, and while inequality has probably continued to decline, the extent is questionable and probably of modest proportions.[52]

After the mid-1950s we would expect the level of overall inequality to remain fairly stable since income shares remained fairly constant for all groups in most countries. We note exceptions, however, in the inequality increase in Finland,[53] and the considerable decrease in the case of Norway. The course of inequality in Sweden is disputable: some series report basic stability, while others show declines of about 4 percentage points. The actual value probably lies in between.[54]

Changes in the share of the top strata certainly have been decisive for the trend in overall inequality. The relative decline of the top incomes appears to have been a general development, most strongly evidenced during both world wars. Where data are available, postwar levels of the upper income shares in almost all countries are considerably lower than prewar. But how do we explain the diverging patterns of development that took place predominantly during peacetime? Why did top income shares rise in some countries like Finland, fall for example in the United Kingdom, and both increase and decline to break predominant trends in others? Can these varying trends be explained by changes in economic development, where beyond a certain threshold of economic performance industrializing societies are characterized by lessening overall inequality? Finland certainly is an industrial latecomer, while the different trends in German Länder prior to World War I also conform to their different levels of economic development.[55] According to the most reliable series, decreasing upper income shares are reported from the turn of the century for the industrial leaders among the Länder (Prussia and Saxony), whereas in the industrial laggards (Hesse, Bavaria, Baden) no trend break appears to have occurred.[56] However, the relationship obviously applies neither to Danish nor Swedish developments, where declining inequality is reported also for early phases of industrialization, nor to the American experience, where the decline in inequality occurred long after her transformation from an agrarian society into an industrial one.

Each of these trends and patterns of change should be evaluated in the context of changes in the distribution of national income by factor shares and the effects of these changes on the composition of total incomes of the various strata. However, historical data on both aspects are very scarce. There is evidence that the share of income from assets over the last century declined markedly in several countries[57] and that the share of employee compensation increased. Table 6.3[58] shows the development of labor's share[59] in national income for most of the West European countries.

Since the share of total national income distributed to households has declined from about 90% at the turn of the century to about 75% currently, labor's share is even higher when compared with private incomes to which all the data collections in principle refer. Inequality in earnings might thus increasingly be responsible for total inequality. There are some indications that earnings probably became more equally distributed between the 1930s and the early 1950s, with the trend reversing thereafter.[60] Changing patterns and trends of income inequality also need to be interpreted within the general rise in total and per capita incomes—which have frequently quadrupled within the century.[61] In fact, we might want to ask whether economic growth is the more dominant feature of income inequality development. Of course, it should be kept in mind that data relating to the

Table 6.3
Labor's Share: Compensation of Employees as Percentage of National Income

Year	AU	BE	DE	FI	GE	IT	NE	NO	SW	SZ	UK
1850											
1855											56
1860											55
1865											52
1870					43						50
1875					45						54
1880					43						54
1885					45						56
1890					45						57
1895					48						57
1900					47						57
1905					47						57
1910					48						58
1915	51⁻⁻				49⁻⁻						66
1920											70
1925	56				61					52⁻	65
1930	59				64			48	51	50	65
1935	57				61			47	52	53	67
1940	55⁻⁻⁻				56				48	49	72
1945	56⁺⁺⁺				55⁺⁺⁺			57⁺	49	54	72
1950	55		53	58	58	49	55	56	51	61	73
1955	59	53	58	56	59	51	54	58	66	60	73
1960	59	57	58	57	60	52	57	63	66	61	73
1965	63	61	63	62	65	57	64	63	72	64	76
1970	64	62	67	64	67	59	69	67	76	63	80

incomes of the poorest segments of the population are extremely scarce or lacking altogether for earlier times. At present, too little is known to evaluate this relationship conclusively.

III. Societal Change and Income Inequality: Selected Studies

While there are various theories that attempt to explain the unequal distribution of incomes,[62] most are ahistorical and tend to focus on a single cause, such as chance, ability, or education. Only a few incorporate broad social change as a primary determinant.[63] Within this vein, we can distinguish three main approaches:

1. changes in income inequality as a result of capitalist industrialization or general economic growth within a country (Simon Kuznets);[64]
2. changes in income inequality as a result of changes in the distribution of power within a country (Gerhard Lenski);[65] and
3. changes in income inequality as a result of changes in the economic and political relationship of a country to the world economy—an international, rather than national, perspective (the dependency theorists).[66]

These approaches are comprised of a variety of factors. While some variables are common to all of these theories, each emphasizes different ones and proposes different structural links.

According to Simon Kuznets, early phases of industrialization are characterized by rapid shifts from agricultural to non-agricultural production; by an increasing centralization and concentration of agriculture; and by an increasing supply of industrial labor due to continuous migration from rural to urban areas. All of these processes contribute to an increase in inequality. In later phases when technological advancements are made in all economic sectors, differences in labor productivity decline to make physical capital less important relative to skilled labor in the production process. As a result, income inequality begins to subside. Although Kuznets concedes the importance of political processes—particularly the introduction and extension of civil, political, and economic rights—he maintains that the production sphere is the primary determinant of changes in income inequality.

Gerhard Lenski argues that inequality is diminished by changes in the distribution of economic and political power as a society advances from an agrarian to an industrial economy. In late agrarian societies, where the social division of labor has sufficiently increased to create an economic surplus, it is predominantly and increasingly distributed on the basis of political power. The formation of modern class structures as a political concomitant of capitalist economic growth simultaneously changes power relationships between these emergent classes. In turn, social mobilization leads to the extension of citizenship rights to disenfranchised social groups, which thus changes the power relations between various classes and the state. In Lenski's theory, the mere extension of these rights in the new industrial societies effects changes in the distribution of power. In later phases, the formation and increasing strength of trade unions and socialist parties causes a decline in the concentration of power and a greater willingness of the economic elite to compromise, thus leading to a more equal distribution of material rewards. In contrast to Kuznets, Lenski does not view economic development as the direct cause of changes in inequality, but as a prerequisite for changes in the distribution of power which are instead primary.

Richard Rubinson[67] has recently critiqued Lenski's theory through the application of *dependency theories* to his data. Here, the capitalist mode of production is characterized not only by an internal division of labor, but also by an asymmetric geographical division of labor.[68] Internal differences in production and occupational and class configurations are viewed as both the result and cause of a world division of labor. The distribution of income within a country is thus predominantly determined by the distribution of economic and political power between nations. While dependency theories are certainly extremely valuable to historical comparative analyses, they are probably less useful for explaining the more recent developments in the advanced Western countries. Since testing the dependency theories in all their complexity would require a separate chapter,[69] we shall limit our consideration to quantitative comparisons of the influence of national developments on inequality.

Most of our evidence must be derived from cross-national analyses despite their many problems regarding historical developmental conclusions. Table 6.4 gives a simplified idea of the framework that selected studies[70] utilize to examine the relationship between inequality and economic and political development, although many factors have obviously been eliminated for this short survey.[71] Most of the cross-sectional studies refer to a highly varied set of countries typically during the mid-l950s or mid-l960s. Only Cutright's study provides a separate analysis of different stages of economic development. Cameron's and Hewitt's are limited to different sets of industrialized countries only. The only available longitudinal study that considers the economic and political dimensions of social change was conducted by Guy Peters[72] and deals with two old nations after their economic take-off.

All studies differ considerably in their conceptual framework, methods, and data sources. *Income inequality,* when measured directly by pretax data on personal incomes, or indirectly by some summary measure of sectoral differences in labor productivity,[73] actually comes closest to our notion of producer inequality. Interpretations, however, often rest on some concept of consumer inequality and thus differ greatly from what has actually been measured.[74] *Economic development* is a factor in all of the analyses and is usually a per capita measure of national product and energy consumption. Interpretations of data range from Rubinson's "degree of the social division of labor" to Peters' "level of surplus available for redistribution." Cameron, Hewitt, and Jackman also include growth rates to distinguish between the short-run and the long-run effects of economic development.[75]

Only some studies consider the *role of the state* and usually stress different aspects. Cameron focuses on its role in supplementing or substi-

Table 6.4
Income Inequality and Social Change:
Framework of Selected Studies

Studies — Author/Sample	Dependent variables — Income inequality (concept measurement)	Independent variables — Economic Development	Rise of the state	Development of mass democracies	Labor movement
Cameron — Industrialized countries (N=13) (mid-sixties)	Primary distribution (a) directly income shares: top 20 %	Level of economic activity; short-run growth	State as a producer (Scope of the state)		Unions; Socialist Parties
Cutright — Industrialized and less developed countries (N=44; early fifties)	Secondary distribution (a) indirectly (b) overall level	Division of labor/ level of Surplus		Index: Political Representativeness (Institutionalization of opposition; electoral procedures)	Power-lessness of labor force
Hewitt — Industrialized countries (N=25) (mid-sixties)	Primary distribution (a) directly (b1) shares: top 5 %, 20 % (b2) earng. gap	Level of economic activity; growth rates		Index: Democratic Experience (longterm tradition of democratic procedures)	Executive strength; Legislative strength
Jackman — Industrialized and less developed countries (N=60; 1960)	Final distribution (a) indirectly (b) overall level	Division of labor/ level o surplus; growth of surplus	Committment of the state to welfare (civilian scope of the state	Index: Democratic Performance (Freedom of press; competitiveness of party system; electoral irregularity; adult voting	Degree of organization
Rubinson — Industrialized and less developed countries (N=47; ca. 1965)	Primary distribution (a) directly (b1) overall levels (b2) share of 3 rd. quintile	Division of labor	State as a producer and a consumer (level of civilian public expenditures)	Cutright's PRI-Index and as an alternative Jackman's Index of Democratic Performance	
Rubinson/Quinlan — Industrialized and less developed countries (N=32; ca. 1965)	Primary distribution (a) directly (b1) overall level (b2) share of 3 rd. quintile	Division of labor	Regulative and control capacity of the state ("Internal State Strength") (Scope of the state)	Cutright's PRI-Index and alternatively Jackman's DP-Index	
Peters — Sweden 1920–1969, United Kingdom: a) 1680–1969, b1) 1880–1939, b2) 1949–1969	Secondary distribution (a) directly (b) overall level	Division of labor; level of surplus		Electoral discrimination (Male franchise rate)	Power-lessness of labor force

tuting markets, while Jackman additionally examines its social welfare role. Rubinson and Rubinson-Quinlan emphasize the state's ability to control and regulate markets. Actual measurements (revenue shares or the level of civilian public expenditure to national product) show much more similarity than do interpretations.[76] It is widely agreed that the *development of mass democracies* is probably a basic determinant of income inequality, especially in its introduction and extension of civil and, above all, political rights (freedom of press, right to form political parties, the franchise, etc.). Except for Hewitt's Index of Democratic Experience, the indicators are devised to measure not only the degree of formal institutionalization, but also that of participation. The *power of associations* is less frequently taken into account, but is usually measured by the strength of the organization of the labor movement—the trade unions or the socialist parties. The strength of the parties is always seen as institutionalized strength, whether legislative (Hewitt, Jackman) or executive (Cameron). Union strength is measured either directly by the degree of organization (Jackman), or more frequently indirectly by the proportion of the labor force that usually has less access and ability to form an interest organization (Cutright, Peters). The indirect measure—the proportion of the labor force employed in agriculture—is, however, probably more an indication of economic development than of union strength.

The social welfare role of the state is examined only sporadically in the studies. Cameron deals with educational opportunity (extent and inequality of higher education), and Jackman and Rubinson with bureaucratic experience and rationality in implementing social security programs. In fact, the attempts to include these factors are either highly speculative (Jackman, Rubinson),[77] or difficult to generalize (Cameron).[78] We have, therefore, excluded them from this survey.

In examining these studies we are faced with many questions. What can they tell us about the relationship between social change and income inequality? Are changes in producer inequality merely the result of changing economic structures as is so often proposed? What part do structural changes of the polity play? What are the relevant core elements and how are they related? Of course, faced with such marked differences in model specification and measurement, we can only arrive at the most tenuous of conclusions.

Cutright, the first to analyze income inequality within the context of social change, devised his study as a partial test of Lenski's stratification theory. In analyzing the entire sample of non-communist nations, he concludes that inequality is affected not only by economic factors, but, more importantly, by political factors. The distribution of political power (or access of the masses to the political elite) as well as economic power (power of propertied class, unions) exerts a strong influence on producer inequality. Since these factors are independently related to inequality, Cutright cannot confirm Lenski's developmental model: class structures are at least not exclusively a function of the degree of economic development. Separate analyses of subsamples with comparable levels of economic development moreover suggest that class structures and democratic performance are explanatory factors only in agrarian and early industrial societies. Whether differences in income inequality in highly industrialized countries are instead due to differences in the strength of socialist parties, as Lenski proposes, must remain open. Cutright made no attempt to test this relationship, although results could be molded to fit a simpler version of Lenski's theory if the proposed linkages between economic and political development are ignored. Kuznets' theory of the direct relationship between economic development and income inequality is partly confirmed. We must keep in mind, however, that these results can be quite misleading, even if one just considers the highly unreliable measurement of income inequality.

Economic and political developments are (among others) basic also to Jackman's much more complex models. Except for education, all the principal aspects of social change, noted in the general framework of Table 6.4, are included. His results suggest that income inequality is deeply rooted in the economic structure. Long-term structural changes in the economy, including increasing (civilian) public expenditures, partly a result of the former, will effect a decline in inequality. As opposed to Kuznets, he sees this relationship as strongest in the early phases of industrialization. Lenski's theory is also unconfirmed. Long-term economic change seems to increase considerably the institutionalization and extension of civil and political rights, especially in the early phases. Democratization, however, appears here to have no impact at all on a society's level of inequality. The formation of associations with redistributive goals seems also to have had little influence: labor unions decreased inequality levels, particularly at their early stage of formation, but socialist parties, the political arm of the union movement, had no effect according to his results. Finally, the short-run growth of surplus, which Lenski anticipates will level inequality, instead seems to have increased it.

Rubinson and Quinlan have recently replicated part of Jackman's and Cutright's findings. Utilizing far more reliable data on inequality, they surprisingly support the finding that long-term economic development, a primary determinant of inequality in the other studies, affected neither overall levels of inequality nor the income shares of particular segments of the labor force. Democratization, although of small impact, tends to level inequalities.[79] Perhaps most important, however, they show that the causality of the relationship is highly questionable.[80] With regard to the role of economic development, however, Rubinson-

Quinlan's results differ somewhat from Rubinson's own findings. He earlier theorized that in economically advanced countries, income shares of the middle strata tend to be higher, and those of the top and bottom quintiles lower than in more underdeveloped countries. Although results are not very strong, the increasing shares of the middle strata and the declining shares of the lowest quintile are possibly a result of structural economic change. In any case, economic development would not seem to be the main determinant of distributive changes, but instead it is the internal governmental strength of a country.[81] Whether the rise of the state is such a dominant factor because of its regulative capacity, as Rubinson suggests, or because of its economic role in the income system remains open, as neither of the proposed structural links has been tested.

The role of the state is also a basic factor in Cameron's explanation of the differences of the top quintile's income share among Western industrialized countries. According to his results, the respective income shares tend to be lowest in those societies that in the medium-term have experienced the most dramatic increases in state revenue shares. State expansion, furthermore, is caused not by economic development, the institutional structure of the state, or tax visibility, but mainly by the policies of left-leaning governments. His data support such a developmental relationship: leftist governments are most inclined to expand state activity, which in turn is associated with comparatively lower income shares of the economic elite. In observing the close ties between state expansion and changes in occupational structure, Cameron concludes that the state's main importance lies in its role as a producer. In contrast, market forces seem to work slightly in favor of the top income recipients. Levels of economic development as well as economic growth rates show a positive association with the income shares of the top 20%. But no general conclusions can be drawn since Cameron neglects to take into account the remaining strata and the overall level of inequality.

Using a broader set of highly industrialized countries, Hewitt reaches rather different conclusions. National differences in the income shares of the top 20% and the top 5% seem due to differences in long-term democratic traditions, the medium-term governmental strength of socialist parties, and differences in economic growth rates and levels of production. All of these factors negatively affect the top income shares. Thus, where economic factors are concerned, Hewitt's findings contradict Cameron's. This model, however, provides no explanation of the spread of earnings. Apparently, for late industrial societies at least, Lenski's model seems most applicable to changes in the top income shares.

It is not surprising to find empirical support for very different theories. But existing evidence tentatively leads us to conclude that economic and—

even more so—political developments are the main causes of change in producer inequality. The relationship between income inequality and economic development is still debatable. Cross-sectional studies based on direct measures of income inequality (the more valid ones) indicate only a limited relationship of a contradictory nature. The results range from finding the economic development limited to the relative impoverishment of the poorest strata and to the incrasing wealth of the middle class (Rubinson) to seeing it as a factor in the deterioration (Hewitt) or improvement (Cameron) of the income positions of the upper strata. Whether findings vary because of different specifications of explanatory variables or because of likely differences in the country samples must be left to direct replication.

The studies lead to more conclusive findings with respect to *the role of political development*. The development of mass democracies, the strength of socialist parties, and the rise of the state seem to be associated with declining inequality. All the cross-sectional studies support this view, except for Jackman's analysis which suffers from the unreliability of its inequality indicator. The most influential factor seems to be the rise of the state. Wherever[82] some measure of the scope of state activity was included, it proved to be highly significant in explaining the overall level of inequality (Rubinson, Cameron). But specific interpretations and proposed linkages vary. The capacity of the state to regulate or to modernize the economy, an intrepretation adopted by Rubinson, seems less valid for industrial countries. Even in the case of Rubinson's study, the extractive capacity of the state might be interpreted as an indirect indicator of its direct economic involvement. This receives solid support by a recent analysis by Steven Stack,[83] who uses a subsample of Rubinson's country set to show that the share of public expenditure in national product "is most closely associated with low income inequality."[84] However, much more work is needed to determine the linkage between the rise of the state and income inequality, as well as its relation to other political factors.

Explanations based on cross-sectional analyses will not necessarily hold in an historical context which can be evaluated only by longitudinal analysis. Peters has attempted such an analysis in comparing the United Kingdom from the late nineteenth century on with Sweden since the end of World War I. His conceptual framework and proposed structural links are similar to those of Cutright's cross-sectional analysis. His measurement differs slightly with regard to the independent variables, and markedly with regard to inequality. Instead of using Cutright's indirect measure (inequality of labor productivity among economic sectors), Peters compiled data on inequality of personal incomes. Employing bivariate analyses, he found that in both countries decreasing overall inequality was associated with long-run economic growth, the extension of franchise and the formation of modern class structures. His variables have since been reduced mechanically[85] to two basic dimensions: elite power and surplus.[86] In both countries the elite power factor was found to have a stronger effect on inequality than the surplus factor. The decline in inequality seems mainly due to the weakening ability of "the upper economic classes to influence the use of economic power for their own benefit."[87] Whether this is really a strong confirmation of Lenski's theory, as Peters suggests, seems questionable: the elite power factor is a combination of several factors, each of which could be interpreted quite differently (e.g., capital formation, trade pattern, defense expenditures). Unfortunately, the effects of increasing mass participation in the political system (franchise rate), cannot be separately assessed.[88] Since this is one of Lenski's key variables, any conclusion about the role of political developments unavoidably must remain only tentative.

We encounter similar problems in the results of Peters' separate regression over equal halves of the United Kingdom period. His findings now suggest that changes in inequality during the first half were overwhelmingly dominated by changes in the distribution of power, and by changes in surplus in the second half. The latter result at least[89] contradicts Lenski's theory. According to Peters, a new stage of development not covered by Lenski's theory may have been reached: the post-industrial society, in which "the general relationship between the economic classes will have been decided in the political system, and changes in the level of inequality. . . . will be functions of the changes in the available surplus."[90] Of course, his interpretation is highly speculative. Alternative intrepretations might hold at least as well. For example, the effect of public intervention in private bargaining, so widespread in postwar Europe,[91] would reflect the political power of the state (a factor outside Peter's model), not the "economic power of the nation."[92] The management of aggregate demand, also common in post-war Europe, might provide another explanation. Several studies have already shown that unemployment is an important source of inequality[93]—and its subjectivity to political constraint has recently also gained empirical support.[94]

It is quite evident that any conclusion concerning the role of the state in generating changes in producer inequality is so far extremely speculative. Very likely, the rise of the state is significantly associated with declining inequality of market incomes. But in which manner? Because of increasing control and regulation or markets? Because of its rising demand for goods and services? In order to reach less ambiguous results, the concept of the state needs to be correspondingly differentiated. In addition, examination of structural links must move beyond conceptual discussion to empirical testing. Because historical data are scarce, it might be necessary to adopt indirect approaches rather than direct ones.

Table 6.5
Data on Income Shares

Denmark (DE)

Income strata	Source	1870	1903	1908	1925	1939	1944	1949	1952	1953	1955	1961	1963	1964	1965
(1) top 5 %	COMP-1					26.7		20.1							
	COMP-2									18			16.9		
	K-1	36.5	28		26										
	K-2			30	26	24.5									
	DE-1					24.6	21.8	19.1	18.0		17.3	17.5		16.5	
(2) top 10 %	COMP-1					37.6		30.7							
	COMP-2									28.0			27.1		
	K-1	50	38		36										
	K-2			39	37	35									
	DE-1					35.2	32.4	29.5	28.6		27.4	27.5		26.5	
	DE-2														26.4
(3) deciles 7-9	COMP-1					37.2		39.8							
	COMP-2									40.3			40.3		
	K-2			30	38	38									
	DE-1					37.9	38.2	38.9	39.6		40.6	40.0		40.5	
	DE-2														40.3
(4) bottom 60 %	COMP-1					25.2		29.5							
	COMP-2									31.7			32.6		
	K-2			31	25	27									
	DE-1					26.9	29.4	31.6	31.8		32.0	32.5		33.0	
	DE-2														33.3

Finland (FI)

Income strata	Source	1881	1900	1950	1952	1954	1956	1957	1958	1960	1962	1964	1965	1966	1967	1968	1969	1970
(1) top 5 %	COMP-2			18						21								
	FI-1	31	40											15				
	FI-2			18.3	19.3	19.0	19.5	19.7	19.9	20.1	21.1	21.6	21.6	21.4	21.5	21.6	21.0	
(2) top 10 %	COMP-2			28.9						32.5								
	COMP-3			26.7			28.6			30.0			30.9					
	FI-1	39	50											25				
	FI-2													32.7	32.7	32.9	33.0	33.2
(3) deciles 7-9	COMP-2			40.1						41.0								
	COMP-3			42.1			42.1			42.8			43.2					
	FI-2													41.3	41.5	41.5	41.9	42.5
(4) bottom 60 %	COMP-2			31						26.5								
	COMP-3			31.2			29.4			27.1			25.9					
	FI-2			31.2	30.9	30.9	29.4	29.4	29.0	27.8	26.9	26.3	26.0	25.8	25.6	25.1	24.3	25.0

Table 6.5
(Continued)

Germany: Prussia (PR) and Saxony (SAX)

PR

Income strata	Source	1854	1873/75	1876/80	1881/85	1886/90	1891/95	1896/00	1901/05	1906/10	1911/13	1928
(1) top 5 %	K-3	21	26				27				30	
	K-4										31	26
	PR-1		27.8	28.4	29.9	31.0	31.3	32.6	32.0	31.1	30.6	
(2) bottom 60 %	K-4										32	31

SAX

Income strata	Source	1854	1873/75	1876/80	1881/85	1886/90	1891/95	1896/00	1901/05	1906/10	1911/13	1928
(1) top 5 %	K-3			34			36				33	
	K-4										33	28
	SAX-1				33.2	33.7	34.2	34.4	33.3	33.3	33.0	
(2) bottom 60 %	K-4										28	31

Germany (GE)

Income strata	Source	1913	1926	1928	1932	1934	1936	1950	1955	1960	1962	1964	1965	1968	1969
(1) top 5 %	COMP-1							27.9	23.6						
	COMP-2									(36.2	35.7) a)				
	K-4	31		27	21 b)										
	K-5			20			23								
	GE-1	31	24.8	26.3	23.2	23.5	25.2								
	GE-2							27.2	23.5						
	GE-3									26.0			27.2	24.3	
	GE-4											24.9			23.3
(2) top 10 %	COMP-1							39	34						
	COMP-2									(44.0	43.5			41.4) a)	
	GE-1	40.5	35	36.5	33.7	34.2	36.0								
	GE-2							37.8	33.5						
	GE-3									36			36.7	32.8	
(3) deciles 7-9	COMP-1							34.5	37						
	COMP-2									(29.5	28.5			29.5) a)	
	GE-1	26.3	27	30.3	37.2	38.2	34.5								
	GE-2							34.5	36.5						
	GE-3									38			33.1	36.1	
(4) bottom 60 %	COMP-1							26.5	29						
	COMP-2									(26.5	28			29.1) a)	
	K-4	32		31	34 b)										
	GE-1	33.2	38	33.2	28.5	27.5	29.5								
	GE-2							27.7	30						
	GE-3									26			30.1	31.1	

a) Figures include undistributed profits of corporations

b) After adjustment for incomplete coverage

Table 6.5
(Continued)

therlands (NE)

come strata	Source	1938	1946	1949	1950	1952	1954	1957	1959	1962	1967
) top 5 %	COMP-1	28.9	27.3	24.6							
	COMP-2				25.0				23.6		
	K-6	19	17			13					
	NE-1						24.4	23.3			21.1
) top 10 %	COMP-1	38.7	38.3		35.0						
	COMP-2				35.0						33.8
	COMP-3					33.6		28.4	31.9	29.5	
	COMP-4										31.1
	NE-1						34.4	33.5			31.1
) deciles 7-9	COMP-1	32.8	35.7	35.5							
	COMP-2					36.6				36.2	
	COMP-3						36.9	37.3		36.9	38.5
	COMP-4										36.5
	NE-1						35.3	35.6			36.3
) bottom 60 %	COMP-1	28.5	26.0	29.5							
	COMP-2					29.4				30.0	
	COMP-3						29.5	34.3		32.0	31.9
	COMP-4										32.6
	K-6	31.0		34.0		40.0					
	NE-1						30.3	31.1			32.6

Norway (NO)

Income strata	Source	1952	1957	1962	1963	1967	1970
(1) top 5 %	COMP-2		17.9	15.4			
(2) top 10 %	COMP-2		27.6	24.9			
	COMP-3	25.6	26.5	24.1		21.4	
	COMP-4						24.5
(3) deciles 7-9	COMP-2		39.4	40.0			
	COMP-3	41.8	40.2	40.9		42.9	
	COMP-4						41.0
(4) bottom 60 %	COMP-2		33.0	35.1			
	COMP-3	32.7	33.2	34.8		35.7	
	COMP-4						34.5

Sweden (SW)

Income strata	Source	1935	1945	1948	1951	1952	1954	1955	1957	1958	1960	1962	1963	1965	1967	1968	1969	1970
(1) top 5 %	COMP-1	28.1	23.6	20.1														
	COMP-1 a)				20.0		17.0											
	COMP-2						17.0						17.6					
(2) top 10 %	COMP-1	39.5	34.1	30.3														
	COMP-1 a)				30.0		27.3											
	COMP-2						27.3						27.9					
	COMP-3					26.2			26.2			28.2			26.4			
	COMP-5						27.3						27.9			29.2		26.6
	SW-1					34.2	33.3	33.0	32.8	33.0	33.0	33.3	32.7	32.6	31.9	32.1	32.1	31.4
(3) deciles 7-9	COMP-1	37.8	39.6	40.6														
	COMP-1 a)				38.3		38.8											
	COMP-2						38.8						40.7					
	COMP-3					40.4			41.6			40.6			41.0			
	SW-1						39.8						40.7			42.4		40.7
(4) bottom 60 %	COMP-1	22.7	26.3	29.1														
	COMP-1 a)				31.7		33.9											
	COMP-2						33.9						31.4					
	COMP-3					33.4			32.3			31.3			32.7			
	SW-1						32.9						31.4			28.4		32.7

a) unadjusted tax data

Table 6.5
(Continued)

Switzerland (SZ)

Income strata	Source	1949/50	1951/52	1953/54	1955/56	1957/58	1959/60	1961/62	1963/64	1965/66	1967/68
(1) top 5 %	SZ-1										
(2) top 10 %	SZ-1	26.3	26.6	27.2	27.7	33.3	32.1	33.1	32.3	31.8	31.3
(3) deciles 7-9	SZ-1	35.1	35.4	35.4	34.7	32.6	35.5	35.6	34.6	35.3	35.3
(4) bottom 60 %	SZ-1	38.6	38.0	37.4	37.6	34.0	32.4	31.3	33.1	32.9	33.4

United Kingdom (UK)

Income strata	Source	1880	1913	1929	1938	1947	1949	1953	1954	1955	1957	1959	1961	1962	1963	1964	1965	1966	1967	1968	1969	1970
(1) top 5 %	COMP-1			29.5	23.7	20.2																
	COMP-2				21.0									19.2								
	K-9	48	43																			
	K-10			33																		
	K-11				31	24																
	K-12				29		23.5				18											
	UK-1				31.5																	
	UK-1						23.1	19.7				18.5				18.3	18.5	17.6	17.4	17.3	17.1	16.6
	UK-2						23.8	20.8					19.9	19.2	19.5	19.2	19.5	19.6	18.8	18.4		
(2) top 10 %	COMP-1				38.0		33.0			29.3												
	COMP-2							30.4						29.3								
	COMP-3								33.1	31.0	30.1	30.1	29.6	29.5	27.2	28.2	28.1	29.7	27.6	28.1	26.3	
	UK-1 a)				40.5																	
	UK-1						32.1	28.3				27.4				27.0	27.3	26.4	26.2	26.0	25.8	25.7
	UK-2						33.2	30.1					29.4	28.9	29.2	28.9	29.1					
(3) deciles 7-9	COMP-1				28.8		35.0			38.0												
	COMP-2							37.9						38.8								
	COMP-3								36.1	37.8	38.5	38.5	38.1	37.3	39.7	40.3	40.4	40.4	40.1	39.7	40.2	
	UK-1 a)				28.0																	
	UK-1						32.8	35.2				35.6				35.7	35.8	36.2	36.4	37.0	36.7	36.9
	UK-2						34.9	38					38.4	38.1	38.7	38.9	39		38.4	38.7	38.9	
(4) bottom 60 %	COMP-1				33.2		32.0			32.7												
	COMP-2							31.7						31.9								
	COMP-3								22.5	22.4	30.8	31.2	32.2	33.1	33.0	31.4	31.4		32.1	32.1	33.4	
	UK-1 a)				31.4																	
	UK-1						35.1	36.5				37.2				37.3	37.0	37.4	37.3	37.1	37.4	37.3
	UK-2						31.9	31.9					32.2	33.1	32.3	32.2	31.9		32.7	32.8	33.2	

a) Data cannot be compared to lates year because of extremely low coverage of income recipients.

Table 6.5
(Continued)

United States (U.S.)

Income strata	Source	1900	1910	1918	1921	1929	1934	1935	1937	1939	1941	1944	1945	1946	1947	1948	1949	1950
(1) top 5 %	COMP-5														22.7			
	COMP-5														22.1			
	COMP-5														18.5			
	COMP-5														21.5			
	US-1	ca.24																
	US-2				30.0		26.5		25.8	24.0	20.7		21.3	20.9		21.4		
	US-3																	
	US-4				32.2		28.8		27.8	25.7	18.7		20.0	19.1	19.4			
(2) top 10 %	COMP-3														28.1	26.0	27.0	25.6
	US-1		32															
	US-5			33.9	34.5	38.2	39.0	33.6		34.4		34.0		29.0	32.0	33.5	30.9	29.8 28.7
(3) deciles	COMP-3														40.4	41.4	41.5	42.7
7-9	US-1		36															
	US-5			31.3	31.2	32.2	31.1	33.5		35.9		38.0		40.0	37.0	36.4	36.7	38.6 38.9
(4) bottom	COMP-3														31.4	32.6	31.5	31.7
60 %	COMP-5 a														26.3			
	COMP-5 b														31.9			
	COMP-5 c														29.8			
	US-1		32															
	US-2				26.3		27.4			28.9	32.0			32.0		31.6		
	US-3																	
	US-5			34.8	34.3	29.6	29.9	32.9		29.7		28.0		31.0	31.0	30.1	32.3	31.6 32.4

United States (continued)

Income Strata	Source	1951	1952	1953	1954	1955	1956	1957	1958	1959	1960	1961	1962	1963	1964	1965	1966	1967	1968	1969	1970
(1) top 5 %	COMP-5									21.9			20.8					21.5			
	COMP-5									20.1			20.9			20.5					
	COMP-5									17.7			17.1			17.5					
	COMP-5									20.0			20.0						19.2		
	US-1																				
	US-2	20.7			20.3		20.2			19.6	19.6		20.0						19.2		
	US-3								16.4	17.0	17.0	17.7	16.7	16.8	17.2	16.6	16.7	16.4	16.8	16.6	16.9
	US-4																				
(2) top 10 %	COMP-3	27.5	28.5	25.5	25.6	26.0	26.2	25.2	25.1	26.2	26.4	27.5	27.1	27.0	26.6	27.8	27.8	25.7	25.0	24.2	24.7
	US-1																				
	US-5	30.9	29.5	31.4	29.3	29.7	30.6	29.4	27.1	28.9											
(3) deciles	COMP-3	40.3	39.7	42.2	42.6	42.0	41.7	42.0	42.3	41.8	41.6	41.6	41.6	41.6	42.0	41.4	41.4	42.5	42.6	43.8	43.8
7-9	US-1																				
	US-5	37.9	38.3	37.0	38.4	39.2	38.1	39.0	40.5	39.2											
(4) bottom	COMP-3	32.2	31.8	32.3	31.8	32.0	32.2	32.8	32.6	32.1	31.9	30.9	31.3	31.4	31.4	30.8	30.8	31.8	32.4	31.9	31.6
60 %	COMP-5 a									23.3			23.3						23.2		
	COMP-5 b									28.7			28.2			27.6					
	COMP-5 c									30.1			30.2			31.4					
	US-1																				
	US-2				32.4					31.8			31.2						31.7		
	US-3								31.9	31.4	31.3	30.5	31.3	31.3	31.0	31.6	31.9	31.7	31.8	31.5	31.2
	US-5	31.2	31.3	31.6	32.3	31.1	31.3	31.7	32.4	31.9											

Table 6.6
Overall Levels of Income Inequality: Gini-coefficients

Land	Source	1935	36	37	38	39	1940	41	42	43	44	1945	46	47	48	49	1950	51	52	53	54	1955	56	57	58	59	1960	61	62	63	64	1965	66	67	68	69	1970
DE	COMP-1					.50																															
	COMP-2																																				
	DE-1				.45											.39		.44	.42	.40		.40						.38		.39							
FI	COMP-2	.49															.45					.42					.49						.46		.50		
	COMP-3																											.47 .45		.47							
NE	COMP-1			.48								.50					.45					.51						.5?									
	COMP-2																.45		.45 .42		.43			.37			.42	.44 .40 .43		.43			.44 .43				
	NL-1																													.47							
NO	COMP-2																							.40 .38				.35		.36			.74				
	COMP-3																																				
SW	COMP-1	.54										.48	.44 .40							.36 .38			.32					.40 .40		.40			.38 .44			.3?
	SW-1																.56 .55	.55	.31	.54 .54	.54	.31		.54 .38		.54 .40	.53 .52	.41	.53		.39	.52 .52	.52 .52	.50		
SZ	SZ-1			.43												.42	.50				.41							.41		.41			.39			
UK	COMP-1			.42												.36	.48 .42													.41 .33						
	UK-2															.41	.43 .42 .42 .40	.42	.40	.40 .40	.41	.50 .43	.42	.42 .42 .42	.47 .42	.43	.51 .52	.44	.42 .43	.42 .40	.40	.51	.46 .41	.42	.39	.40	.40
US	COMP-5a																.48					.50						.51		.39 .40		.51	.45 .46	.50			.51
	COMP-5c																																	.42			.40
	US-2												.42																					.78			.40

Sources

COMP-1	United Nations 1957. Income shares and Gini coefficients are from chapter 9, p. 6, Table 3. The distributions are based on adjusted income tax data.
COMP-2	United Nations 1967. Income shares and Gini coefficients are from chapter 6, p. 15, Table 6.10. Data refer to tax units and taxable incomes. They are not adjusted for incomplete coverage or any other deficiency.
COMP-3	Roberti 1974. Income shares are from Appendix Tables 1b and 1c. Gini coefficients have been calculated according to a method suggested by Morgan 1962. Data are based on raw income tax data.
COMP-4	Sawyer 1976. Income shares are from Table 3, p. 14. Gini coefficients are from Table 5, p. 16. Data are based on income tax data matched with surveys, or merely on surveys.
COMP-5	Stark 1977.

COMP-5 (cont.) For *Sweden* (SW) income shares and Gini coefficients are from Table 99, p. 147. They are based on unadjusted income tax returns. Data refer to the taxable incomes of individuals aged 15 and above. For the *United States* (US) income shares are from Table 113, pp. 113-114. Gini coefficients are from Table 114, p. 172.

- *Comp-5a* ("CPS/Persons") is based on the Current Population Survey. Data refer to total money income of persons over 14 years of age (including transfer incomes).

- *Comp-5b* ("TM/all returns") is based on tax statistics. Data refer to tax units and their taxable income exclusive of transfer incomes and net of social security contributions. No adjustments are made for incomplete coverage of recipients.

- *Comp-5c* ("CPS/consumer units") is based on the Current Population Survey. In contrast to COMP-5a, distributions are shown for consumer units. Similar to COMP-5a incomes are total monetary incomes (including transfer incomes).

DE-1	Bjerke 1965. Income shares are from Table 1, p. 223. Gini coefficients have been calculated using the method suggested by Morgan 1962. Data refer to tax units and their taxable incomes.
DE-2	Okonomiske Rad 1967. Income shares are from Table 3, p. 21. The Gini coefficient has been calculated according to Morgan 1962. Data refer to tax units and their taxable incomes.
FI-1	Hjerppe and Lefgren 1974. Income shares are from Table 4, p. 113. The data refer to tax units and their taxable incomes after adjustment for incomplete coverage of income recipients.
FI-2	Central Statistical Office of Finland (CSOF) 1975, 1974, 1972, 1965, 1960. Income shares for 1950 to 1957 are from CSOF 1960, Table IV, p. 15; for 1958 to 1961 from CSOF 1965, Table IV, p. 15; for 1962 to 1968 from CSOF 1972, Table V, p. 15; for 1969 from CSOF 1974, Table 4, p. 12, for 1970 from CSOF 1975, Table 7, p. 19. The data refer to tax units and their taxable incomes; this source embraces in principle all income recipients.
GE-1	Statistisches Reichsamt 1939. Income shares are based on the table at p. 660; they have been derived by linear, graphical interpolation.

Data refer to tax units and their taxable incomes. They cover all persons actually employed as well as the elderly irrespective of income size.

GE-2   Statistisches Bundesamt 1954. Income shares are based on Table 2, p. 462; they have been derived by linear, graphical interpolation. Data are based on tax statistics corrected for incomplete coverage of recipients and other outstanding incomparabilities.

GE-3   Statistisches Bundesamt 1973, 1969 and 1954. Income shares are based on T.3, p. 459 (1973); T.2, p. 620 (1969); T.1b, p. 461, cols. 1 and 4 (1954). They have been derived by linear, graphical interpolation. Data are based on adjusted tax statistics.

GE-4   Glatzer 1978. Income shares and Gini coefficients are from T.2a, p. 350, col. 1. Data are based on surveys.

K-1   Kuznets 1963. Income shares are from Table 16, p. 61, "Zeuthen I."

K-2   Kuznets 1963. "Zeuthen II."

K-3   Kuznets 1963. Income shares are from Table 16, p. 60, "Procopovitch."

K-4   Kuznets 1963. "Reich Statistical Office."

K-5   Kuznets 1963. "Müller."

K-6   Kuznets 1963. "Wit."

K-9   Kuznets 1963. "Bowley."

K-10   Kuznets 1963. "Clark."

K-11   Kuznets 1963. "Seers."

K-12   Kuznets 1963. "Lydall."

NE-1   Centraal Planbureau 1975. Income shares are from Table V.1.1b, p. 79; Gini coefficients are from Table 3, p. 161.

SW-1   Schnitzer 1974. Income shares and Gini coefficients are from Table 3.4, p. 79. The data refer to all persons over 20 years and are based on tax statistics, corrected for incomplete coverage of income units and incomes. For the original source see Spant and Seelander 1966.

SZ-1   Noth 1975. Income shares are from Table 17, p. 91. Gini coefficients have been calculated according to Morgan 1962. Data refer to tax units and their taxable incomes. The income tax data are corrected for incomplete coverage and underreporting.

UK-1   Royal Commission on the Distribution of Income and Wealth 1975. Income shares and Gini coefficients are from Table G.1, p. 200. The data refer to tax units and their taxable incomes without adjustments for incomplete coverage of income recipients.

UK-2   Royal Commission on the Distribution of Income and Wealth 1975. Income shares and Gini coefficients are from Table G.5, p. 205. In this source UK-1 is adjusted mainly for incomplete coverage of income recipients and incomes.

US-1   Lebergott 1976. Income shares are based on Table 1, p. 321. Income shares have been derived by linear, graphical interpolation. Data refer to households and their money incomes as well as some incomes in kind (excluding transfer incomes).

US-2   Taussig 1977. Income shares are from Table 4, p. 13. The basic source is Radner and Hinrichs 1974 and refers to the series of the Bureau of Economic Analyses ("BEA"). Data show money incomes (including transfer incomes and net of social security contributions) plus a number of incomes in kind of consumption units. They are based on adjusted tax statistics which are matched by other sources for recent times (Cf. Stark 1977, Taussig 1977).

US-3   Taussig 1977. Income shares are from Table 2, p. 6. Gini coefficients are from Table 3, p. 7, column 4. The basic source is U.S. Bureau of the Census, unpublished estimates. Data refer to the money income (including transfer incomes and gross of social security contributions) of families and unrelated individuals. This source covers almost the whole population.

US-4   Kuznets 1953. Income shares are from Table 122, p. 635. Data are based on tax statistics and are adjusted for numerous deficiencies (most important of which is the correction for incomplete coverage of income recipients).

US-5   Kolko 1962. Income shares are from Table 1, p. 14. The data are based on tax statistics adjusted for incomplete coverage of income units and incomes. American series on income distribution are discussed at length in Lindert and Williamson 1976, Stark 1977 and Taussig 1977.

Notes

1. For a comprehensive overview of the major conceptual problems involved and of imputation procedures used in empirical research see Pfaff and Asam 1978.

2. We are less interested in the distribution of overall welfare than in the generation and transformation of economic inequality by the growth and differentiation of markets, associations, and public bureaucracies. Hence, the graph is based on a concept of income that does not refer to a person's command over *all* goods which are scarce in society—the comprehensive concept of income widely accepted by economists (cf. Atkinson 1975)—but only to those produced by enterprises and by public institutions. Three means of command are distinguished in the graph: disposition of monetary entitlements (to which the first three inequality types in Fig. 6.1 refer), legal entitlements, or mere factual access (which the Final Distribution also takes into account). Those "flows" in Fig. 6.1 marked by double lines indicate additions to and subtractions from the command of private households over goods and resources. "Producer Inequality" refers to unequal factor remuneration in production; any indicator should therefore be based on the total number of individuals and on total gross incomes (including also cash in kind and unrealized capital gains). "Consumer Inequality" refers to access to consumption; hence, inequality indicators should be based on the potential command over goods and services exercised by consumption units.

3. This holds at least in two respects. First, the graph refers only to those flows of goods and money in which private households are directly involved. It does not show transactions among public institutions and enterprises (such as public expenditures for privately produced goods and services, taxes on corporations, etc.). Although certainly important, these are indirect determinants of income inequality. Second, the graph does not provide a complete list of relevant market exchanges and bureaucratic transactions. With respect to the Tertiary Distribution, for example, one might impute the benefits in kind derived from nonfinancial assets (such as the use of owner-occupied dwellings), since at this stage they are economically comparable to the (monetary) benefits of financial assets that are already included in the Primary Distribution. In contrast to the graph, fees might be treated as consumption expenditures, and consequently only the difference between

fees and (estimated) market prices of the consumed public services would be imputed. With respect to the Tertiary Distribution one might also include the effects of producer externalities on consumption (air pollution, etc.).

4. Such an approach is used in Peters' (1974) time series study of redistribution in France, the United Kingdom, and Sweden.

5. Notable exceptions are the early representative studies on income inequality in Norway during the second half of the nineteenth century: Kiaer 1892 and 1911; Kiaer and Hanssen 1898; Statistiske Centralbureau 1897. For a thorough review of sample surveys currently undertaken in Western countries (France, Germany, Ireland, Sweden, the United Kingdom and the United States) see Stark 1977. On the problems of survey-based information in OECD-countries see also Sawyer 1976.

6. Since tax statistics, especially in earlier times, tend to provide only scarce information on the distribution of lower incomes, they need to be supplemented by additional sources (payroll tax statistics, wage and occupational censuses) to approximate the entire distribution.

7. Cf. Seligman 1921, pp. 34-38. Seligman, however, also distinguished a third type, the presumptive income tax: "The system introduced at the outset was not to make any effort to ascertain the exact income of the individuals, but to attempt to reach it approximately by a series of presumptions" (Seligman 1921, p. 35). In our view, this is a predecessor rather than a special type of income tax. For the history of the income tax see also Popitz 1926, and above all Ardant 1971.

8. Both are lump-sum taxes.

9. Popitz 1926, Seligman 1921, Gerloff and Meisel 1928 were the main sources used. Additional information has been derived from several monographs: Brudno and Bower 1957; Chirelstein, Day, Owens, and Surrey 1963; Cobb and Forte 1964; Hoek 1966; Lardi 1970; Norr, Duffy and Sterner 1959; Norr and Kerlan 1966; Statistike Centralbureau 1885.

10. The introductory years refer to "Eidgenössische Krisenabgabe" (Swiss crisis tax)—an extraordinary, but comprehensive income tax of the central government. It was levied for the years 1933-1937. Since 1941, the "Eidgenössische Wehrsteuer" (Swiss military tax), also a comprehensive income tax, is raised at two-year intervals. Cf. Lardi 1970.

11. This applies to income-tax systems where levies are divided into two, i.e., the wage tax and the income tax. In these cases certain income recipients are covered in the wage-tax statistics (with their employment incomes), as well as in the income tax statistics (with their entrepreneurial and property incomes).

12. According to this broad concept, not only the income of children, but also of relatives living in the same household are pooled together and treated as one income (as was the case in Prussia prior to 1891, for example). At the present time, the household concept is generally restricted to married couples only. In practice, therefore, the income units shown in tax statistics are composed partially of households and partially of individuals.

13. Stark 1977 provides income distributions for consumer units, households, individuals, and tax units. However, since the data are from different sources, biases cannot reliably be judged. See also Sawyer 1976 and Titmuss 1962.

14. The data for tax units are from various statistical yearbooks and income tax statistics. The data for active population are from Alber 1976. They are based essentially on Bairoch et al. 1968 and OECD 1972 and 1974 and are linearly interpolated between census years. Except for Austria (prior to World War I) and Prussia, no provision has been made for differences in the definition of

income units. Since the method of interpolation used is rather crude, and because recipients of *taxable* transfer payments are included in the number of tax units, the coverage can well exceed 100%. See also United Nations 1957, p. IX-3, Table 1 for alternative coverage data for several western European countries immediately prior to and after World War II. These figures differ from each other, because the United Nations data refer to adjusted tax records and to population aged 15 and over.

15. They are, however, of minor importance until very recently.

16. Cf. United Nations 1957, Appendix B, pp. 33-35, and Stark 1977. For an attempt to assess the likely impact of items missing from official statistics on the distribution of incomes see Atkinson 1975.

17. Data on an appropriate basis, i.e., total private incomes of households, are very scarce prior to World War II. See Kraus 1979. For sparse data on income coverage immediately before and after World War II see United Nations 1957, p. IX-3, Table 1.

18. For recent income-coverage ratios of survey-based distribution for OECD-countries see Sawyer 1976.

19. Except for Denmark, where taxable incomes come close to the posttax distribution. See Bjerke 1965 and 1956.

20. For Italy, no tax-record based statistics could be found up to the present day. For the post-World War II period, however, survey-based information is available. For the Republic of Ireland, tax statistics provide size-distribution data only for those incomes subject to the supplementary income tax. Since it is a surtax, only top incomes are covered. Survey-based distributions are available, but are rather scanty (Stark 1977).

21. Reference could be made to total active population or to the population aged 15 and over.

22. This is due to low coverage prior to World War I. For a fine example see the study by Schultz 1967 on Dutch inequality.

23. Such as comparability of definitions and concepts between tax statistics and additional sources.

24. For example, the income share of the top x% in the total income of all private households. This procedure has been adopted by Kuznets 1963, and by Müller and Geisenberger 1972.

25. Schmoller 1896.

26. Kiaer 1914.

27. Pareto 1897.

28. United Nations/ECE 1957. This study provides data on the structure and the overall level of income inequality before and after tax. For a few countries, pretax distributions are also shown by industrial sector and by occupational status. The data are from tax statistics; several weaknesses have been adjusted to ensure comparability.

29. Kuznets 1963.

30. United Nations/ECE 1967. This collection is based on tax statistics, which, contrary to the 1957 study by the same commission, have not been adjusted.

31. The author provides decile distributions of pretax incomes. The data are from unadjusted tax records.

32. Sawyer 1976. The study provides data on the structure and overall level of income before and after tax. Data are from tax statistics and surveys. For no country are figures on trends in income distribution based merely on tax returns. Thus, comparability of the figures is relatively high.

33. Stark 1977. This study provides the most comparable data available to date.

Data refer to inequality before and after taxation. Data are from surveys and/or adjusted tax records. Stark also gives detailed information on the data sources for each country.

34. For a different kind of survey of trends in income distribution in some Western countries, see Tinbergen 1975a. Tinbergen also provides some data on posttax inequality and on redistribution. See in addition Tinbergen 1975b.

35. Low coverage in earlier periods restricts long-term information to these top strata.

36. See the detailed distributions in United Nations/ECE 1957, 1967 and in Roberti 1974.

37. An increase of the income share of the bottom 60% tentatively (neglecting distributive changes within the respective groups) represents a movement toward greater equality (in the sense of the proposed equality line), while in the case of the remaining upper deciles an increase means greater inequality.

38. That is, the total degree of inequality. A variety of statistics can be used to summarize the entire distribution in a single value. All summary statistics evaluate the actual distribution against a hypothetical one of perfect equality. These statistics differ from each other with respect to implicit definition of equality. Hence, a comparison of the same actual distributions by different summary statistics leads to different conclusions with respect to the exact margins of change in the overall level of inequality. Results become ambiguous in those cases where the Lorenz-curves of the actual distributions do intersect, i.e. where the cumulative income shares of an actual distribution A are not consistently lower (or higher) than those of an actual distribution B throughout the entire distributions. These questions are discussed at length in Atkinson 1970, Sen 1973, Stark 1972, Allison 1978. For differences in the sensitivity of various summary statistics to a given change in the distribution see Sawyer 1976. For a completely different view on appropriate inequality measures see Wiles 1974.

39. The Gini coefficient, a measure of concentration, is the most popular summary statistic. It is the ratio of the extent of the deviation of the actual distribution from one of perfect equality (i.e. where everyone has the same income) to the maximum degree of inequality (i.e. where one recipient gets all the income). Stated technically: the Gini-Index is exactly one-half of the arithmetic average of the absolute values of differences between all pairs of income (cf. Sen 1973, p. 30). The coefficient can range from 0, indicating perfect equality, to 1, indicating maximum inequality. For a graphic explanation of the Gini coefficient see Sen 1973, p. 29.

40. In the case of Prussia, however, alternative estimates show different trends. This is due predominantly to differences in the series on national income. Source "PR-1" is to be preferred, since both the underlying estimate of national income and the adjusted data from tax records are much more reliable.

41. Hence, interpretations of cross-national patterns of the levels of income shares are much more tentative than are those of trends.

42. Hjerppe and Lefgren 1974 (Table 4, p. 113) report a similar experience for Finland: according to their study the top 5% of all income recipients received about 31% in 1881 but only about 15% in 1966. This study has not been included in our survey, because data are provided for three time points only.

43. Of course, income shares are difficult to compare over such a long period. Figures on initial shares are clearly subject to greater margins of error than

are recent shares. It should also be noted that initial shares are far less reliable for Denmark and the United Kingdom (extremely defective and scarce data bases for earlier periods) than for the United States or particularly for Prussia. Nonetheless, the exact magnitude of change is clearly also disputable for the latter two countries. The income share for Germany in 1968 is very likely overestimated, and hence the long-term decline underestimated: survey-based information suggests a share of 23.3% in 1969 (cf. Glatzer 1978). Although data for the initial American share are not from Kolko 1962, who has recently been criticized for considerable underestimation of early inequality and hence also of the long-run decline (cf. Lindner and Williamson 1976), but have been derived instead from the fairly well-based estimate by Lebergott 1976, early inequality might still be underestimated. Despite these weaknesses and imponderabilities, the main conclusion should nevertheless hold: the long run behavior of income shares in Denmark and the United Kingdom are too different from the American and German one.

44. Although Lebergott's data are difficult to compare with the estimates for successive years provided by Kolko (1962) or by Kuznets 1953, this view is tentatively supported by several other inequality "proxies," presented in Williamson 1975. It can reasonably be assumed that upper income shares around 1930 were markedly higher than around the turn of the century, although the exact order of magnitude might be questioned.

45. According to Hjerppe and Lefgren 1974 in Finland the top 5% (as well as the top 10% of all recipients markedly increased income shares in the late nineteenth century (from 31 or 39% in 1881 to about 40 or 50% in 1800) and probably even up to the outset of World War I.

46. For a much more detailed view of the historical inequality experience of the United States see Williamson 1975 and Lindert and Williamson 1976.

47. Compare the respective income shares listed in the Appendix across time.

48. Data provided by the Royal Commission on the Distribution of Income and Wealth 1975 seem to indicate a rise of about 4% between 1938 and 1949. As the commission points out, however, "the table for 1938 is not comparable to the distributions covering the postwar years" (p. 197). In contrast, United Nations/ECE 1957 adjusted data for the low coverage in 1938; these roughly comparable estimates suggest basic stability.

49. It should be pointed out, however, that the German tax based data suffer from a number of shortcomings. In addition, decile shares have been derived rather crudely by linear interpolation. Nonetheless there is some indication that the trend pattern is by and large correct. A comparison with survey-based information (cf. Glatzer 1978) shows differing levels for the available two years, but a similar—though less spectacular—trend. The trend pattern of the tax-based distributions also roughly corresponds to that of the series shown in United Nations/ECE 1967, which includes, however, undistributed profits of corporations.

50. See p. 323 as well as note 36. In terms of the Lorenz-curve, the lower part of the curve tentatively moves toward the line of perfect equality while in the medium part it tends to move away from it. Thus, intersecting curves are not unlikely. Where intersections occur, different summary statistics might yield quite different changes in the overall level of inequality. See Atkinson 1975 and notes 38 and 39 above.

51. Due to low coverage, prior to World War II the proportion of income units belonging to the lowest income range is too large to allow for confident calculation of overall levels of inequality.

52. According to source "UK-1," most of the change seems to have occurred during the decade from 1939 to 1949. Source "COMP-1," however, reports basic stability. The divergent results cannot be explained by internal incomparabilities of source "UK-1"(see note 48 above): source "COMP-1" reports the same Gini coefficient for 1939, although it is based on a much more comprehensive distribution for that year. For the successive years source "UK-1" in addition reports a stronger decline than does the far more reliable source "UK-2." Thus it might well be that inequality remained basically stable during 1939 to 1949; for successive years a moderate decline in inequality seems most realistic. For a review of several studies on postwar changes in the distribution of pretax incomes see Roberti 1975.

53. Finnish tax statistics cover also income recipients with extremely low incomes. Young people still living with their parents are separately assessed. Thus, the rising entrance age of work-force participants and increasing part-time work are at least partially responsible for the reported rise in inequality. Although in none of the other West European countries are tax statistics limited only to the incomes of adult, full-time employed, the inclusion of part-time incomes is most extreme in the Finnish case. Thus, compared to the other countries Finland might in fact have experienced basic stability. Actually, the recent study on long-run trends in Finland's income distribution by Hjerppe and Lefgren concludes that "from the early 1950s to 1967 there appears to have been a stability of income inequality if not a slight widening" (cf. Hjerppe and Lefgren 1974, p. 118). However, whether the strong increase in the share of the top income recipients is due to these factors alone seems disputable. For a discussion of tax-record based inequality data as well as survey-based data for the Scandinavian countries see Uusitalo 1973.

54. Source "SW-1" refers to adult persons only and therefore tends to overestimate the decline in overall inequality when compared to the coverage of tax records. For a discussion of these data see Stark 1977, p. 146. Source "COMP-3" refers to unadjusted tax data. The variability of the level of inequality over time thus might be due to variations in tax thresholds and inflation.

55. Cf. Müller and Geisenberger 1972.

56. A similar pattern is reported for Prussia at the regional level: in predominantly agrarian regions the upper income shares generally have risen up to World War I, whereas in industrializing regions trend breaks can be observed. See Geisenberger and Müller 1972, pp. 46 ff.

57. Cf. Kuznets 1966.

58. This kind of distribution should not be confused with the functional distribution, which also includes imputed labor incomes of the self-employed in labor's share.

59. For the period 1952 to 1970 shares have been calculated from national accounts statistics, which are based on the accounting system of the Statistical Office of the European Communities (1973). See Statistical Office of the European Communities 1974 and 1973. Prior to World War II data are from country studies: Austria: Kausel, Németh, and Seidel 1965; Finland: Central Statistical Office of Finland 1958; Germany: Jeck 1970, Statistisches Bundesamt 1972; Norway: Statistisk Sentralbyrg 1965; Jungenfelt 1966; Eidgenössisches Statistisches Amt 1965 and 1941; United Kingdom: Feinstein 1972.

60   Cf. United Nations/ECE 1957, 1967 and above all Lydall 1968. See also Phelps-Brown 1977.

61. See Kuznets 1966; Kraus 1979.
62. For general overviews, see Bjerke 1961; Bronfenbrenner 1971; and above all Sahota 1978.
63. This section is confined to those statistical studies that deal with inequality in the context of economic and political development. Studies which deal with more specific aspects are already well reviewed: Mincer 1970; Blaug 1976; Carnoy 1977 survey the empirical work on education, skill, and earnings inequality. With respect to schooling and inequality see also Levine and Bane 1975. Wilensky 1978 compares the sociologist's approach to earnings inequality with that of the labor market economists and provides a very useful summary of the major findings. We have also excluded studies that attempt to explain changes in income inequality by economic developments only. Some of these studies are highly relevant and sophisticated—apart from the pioneering works of Tinbergen, e.g., the quantitative historical studies by Williamson 1975 on the United States, by Schultz 1967 on the Netherlands, and the study by Müller and Geisenberger 1972 on Prussia and not yet summarized elsewhere, but they clearly deserve separate attention.
64. Kuznets 1955, 1963, and 1966.
65. Lenski 1966.
66. For an introduction see Lall 1975; Portes 1976.
67. Rubinson and Quinlan 1976.
68. Core-states of the world-economy exploiting peripheral areas. See Wallerstein's study on the origins of the European world-economy in the sixteenth century (Wallerstein 1974).
69. For a recent survey of cross-national findings on the impact of foreign investment and aid on inequality, see Bornschier, Chase-Dunn, and Rubinson 1978.
70. The following cross-national studies have been selected: Cameron 1976; Cutright 1967; Hewitt 1977; Jackman 1975; Rubinson and Quinlan 1976; Rubinson and Quinlan 1977. Steven Stack's study (Stack 1978) appeared too late to be included.
71. Most common are dependency aspects. They are taken into account by Cutright 1967 (indirect measures of penetration), Jackman 1975 (trade patterns), Rubinson and Quinlan 1976, 1977 (size and pattern of foreign trade; strength of the state in the world economy), and by Peters 1973 (indirect measures of penetration). Thus, the relationships reported are controlled for these aspects, which means that the reported impacts of national developments hold independent of external factors.
72. Peters 1973.
73. Such a proxy is used in the studies of Cutright and of Jackman. Kuznets (1963) originally proposed this indicator as an approximation of unequal factor remuneration. The validity of this indicator, however, is highly debatable. According to Jackman 1975 (p. 20), a study by J. Romaninsky reports a .82 correlation between Gini coefficients of intersectoral income inequality with those of personal income inequality for a cross-section of 48 American states in 1950. However, our own crude calculations for a subsample of Jackman's country set have shown a very modest correlation between his indirect measure of equality and Gini-Indexes of inequality of pretax incomes ($r = -.64$).
74. Interpretation and measurement are likely most discrepant in Jackman's study, in which sectoral differences in labor productivity—a proxy at best for

producer inequality—is used as an indicator even for inequalities in the potential command over goods and resources (i.e. the most comprehensive concept of consumer inequality). Since this is extremely speculative—no theoretical link seems plausible—we have reinterpreted it as a measure of producer inequality.

75. In line with Jackman, rates of economic growth in the following are taken as an indicator of short-run growth of surplus, and consequently interpreted as a test of Lenki's hypotheses on rising surplus and inequality. See Jackman 1975, p. 43.

76. Jackman uses the share of civilian public expenditures in national product as an indicator of the state's commitment to welfare. Since his inequality indicator at best measures producer inequality, i.e. does not tap aspects of redistribution, the proposed relationship should be dropped. To arrive at more consistent conclusions, this indicator is reinterpreted as a measure of the direct economic involvement of the state in the economy.

77. In both studies the inequality data at best indicate inequalities in factor remuneration, but hardly in posttransfer incomes—which these approaches actually presuppose.

78. This is due to the fact that Cameron refers to the relationship between higher education and the income share of only the top 20%

79. The effects are similar irrespective whether Jackman's index of Democratic Performance or Cutright's Political Representativeness Index was used.

80. An alternative specification, that inequality affects democratization, has also gained empirical support. This view was even strenghtened in a reciprocal model which was developed to assess the relative validity of each specification.

81. Similar results have been found for the effects of inequality on state strength in the international system as well as of trade relations and direct economic penetration. Internal governmental state strength, however, showed the most robust effects.

82. With the exception of Jackman, where the scope of the state, measured by the share of civilian public expenditure in national product, was not related to inequality in a statistically significant manner. Because of the extreme unreliability of the inequality indicator used, however, not too much stress can be placed on this contradictory finding.

83. Stack 1978.

84. Stack 1978, p. 886.

85. That is, these two factors have not been deduced by theoretical reasoning, but instead by interpreting the loadings that emerged as a result of a rather restrictive kind of factor analysis (principal component approach with varimax rotation).

86. The pattern of factor loadings is somewhat ambiguous, however. In both countries political factors clustered together with economic factors. Surplus, one of the two extracted basic factors, is characterized by the loadings of the two indicators of economic development (energy consumption, per capita incomes), an indicator of class-structure (share of agricultural labor force— probably an indicator of economic development as well) and extension of franchise. To take account of the latter, Peters labels this factor somewhat vaguely "availability of an economic surplus which could be used for redistribution along with the access of the total population to political means of affecting the character of that redistribution" (p. 113). The second basic factor, the power factor, is characterized by the loadings of rather heterogen-

ous factors like propertied class interest (farm rental) and a conglomerate of rather different elite decision variables (capital formation, external trade, defense expenditures, etc.).

87. Peters 1973, p. 114.
88. This is due to technical reasons: high intercorrelations among the independent variables prohibited the use of corresponding statistical techniques (cf. Peters 1973, p. 113).
89. Most of the variations in franchise occurred during the first subperiod. As franchise is one of the components of the surplus factor, a different intrepretation of this factor has to be adopted for the first and for the second subperiod. While for the latter interpretation as economic surplus seems appropriate, for the former the political component (i.e. class relations) needs to be strengthened. In line with Lenski's reasonings, the surplus factor theoretically should have played a dominant role during the first subperiod, which it obviously did not.
90. Peters 1973, p. 117.
91. Cf. Flanagan and Ulman 1971.
92. Peters 1973.
93. See for example Kuznets 1963; Lydall 1959; Schultz 1967, 1969 and 1971; Metcalf 1969; Chiswick and Mincer 1972; Beach 1976. Budd and Whiteman 1978 report a much smaller impact, however.
94. See Nordhaus 1975, Hibbs 1977.

References

Alber, Jens. 1976. "Social Security I: Participants of Social Insurance Systems in Western Europe." HIWED - Research Project. University of Cologne. Report No. 4. Mannheim: mimeo.

Allison, Paul D. 1978. "Measures of Inequality." *American Sociological Review*, 43, pp. 865-880.

Ardant, Gabriel. 1971. *Histoire de L'impôt*. Paris: Librairie Arthéme Fayard.

Atkinson, Anthony B. 1975. *The Economics of Inequality*. Oxford: Oxford University Press.

Atkinson, Anthony B. 1970. "On the Measurement of Inequality." *Journal of Economic Theory*, 2, pp. 244-263.

Bairoch, P.; Deldycke, T.; Gelders, H. and Limbor, J. M. 1968. *La Population active et la Structure*. Bruxelles; Editions de L'Institut de Sociologie.

Beach, C. M. 1976. "Cyclical Impacts on the Personal Distribution of Income." *Annals of Economic and Social Measurement*, 5, pp. 29-52.

Bjerke, Kjeld. 1965. "Forskydninger i den personlige indkomstfordeling 1939 til 1964." *Socialt Tidsskrift*, 41, pp. 220-230.

Bjerke, Kjeld. 1961. "Some Income and Wage Distribution Theories." *Weltwirtschaftliches Archiv*, 86, pp. 46-68.

Bjerke, Kjeld. 1956. "Changes in Danish Income Distribution 1939-1952." In *Income & Wealth*, Series VI, pp. 98-154. London: Bowes and Bowes.

Blaug, Mark. 1976. "The Empirical Status of Human Capital Theory: A Slightly Jaundiced Survey." *Journal of Economic Literature*, 14 pp. 827-855.

Bornschier, Volker; Chase-Dunn, Christopher and Rubinson, Richard. 1978. Cross-national Evidence of the Effects of Foreign Investment and Aid on Economic Growth and Inequality: A Survey of Findings and a Reanalysis." *American Journal of Sociology*, 84, pp. 651-683.

Bronfenbrenner, Martin, 1971. *Income Distribution Theory*. London: Macmillan.

Brudno, Walter and Bower, Frank. 1957. *Taxation in the United Kingdom.* World Tax Series. Boston; Toronto: Little, Brown and Company.

Budd, Edward and Whiteman, T.C. 1978. "Macroeconomic Fluctuations and the Size Distribution of Income and Earnings in the United States." In *Income Distribution and Economic Inequality,* eds. Zvi Griliches; Wilhelm Krelle; Hans-Jürgen Krupp and Oldrich Kyn, pp. 11-27. Frankfurt: Campus-Verlag; New York: Halsted Press, John Wiley & Sons.

Cameron, David R. 1976. *Inequality and the State: A Political Economic Comparison.* Paper prepared for delivery at the 1976 Annual Meeting of the American Political Science Association.

Carnoy, Martin. 1977. "Education and Economic Development: The First Generation." *Economic Development and Cultural Change,* 25, Supplement, pp. 428-448.

Centraal Planbureau. 1975. "De personele inkomensverdeling 1952-1967." Monografien No. 19. s'Gravenhage: Staatsuitg.

Central Statistical Office of Finland. 1975. "Statistics of Income Property. 1970, 1971." Official Statistics of Finland, IV B:37. Helsinki.

Central Statistical Office of Finland. 1974. "Statistics of Income and Property. 1974, 1969." Official Statistics of Finland. IV B: 36. Helsinki.

Central Statistical Office of Finland. 1972. "Statistics of Income and Property. 1968." Official Statistics of Finland. IV B: 35. Helsinki.

Central Statistical Office of Finland. 1965. "Statistics of Income and Property. 1965." Official Statistics of Finland. IV B: 32. Helsinki.

Central Statistical Office of Finland. 1960. "Statistics of Income and Property. 1957." Official Statistics of Finland. IV B: 24. Helsinki.

Central Statistical Office of Finland. 1958. "National Accounting in Finland, 1948-1964." Helsinki.

Chirelstein, Marvin; Day, Langdon; Owens, Elisabeth and Surrey, Stanley. 1963. *Taxation in the United States.* World Tax Series. Chicago: Commerce Clearing House, Inc.

Chiswick, Barry R. and Mincer, Jacob. 1972. "Time-Series Changes in Personal Income Inequality in the United States from 1939, with Projections to 1985." *Journal of Political Economy,* 80, pp. 34-66.

Cobb, Charles K. and Forte, Francesco. 1964. *Taxation in Italy.* World Tax Series. Chicago: Commerce Clearing House, Inc.

Cutright, Phillips. 1967. "Inequality: A Cross-national Analysis." *American Sociological Review,* 32, pp. 562-578.

Eidgenössisches Statistisches Amt. 1965. "Volkswirtschaftliche Gesamtrechnung der Schweiz für die Jahre 1938 und 1948 bis 1963." Die Volkswirtschaft. Bern.

Eidgenössisches Statistisches Amt. 1941. "Schweizerisches Volkseinkommen 1924, 1929 bis 1938." Beiträge zur Schweizerischen Statistik, Heft 9, Reihe G a 1. Bern.

Feinstein, Charles H. 1972. *National Income, Expenditure and Output of the United Kingdom 1855-1965.* Cambridge: Cambridge University Press.

Flanagan, Robert and Ulman, Lloyd. 1971. "Wage Restraint. A Study of Incomes Policies in Western Europe." Berkeley: University of California Press.

Gerloff, Wilhelm and Meisel, Franz (eds.). 1925-1929. *Handbuch der Finanzwirtschaft,* 3 volumes. Tübingen: Mohr.

Glatzer, Wolfgang. 1978. "Einkommenspolitische Zielsetzungen und Einkommensverteilung." In *Lebensbedingungen in der Bundesrepublik,* ed. Wolfgang Zapf, pp. 323-384. Frankfurt/Main: Campus.

Hewitt, Christopher. 1977. "The effect of political democracy and social democracy on equality in industrial societies: A cross-national comparison." *American Sociological Review,* 42, pp. 450-464.

Hibbs, Douglas A. Jr. 1977. "Political Parties and Macroeconomic Policy." *American Political Science Review*, 71, pp. 467-487.

Hjerppe, Riitta and Lefgren, John. 1974. "Suomen tulonja kaufman kehityksestä 1881-1967." *Kansantaloudellinen aikakauskirja*, pp. 97-119.

Hoek, Jan. 1966. "Die Entwicklung der Einkommensbesteuerung in Belgien vom Ende des Ancien Régime bis heute."'(Dissertation). Riehan: Merkel Druck.

Jackman, Robert W. 1975. *Politics and Social Equality: A Comparative Analysis*. London; New York: John Wiley & Sons.

Jeck, Albert. 1970. *Wachstum und Verteilung des Volkseinkommens*. Tübingen: J. C. B. Mohr.

Jungenfelt, Karl G. 1966. *Löneandelen och den ekonomiska utvecklingen*. Uppsala: Almqvist & Wiksell.

Kausel, Anton; Németh, Nandor and Seidel, Hans. 1965. Österreichs Volkseinkimmen 1913-1963." Sonderheft des "Österreichischen Statistischen Zentralamtes. Wien: Carl Ueberreuter.

Kiaer, Anders N. 1914. "Indtaegtsforhold i Sverige og Norge for personer av forskjellig kjön, alder og aegteskapelig stilling." *Statsvetenskaplig Tidskrift*, 17, pp. 215-253.

Kiaer, Anders N. 1911. "Tillaegsopgaver Vedkommende Indtaegtsforhold." Udarbeitet til Bruk for den Departementale Folkeforsikringskomite. Kristiania: Bjørnstads Boktrykkeri.

Kiaer, Anders, N. 1892. "Indtaegts- og formuesforhold i Norge." Tillaeg til *Staatsøkonomisk tidskrift*, 1892, pp. 1-50.

Kiaer, Anders N. and Hanssen, Paator E. 1898. "Socialstatistik." Vol. 1. Bilag tilden parlamentariske Arbeiderkommissions Indstilling. Kristiania: O. Christiansens.

Kolko, Gabriel. 1962. *Wealth and Power in America*. London: Thames and Hudson.

Kraus, Franz. 1979. *Growth and Structure of National Income in Western Europe*. HIWED-Report No. 10, Köln: mimeograph.

Kuznets, Simon. 1966. *Modern Economic Growth. Rate, Structure, and Spread*. New Haven and London: Yale University Press.

Kuznets, Simon. 1963. "Quantitative Aspects of the Economic Growth of Nations: VIII. Distribution of Income by Size." *Economic Development and Cultural Change*, IX, part II, pp. 1-80.

Kuznets, Simon. 1955. "Economic Growth and Income Inequality." *American Economic Review*, 45, pp. 1-28.

Kuznets, Simon. 1953. *The Share of the Upper Income Groups in Income and Savings*. New York: National Bureau of Economic Research.

Lall, Sanjaya. 1975. "Is 'Dependence' a Useful Concept in Analyzing Underdevelopment?" *World Development*, 3, pp. 799-810.

Lardi, Peter. 1970. "Empirische Untersuchungen zur personellen Einkommensverteilung in der Schweiz. (Dissertation). Riehan: A. Schudel & Co. AG.

Lebergott, Stanley. 1976. *The American Economy*. Princeton: Princeton University Press.

Lenski, Gerhard. 1966. *Power and Privilege: A Theory of Social Stratification*. New York: McGraw-Hill Book Company.

Levine, Donald and Bane, Mary. 1975. *The "Inequality" Controversy: Schooling and Distributive Justice*. New York: Basic Books, Inc.

Lindert, Peter H. and Williamson, Jeffrey G. 1976. *Three Centuries of American Inequality*. Institute for Research on Poverty, Discussion Papers 333-76. University of Wisconsin - Madison.

Lydall, Harold. 1968. *The Structure of Earnings*. Oxford: Clarendon Press.

Lydall, Harold. 1959. "The Long-term Trend in the Size Distribution of Income." *Journal of the Royal Statistical Society*, 122, series A, part 1: pp. 1-46.

Metcalf, Charles E. 1969. "The Size Distribution of Personal Income during the Business Cycle." *American Economic Review*, 59, pp. 657-668.

Mincer, Jacob. 1970. "The Distribution of Labor Incomes: A Survey." *Journal of Economic Literature*, 8, pp. 1-26.

Morgan, James. 1962. "The Anatomy of Income Distribution." *Review of Economics and Statistics*, 44, pp. 270-283.

Morley, Samuel and Williamson, Jeffrey. 1977. "Class Pay Differentials, Wage Stretching, and Early Capitalist Development." *Economic Development and Cultural Change*, 25, Supplement, pp. 407-427.

Müller, J. Heinz and Geisenberger, Siegfried. 1972. *Die Einkommensstruktur in verschiedenen deutschen Ländern 1874-1913*. Berlin: Duncker & Humblot.

Nordhaus, William D. 1975. "The Political Business Cycle." *Review of Economic Studies*, 42, pp. 160-190.

Norr, Martin and Kerlan, Pierre. 1966. *Taxation in France*. World Tax Series. Chicago: Commerce Clearing House, Inc.

Norr, Martin; Duffy, Frank J. and Sterner, Harry. 1959. *Taxation in Sweden*. World Tax Series. Boston, Toronto: Little, Brown and Company.

Noth, Albert. 1975. "Die personelle Einkommensverteilung in der Schweiz. (Dissertation). Freiburg (Switzerland): mimeograph.

O. E. C. D. 1974. "Labour Force Statistics." Paris.

O. E. C. D. 1972. "Labour Force Statistics." Paris.

Okonomiske Råd. 1967. "Den personlige indkomstfordeling og indkomstudjaevningen over de offentlige finanser." København: Statens Trykningskontor.

Pareto, Vilfredo. 1897. *Cours d'Economie Politique*. Lausanne: Rouge.

Peters, B. Guy. 1974. "Income Redistribution: A Longitudinal Analysis of France, Sweden and the United Kingdom." *Political Studies*, XXII, 3, pp. 311-323.

Peters, B. Guy. 1973. "Income Inequality in Sweden and the United Kingdom: A Longitudinal Analysis." *Acta Sociologica*, 16, pp. 108-120.

Pfaff, Martin and Asam, Wolfgang. 1978. "Distributive Effects of Real Transfers via Public Infrastructure: Conceptual Problems and Some Empirical Results." In *Income Distribution and Economic Inequality*, eds. Zvi Griliches, Wilhelm Kreue, Hans Jürgen Krupp, and Oldrich Kyn, pp. 66-96. New York; Toronto; Chichester; Halsted Press, John Wiley & Sons; Frankfurt/Main; Campus-Verlag.

Phelps-Brown, Henry. 1977. *The Inequality of Pay*. Oxford: Oxford University Press.

Popitz, Johannes. 1926. "Einkommenssteuer." In *Handwörterbuch der Staatswissenschaften*, eds. Ludwig Elster, Adolf Weber and Friedrich Weiser, 3, pp. 400-491. Jena: Verlag von Gustav Fischer.

Portes, Alejandro. 1976. "The Sociology of National Development." *American Journal of Sociology*, 82, pp. 55-85.

Radner, Daniel B. and Hinrichs, John C. 1974. "Size Distribution of Income in 1964, 1970, and 1971." *Survey of Current Business*, 50, No. 10.

Roberti, Paolo, 1975. "Did the UK Trend towards Equality Really Come to an End by 1957?" *International Journal of Social Economics*, 2, No. 1, pp. 53-59.

Roberti, Paolo. 1974. "Income Distribution: A Time-Series and a Cross-Section Study." *Economic Journal*, 84, pp. 629-638.

Rubinson, Richard and Quinlan, Dan. 1977. "Democracy and Social Inequality: A Reanalysis." *American Sociological Review*, 42, pp. 611-623.

Rubinson, Richard and Quinlan, Dan. 1976. "The World Economy and the Distribution of Income within States: A Cross-national Study." *American Sociological Review*, 41, pp. 638-659.

Royal Commission on the Distribution of Income and Wealth. 1975. "Initial Report on the Standing Reference." London: Her Majesty's Stationary Office.

Sahota, Gian S. 1978. "Theories of Personal Income Distribution: A Survey." *Journal of Economic Literature*, 16, pp. 1-55.

Sawyer, Malcolm. 1976. "Income Distribution in OECD Countries." *OECD Economic Outlook (Occasional Studies)*, July 1976, pp. 3-36.

Schmoller, Gustav. 1896. "Die Einkommensverteilung in alter und neuer Zeit." *Bulletin de L'Institut International de Statistique*, IX, 2e et derniére Livraison, pp. 1-22.

Schnitzer, Martin. 1974. *Income Distribution. A Comparative Study of the United States, Sweden, West Germany, East Germany, the United Kingdom, and Japan.* New York; Washington; London: Praeger Publishers.

Schultz, T. Paul. 1971. *Long-term Change in Personal Income Distribution: Theoretical Approaches, Evidence and Explanations.* Santa Monica: Rand Corporation.

Schultz, T. Paul. 1969. "Secular Trends and Cyclical Behavior of the Income Distribution in the United States: 1944-1965." In *Six Papers on the Size Distribution of Income and Wealth*, ed. Lee Soltow, Studies in Income and Wealth, 33, pp. 75-100.

Schultz, T. Paul. 1967. "Secular Equalization and Cyclical Behaviour of Income Distribution." *Review of Economics and Statistics*, 49, pp. 259-267.

Selander, Pebbe and Spant, R. 1966. "Inkomstfördelningen i Sverige 1951-1966." Uppsala University (unpubl. study).

Seligman, Edwin. 1921. *The Income Tax. A Study of the History, Theory and Practice of Income Taxation at Home and Abroad.* New York: The Macmillan Company.

Sen, Amartya K. 1973. *On Economic Inequality.* Oxford: Clarendon Press.

Stack, Steven. 1978. "The Effect of Direct Government Involvement in the Economy and the Degree of Income Inequality: A Cross-national Study." *American Sociological Review*, 43, pp. 880-888.

Stark, Thomas. 1977. "The Distribution of Income in Eight Countries." Royal Commission on the Distribution of Income and Wealth, Background Paper No. 4. London: Her Majesty's Stationary Office.

Stark, Thomas. 1972. *The Distribution of Personal Income in the United Kingdom 1949-1963.* London: Cambridge University Press.

Statistical Office of the European Communities. 1974. "National Accounts. 1960-1973." Luxembourg.

Statistical Office of the European Communities. 1973. "National Accounts. 1951-1972." Luxembourg.

Statistisches Bundesamt. 1973. "Einheitliche Schichtung der Lohn- und Einkommensteuerpflichtigen nach der Höhe ihrer steuerlichen Einkünfte 1968. Ergebnis der Lohn- und Einkommensteuerstatistik 1968." Wirtschaft und Statistik, pp. 457-461.

Statistisches Bundesamt. 1972. "Bevölkerung und Wirtschaft 1872 bis 1972." Stuttgart; Mainz: W. Kohlhammer.

Statistisches Bundesamt. 1969. "Einheitliche Schichtung der Lohn- und Einkommensteuerpflichtigen nach der Höhe ihrer steuerlichen Einkünfte 1965. Ergebnis der Lohn- und Einkommensteurstatistik 1965." Wirtschaft und Statistik, pp. 617-621.

Statistisches Bundesamt. 1954. "Versuch eines Vergleichs der Einkommensschichtung in der Bundesrepublik Deutschland 1950 und im Deutschen Reich 1936." Wirtschaft und Statistik, pp. 457-460.

Statistisches Reichsamt. 1939. Die Einkommensschichtung im Deutschen Reich. Wirtschaft und Statistik, 19, pp. 660-664.

Statistisk Sentralbyrå. 1965. "Nasjonalregnskap 1865-1960." Oslo.

Statistiske Centralbureau. 1897. "Statistiske Opylsninger om Indtaegts - og Formuesforhold." Socialstatistik II, Norges Officielle Statistik, Tredie Raekke No. 255. Kristiania: H. Aschehoug & Co.

Statistiske Centralbureau. 1885. "Öfversigt af inkomstbevillningens resultater år 1881." Bidrag till Finlands Officiela Statistik, IV, Förmögenhets-Förhallanden, 4. Helsingfors: Kejserliga Senatens Tryckeri.

Taussig, Michael K. 1977. *Trends in Inequality of Well-Offness in the United States since World War II.* Madison: Institute for Research on Poverty at the University of Wisconsin-Madison.

Tinbergen, Jan. 1975a. *Income Distribution. Analysis and Policies.* Amsterdam: North Holland Publishing Company.

Tinbergen, Jan. 1975b. *Income Differences, Recent Research.* Amsterdam: North Holland Publishing Company.

Titmuss, Richard M. 1962. *Income Distribution and Social Change.* London: Allen & Unwin Ltd.

United Nations. Research and Planning Division. Economic Commission for Europe. 1957. Economic Survey of Europe in 1956.

United Nations, Secretariat of the Economic Commission for Europe. 1967. "Incomes in Postwar Europe: A Study of Policies, Growth and Distribution." Economic Survey of Europe in 1965, Part 2.

Uusitalo, Hannu. 1973. *On the distribution of income in Scandinavia.* Research Group for Comparative Sociology. University of Helsinki. Research Report No. 2, Helsinki.

Wallerstein, Immanuel. 1974. *The Modern World System: Capitalist Agriculture and the Origins of the European World-Economy in the Sixteenth Century.* New York: Academic Press.

Wilensky, Harold L. 1978. "The Political Economy of Income Distribution: Issues in the Analysis of Government Approaches to the Reduction of Inequality." In *Major Social Issues: A Multidisciplinary View,* eds. Milton, Singer and Stephen J. Cutler, pp. 87-108. New York: The Free Press.

Wiles, Peter. 1974. *Distribution of Income: East and West.* Amsterdam: North Holland Publishing Company.

Williamson, Jeffrey G. 1975. "The Sources of American Inequality, 1896-1948." Institute for Research on Poverty, Discussion Papers 260-75. University of Wisconsin-Madison.

Part Five

Educational Opportunities: Access to Education and Priorities in Welfare State Development

Chapter 7

Educational Opportunities and Government Policies in Europe in the Period of Industrialization

Hartmut Kaelble

Educational opportunities in nineteenth-century Europe have attracted the interest of a growing number of scholars in recent years. Stimulated by the debate on present educational systems in Europe, the studies have dealt with the causes and consequences of the long-term expansion of secondary and higher education, with educational crisis, and with the social structure of the educators and educated. Relating socioeconomic factors and interests in educational policy to decisions and non-decisions of governments in this field, they have complemented the hitherto one-sided intellectual and institutional history of education. For the first time, we have an idea of the long-term structures and changes of educational opportunities in industrializing Europe.

So far, however, most of the research has had a very limited scope in space and time. On the one hand, the comparative perspective was almost always neglected. Scholars dealing with one European country rarely knew about the studies even from neighboring parts of Europe.[1] On the other hand, the research rarely touched the debates on long-term change of educational opportunities in the framework of economic development, on changes of social structures and mentalities, and on long-term alterations of the political power structure and the rise of the welfare state. Departing from these shortcomings, this chapter tries to place the findings of the available studies in an intra-European comparative context, and to put

239

forward a concept of long-term development of educational opportunities in the context of social change in nineteenth-century Europe. The chapter is divided into three sections. The first section contains a sketch of a historical conception of the development of educational opportunities, including the relationship to the main topic of the volume—the rise of the welfare state. The second section describes the common European characteristics of opportunities in higher education and the related parts of secondary education.[2] The third section tries to explain why these common characteristics existed, and to what degree this was due to the emergence of the welfare state.

My chapter and the following one by Arnold Heidenheimer are intended to complement one another. I concentrate on comparing the social history of postprimary educational institutions in three European countries, whereas Heidenheimer presents more explicit analyses of the evolution of political structures, and of how the extension of education benefits was related to the extension of social security benefits. We both emphasize German educational development within the context of our comparative analyses, but Heidenheimer compares that development especially with that of the United States over a longer timespan. My comparison of German, British, and French developments concludes in the era when government gradually intervened more consciously in structuring educational institutions and opportunities. Heidenheimer seeks to trace how policies were chosen among alternative options, whereas I tend to place these interventions more in the context of stratification and selection patterns. Partly due to the nature of our research approaches and to the time period under examination, Heidenheimer's article tends to accentuate differences in how educational opportunities were cast in the different national settings, while I tended to accentuate the similarities.

I. A Conceptual Framework for the
Development of Educational Opportunities

Current historical and sociological research on nineteenth-century educational opportunities in Europe has reached the point at which it can benefit from a conceptual framework covering the definition and general determinants of educational opportunities and long-term changes in the pattern of educational opportunities during the nineteenth and twentieth centuries. Since these theoretical components are closely intertwined, all of them are dealt with briefly at the outset.

The term *educational opportunities* can be variously employed. With regard to postprimary education, it seems most appropriate to define it in terms of the proportion of children of different social or occupational classes obtaining secondary or higher education; similar definitions could be used for the regional, sexual, or ethnic distribution of educational opportunities not covered here. Relevant to this definition, therefore, are both the origin of students and the overall development of the enrollment levels in postprimary education. Educational opportunity thus defined also embraces closely related structural changes that are often neglected in historical studies.[3] The only disadvantage of the definition is the reduction of a very complex phenomenon to a few numbers. Therefore, two distinct dimensions of educational opportunities are employed in this essay: the social distribution of educational opportunities (the social origin of students in relation to the social structure of a society) and the magnitude of educational opportunities (the volume of enrollment figures in relation to respective age cohorts).[4]

Four determinants warrant examination for their role in shaping the magnitude and distribution of educational opportunities in modern societies. They are:

1. Variations in the demand for highly trained manpower due to economic development and the growth of public bureaucracy, with its attendant impact on the social prestige of education and occupational mobility;
2. Variable class perceptions of the utility of higher education as a guarantor of social status, shaped by class differentials in information and in the financial resources available for education, as well as by the prevalent cultural values and their conformity with educational inequality;
3. The permeability of educational institutions to a broad social range of students, the availability of financial support for them, and the related social consequences stemming from competition and conflict over the social distribution of postprimary education;
4. The changing role of the government, its educational goals and underlying interests, and its capacity to implement them.

Obviously, a brief essay can touch only lightly upon such complex determinants, but it is clear that their impact on educational opportunities varied widely in the course of the historical development of modern society. For the purpose of historical analysis, in fact, these determinants operated to produce a definable pattern, constituting three successive eras of educational opportunities.[5]

A. The Era of Charity Opportunities

Although industrialization may have commenced, European postprimary education during this period was rarely linked to economic development. Industrial innovation was not usually triggered by scientific research, nor was the qualified labor force in the economy trained in institutions of secondary and higher education. The major traditional markets for university graduates were the church, some professions, and public administration; this market was small in relation to the total workforce and showed no long-term expansionary tendencies. Therefore, only a very small proportion of a given cohort attended secondary and higher education. The chief variable governing crossnational differences in the social prestige of higher education and its role in facilitating occupational mobility was the status of the higher civil service. The European nobility and the traditional elites recognized higher education as a channel for mobility into top positions in the church and partly also in public administration. This awareness might have increased the demand for higher education in the long run. In lower and lower middle class families, limitations in information and income precluded substantial investments in the secondary or higher education of children. However, an uncoordinated charity system for low income students did exist, sustained by churches, small private foundations, individual notables, family connections, and university members. At some universities, the job market for students was quite favorable.

Weak competition in secondary and higher education inhibited the formalization of the educational system, making it easier to transfer between educational institutions. To be sure, in the absence of systematic government intervention in favor on nonprivileged groups, educational opportunities were of limited magnitude, a matter of chance and charity. Nevertheless, contingent on the strength of demand for higher education from the nobility and the educated classes, this environment could produce a relatively high proportion of students from families below the middle classes, such as master artisans, dependent artisans, traditional white collar employes, and farmers.

B. The Era of Competitive Opportunities

This transitional era could be divided into two periods, the first characterized by fluctuating enrollment, followed by a second period of gradual long term growth. To simplify this short sketch, however, I shall join the two periods into a single category.

During this era, the links between education and the industrialization process intensified. Scientific research began to contribute to industrial innovation, especially in iron and steel manufacture, but later in the chemical and electronics industries as well. Even more important was the rising industrial demand for university graduates. The proportion of university graduates rose steadily among both executives and to a lesser extent, white collar employees. In some countries, this demand for university graduates was reinforced by the expansion of public administration and the higher ranks of the civil service. Therefore, enrollment figures in relation to the population and educational investments started to rise slowly in the later part of this era, though the proportion of respective age cohorts attending secondary and higher education remained small before 1914. The demand for higher education among the traditional upper classes increased in response to the growing recognition of education as a gateway to well-paid and prestigious positions, and perhaps also because of rising relative family size. Secondary and higher education began to gain recognition as a transmitter of social status, though it was still not as important as in the second half of the twentieth century relative to other instruments such as property and family. The demand for higher education among the lower middle class expanded as well, partly because of declining economic prospects for small artisans and partly in response to the expansion of the lower ranks of the civil service. Rising demand made secondary and higher education more competitive. This was one reason for the greater formalization of access to postprimary education, especially regarding separation of primary and secondary education, and the declining permeability of institutions of postprimary education. Even where the relevant policy was not tightened, scholarships for gifted students from the lower classes became scarcer because of stronger competition or, later on, because of rising enrollments.

Government policy aimed primarily at financing expansion of secondary and higher education, upgrading the quality of teaching and research, and modernizing the curricula to meet new social and economic needs. The nonprivileged social classes lacked sufficient political influence to counteract the growing trend toward educational inequality. All these factors led to static or deteriorating educational opportunities for the lower classes. Educational opportunities improved mainly for the petit bourgeoisie and sometimes for the lower white collar workers. This limited growth in educational opportunities was a by-product of rising student enrollments, rising standards of living, and changing occupational prospects for the lower middle classes, rather than a result of purposeful government reforms.

C. The Era of Welfare Opportunities

This era is one of transition characterized by growing government intervention and by a further increase in the demand for university graduates in business. Gradually, university graduates came to dominate managerial and executive positions, at least in large corporations. Among white-collar employees, new markets emerged for university credentialed skills in such fields as scientific management and marketing. The expansion of public administration and professional services further reinforced demand for highly educated manpower, causing student enrollments to rise more sharply than before. As university graduates became a significant part of the labor force, filling well-paid, secure and prestigious positions, secondary and higher education gradually became the major access to the upper middle class and to the elite. Hence it became the main instrument of status inheritance and social ascent, although the pattern varied from country to country. Broad social awareness of this development intensified competition for secondary and higher education, particularly inasmuch as educational institutions were still characterized by the high formalization of access and low permeability typical of the era of competitive opportunities.

The most important characteristic of the era of welfare opportunities is the change in political structure and in educational policy goals. Political systems emerged from a long and contradictory period of transition with decision-making processes dominated by three groups: the bureaucracy, organized labor, and organized big business. In contrast to former eras, some politically influential groups were composed of members who were not highly educated. Such prospective or actual changes in the power structure generated three new and interrelated educational policy goals, all tied to the issues of welfare state policy. The first was a policy of active provision for sufficient educational facilities through the expansion of educational investment and teaching staffs. The two additional goals centered on the reduction of educational inequality, either by extending, modernizing, and equalizing basic education or by enhancing the institutional permeability of postprimary education through scholarship programs, tuition reduction, and more flexible access rules.

In contrast to the unsystematic educational options of the era of charity opportunities, the new educational entitlements were often recognized as constitutional or at least legal rights. Even so, educational opportunities improved only slowly, the magnitude of educational opportunity usually changing more measurably than did social distribution. Changes in access were most noticeable in secondary education, much less so in higher education, and least of all in entry to the professions. Indeed, the emergence of welfare opportunities in education was a very slow and sometimes even strongly regressive process. The range of contrasting Western European political systems during the first half of the twentieth century assured that the era of transition to welfare opportunities was a period of highly variable educational policy in which a common pattern of educational opportunities was hard to discern.

The preceding discussion characterizes these three eras of educational opportunities as sequential stages without designating a specific time frame for each. The following discussion investigating the dimensions and determinants of educational opportunity before 1914 will attempt to distinguish one era from another where possible. In particular, it will question whether the era of welfare opportunities could be observed in European education before 1914.

II. Commonalities in the Pattern of
Educational Opportunities in Europe

Before delving more fully into the determinants of educational opportunity, I need to describe the evolving pattern of educational opportunities during the nineteenth century in detail and relate it to the conceptual framework proposed here. The most striking and unexpected comparative observation is the similarity of opportunities in higher and related secondary education throughout Europe. Undoubtedly, a more exhaustive and comprehensive investigation is necessary to confirm this impressionistic conclusion. However, research on at least three major European countries largely supports this impression. This is true for both the magnitude and the social distribution of educational opportunity, the two main dimensions defined above.

A. The Magnitude of Educational Opportunities

One common European characteristic concerns developments in the magnitude of postprimary education during the nineteenth century, as measured by how the enrollment figures related to the respective age cohorts. Most available European data cover only the last decades before 1914 for a rather wide range of mostly industrializing countries.[6] Such data shows that enrollments in secondary and higher education increased slowly, but distinctively and continuously (Tables 7.1 and 7.2). Hence, in all the countries, the chances for children and young adults to acquire secondary and higher education improved, but in almost all European countries a very small minority of any given cohort in fact entered secondary and higher education. The change of magnitude occurred at such a low level that the majority of nineteenth-century citizens might not even have noticed it. Furthermore, the limitation of data to the period between about 1870 and 1914 seems to be crucial. Investigations trying to reach further back show that growth in the magnitude of educational opportunities was not consistent throughout the whole nineteenth century. Studies of France, England, and Germany conclude that the takeoff in higher education occurred in the 1870s and 1890s. Hence, it was only in the latter part of the era of competitive opportunities that educational opportunities seem to have expanded at all.[7]

Just as there are commonalities in the pattern of enrollment growth, so are there similarities in the enrollment levels reached before the First World War. In most European countries a strikingly similar proportion of school-age youth in fact attended institutions of secondary and higher education; the percentage receiving some secondary education clustered between 2 percent and 3 percent (Table 8.1). Only Portugal and Romania had a far lower secondary schooling ratio and so give the impression of the less-developed European countries, for which data is scarce. Furthermore, in most countries, about 1 percent of the young adults attended institutions of higher learning (Table 7.2.). Therefore, the prevailing scholarly impression that significant differences existed among industrializing European countries is not supported by the available data. On the contrary, the range of variation seems rather narrow.[8]

Table 7.1
Extent of Opportunities in Secondary Education:
Students Related to Respective Age Cohorts
(10 through 19)

	Austria (1)	Belgium (2)	Denmark (3)	Finland (4)	France (5)	Germany (6)	Britain Engl-land (7)	Scotland (8)	Hungary (9)	Italy (10)	Netherlands (11)	Norway (12)	Portugal (13)	Romania (14)	Sweden (15)	Switzerland (16)
1840	.	.	.	.	.	.	.	.	.	.	(0.2)h	.	.	.	0.9m	.
1850	.	1.3b	.	.	.	.	.	.	.	.	(0.3)h	.	.	.	0.9m	.
1860	.	1.8b	.	.	.	.	.	.	.	.	(0.3)h	.	.	.	.	.
1870	1.1a	2.5	.	.	2.4	2.3	.	.	3.0f	0.4g	(0.2)h	1.1i	.	.	1.7m	4.7
1880	1.6	2.3	.	.	2.4	2.6	.	.	1.1	0.5g	0.9	2.8	.	.	1.6m	6.1k
1890	1.5	2.4	1.4c	2.1	2.5	2.5	.	.	1.3	0.7g	1.1	2.8	0.4	.	1.9m	7.8
1900	1.9	2.4	1.4c	2.6	2.5	2.7	1.4e	1.9l	1.6	1.4g	1.2	2.9	0.5	0.5	2.3m	.
1910	2.8	2.5	2.6c	4.1	2.6	3.2d	2.4e	2.2l	1.8	2.4g	1.7	3.0	1.0	0.5	.	10.0

a. 1869
b. 1856, 1866
c. 1901, 1911
d. 1911
e. 1901/05, 1911 (state and state-aided schools only)
f. 1869

g. 1871, 1881, 1891, 1901, 1911 (1901, 1911 including training schools for teachers)
h. 1849, 1859, 1869, 1879, 1889, 1899, 1909 (in brackets: only parts of secondary education)
i. 1875 (without private schools)
k. 1888
l. 1901, 1911
m. 1843, 1853, 1862, 1881-85, 1891-95, 1901-05, 1911-15

Annot. to table 7.1: cf. for the use of the data annot. to table 7.2. Moreover, the table comprises more or less all secondary schools, not just the branches which lead to higher education and which this article is focusing upon. So the data are used here as a substitute. Col. 1-4, 7-16: B.R. Mitchell, European Historical Statistics (London: Macmillan 1975), pp. 29 ff.. 750 ff.; col. 5-6: Fritz Ringer, Education and Society (Bloomington, Indiana U.P. 1979, pp. (other calculations for France: V. Isambert-Jamati, Crises de la société, crises de l'enseigne-ment, Paris 1970, p. 377; J. Maillet, L'évolution des effectifs de l'enseignement secondaire de 1803 à 1961, in: La scolarisation en France depuis un siècle, Paris: Mouton 1974, pp.129 ff.; J.-C. Toutain, La population française (Paris 1963), p. 238; col. 15: L. Jörberg, Some notes on education in Sweden in the 19th century, in: Annales Cisalpines d'histoire sociale No. 2, 1971, pp. 70 f.

Table 7.2
Extent of Opportunities in Higher Education:
Students Related to Respective Age Cohorts
(20 through 24)

Year	Au-stria (1)	Bel-gium (2)	Den-mark (3)	Fin-land (4)	France (5)	Ger-many (6)	Britain Eng-land Wales (7)	Scot-land (8)	Hun-gary (9)	Italy (10)	Nether-lands (11)	Nor-way (12)	Por-tu-gal (13)	Roma-nia (14)	Sweden (15)	Swit-zer-land (16)
1840	.	.	.	.	.	.	.	.	.	.	0.6	.	.	.	0.6^p	.
1850	.	0.4^b	.	0.3	.	.	.	.	.	.	0.4^k	.	.	.	.	.
1860	.	0.6^b	.	.	.	0.5^g	.	1.1^f	.	.	0.5^k	0.5^l	0.2^m	.	0.7^q	.
1870	0.7	0.6^b	.	0.4	.	0.7	.	.	0.2^h	0.4^i	0.5^k	0.5^l	.	.	0.7^q	4.7
1880	0.7	.	.	0.4	.	0.8	.	1.9^f	0.3	0.5^i	0.5^k	0.5^l	0.3^m	.	2.8^q	6.1^o
1890	0.9	1.1	.	1.1	0.6^d	0.9	0.5^e	.	0.3	0.5^i	0.7^k	1.0	0.3	.	1.1^q	7.8
1900	1.1	0.9	0.2^c	1.1	0.9^d	.	0.5^e	.	0.6	1.0^i	0.7^k	0.8	0.3	1.1^n	2.2^q	10.0
1910	1.7	1.3	0.4^c	1.2	1.2^d	1.3	0.7^e	1.8^f	0.8	1.0^i	0.8^k	0.8	0.2	0.9^n	.	.

a. 1969
b. 1856, 1866
c. 1901, 1911
d. 1891, 1901, 1911
e. 1891, 1901, 1911
f. 1861, 1881, 1901, 1911, (universities only), 1891-95, 1901-95
g. 1869, 1879, 1889, 1911, 1871-75 (universities only), 1881-85 (universities only)
h. 1901, 1910-15
i. 1861
k. 1849, 1859, 1869
l. 1855, 1865, 1875
m. 1864, 1875, 1912
n. 1899, 1909
o. 1888
p. 1830
q. 1871-75, 1901-05, 1910-15

Annot. to table 7.2: col. 1-4, col. 9-16: B.R. Mitchell, European Historical Statistics, (London: Macmillan 1975), pp. 9-16; 771 ff.; col. 5-8: P. Flora, Indikatoren der Modernisierung (Opladen: Westdeutscher Verlag 1975), pp. 110 ff. (for student enrollments); col. 15: L. Jörberg, Some notes on education in Sweden in the 19th century, in: Annales cisalpines d'histoire sociale No. 2, 1971, p. 71. The data can be used only for rather general arguments; they are inappropriate for any conclusions on precise differences among countries or for calculations of rates of growth, since there are strong variations of the completeness of enrollment figures, of the duration of higher education, of the inclination to attend foreign universities etc.

B. Social Distribution of Educational Opportunities

There are also commonalities in the social distribution of educational opportunities in secondary institutions leading to higher education. To be sure, long-term changes in the social origins of secondary school students are still unclear and have rarely been investigated even in recent research. However, the few social scientists who have entered this field come to similar conclusions. T. W. Bamford demonstrated that during the first half of the nineteenth century the aristocracy and the professions became more dominant in the English public schools, which in turn became more important for access to the university. Theodore Zeldin and Robert Anderson hold that in French secondary education, which had been almost comprehensive during the Second Empire, the proportion of pupils from the lower and lower middle classes had decreased by the beginning of the twentieth century. In a case study of the academic high school (*Gymnasium*) of the German town Minden, Margret Kaul argues that Prussian secondary education before 1848 was competitive and socially open, rather than elitist as it later became. In another case study on secondary education in nineteenth-century Berlin, Detlev K. Müller also argues that Prussian education deteriorated from a socially open, comprehensive school system into a much more formalized, exclusive institution with primary and secondary education becoming largely strictly separated. Müller's assessment has not been fully accepted by other scholars. In fact, his unique long-term time series on the social origin of students in the last grade of secondary education (*Abiturienten*) supports his pessimistic view only until about the 1880s. Up to this time, the proportion of lower-middle-class students dwindled, while general enrollment levels stagnated, in what has been described as the early period of competitive opportunities. However, in the last decades before 1914, the share of students with this background expanded again, along with expanding enrollment levels for the last grades of secondary education.[9]

The relative openness of secondary education during the last decades before 1914 is supported by studies focussed on one point in time rather than on long-term change. As far as all grades of secondary education are concerned, the majority of secondary students came from the lower middle class—that is, from families of small independent artisans, shopkeepers, white collar employees, lower civil servants, and small farmers. This has been shown for a London grammar school as well as for *Gymnasien* in Hessen, Baden, and in various German cities such as Berlin, Breslau, Hannover, Bochum (Tables 7.3, 7.4, and 7.5). To be sure, children of these social groups did not have fully equal chances. If the social origin of students is related to the social structure as a whole, the children of farmers, white collar employees (except for lower civil servants in Germany), and maybe even the children of the petty bourgeoisie, were still underrepresented when compared to the children of the middle class (Table 7.4). To a lesser extent, this is also true for secondary school graduates, though the social distribution of educational opportunities seems to have been more unequal at that level than among secondary students overall (Tables 7.3 and 7.5). Among graduates from Prussian secondary schools between 1875 and 1899, students were almost equally divided into sons of the lower middle class and sons of the middle class. Probably, this also applies to the Württemberg graduates of 1873 and the French secondary graduates of 1865–66 (Table 7.3). This finding too is consistent with what has been defined above as the later part of the era of competitive opportunities.

Just as in secondary schools, the social distribution of higher education also manifested common patterns and changes. During the first half of the nineteenth century, higher education was dominated by the offspring of landed aristocrats, professionals, merchants, and higher civil servants. Sons of the lower middle class were relatively rare. This has been shown for Cambridge and for Oxford in England, for the *école centrale* and the *école polytechnique* in France, for the German universities of Heidelberg, Berlin, Halle, and for Württemberg students (Table 7.6). There are indications that this was the final stage in a long-term early modern process of growing exclusiveness in European higher education. Lawrence Stone and C. A. Anderson have demonstrated this process clearly for Oxford and Cambridge. It might be that there was a similar process in Germany,[10] which again would accord with the transition from charity opportunities to early competitive opportunities. A few cases deviate distinctly from the general pattern just described. The most important is the University of Glasgow whose structure is probably typical of other Scottish universities. A study by W. M. Mathew finds that educational opportunities at that university between 1740 and 1839 were exceptionally well distributed. The proportion of students from aristocratic and large landowning families was low and tended to decline. The proportion of students from the working class, especially from families of skilled artisans and small masters, was high (25 percent), even by the standards of modern European higher education. The proportion of farmers' sons fell, but remained at the rather high level of 15 percent. In addition to the university of Glasgow, less spectacular cases are the *écoles des arts et métiers* in France, including the *conservatoire national des arts et métiers* in Paris. Only one-third to one-seventh of the students stemmed from families of landowners, businessmen, and professionals; the overwhelming majority came from the lower middle classes (Table 7.6).[11]

In the second half of the nineteenth century, the social distribution of educational opportunities in higher education seems to have changed. In the countries investigated so far, this change had several common aspects.

Table 7.3
Social Origins of Secondary School Students in France, England,
and Germany, 1864-1908 by Percentage

	France Secondary Graduates 1864/65 (1)	England Public Schools 1801-1850 (2)	England Grammar Schools 1884-1900 (3)	England Grammar Schools 1904-1918 (4)	Württemberg Secondary Graduates 1873 (5)	Prussia Secondary Graduates 1875-1899 (6)	Hessia 1891/1892 (7)	Hessia 1904 (8)	Baden 1908 (9)
Higher Civil Servants	12[a]	21	13	11	11[c]	19	26[a]	32[a]	10[1]
Professionals	18				30[g]		5	5	4
Large landowners	17[b]	38				2			
Businessmen	13		10	20	21	23	52	43	35
Petit bourgeois	15	3	35[d]	22		10			6
Farmers	12				13	10	8	9	
Lower Civil Servants	.[a]				18	23	.[a]	.[a]	24
White collar employees	2		17	24		3	7[h]	10[h]	3
Workers	8	2[e]	11	15		0			9
Others	4	25	13	8	8	10	9		9
No answer	.	100[f]	.	.		0			.
Total	100	100[f]	100	100	100	100	100	100	100
No. of cases	12 605	25 931	517	873	659	85 034	8 649		12 962

a. all civil servants in category "higher civil servants" including clergy (1%)
b. proprietairestrentiers
c. only higher civil servants in public administration
d. including formen whose proportion is not given
e. lower classes
f. including "titled" (12%)
g. including clergy (16%)
h. category not fully clear. Could also be white collar employees only.

Annot to table 3:
Col. 1: P.J. Harrigan, The social origins, ambitions and occupations of secondary students in France during the Second Empire, in: L. Stone (ed.), Schooling and society (Baltimore London 1976), p. 210 (all students likely to graduate in the next two years); col. 2: T.W. Bamford, Public Schools and Social Class, British Journal of Sociology 12 (1961) p. 229; col. 3 and 4: J. Floud/ F.M. Martin/A.H. Halsey, Educational opportunity and social selection in England, Transaction of the third World Congress on sociology (London 1954) vol. 2, p. 198 (case study in the London area); col. 5: Statistik der Universität Tübingen (Stuttgart 1877), p. 51; col. 6: H. Kaelble, Chancenungleichheit und akademische Ausbildung in Deutschland, 1910-1960, Geschichte und Gesellschaft 1 (1975), pp. 142-143; col. 7: Statistisches Handbuch des Großherzogtums Hessen 1(1903), pp. 142-143 (schools included: Gymnasien, Progymnasien, Realgymnasien, Oberrealschulen, Realschulen, Progymnasien); col. 8: "Mitteilungen der großherzogl.hess. Zentralstelle für die Landesstatistik 35 (1905), pp. 12-15 (schools included as above); col. 9: Badische Schulstatistik vol. 2 (Karlsruhe 1914), p. 139 (schools included as in col. 7 except of Realschulen).

Table 7.4
Social Distribution of Opportunities for Secondary School Students in France, England, and Germany, 1864 - 1918

Social origin	France Secondary Graduates 1864/65 (1)	Prussia Secondary Graduates 1875-99 (2)	Hessia 1891/92 (3)	Hessia 1904 (4)	Baden 1908 (5)	England Grammar School 1904-18 (6)
Higher civil servants	1.00[b]	6.74	3.25[b]	3.67[b]	3.35	11.00
Professionals	6.00		6.37	6.00	4.56	
Large Landowners	.[a]	.[a]	.[a]	2.93	.[a]	4.16
Businessmen	4.59	2.36	3.47	0.36	2.80	
Petit bourgeois	0.34	0.75	0.49		0.35	
Farmers		3.83			3.45	1.40
Lower civil servants	.[b]	0.79	.[b]	.[b]	0.55	
White collar employees	0.13[(?)]	0.01	0.12	0.18	0.17	0.20
Workers	0.20					

[a] included in category "farmer".
[b] all civil servants included in category "higher civil servants"
   "higher civil servants"

Annot. to table +

The recruitment index is to express the relation between the social origin of students and the occupation of their fathers. The index is calculated in a very simple way:

$$i = \frac{s}{f}$$

i = recruitment index; s = proportion of students stemming from fathers with a certain occupation (%); f = proportion of the members of that occupation among the employed population (%). The purpose of the index is only to measure, not to judge or to explain the distribution of educational opportunities. The basic idea of the index is that students from a certain family background have full educational chances if their proportion of the student body is the same as the proportion of their fathers occupation among the employed population. In this case the index is 1. If the index is below one, this indicates low chances; if the index is above one, this indicates privileged chances. If the index falls or rises in direction of 1, this indicates improving educational opportunities or a reduction of educational privileges. The reverse trends is indicated, if the index moves away from 1. - table 2 is based on data of table 1 and on data of occupational structure from the following sources: col. 1 (France 1866: J.-C. Toutain, La population de la France de 1700 à 1959 (Paris 1963), table 66, 67, 148, 154; col. 2 (Prussia 1895): Statistik des Deutschen Reichs, vol. 104; col. 3 (Hessia 1895): ibid., vol. 105; col. 4-5 (Hessia and Baden 1907): ibid., vol. 205; col. 6 (England and Wales 1911): A.H. Halsey, ed., Trends in British society since 1900, p. 113.

Table 7.5
Social Origins of Secondary School Students
in Large German Cities, 1882-1912

Occupation of fathers	Berlin		Hannover	Bochum		Barmen	
				entering classes			
	secondary graduates		all students	Gym-nasium	Oberre-alschule	Gym-nasium	Oberre-alschule
	1882-1886	1907-1911	1912	1906	1901		
	(1)	(2)	(3)	(4)	(5)	(6)	(7)
Higher civil servants	-	22	} 8	14	6	} 19	} 4
professionals	2	5		14	2		
Large landowners	-	-	-	-	-	-	-
Businessmen	16	13	} 41	2	5	31	24
Petty bourgeosie	33	28		21	25	13	35
Farmers	-	-	-	-	-	-	-
Lower civil servants	18	22	5	} 24	} 31	27	11
White collar employees	5	8	13			6	12
Workers	1	1	3	11	20	1	4
Others	-	-	11	5	2	3	10
Total	100	100	100	100	100	100	100
No. of cases	1058	2098	5136	-	-	-	-

Annot. to table 5 :
Col. 1-2: D.K. Müller, Sozialstruktur und Schulsystem (Göttingen 1977), p. 523; col. 3: Mitteilungen des Statistischen Amts der Stadt Hannover 18 (1912), no. 3 p. 7; col. 4-5: D. Crew, Definitions of modernity, Journal of Social History 7.1973,p.64; col. 6 and 7: H. Titze, Die Politisierung der Erziehung (Frankfurt 1973), p. 203.

The traditional economic and educational elites became less visible. The proportion of students from families of large landowners and from the clergy declined. In countries with strong bureaucratic traditions, such as France and Prussia, the same is true for the children of top bureaucrats. Students from the rising economic elite of businessmen increased. Furthermore, higher education became somewhat more open to the sons of the petit bourgeoisie and also some lower white-collar employees. These changes have been shown for Oxford students, for students of the *école des arts et métiers* and of the *école polytechnique* in France (the *école centrale* being an exception), for students of Prussian universities, and for Württemberg students (Table 7.6). These changes do not merely reflect alterations in occupational structure. Rather, they represent distinct reductions

Table 7.6
Social Origins of University Students in Great Britain, France, and Germany during the Nineteenth Century (percentage)

Country groups: England (cols 1–4), France (cols 5–9), Germany (cols 10–14).

Social origin	Cambridge 1800-1849 (1)	Cambridge 1850-1899 (2)	Oxford 1877 (3)	Oxford 1910 (4)	Ecole polytechnique 1815-1840 (5)	Ecole polytechnique 1860-1875 (6)	Ecole centrale 1829-1875 (7)	Ecole centrale 1870-1881 (8)	Ecole centrale 1900-1925 (9)	Students from Württemberg 1835-1844 (10)	Württemberg 1871-1881 (11)	Württemberg 1901-1911 (12)	Prussia 1886-1887 (13)	Prussia 1911-1912 (14)
Higher Civil Servants	2	3	49[a]	48[a]	32	26	12	16	25	18[e]	9[e]	8[e]	21[f]	21[f]
Professionals	51[b]	54[b]	.	.	.	.	.	.	.	27[d]	25[d]	21[d]	.	.
Large landowners	31	19	40[c]	15[c]	30[d]	19[d]	29[d]	31[d]	25[d]	1	1	1	9	1
Businessmen	6	15	7	21	14	16	36	31	28	3	6	11	34	12
Petit Bourgeoisie	.	.	.	7	4	12	6	7	5	23	17	17	4	24
Farmers	.	.	.	.	2	6	2	2	2	7	14	10	.	9
Lower civil servant					21	28	13	10	14	21	21	25	2	27
Lower white collar	.	.	0	1	.	.	3	2	1	0	1	3	0	3
Workers	.	9	.	.	.	.	.	.	.	0	1	3	6	2
Others	10	.	2	5	.	.	.	.	.	0	3	3	0	.
No answer	.	.	.	.	.	.	.	.	.	.	.	.	.	.
Total	100	100	100	100	100	100	100	100	100	100	100	100	100	100
No. of cases	319	352	418	1030	.	.	.	.	.	818	1724	3051	.	5346

a. including clergy (1870: 28%, 1910: 17%)
b. including clergy (1800-49: 32%, 1850-99: 31%, 1937-38: 7%)
c. mainly aristocrats without specification of occupation
d. "rentiers-propriétaires"
e. administration and army only
f. including clergy (1886/87: 7%, 1911/12: 4%)
g. including clergy (1835/40: 14%, 1871/81: 14%, 1901/11: 10%)

Annot. to table 6:
The table covers only institutions whose students have been investigated at least at two different points of time. Col. 1-2: H. Jenkins/D.C. Jones, Social Class of Cambridge University Alumni of the 18th and 19th Centuries, in: British Journal of Sociology 1 (1950), p. 99; col. 3-4: L. Stone, The Size and Composition of the Oxford Student Body 1580-1910, in:id. (ed.), The University in Society (Princeton 1974), p. 103; col. 5-9: M. Lévy-Leboyer, Le patronat français a-t-il été malthusien? in: Le mouvement social No. 88 (1974), p. 25; col. 9-13: id., Innovation and business strategies in 19th and 20th century France, in: E.G. Carter et.al.(eds.), Enterprise and entrepreneurs in 19th and 20th century France (Baltimore 1976), p. 104 ff. (English version has a better temporal grouping of the data for the 19th century); col. 10-12: A. Rienhardt, Das Universitätsstudium der Württemberger seit der Riechsgründung (Tübingen 1918), p. 27 ff. col. 13-14: Preussische Statistik, vol. 102, p. 68; vol. 236, p. 236, p.

Table 7.7
Social Distribution of Opportunities in Universities in England, France, and Germany, 1850-1913 (recruitment index)

	England		France				Germany				
	Cambridge 1850-1899	Oxford 1910	Ecoles des arts et mét. 1860-1875	Ecole centrale 1870-1899	Ecole centrale 1900-1925	Ecole poly-technique 1860-1875	Students from Wurt. 1871-1881	Students from Wurt. 1901-1911	Prussia 1886/87	Prussia 1911/12	Bavaria 1913
	(1)	(2)	(3)	(4)	(5)	(6)	(7)	(8)	(9)	(10)	(11)
Higher civil servants	57.00	48.00	·	·	·	·	15.00	9.67	10.50	7.00	7.00
Professionals							·	·	·	·	9.00
Large landowners											·
Businessmen	2.24	6.41	2.94	5.11	8.29	2.77	1.64	2.15	2.43	3.00	2.67
Petit bourgeoisie			1.10	0.08	0.09	0.25					
Farmers							0.61[a]	0.71[a]	0.93[a]	0.91[a]	0.46
Lower civil servants			1.06	0.59	1.17	1.75	5.25	5.00	1.13	4.50	3.80
White collar employees							1.00	0.60	1.00	0.40	0.50
Workers			·	·			0.02	0.06	0.00	0.03	0.11

a. Large landowners plus farmers. Farmers only: Wurt. 1871-1888: 0.61; Wurt. 1901-11: 0.71; Prussia 1886/87: 0.29; Prussia 1901-11: 0.71; Prussia 1911/12: 0.82.

Annot to table 7.7: For the calculation of the index see table 7.4; for social origin of students cf. table 7.6 for occupational structure in col. 1-2 (England and Wales 1911): A.H. Halsey, Trends in British society since 1900 (London 1972), p. 113; col. 3-6 (France 1866, 1886, 1906): Toutain, Population, table 53, 67, 75, 85, 149, 155; col. 7 (Wurtemberg 1882): Statistik des Deutschen Reichs, vol. 4 (NF); col. 8-11 (Wurtemberg, Bavaria 1907): ibid., vol. 205; col. 9 (Prussia 1882): ibid., vol. 4 (NF); col. 10 (Prussia 1907): ibid., vol. 204. Only parts of the table 7.6 could be used, since informations on occupational structure are not available otherwise. The recruitment index is to be used very carefully, because informations on occupational structure are rarely standardized across nations as well as in time series.

in the inequality of educational opportunities (Table 7.7). The timing and strength of this trend varied strongly from country to country, but no country so far studied remained untouched by this common pattern.

The changes in social distribution that did occur ought to be qualified in various respects. The distribution of opportunities changed only for limited segments of the population; for some social classes, opportunities in higher education improved very slowly or not at all. This is especially true for unskilled and skilled workers, for peasants, and partly also for white-collar employees. Large differences in educational opportunities appear to have persisted. The prototypical rank order of educational opportunities had started at the top with the offspring of higher civil servants and professionals, followed by the children of businessmen, then the petit bourgeoisie and sometimes the lower civil servants; children of peasants and white collar employees trailed by a clear margin, with children of workers at the bottom of the ladder. This order of priority was somewhat modified in the middle ranks, rather than completely transformed before 1914 (Table 7.7). What had occurred was an extension of educational privileges, rather than a general democratization of higher education.

These common characteristics should not overshadow the existence of significant crossnational variability. The brief enumeration of such differences offered here is suggestive rather than comprehensive and points to the necessity of further research. Regional differences are a case in point; although data on regional differences currently exists only for Germany and Great Britain (Tables 7.3, 7.5, and 7.6),[12] these differences are so pronounced as to raise doubts about the validity of any comparison limited to the national level, especially for secondary education. It is also apparent that the relative opportunities for various social classes differ crossnationally and over time. For example, sons of artisanal workers were less limited in their opportunities in France during the 1860s than was the case elsewhere, while sons of lower civil servants enjoyed a rather favorable position in German secondary and higher education. To class and regional variations should be added sizeable differences in the sexual distribution of educational opportunities; although the percentage of school age males obtaining postprimary education was relatively similar from country to country, the comparable percentage of females varied significantly.[13] It also appears, though data is scarce, that the undeveloped parts of Europe differed markedly from the industrializing ones. Finally, there are indications of substantial variability in the role of higher education for occupational mobility. The available data for the period before 1914 do not permit the application of modern methods of measuring the impact of education, but the diverging patterns of recruitment for the professions, higher civil servants, teachers on various levels, and businessmen indicate that the impact of higher education on European career patterns varied distinctively from country to country.[14]

One should add that the common and diverging characteristics described only cover some of the dimensions of educational opportunities. When data is available, it will be of great interest to compare other aspects, such as the contrast between rural and urban educational opportunities, and the educational chances of ethnic, religious, national, and regional minorities.

To sum up, the nineteenth century seems to have been a period in which educational opportunities showed definite cross-national similarities over time in industrializing Europe. There are indications that the first part of the century was a period of growing inequality in the social distribution of educational opportunities, probably as a final stage in a process that had started in previous centuries. This period was also characterized by small and stagnant enrollments. As such it could be considered the transition from charity opportunities to competitive opportunities. Generally, information is far from exact enough to draw any final conclusions or to pinpoint the precise time of the change. Much more research is needed. In the last decades before 1914 the trend seems to have reversed; the social distribution of educational opportunities seems to have become somewhat less unequal, while the magnitude of educational opportunities began a slow growth. However, the beneficiaries of this modest advance were limited to the lower middle class; the lower classes were excluded from it.

III. Determinants of Educational Opportunities

The commonalities just described in nineteenth century Europe would hardly have existed had they not been generated by common determinants. Four such major determinants were identified in conjunction with the proposed conceptual framework at the beginning of this essay: the demand for higher education by the traditional upper classes and educational elites, especially in the first part of the nineteenth century; the permeability of educational institutions, the demand for university graduates, and the role of the government. Changes in these determinants are closely related to the industrialization process, but also, in contrast to events in new nations such as the United States, to enduring preindustrial and precapitalist remnants in European societies.

A. Socially Differential Perceptions of the Utility of Higher Education

Most scholars agree that the demand for higher and related secondary education by traditional elites and by the educated middle class such as the landed aristocracy, the clergy, the professionals, and, in countries with strong bureaucratic traditions, the higher civil servants, was strong and even increased somewhat up to the nineteenth century. This reflects a situation in which meritocratic liberalism was more widely accepted, while positions of traditional elites were threatened by the process of industrialization. This threat to the traditional elite is the most important reason why educational opportunities in Europe differed from those in new nations such as the United States.

For nineteenth-century Germany, various studies testify to the strength of this demand from the traditional economic and educational elites. Karl-Ernst Jeismann points to the eagerness of the rising educational elite to preserve educational privileges, in contravention of the original purposes of the educational reforms in the early nineteenth century. Konrad Jarausch emphasizes that the limited broadening of recruitment in the 1820s and 1830s was reversed in the 1840s, a time of crisis in the job market for trained manpower. Detlev Müller holds that it was political pressure from the educated middle class that made Prussian secondary education shift from an early "comprehensive" strategy to a socially exclusive strategy during the later nineteenth century. Fritz Ringer argues that higher education was the main instrument for the preindustrial or early industrial elites to transfer high social status to their offspring in an industrial society. Though there is marked dissent among scholars about the evolution of educational opportunities in Germany, they do agree on the strong impact of educational demand, especially from these traditional elites.[15] Hence during the period of stagnation in both student enrollments and in the academic job market, a substantial proportion of students came from those classes. Furthermore, the privileged classes faced a growing rather than diminishing demand for higher education from other social classes: the rising industrial bourgeoisie sought higher education more for social prestige than for economic advancement; the petty bourgeoisie sought broader occupational prospects; and the lower civil servants sought jobs within the strict formalization of occupational advancement in German bureaucracy. As long as student enrollments and jobs for university graduates failed to increase, these converging demands for higher education could only intensify competition and increase political pressure from the privileged classes for the limitation of educational opportunities.

Research on England is even more controversial. There is consensus on the strong educational demand from the upper and middle classes, but dissent about the specific class from which the demand came most vigorously. Nicholas Hans and Brian Simon argue that it was the rising industrial bourgeoisie who most strongly demanded higher education for their offspring and who were thus instrumental in bringing about a reduction in the proportion of students from the lower classes and a shift from charity opportunities to competitive opportunities. Other scholars come to opposite conclusions. T. W. Bamford finds that it was the nobility and the professionals who increasingly predominated among the pupils of the top public schools in the first half of the nineteenth century, as the public school became integrated into the life of the English aristocracy. Lawrence Stone argues that the numbers of students from the lower classes started to diminish much earlier than the industrial revolution and that it was the clergy and the nobility rather than the industrial bourgeoisie who profited from the process. Only in the 1860s did the aristocratic character of Oxford reach its peak. The contrasting situation at the Scottish universities supports this position. To be sure, there were several reasons for the extraordinarily open access to Scottish postprimary education; at least one reason was the absence of the Scottish aristocracy from local universities and their strong preference for the aristocratic style of life at English universities.[16]

B. The Permeability of Educational Institutions

A second major determinant of educational opportunity during the nineteenth century was a complex of institutional changes that reduced the permeability of higher education. These included a gradual separation of primary and secondary education and a clear differentiation among institutions of postprimary education according to their role for social mobility. Scholarships for students from low-income families became scarcer; access to higher education became more competitive and formalized. Though the impact of these changes varies from country to country, they seem to have had some importance everywhere, reinforcing rather than alleviating the inequality of educational opportunities.

For France, recent studies by Robert Anderson and by Patrick Harrigan show that secondary education was used not only by the upper classes for the preservation or their social status, but also by the lower middle classes as a means of social ascent. Scholarship policy favored families that had served the state rather than low-income families, but the low school fees seem to have been in the reach even of artisanal workers. However, in the view of Robert Anderson and Theodore Zeldin, French secondary education retained its almost comprehensive character only until the Second Empire. Educational reforms starting in the Second Empire led to a stronger separation of primary and secondary education and to more marked differences within secondary education. Harrigan shows that the social origins of pupils in the *lycées*, who had access to the *grandes écoles*, were more elitist than those in the *enseignement special*, which was introduced in the 1860s and did not lead to higher education. Zeldin even argues that, as a consequence of these and other reforms, the overall social structure of pupils in French secondary education became more exclusive in the decades before 1914 for reasons that are still unclear. Differences in higher education were even more pronounced. Graduation from the universities, which were open to everybody who could pay the fees and who had passed the *baccalauréat*, did not pave the way for much occupational success. However, access to the *grandes écoles* which were a channel to higher positions in public administration, business, and the professions had become highly competitive during the early nineteenth century.[17]

Studies dealing with Germany reveal similar institutional changes beginning some decades earlier. From the 1830s on, primary and secondary education by and large became distinct sectors with diminishing possibilities of transition from the one to the other. Furthermore, secondary education was gradually subdivided into separate branches with different curricula stratified by occupational career and social class. Scholars including Max Weber agree on the negative consequences of these institutional changes for the social distribution of educational opportunities. Distinct contrasts in the social recruitment of pupils emerged within secondary education; *Gymnasien* affording access to higher education and to the higher ranks of the civil service and the professions were more elitist socially than other institutions of secondary education.

Moreover, access to higher education became more formalized and competitive, though in a different sense than in France. In the first place, the access routes to university education underwent a transformation. Starting with the first crisis of the academic job market in the 1830s and 1840s, access to universities was limited gradually to graduates from the *Gymnasium*, with its strong emphasis on classics. This change was motivated by the desire to relate education and occupational careers more closely and by the fear that an excess of university trained manpower would threaten occupational prospects for the offspring of the educated social classes. Although access to universities was extended in the late nineteenth century to graduates of other secondary schools with a somewhat stronger emphasis on modern languages and science, only a small percentage of secondary pupils entered higher education. It may also be that university scholarship policies became less favorable for educational opportunities. In the decades before 1914, the proportion of university students receiving scholarships in Prussia dropped from about 20 percent in 1887 to 1888, to about 10 percent in 1911. Furthermore, clear contrasts existed especially between the socially more elitist law faculty, which was the main channel to the prestigious positions in higher administration and the judiciary, and the other sections of the university.

These changes in the university access structure were paralleled by changes in technical education. Access to technical education, which had been rather flexible and open in the first half of the nineteenth century, later adapted to the university system of admittance. This process was reinforced by scholarship policies; as Peter Lundgreen has demonstrated, financial support for low income students was drastically reduced by the middle of the nineteenth century and replaced by competitive grants. Perhaps the most competitive part was the postuniversity trainee program for public administration, the judiciary, and secondary teaching. Especially when there was a surplus of university graduates, competition at this educational level was intense and even seems to have been used as a deterrent to university study.[18]

Studies dealing with English secondary and higher education describe decisive institutional changes that led in the same direction, though with different institutional manifestations. As in France and Germany, primary and secondary education became distinct branches during the nineteenth century without linkages or possibilities for transition. Certainly, this was a much more gradual and ambiguous process in England because of the extreme decentralization of the English school system and the strong impact of the local clientele on the curricula. Only in the second half of the nineteenth century did government intervention in favor of distinct secondary education become more apparent. Furthermore, the emergence of the public school reinforced the demarcation of secondary education. In the late eighteenth and the early nineteenth century, public schools developed from endowed schools for local educational needs taking in children from all social classes to institutions designed to prepare a national, mainly aristocratic, elite for university studies. To this end, public schools became boarding schools with a nationwide intake, high fees, and few free places; they emphasized classics, abolishing all curricula not related to university studies. In spite of strong variations among public schools, the social structure of the students was clearly different from that of other secondary schools less important for social advancement.

Recent studies also pinpoint institutional changes that brought about the growing exclusiveness of Oxford and Cambridge mentioned earlier. One such change was the growing dominance of access to these two universities by the public schools. An additional obstacle was financial, although the fees and actual cost of living were less prohibitive in this regard than the high cost of maintaining the eccentric aristocratic student lifestyle. Prospective students also confronted a widening gulf between university curricula and the educational expectations of the middle class, as well as university disinterest in raising student enrollments or changing the social structure of the student body. Consequently a marked contrast existed between the social origins of Oxbridge students and those of students at the new civic universities, most of which were founded in the second half of the nineteenth century.[19]

One might question whether these institutional changes in fact abolished a truly comprehensive system; what existed under the *ancien regime* and survived into the early nineteenth century was clearly different from the modern comprehensive school system, above all in its size and in its role as a gateway to occupational mobility. Nevertheless, these institutional changes did contribute to the erection of strong barriers to educational opportunities during the period of slow growth in student enrollment and academic jobs. In fact, they may well have been a response to rising educational competition that generated fears among upper and educated middle classes of overcrowding in postprimary education and of an excess of trained manpower. As education became more important for social mobility, the need to formalize educational access to higher education also induced institutional change. Hence, in the conception put forward above, one could consider these institutional changes as the transition from the era of charity opportunities to the era of competitive opportunities.

C. The Changing Demand for Highly Trained Manpower

The situation changed markedly when the demand for university trained manpower started to increase in the last decades before 1914. There are various reasons for this increase. The proportion of university graduates among members of the European business elites as well as among white collar employees began to rise. Public administration expanded, though at very different rates, throughout Europe. The enlarging private service sector also included a growing number of jobs for university graduates, especially for lawyers and physicians. As a consequence, more teachers in secondary and higher education were needed to train the rising number of future university graduates. These occupations and/or the proportion of university graduates in these occupations expanded more rapidly than the population. To be sure, the expansion was only the beginning of a much more substantial increase following the Second World War, but the take-off clearly occurred before 1914.[20]

The expanding demand for university graduates had a distinctive impact on both of the dimensions of educational opportunities discussed in this essay. First, the growth in enrollment figures and hence in the magnitude of educational opportunities has been already shown. Certainly, the growth rates were still low compared to the postwar period and did not coincide precisely with demand; for instance, the oversupply of educated manpower produced a severe crisis in the job market, especially in the 1880s. Nevertheless, the long-term increase in enrollment could not be explained without the rising demand for university graduates. Secondly, the growth in demand exercised an indirect impact on the social distribution of educational opportunities by reducing competition in secondary and higher education. The demand for higher education from the traditional upper classes and educated elites was satisfied more easily, allowing somewhat more open access to secondary and higher education for children of the lower middle class and also for female graduates.[21]

D. The Role of Governments

There are few indications that this limited change in educational opportunities was the consequence of direct government intervention in favor of a more equal distribution of educational opportunities. Except for the

British reform bill of 1902, the educational policies of European government were primarily concerned with adapting educational institutions to the needs of the rising industrial society, rather than with reducing inequality in educational opportunities. Political parties and organizations that influenced or participated in educational policy decisions usually took an elitist rather than an egalitarian view before 1914.

On this point, available research seems in full accord. Studies of France describe the strong preoccupation of educational policy with the proportion of classics to the more modern topics in secondary school curricula, with church control of a large sector of secondary education, and with the modernization and integration of university education into a coordinated system and its relation to the *grandes écoles* and special research institutions. For most of the nineteenth century, equality of educational opportunities seems to have been ignored by the French political elite. Studies on Germany point to a parallel political debate on the share of classics, sciences, and modern languages in the curricula of the secondary level, to the revaluation of institutions of higher technical training, and to the development of intra- and extrauniversity research, above all in the sciences. Especially in the second half of the nineteenth century, those involved in educational decision making were concerned with the preservation of privilege and the exclusion of the lower and lower middle classes, rather than with furthering egalitarian approaches.

Studies on English educational policies also fall into a similar pattern—the debate over classics versus modern topics in the curricula of public schools, grammar schools, and the major universities, the relation of university training to the needs and expectations of the business sector, the special English problem of an extremely decentralized system of nonprivate endowed schools and the problem of Anglican control of the most prestigious institutions of secondary and higher education. Once again, the participants in the various reform bill controversies looked at the distribution of educational opportunities from an elitist viewpoint.

The similar orientation of educational policies in these three major European countries stems from several causes. One was the extensive exchange of ideas among educational institutions. Moreover, in all three countries, educational institutions confronted the needs of the industrialization process. It should also be noted that in each case those excluded from educational privileges did not participate or receive consideration in the political decision making on education before 1914. Furthermore, secondary and higher education were not yet widely regarded by these social classes as an instrument of social advancement that ought to be distributed more equally.[22] All this indicates that the limited change of educational opportunities in pre-1914 Europe ought to be considered—in terms of the conception put forward at the beginning—as the last stage in the era of competitive opportunities, with rising demand for university-trained manpower, rather than a period in which purposeful, efficient, and egalitarian educational policies led to a reduction of inequality. It is true that the rising demand for university graduates was partly a consequence of the evolution of social policy with subsequent effects on the increase of civil servants, physicians, and teaching staffs. However, direct government intervention in favor of more equity in educational opportunity was yet to come. This characterization would fit into the periodization proposed by Peter Flora and Hugo Heclo with respect to the emergence of the welfare state in a broader sense.[23]

Notes

1. The most important exception seems to be Ringer 1979. As I saw only a small section in manuscript, the conclusions of the book are not reflected in this essay. A very interesting step in the same direction is Kocka 1978. For the comparative investigation of one major component of educational opportunity, the enrollment figures in secondary and higher education, see Flora 1975. For an important effort to bring some current projects into relation with each other, see Stone 1974 and 1976. For a summary of the studies on educational opportunities in West Europe during the nineteenth and twentieth centuries, see Kaelble 1978. For the beginnings of a comparative discussion on early modern times, see Chartier and Revel 1978; very valuable comments on earlier versions of this paper came from Peter Flora, Roy Hay, Arnold Heidenheimer, Jürgen Kocka, Peter Lundgreen, Bo Öhngren and Konrad Jarausch.
2. Other sections of secondary education that did not lead to university studies have been largely omitted in this essay since a comparison turned out to be very difficult. The whole of secondary education has been included only as a substitute if information on the sections linked to higher education were lacking.
3. Two structural components are very often omitted in historical investigations of educational opportunities: on the one hand, enrollment figures are frequently not related to the respective age cohorts and so might lead to mistaken conclusions about the historical changes or differences between countries; on the other hand, the social origin of students usually is not related to the social structure of a society; so changes of social origin that might be mere consequences of changes of the social structure can be considered erroneously as alterations of educational opportunities. The definition put forward above avoids these shortcomings. It has been introduced by sociologists dealing with present education such as Bourdieu, Westergaard, Bühl, Anderson (see Bourdieu 1964, pp. 136 ff.; Little and Westergaard 1964; Bühl 1968; Anderson 1965, p. 253).
4. Furthermore, the social origin of the students is given separately in the following tables, in order to make it easier to follow up separately the two main components of the social distribution of educational opportunities. Unfortunately, an important demographic component of the definition, the social or occupational differential of family size, cannot be dealt with for lack of any data covering the nineteenth century. This component could be

neglected if the differential of family size had remained constant during the nineteenth century. However, this was probably not the case. Hence, I would see here a strongly neglected and so far uncalculable aspect that limits the conclusion of the essay.

5. Apart from the special studies to which references are made in the next sections the general works most stimulating for the following conception were Ringer 1979; Rimlinger 1971; the essays by Kocka 1974 and by Wehler 1974; Maier 1975; and the essays by Heidenheimer and Heclo in this volume.

6. For the previous time information either on enrollments or on the population size broken down by age cohorts is lacking.

7. England: Stone 1974, pp. 6 f., 65 ff; Germany: Ringer 1979; Jarausch 1976; Lundgreen 1976, pp. 27 ff.: Müller 1977, pp. 441 ff. (cause study on Berlin secondary education); France: Ringer 1979; Mouton 1974, pp. 176 ff. (covering also the period before 1890); Maillet 1974, pp. 129 ff. (stressing the small rates of growth before 1914 rather than dealing with the take-off of growth); Toutain 1963, pp. 231 ff.

8. Ringer comes to the same conclusion in his comparison between France and Germany which are usually referred to as examples of different magnitudes of educational opportunities (cf. Ringer 1979).

9. Bamford 1961, pp. 229 ff.; Zeldin 1977, pp. 294 ff.; Anderson 1971; Kraul 1976 and 1977; Müller 1977, pp. 430 ff., 517 ff.; for early modern Europe cf. Chartier and Revel 1978, pp. 357 ff.

10. Stone 1974, pp. 37 ff., p. 93; Anderson and Schnaper 1952; McClelland 1976; Zorn 1964.

11. Mathew 1966; Lévy-Leboyer 1976, pp. 108 f.

12. For the strong contrasts among English universities, see the information on various civic universities in Sanderson 1972, pp. 97 ff.

13. Female students in higher education related to their age groups (20 through 24) in 1910: Netherlands 2.13 percent, Switzerland 0.90 percent, France 0.24 percent, Sweden 0.21 percent, Germany 0.09 percent (calculated from Edding 1958, pp. 55 ff.; Mitchell 1975, pp. 29 ff.).

14. Cf. Heidenheimer in this volume and the studies by Ringer, Kocka, Jarausch referred to in note 15; Armstrong 1973, pp. 73 ff.; Kaelble 1978, 1980; Ringer 1978b.

15. Jeismann 1977, pp. 55 f.; Jarausch 1974, pp. 551 ff. and 1978; Zorn 1964; Müller 1977; Ringer 1967 and 1978a; Kocka 1978; for the eighteenth century, see McClelland 1976.

16. Hans 1951, pp. 43 ff., 210 ff.; Simon 1960, pp. 298 ff.; Bamford 1961; Stone 1975, pp. 37 ff.; Mathew 1966; see also Thompson 1963, pp. 81 ff.

17. Anderson 1971 and 1970; Harrigan 1975 and 1976; Zeldin 1967; Chevallier, Grosperrin, and Maillet 1968; Ringer 1979.

18. See Zorn 1964; Ringer 1967, pp. 337 ff.; Jarausch 1978; Jeismann 1977; Müller 1977, pp. 37 ff.; Meyer 1968; Lundgreen 1975, pp. 85 ff. and 1977; Herrlitz and Titze 1976.

19. Sanderson 1962 and 1972, pp 97 ff. (social structure of students outside Oxford and Cambridge); Adamson 1964, pp. 62 ff., 258 ff.; Bamford 1961 (social structure of students); Simon 1960 and 1965; Stone 1970 and 1975, pp. 60 ff.

20. For England see Stone 1975; for France see Toutain 1963; for Germany see Kaelble 1976, pp. 282 ff.; for the business elite see Perkin 1976, Table 5; Erickson 1950; Kaelble 1977, Table 4; Kocka 1978.

21. See Tables 7.1-7.3, 7.6; Stone 1975; Ringer 1979; Jarausch 1979.
22. France: Anderson 1971; Duveau 1947; Germany: Müller 1977; Herrlitz and Titze 1976.
23. See Flora 1976 and the essay by Hugh Heclo in this volume.

References

Adamson, John W. 1964. *English Education 1789-1902*. Cambridge: Cambridge University Press.

Anderson, Charles A. 1965. "Access to Higher Education and Economic Development." In *Education, Economy, and Society*, eds. Albert H. Halsey et al., pp. 253 ff. New York: Free Press of Glencoe.

Anderson, Charles A. and Schnaper, Miriam. 1952. *School and Society in England: Social Background of Oxford and Cambridge Students*. Washington, D. C.: Public Affairs Press.

Anderson, Robert D. 1971. "Secondary Education in Mid-nineteenth Century France: Some Social Aspects." *Past and Present* 121-146.

Anderson, Robert D. 1975. *Education in France, 1848-1870*. Oxford: Clarendon Press.

Bamford, Thomas W. 1961. "Public Schools and Social Class 1801-1850." *British Journal of Sociology* 12: 229 ff.

Bourdieu, Pierre and Passeron, Jean-Claude. 1964. *Les héritiers*. Paris: Ed. de Minuit.

Bühl, Walter L. 1968. *Schule und gesellschaftlicher Wandel*. Stuttgart: Klett.

Chartier, R. and J. Revel. 1978. "Université et société dans l'Europe Nouvelle." *Revue d'histoire moderne et contemporaine* 25.

Chevallier, Pierre, Grosperrin, Bernard, and Maillet, Jean. 1968. *L'enseignement francais de la révolution à nos jours*. Paris: Mouton.

Duveau, Georges. 1947. *La pensée ouvrière sur l'education pendant la Seconde République et le Second Empire*. Paris.

Erickson, Charlotte. 1959. *British Industrialists*. Cambridge: Cambridge University Press.

Flora, Peter. 1975. *Indikatoren der Modernisierung*. Ein historisches Datenhandbuch. Opladen: Westdeutscher Verlag.

Flora, Peter. 1976. "On the Development of the Western European Welfare States." *HIWED Report*, No. 5. Mannheim: Universität Mannheim.

Floud, Jean, Halsey, Albert H. and Martin, Felipe R. 1955. *Social Class and Educational Opportunity*. London.

Halsey, Albert H. 1972. "Higher Education." In *Trends in British Society since 1900*, ed. Albert H. Halsey, pp. 192-226. London: Macmillan/St. Martin's Press.

Halsey, Albert H., Sheehan, John, and Vaizey, John. 1972. "Schools," In *Trends in British Society since 1900*, ed. Albert H. Halsey, pp. 148-191. London: Macmillan/St. Martin's Press.

Hans, Nicholas. 1951. *New Trends in Education in the 18th Century*. London.

Harrigan, Patrick J. 1975. "Secondary Education and the Professions in France during the Second Empire." In *Comparative Studies in Society and History* 17: 349-371.

Harrigan, Patrick J. 1976. "The Social Origins, Ambitions, and Occupations of

Secondary Students in France during the Second Empire." In *Schooling and Society*, ed. Lawrence Stone, pp. 206-235. Baltimore: Johns Hopkins University Press.

Herrlitz, Hans-Georg, and Titze, Hartmut. 1976. "Überfüllung als bildungspolitische Strategie." In *Schuleund Gesellschaft*, ed. Ulrich Herrmann. Weinheim: Beltz.

Jarausch, Konrad H. 1974. "The Sources of German Student Unrest 1815-1848." In *The University in Society*, vol. 2, ed. Lawrence Stone, pp. 551 ff. Princeton, N. J.: Princeton University Press.

Jarausch, Konrad H. 1976. "Die Studenten in Kaiserreich: Bildung, Gesellschaft und Politik." unpubl. paper, appendix (enrollments in relation to the population in Germany 1820-1914).

Jarausch, Konrad H. 1978. "Die neuhumanistische Universität und die bürgerliche Gesellschaft, 1800-1870." *Vierteljahrschrift für Sozial- und Wirtschaftsgeschichte* 65, no. 4.

Jarausch, Konrad H. 1979. "The Social Transformation of the University. The Case of Prussia 1865-1914." *Journal of Social History* 12:609-636.

Jeismann, Karl-Ernst. 1977. "Gymnasium, Staat und Gesellschaft in Preußen. Vorbemerkung der politischen und sozialen Bedeutung der 'höheren Bildung' im 19. Jahrhundert." In *Schule und Gesellschaft im 19. Jahrhundert*, ed. Ulrich Herrmann, pp. 55 ff. Weinheim: Beltz.

Kaelble, Hartmut. 1975. "Chancenungleichheit und akademische Ausbildung, 1910-1960." *Geschichte und Gesellschaft* 1: 121-149.

Kaelble, Hartmut. 1976. "Sozialer Aufstieg in Deutschland, 1850-1914." In *Quantifizierung in der Geschichtswissenschaft*, ed. Konrad H. Jarausch, pp. 279-303. Düsseldorf: Droste.

Kaelble, Hartmut. 1980. "Long-term Changes of the Recruitment of the Business Elite: Germany Compared to te USA, France, and Great Britain since the Industrial Revolution." *Journal of Social History*, Spring.

Kaelble, Hartmut. 1978. *Historische Mobilitätsforschung. Westeuropa und USA im 19. und 20. Jahrhundert*. Darmstadt: Wissenschaftliche Buchgesellschaft.

Kocka, Jürgen. 1974. "Organisierter Kapitalismus oder Staatsmonopolistischer Kapitalismus." In *Organisierter Kapitalismus*, ed. Heinrich A. Winkler, pp. 19-35. Göttingen: Vandenhoeck & Ruprecht.

Kocka, Jürgen. 1978. "Bildung, soziale Schichtung und soziale Mobilität im Deutschen Kaiserreich am Beispiel der gewerblich-technischen Ausbildung." In *Industrielle Gesellschaft und politisches System*, ed. Bernd J. Wendt, Dirk Stegmann, and Peter C. Witt, pp. 297-314. Bonn: Neue Gesellschaft.

Kocka, Jürgen. 1978. "Entrepreneurs and Managers in the German Industrial Revolution." In *Cambridge Economic History of Europe*, vol. 7. Cambridge: Cambridge University Press.

Kraul, Margret. 1976. "Untersuchungen zur sozialen Struktur der Schülerschaft des preußischen Gymnasiums im Vormärz." *Bildung und Erziehung* 29: 509-519.

Kraul, Margret. 1977. Das neuhumanistische Gymnasium - eine integrierte Gesamtschule? Studien zur Sozialgeschichte der Schülerschaft von preußischen Gymnasien im Vormärz. Dissertation. Hanover: Technische Universität.

Lawson, John and Silver, Harold. 1973. *A Social History of Education in England*. London: Methuen.

Leschinsky, Achim and Roeder, Peter M. 1976. *Schule im historischen Prozeß*. Stuttgart: Klett.

Lévy-Leboyer, Maurice. 1976. "Innovation and Business Strategies in 19th- and 20th-Century France." In *Enterprise and Entrepreneurs in 19th- and 20th-Century France,* eds. Edward C. Carter, Robert Forster, and Joseph N. Moody, pp. 108 ff. Baltimore: Johns Hopkins University Press.

Little, Alan and Westergaard, John. 1964. "The Trend of Class Differentials in Educational Opportunity in England and Wales." *British Journal of Sociology* 15: 301-316.

Lundgreen, Peter. 1976. "Educational Expansion and Economic Growth in Nineteenth Century Germany: a Quantitative Study." In *Schooling and Society,* ed. Lawrence Stone, pp. 20-66. Baltimore: Johns Hopkins University Press.

Lundgreen, Peter. 1977. "Historische Bildungsforschung." In *Historische Sozialwissenschaft,* ed. Reinhard Rürup, pp. 96-125. Göttingen: Vandenhoeck & Ruprecht.

Maier, Charles S. 1975. *Recasting Bourgeois Europe: Stabilization in France, Germany, and Italy in the Decade after World War I.* Princeton, N. J.: Princeton University Press.

Maillet, Jean. 1974. "L'évolution des effectifs de l'enseignement secondaire de 1809 à 1961." In *La scolarisation en France depuis un siècle,* ed. Pierre Chevallier. Paris: Mouton.

Marceau, Jane. 1974. "Education and Social Mobility in France." In *The Social Analysis of Class Structure,* ed. Frank Perkin, pp. 205-235. London: Tavistock Publications.

Mathew, W. M. 1966. "The Origins and Occupations of Glasgow Students, 1740-1839." *Past and Present* 33: 74-94.

McClelland, Charles E. 1976. "The Aristocracy and University Reform in Eighteenth-century Germany." In *Schooling and Society,* ed. Lawrence Stone, pp. 146-173. Baltimore: Johns Hopkins University Press.

Meyer, Ruth. 1968. "Das Berechtigungswesen in seiner Bedeutung für Schule und Gesellschaft im 19. Jahrhundert." In *Zeitschrift für die gesamte Staatswissenschaft* 124: 763-776.

Mitchell, Brian R. 1975. *European Historical Statistics.* London: Macmillan.

Mouton, Marie-Renée. 1974. "L'enseignement supérieur en France de 1890 à nos jours." In *La scolarisation en France depuis un siècle,* ed. Pierre Chevallier, pp. 176 ff. Paris: Mouton.

Müller, Detlef K. 1977. *Sozialstruktur und Schulsystem. Aspekte zum Strukturwandel des Schulwesens im 19. Jahrhundert.* Göttingen: Vandenhoeck & Ruprecht.

Perkin, Harold. 1976. 1977. "Die Rekrutierung der Eliten in der britischen Gesellschaft seit 1880." In *Geschichte und Gesellschaft* 3: 485-502.

Peyre. 1958. "L'origine sociale des élèves de l'enseignement secondaire en France." In *Ecole et société,* ed. Pierre Naville. Paris.

Rimlinger, Gaston V. 1971. *Welfare Policy and Industrialization in Europe, America, and Russia.* New York: John Wiley & Sons.

Ringer, Fritz K. 1967. "Higher Education in Germany in the 19th Century." *Journal of Contemporary History* 2: 123-138.

Ringer, Fritz K. 1978. "The Education of Elites in Modern Europe." *History of Education Quarterly* Summer: 159-172.

Ringer, Fritz K. 1978. "Education, Economy, and Social Structure, 1800-1860: German Development in Comparative Perspective." *Education and Society in Modern Europe.* Bloomington, Indiana: Indiana University Press.

Sanderson, Michael. 1962. "The Grammar School and the Education of the Poor, 1786-1840." *British Journal of Educational Studies* 11.

Sanderson, Michael. 1972. *The Universities and British Industry 1850-1870.* London: Routledge & Kegan Paul.

Silver, Harold. 1965. *The Concept of Popular Education.* London: MacGibbon & Kee.

Simon, Brian. 1960. *Studies in the History of Education 1780-1870.* London: Lawrence & Wishart.

Simon, Brian. 1965. *Education and the Labour Movement, 1870-1920.* London: Lawrence & Wishart.

Stone, Lawrence. 1970. "Japan and England: A Comparative Study." In *Sociology, History, and Education,* ed. Peter W. Musgrave, pp. 101-114. London: Methuen.

Stone, Lawrence, ed. 1974. *The University in Society,* vol. 2. Princeton, N. J.: Princeton University Press.

Stone, Lawrence. 1975. "The Size and Composition of the Oxford Student Body, 1580-1910." In *The University in Society,* vol. 1, ed. Lawrence Stone, pp. 37 ff. Princeton: Princeton University Press.

Stone, Lawrence. 1976. *Schooling and Society.* Baltimore: Johns Hopkins University Press.

Sturt, Mary. 1967. *The Education of the People.* London: Routledge & Kegan Paul.

Sutherland, Gillian. 1971. *Elementary Education in the Nineteenth Century.* London: Historical Association.

Thompson, F.M.L. 1963. *English Landed Society in the Nineteenth Century.* London: Routledge & Kegan Paul.

Toutain, Jean-Claude. 1963. *La population de la France de 1700 à 1959.* Paris: I.S.E.A.

Wehler, Hans-Ulrich. 1974. "Der Aufstieg des Organisierten Kapitalismus und Interventionsstaates in Deutschland." In *Organisierter Kapitalismus,* ed. Heinrich A. Winkler, pp. 36-57. Göttingen: Vandenhoeck & Ruprecht.

Westergaard, John and Little, Alan. 1970. "Educational Opportunity and Social Selection in England and Wales." In *Family, Class and Education,* ed. Maurice Craft. London: Longman.

Zeldin, Theodore. 1967. "Higher Education in France, 1848-1945." *Journal of Contemporary History* 2: 53-80.

Zeldin, Theodore. 1977. *France 1848-1945,* vol. 2. Oxford: Clarendon Press.

Zorn, Wolfgang. 1964. "Hochschule und höhere Schule in der deutschen Sozialgeschichte der Neuzeit." In *Spiegel der Geschichte.* Festgabe Braubach, eds. Konrad Repgen and Stephan Skalweit. Münster: Aschendorff.

Chapter 8

Education and Social Security Entitlements in Europe and America

Arnold J. Heidenheimer

Trends noted and analyzed in previous chapters, dealing with the development of social security and education policies in Western Europe and North America, are interrelated and subjected to intensive scrutiny in this essay. The central themes emerge from a set of questions that seek to probe how and why education and social security entitlements were historically broadened in such very different ways in the larger European states on the one hand, and the United States on the other. Postprimary education is perceived here as an instrument for the realization of states' concern with equality and security goals, and hence the emphasis on education and social security programs are viewed as the cores of alternative strategies pursued by emerging welfare states.

The relevant policy developments were characterized by me in an earlier article in these terms:

- Public social insurance and some other kinds of income maintenance programs were introduced in the United States with about a one generation lag behind Europe, but then exhibited growth rates that tended to bring the scope of American programs closer to those of Europeans.
- With regard to public education, the broadening of U.S. postprimary school opportunities occurred a generation earlier than in Europe, and European systems have only in the past few decades allowed their secondary and tertiary systems to enter the take-off stage.[1]

269

In this chapter I attempt an explanation of these divergent developments, primarily by analyzing how the two policy areas are linked to labor market problems, and thus indirectly to each other.

I. Education and Citizenship in Emerging Welfare States

A. *Education Development in "Bureaucratic" and "Pluralist" Systems*

Political systems can be classified according to whether they developed articulated party systems before, after, or concurrent with the establishment of centralized national bureaucracies. "In France and Germany powerful bureaucracies were built up as social-control mechanisms long *before* non-bureaucratic social groups had learned to use the weapon of political organization to secure influence."[2] In Britain, on the other hand, the emergence of a strong national bureaucracy in the mid-nineteenth century came nearly a century after political parties had begun to crystallize in a relatively decentralized polity. In the United States, as well, the start of party organization in the Jeffersonian period preceded by almost a century the steps leading to the creation of a career civil service whose members would be safeguarded against the "spoils tradition." The "constitutional" and "religious" character of political systems was related to the manner and sequence in which they gradually "nationalized" social services:

- National States found it necessary to sustain the minimal material needs of their residents earlier than they provided means of improving their moral and knowledge faculties.[3] But this "lag" tended to be shorter in the Protestant systems.
- The transferral of duties and services from associations to public bureaucracies, and from local to national officials, though everywhere gradual, was a more rapid process in the "early bureaucratic" systems, because these could command relatively greater resources to "police" and assimilate the functions of local authorities.
- As regards educational services, the pace of transfer from church to state was affected by both "constitutional" and "religious" characteristics. It was especially rapid in the Lutheran absolutist states which encouraged "the first crusade for mass education that the West has ever seen."[4]
- The two "party first" systems remained more "pluralist" because religious, local, and entrepreneurial interests remained freer to offer a variety of services in competition with the public services which the national and state governments were gradually evolving.

English experience can be interpreted to identify the state's concern with material wants through the Elizabethan Poor Laws, but its response to schooling needs only in the Victorian era. Equivalent state interventions in Prussia, by contrast, both commence in the seventeenth and eighteenth centuries. Edicts that sought to universalize at least a reading ability were adopted at this time in Sweden as well as in Prussia, as a "form of educational conscription" that sought to "throw the cost of execution on parents and communes."[5] In Sweden it was the parents who had to teach their children to read well enough to pass the annual public village exams in Bible reading, for a 1686 law provided that those who failed the exams were excluded from both communion and marriage.[6] Thus we find that the pace at which nation-states intervened to control or directly administer education varied mainly with whether they were Protestant or Catholic, and whether they gave priority to the creation of strong national bureaucracies.

In England the struggles between the Church of England and the non-conformist churches retarded the state system of primary education, while public secondary schools were not established until 1902. In Prussia, Frederick the Great had already succeeded in the late eighteenth century in "bringing secondary and university education under the control of a state department, and in establishing a leaving examination in secondary schools which ultimately became a condition of entry both to the universities and to the ranks of the Prussian administration."[7]

In America, with its slower pace of bureaucratic development, and its conspicuous history of denominational struggles, we might have expected later and less extensive advances for public education than in Europe. Indeed, the federal government became significantly involved in education policy some two generations later than even the British central government. But if we regard the American political culture as being shaped largely by pre-Tudor, anticentralist political traditions,[8] we can better understand why many educational initiatives flourished uniquely at American subnational levels. In the "denominational complexity of 18th century America a common interest of minority groups developed to neutralize the state, to deny its right to a separate interest dominant over all others, and to create of its benefits not privileges but rights."[9] In America, the competing denominations were freer to work out ad hoc solutions, in the varying colonies and states, to the question of how families, churches, and local and state governments should share in providing educational functions. Whereas, even if an English government had wanted to impose a central educational system on the country, it would have lacked the bureaucratic ability to do so in the early nineteenth century.

The capacities of modernized bureaucracies contributed to the diffusion of literacy. They extended its scope by transferring learning functions from informal to formal settings where both the extent and intensity of primary learning efforts became subject to more direct hierarchical control. The timing of compulsory education laws somewhat exaggerates the innovation of bureaucratic systems—since these generally preceded the spread of schools to the periphery—whereas in pluralist systems they tended to come after schools had sprouted more widely on a voluntary basis. But the bureaucratic "high stateness" systems could mobilize and coordinate the efforts of local school boards and clergy toward the achievements of national minima better than the pluralist systems could.

When attention is focused on the expansion of opportunities at the secondary and university level, the impact of earlier bureaucratization can be divergent. On the one hand, these systems possess greater leverage in inducing youth to pursue more formalized, longer, and more uniform degree programs because they can more easily impose systematic credential requirements for entry into developed public service bureaucracies. Since these civil services encompassed larger proportions of the prestigious professions, they could accentuate formalized education and more quickly phase out clerkship and other forms of informal training.[10]

On the other hand, some pluralist systems, whose public services were less integrated and less dominant in the labor market for professionals, could leap in higher education growth. The conditions under which this occurred are best illustrated by the American case. This shows that post-primary education can grow at an even faster rate if the various denominations and local communities are able to establish academies, high schools, but especially colleges and universities, without having to meet the selective chartering criteria of an elitist national bureaucracy. If these institutions are freer to compete for prestige in the larger society on a variety of criteria dimensions, they may be able to generate demand for their graduates in a larger variety of both private and public employment settings. The growth potential of higher education in the bureaucratic systems, by contrast, tends to be limited when large numbers of applicants, or reduced public finances, create periods of "qualification crisis," when the credentialled cannot be quickly absorbed by the public services for which their training is largely targeted.

B. Certification and Stratification in Britain and the United States

By the early nineteenth century Prussia made appointment to public offices dependent on qualifications like the *Abitur* and *Staatsexamen,* whereas in England the bulk of public and political offices continued to be filled more with recruits from the leisured classes than with holders of formal qualifications. In England, the institutions that dominated higher learning—the Church of England, Oxbridge, the Royal Colleges, and other professional elite bodies—bestowed credentials more by cooptation than by merit, and were not yet significantly accountable either to political executives or legislatures. In this setting, franchise extensions notwithstanding, secondary educational opportunities remained in a parlous state.

The effect of the extension of political rights on educational opportunities was meanwhile quite different in most parts of the United States. There, the extension of universal white male suffrage was followed by a severing of the ties not only between church and state, but also between the state and professional licensing bodies that sought to maintain monopolies or to guard the value of particular kinds of credentials. A seven-fold expansion of the electorate between 1824 and 1840 enabled "the various churches close to the people, such as the Baptists and Methodists," to push for the "wiping out of all survivals of old church-state connections."[11] Local interests generated the common school movement of the 1840s to make schooling both a more regularized and a more distinctly public concern at a time when in England, Tory opposition to the principle of mass education was strong in the wake of the Chartist challenge.[12]

"The fact that schooling became public in a de jure sense at precisely the time that churches remained public solely in a de facto sense had prodigious consequences for the future; for localities and states found a political leverage with respect to the schools that they no longer enjoyed with respect to the churches."[13] They used this prodigally so as to charter vast numbers of assorted postprimary academies and colleges that offered a variety of unstandardized curricula and degrees. Associational control yielded to market forces; if a potential entrepreneur had difficulty in getting a license or recruiting students in one place, he could simply try his luck in another. In this setting, it was easy to press the de facto claim that a citizen had the right not to be denied admission to some kind of higher education institution. But entitlements remained closely linked to enfranchisement. When the blacks were excluded from voting following the Reconstruction period, Southern counties spent about ten times as much per child for teachers' salaries in the white as in the black schools.[14]

Two ways of linking the extension of social rights to citizenship status can serve to distinguish the consequences of expansion of public education in these two pluralist systems. Bendix's formulation that "social rights as an attribute of citizenship may be considered benefits which compensate the individual for his consent to be governed under the rules and by the agents of his national political community,"[15] covers well the sequence of franchise, social policy, and educational changes in Britain after 1870. Thus the consent of the newly enfranchised lower classes was compensated by a package of insurance and education benefits resembling those adopted in the early bureaucratic systems; especially important was a close link between school certificates and employment opportunities. As Marshall was to note, attendance in various schools fixed lifelong patterns of expectations. Admission to the academic secondary schools had to be limited because "if a boy who is given a Grammar School education can then get nothing but a Modern School job, he will ... feel that he has been cheated." Therefore, "the ticket obtained on leaving school or college is for a life journey. The man with the third-class ticket who later feels entitled to claim a seat in the first-class carriage will not be admitted, even if he is prepared to pay the difference."[16]

Marshall's conclusion is that "through education in its relation with social structure, citizenship operates as an instrument of social stratification."[17] But this statement fits poorly with the empirical data on American educational opportunity. Whereas Americans too eventually received social security benefits from their national political leaders, the American lower strata used their franchise much earlier to win educational opportunities from local political leadership. Since more local officials were elected rather than appointed, they themselves were often graduates of night school and other marginal institutions, which were upgraded in a way that European equivalents—like folk high schools and workers' educational centers—were not. In part the American citizenship-education-occupation linkage can be viewed as a form of "class abatement, consciously aimed at making the class system less vulnerable to attack by alleviating its less defensible consequences." At worst, this implied that public education, as in the case of the "separate-but-equal" black institutions, "offered alternatives to the rights of citizenship, rather than additions to them,"[18] for in *Plessy v. Ferguson* (1896), the Supreme Court had declared that, "If one race be inferior to the other socially, the Constitution of the United States cannot put them upon the same plane." For several generations of black college graduates, this meant that the most they could aim for in social service positions was either to serve as undertakers for the black community or as porters for the whites who used Pullman railroad cars.

For the society as a whole, however, we can agree with Janowitz that "perhaps the most significant difference between the institutional bases of the welfare state in Great Britain and the United States was the emphasis placed on public education—especially for lower income groups—in the United States. Massive support for the expansion of public education, including higher education, in the United States, must be seen as a central component of the American notion of welfare—the idea that through public education both personal betterment and national and social and economic development would take place."[19]

C. Options and Priorities in Emerging Welfare States

If we ask how previous education opportunities were adapted in the era of the welfare state, we need to turn our attention, as regards three of our four countries, to the 1880s. It was in that decade that Britain, Germany, and the United States all came to combine mass enfranchisement with the bureaucratic potential for policy steering and implementation in rapidly industrializing systems. Germany and the United States achieved the relevant levels of industrialization and urbanization; the United States also began to endow itself with the necessary bureaucratic instruments; Britain extended enfranchisement. Sweden did not achieve the relevant thresholds until the decade of 1910-1920.

We can perceive the three countries selecting alternative governmental responses to the needs and demands for equality and security that came to be more strongly articulated at this time. Germany gave priority to meeting security needs of the lower classes by introducing compulsory insurance programs. The United States responded more to equality demands by enhancing mobility opportunities for individuals through the initiation of an unprecedented expansion of postprimary education opportunities, largely through state and local governments. Germany used its expanded social security system to deflect upward mobility ambitions, and imposed a system of "tight coupling" between its educational, labor market and social security systems. The United States continued a strategy of "substituting education for techniques of social action,"[20] and encouraged a system of "loose coupling" which accommodated more varied meritocratic accumulation tactics by individuals. Britain did not initiate radical departures in either education or social insurance, but rather enhanced the ability of various subnational collectivities to offer both kinds of benefits on a voluntary basis. Unions, friendly societies, local governments, and professional groups were stimulated by national bureaucratic and political reformers to expand local health services, found secondary schools and new universities, workers' education societies, and a vast panoply of other services, which began to reduce the previous class and regional inequalities in the availability of these benefits.

Ideological proclivities, of course, played a strong role in deciding these choices. But there were also important structural reasons that foreclosed the other choices at this time. Germany could not have selected the "British option" because the bulk of voluntary organizations were under the control of political organizations—Catholic, Socialist and Liberal—which had been alienated by Bismarck's Reich. Why it could not adopt the "American option" will be explored at greater depth in Part II.

The United States could not follow the "German option" both because it lacked an experienced bureaucracy and also because the high level of tension between economic and regional interests foreclosed the possibility of agreement on new policy departures in the socioeconomic area. The lack of a developed labor movement and the heterogeneous interests of ethnic and religious subgroups largely foreclosed the "British option."

Britain could not follow the "American option" of greatly expanding education without engendering the fierce resistance of the elitist groups who still dominated its traditional educational, cultural, and religious institutions. It also could not, at this time, follow the German "tight coupling" technique because "there was no meritocratic civil service in England before 1870 . . . nor . . . a state examination system of the German type."[21] It did move in the German direction after its bureaucratic capacity was enhanced and its party system altered to include a working class party.

In the three European systems, state-mandated insurance systems initially benefited the lower class, while state-supported higher education primarily benefited the upper strata. Eligibility for social insurance programs was extended "up" the social scale, more quickly than educational opportunities were broadened "down" to the lower social strata. This was more conspicuously the case in Germany. Probably greater exposure to the consequences of war and regime change led the German higher strata to press more vehemently for safeguards against downward social mobility and economic insecurity. After both world wars this led to the abortion of strong efforts to open up the postprimary education systems. At the same time, social security mechanisms were adjusted to protect the more highly educated unemployed from having to take jobs that were below their skill levels.

In both Britain and Sweden twentieth-century development altered more rapidly the ways in which social and education policies stratified the population. Britain set the stage for the rapid universalization of social security benefits, and initiated an education development which "combined low enrollments per age group with a comparatively democratic distribution of access chances."[22]

American welfare state development must be interpreted in light of a marked "low stateness" profile that the political system exhibited well into the twentieth century. One manifestation was that the federal government remained constitutionally and politically inhibited from significant direct initiatives in either education or welfare, although it did encourage the spread of higher education indirectly through resource (mainly public land) transfers throughout the nineteenth century. In sharp contrast to Europe, the lower levels of government generally retained higher levels of legitimacy and financial capability. When states founded universities, counties and localities bid for their location through pledges of cash and land. This situation sharply circumscribed the meaning of national, or even state, citizenship rights. Thus a welfare state infrastructure had to be developed even in the absence of effective national policymaking potential in many areas.

But the network of high schools and universities, which expanded so rapidly from the 1880s, constituted important delocalizing agents. Credentialing systems, which were being reintroduced by revived professional interests, provided coupling between education and employment markets. Coupling was established not by standardizing a particular general degree—as had been done for the *Abitur* in Germany—but rather by sectoral efforts to upgrade and standardize entrance requirements to professional schools. The desire to enter the professions triggered a "rush to the universities," as the lower-middle-class families sought to achieve security goals by "investing hopes in their children."

Whereas in Germany the possession of a university law degree long remained virtually a prerequisite for entry into the higher civil service, equivalent American positions have remained accessible through a much more varied set of credentials and experience. Conversely, in Germany a given credential signified, for its holder, a more standardized, and at most times, surer, claim to a particular career pattern. The combination of the *Laufbahn* career pattern with the guaranteed lifetime tenure for *Beamten*, meant that the *Berechtigungen* of most postprimary school credentials were linked to postretirement pensions in one fairly continuous chain of entitlements. The adoption, in Bismarck's time, of compulsory pensions and other social security coverage for industrial workers, may be seen as the extrapolation of this entitlement model to the lower-class workers in private employment when economic growth had begun to make this feasible and political enfranchisement had made it expedient.

II. The Divergence Between German and United States Educational Development, 1880-1920

Why did the United States initiate an unprecedented expansion of secondary and higher education, while Germany yielded its hitherto leading education position as it began to concentrate resources on a social security build-up? In this part we shall attempt to analyze in greater detail just how the two leaders came to be propelled in such divergent policy directions during the initial phase of welfare state development. Since the two countries were strikingly similar in the nature and rate of their macroeconomic change—that is, both came to overtake Britain as industrial producers in this period—we can focus attention on how their political and cultural institutions reacted to the conditions of capitalist development at that time: how they adjusted to the exigencies of business cycles and changed manpower needs. We therefore seek insight into the links between changes in labor markets and changes in education and social security systems. In the background is the contrast between German social security development and the American inaction. In the foreground are the conditions that impelled German policy makers to shift to a restrictive education policy, while Americans undertook a sharply expansive one.

A. Bureaucratic Dominance and Secondary School Models

In both countries, educational policy was in the jurisdiction of the states rather than the federal governments, but Prussia had two-thirds of the total Reich population, and policy was much more the result of conscious central direction. The function of American government at the time has, by contrast, been well described as serving "primarily as an *underwriter*, secondarily as the *coordinator* . . . rarely as the *integrator*, never as the *architect*.[23] Policy within the especially decentralized education system was laid down by ad hoc commissions, such as the one that produced the report, *Cardinal Principles of Secondary Education* (1918), of which the United States Bureau of Education then sold more than one hundred thousand copies. But when, ten years later, 1,228 school superintendents were surveyed about their familiarity with this report, less than one-fifth said they had heard of it,[24] illustrating extremely poor articulation.

The result of public high school expansion was that the proportion of fourteen to seventeen year olds who were in full time school attendance increased five-fold—from 6.7 percent in 1890 to 32.3 percent in 1920—and kept on increasing from there. At the same time, the number of public high schools increased six-fold—from 2,526 to 14326—and the number of high school teachers more than ten-fold.[25]

Trying to fit together the pieces, historians today are still "unable to explain completely the reasons for this remarkable increase in high school attendance over the thirty-year period, 1890-1920. Enrollments in public high schools increased gradually throughout the second half of the nine-teenth century, but why that secular trend increased sharply when it did remains something of a mystery."[26] Perhaps the mechanization of many of the simple factory operations that children had performed propelled more youth into high school for lack of job alternatives; then child labor and compulsory education laws generalized the pattern.[27]

When mechanization brought the typewriter and the duplicator to offices it engendered demand for skilled office personnel, and somehow "this kind of job became reserved for the person who had some high school education." Thus Church speculates that "high school enrollments rose because it became increasingly evident to those interested in the status and income accompanying white-collar occupations that a high school educa-tion was a valuable—perhaps the most valuable—guarantee of securing such positions. Anxiety about decreasing opportunity in America and intensified job competition may have caused many to want the *insurance* of added education—an *insurance* that in the nineteenth century few had thought it necessary to obtain."[28] In the private sector, meanwhile, com-panies were responding to workers' needs at the end of the employment period by beginning to introduce company pension programs. But only about a half-dozen firms offered such programs before 1900; the number expanded to about fifty by 1910.[29] By 1924, only some thirty-six thousand workers were drawing benefits from these programs, whereas about one out of every twenty-five Americans was enrolled as a public high school student.

In Germany the decade that marked the introduction of social security legislation saw education policy makers greatly enhancing their bureau-cratic steering potential over the school system. In 1882, the Prussian Education Ministry issued the first modern set of comprehensive regula-tions covering instructional goals and examination functions in all types of secondary schools. They spelled out in detail which leaving credentials of the various schools could serve as entry entitlements to higher education and to positions in the public service. Individual ministries had, up to then, implemented their own recruitment criteria, but in 1884 they yielded this authority to the education ministry; it was then in a much stronger position to try to match the supply of secondary and tertiary graduates to the anticipated demand in the public sector, which for most types of credential bearers encompassed the bulk of employment opportunities. The thrust was to reward those who had completed some formal course; the student who attended a *Realschule* for four years and then "dropped out" came out worse than a student who had opted for the four-year vocational course in the first place.

The German and American developments can be seen as exemplifying diametrically opposed longer-term trends as regards the elitization of secondary education and the resulting selection of the modal secondary school type. In 1830 the *Gymnasia* were still utilized as a kind of comprehensive school, catering to the early leaver who would enter commerce or white-collar work, as well as to the prospective university student.[30] But then the prerequisite of a *Gymnasium Abitur* for university entrance was made absolute, and a rapid process of differentation between the various secondary school types was implemented. Whereas in 1830 about half of the urban youth subject to compulsory schooling were enrolled in *Gymnasien* and other "higher schools," by the end of the century the proportion in these elite schools had been reduced to about 15 percent.[31] Most of these were aiming for either the prized *Abitur,* or at least the tenth year leaving certificate which made the bearer eligible for fulfilling his military obligation through a one-year stint as a reserve officer (Einjährige). *Gymnasia* were enabled to compensate for the loss of tuition from the "early leavers" by raising tuition for the higher grades, eliminating progressive, income-related tuition schedules, and by receiving the bulk of state secondary school subsidies.[32] Thus the "majority of the *Gymnasien* and *Realschulen* were transformed from differentiated comprehensive schools (*Gesamtschulen*) at the beginning of the nineteenth century, to essentially elite schools at its end."[33] With the adherence of South German *Laender* to the North German Federation (1867) and then the empire (1871), they found it necessary to adapt their school systems to the pattern shaped by the Prussian *Berechtigungswesen.* In the case of Württemberg and the Hanseatic states this meant diluting a highly developed system of middle schools that had been less oriented toward the needs of the public service and more toward those of private employers.[34]

"The use of the post-primary schools as 'comprehensive schools' for the majority of the urban population, which persisted into the mid-19th century, facilitated intergenerational mobility. The pupil, who because of his family background and other limitations leaves school at an intermediate level, will later encourage his children to go further in the same type of school, thereby facilitating some upward social mobility."[35] This development aborted in Prussia was generally pursued in America where the lower middle class was "an important constituent in the creation of the high school."[36] It is difficult to compare German school types with contemporary American models, but the *Gymnasium* had the closest functional resemblance to the private, mainly classically-oriented, academies, while the *Realschulen* were more similar in curricula and social recruitment to the emerging public high schools. In the United States, by the end of the century, academies "survived largely as an elite system overshadowed by the public high schools."[37]

B. Determinants of Restrictive and Expansive Education Policies

If German workers came to see the late nineteenth-century *Gymnasium* and *Realschule* as bastions of middle-class privilege, there were some parallels in the early phases of the American high school development. In 1873 President Eliot of Harvard related that mechanics, blacksmiths, and other members of the "masses of Massachusetts," were asking, "Why should I pay for the professional education of the lawyer's son, the minister's son? The community does not provide my son his forge or loom?" A little later on, the Knights of Labor, who organized the heavily Catholic manual workers with some success in the 1880s lined up "with the forces opposing the high school 'craze'"[38] But while the depression of the 1880s initially favored the Knights, it also ushered in their demise when their freer use of strike and boycott weapons came to appear discredited by violent confrontations like the Haymarket bombings of 1886. The American Federation of Labor, founded that year, quickly surplanted them as the dominant force. Whereas the Knights were skeptical of formal schooling as unlikely to serve their members' political or economic needs, the leadership of the AFL endorsed formal education with dedication and persistence.

The AFL's opposition to government intervention led it to oppose child labor laws and public social security legislation, yet it strongly favored raising the compulsory school-leaving age, a device that would reduce competition in labor markets while also being highly consonant with middle-class values. In 1894, AFL spokesmen "heartily concurred in the sentiment that education shall be the watchword of the labor movement." In 1898, Gompers declared that "much of our misery as enforced wage-workers springs not so much from any power exerted by the upper or ruling classes, as it is the ignorance of so many in our own class who accept conditions by their own volition."[39]

Thus a very similar experience—exposure to the economic recession of the 1880s—triggered an expansionist school development in a less stratified society where links between education and labor market were highly flexible, while it led to a sharply restrictive policy development in a more stratified society with highly formalized entitlements. In Germany holders of *Abitur, Staatsexamen*, and other credentials held expectations for positions in the bureaucracy and the professions that were largely fulfilled in a "seller's market," such as that of the 1870s. But in a depression decade both public bureaucracies and private employers curtailed new hiring, thus bringing about a qualification crisis in which the value of these degrees sharply depreciated. Experts, who had called for an expansion of educational opportunities only a few years earlier, reversed course to urge the reintroduction of barriers so as to contain the surplus of unemployed or underemployed academic manpower.

In this setting the upward trend in university enrollment was arrested,[40] but not before Bismarck was able to use the spectre of an emerging academic proletariat to manipulate the educated middle classes in a more conservative political direction. With education policy joined to the antisocialist laws and colonial claims as key issues in the election campaign of 1884, the conservative coalition was able to lay the basis for the recapture of a stable pro-Bismarck Reichstag majority by 1887. It was against this background that gatekeepers at all levels raised the thresholds of school admission. At the level of the school, teachers and principals took pride in discouraging parents from the lower strata from trying to enter their children in the higher-level schools. These reorientations made it easier for the minister of education to tell the Prussian Diet in 1889 that he would limit the number and capacity of the academically oriented schools according to "what is needed for the replenishment of the so-called ruling classes."[41] A year later the national School Conference of 1890 rejected the claims of the other secondary schools and reaffirmed the monopoly of *Gymnasium* graduates for admission to most types of university education and higher bureaucratic offices.[42] In Prussia, the increased capacity provided by the 43 gymnasia and 77 other secondary schools established between 1876 and 1896 helped to keep up with population growth; but the overall ratio of one secondary pupil for some 230 inhabitants remained almost static.[43]

An economist like Johannes Conrad asserted that "it should be one of the tasks of the developing social policy to bring social needs and economic constraints into closer equilibrium."[44] He clearly recognized the substitution potential of educational and social welfare benefits. For him "integrating education policy into social policy" implied the development of trade-offs that could discourage lower strata children from utilizing their potential claims to higher education. Thus he called for an improvement of apprenticeship training, adoption of laws regulating the length of the working day, and the increase of wage levels, all toward the end of "raising the social position of the lower classes." His basic recommendation, as a "necessary correlate" of the restrictionist schools admission policy, was the "improvement of the position of the working class . . . *in order to reduce the aspirations for trying to get out of it.*"[45] This goal could be accepted both by Bismarck and his Socialist opponents.

The Social Democrats opposed Bismarck's social insurance laws, but the Social Democratic union leaders won control of the sickness funds that were given the tasks of implementing the sickness insurance system. Their staffs quickly grew in size and constituted the largest category of white-collar positions to which entry was not contingent upon the school-centered credentials system. This meant that the party and unions possessed greater means of providing social mobility for meritorious functionaries, probably causing skilled workers to downgrade utilization of more advanced formal education enrollment, as opposed to enrollment in party and union positions,[46] for their children.

Ringer argues that the higher formalization of the German as compared to the English system encouraged more lower-middle-class youth to work their way up into the university system.[47] Kaelble confirms that the utilization of higher education by the lower middle class was more prevalent in Germany than in England or France, but it was developed less consistently than in the United States. In periods like the 1880s, the German lower middle class, "attuned to law and order thinking, is alarmed by the notion that danger lurks both in the factories and the universities. Its fear of sinking into the proletariat is reenforced by its fear of rising into the proletariat."[48] Slogans floated from above, like that of the "academic proletariat," meshed with those generated from below, like "cobbler, stick to your last," to reenforce motivational barriers against the use of potentially accessible entitlements.

C. Credentialling Modes and Employment Mobility

How, then, did the United States nurture a trend which, on the one hand brought larger proportions of youth into formal postprimary education, while on the other hand maintained greater flexibility than was the case in the European countries? The key to the answer lies in the complementary functions of associational and governmental bureaucracies which a "low stateness" system facilitated.

In the United States, credentialling authority was established and extended through accreditation systems operated mainly by educators on the basis of broad legislative authority and close coordination with practitioners and employers. Historians are not sure whether the accredition model was shaped by a state board of education, a church organization, or a woman's organization,[49] but it was definitely not invented by the national bureaucrats.

The stringency of entry controls to higher education and occupational licenses differed greatly by occupation and region. This contributed to a lower degree of standardization of educational credentials and to a relatively high substitutability between credentials and job experience. Bureaucracies remained powerless or hesitant to police the use of degrees and titles. As a result most states continued to "grant charters to educational institutions in an almost profligate manner," while at the same time "requiring that candidates for a profession be graduates from accredited colleges in order to take state licensing examinations."[50]

This situation encouraged foundations to play a key role in setting standards, as the Carnegie Foundation for the Advancement of Teaching did when it imposed entrance and curricular standards on the private nondenominational colleges which it helped finance. In 1906 it declared that a college had to have at least six professors, offer a four-year liberal arts program, and admit only students who had completed a four-year high school course. The last condition was crucial insofar as the distinction between secondary and higher education had not hitherto been clearly established. Its planners further specified that high school graduation had to entail the completion of fourteen "Carnegie units" of instruction in basic subjects, a definition which in effect bound the high schools to a four-year curriculum.[51]

An analysis in the context of welfare state development makes it appropriate to underline that the incentive which the foundation held out to the colleges for the adoption of these rules, was the financing, until 1915 completely from its own resources, of a pension program for college faculty. Thus the foundation was replicating the role of the Prussian Education Ministry not only by imposing credentials, but also by providing the equivalent of the German *Beamten* retirement security. Thus were enticements linked to entitlements: "A second-rate college could no longer take students from the midst of their high school studies, or its faculty would lose their pensions; high schools had to offer a four-year program, or their students would be ineligible to attend any college which wanted pensions for its faculty."[52] The foundation succeeded in imposing on the private sector that which the U. S. Office of Education had failed initially to impose on the system as a whole; for that bureaucracy's attempt at classification had unleashed a storm of protest that "there are no second and third and fourth class colleges; that it was an outrage and an infamy so to designate institutions whose sons reflected honor on the state and nation." Thus citizens who had enjoyed equal suffrage for three generations rejected a hierarchial model in the way that Prussians, voting under a three-class electoral law, could and did not.

Overall, the American development led within two generations to a reduction from 4:1 to 2:1 in the percentage share of all schooling received by the most and the least educated third of American males. During some phases indeed the broadened equality of opportunity led to some surprising equality of at least intermediate results. Thus, "in the years 1915-1925, it was college freshmen from poorly educated families who were actually more likely to earn degrees than were freshmen from well-educated families."[53] Later, as the value of college credentials became more evident, one finds that "upper middle class parents make aggressive efforts to provide their offsprings with a college education superior to that usually given to the middle majority and the poor," as Wilensky describes the California experience.[54] The theorem that perhaps best captures the essentials of this complex development is Bendix's dialectical proposition that "the extension of citizenship to the lower classes involves at many levels an institutionalization of abstract criteria of equality, which gives rise to new inequalities and new measures to deal with these ancillary consequences."[55]

The spread of the accreditation system meant that credentials which bore the same title, such as high school diplomas or B.A. degrees, could lead to quite different entitlements regarding admission to college or postgraduate study, depending on the status of the institution that awarded it. Consequently the students utilizing entitlements to free public education encountered options in the higher regions of the systems, which varied with such factors as the per capita tax income of the school district and the racial and social composition of the school. Where the typical European lower-class students encountered *de jure* barriers, his American equivalent often encountered almost equally severe *de facto* barriers. Graduates from midwestern state colleges often became managers and teachers, seldom medical school professors. Graduates from Catholic colleges often became accountants and lawyers, seldom physicists or nationally known social scientists. Graduates from southern black colleges often became teachers in black schools, but for a long period had few other professional opportunities.

Qualitative differentials in the bestowal and utilization of credentials produced striking crossnational differences in the degree of cohesion and common interest among those who concluded higher studies. In Germany, all holders of university degrees remained sharply distinguished as *Akademiker* from even graduates of other higher education institutions. In Britain the term "graduate" remained less meaningful and ambiguous. There and in the United States the label of "professional" also remained susceptible to usurpation; in America one could advertise oneself as a "professional gardener" in a way that no German could label himself as an "academic gardener."

The credentialing patterns that evolved within the increasingly formalized German higher education system were also imposed to reinvigorate the more informal, apprenticeship-based training systems for German skilled manual workers. Amendments to the *Gewerbeordnung* required the artisans' guilds to erect training schools and introduce examinations. Those who taught apprentices had to possess adequate credentials and, by 1908, were required to have passed the masters' exams in their trades. In England, by contrast, the state lost control of apprenticeship systems in the early nineteenth century, and later its use by unions as an entry control device with lower learning content led to its qualitative decline. In America, the greater mobility of labor caused "the individual manufacturer to feel that it is of little advantage to him to educate boys, who, once trained, may leave him to enter the employ of a rival concern."[56] Lacking sufficient pressures for the upgrading and updating of their programs, American apprenticeship programs also "stopped being educative . . . and became exploitative—that is, an initial career stage in which the worker was paid very little for repetitive performance of an unskilled job . . . with the result that industry began to demand vocational preparation of the schools."[57]

Increased differentiation and specialization produced strong elitization tendencies, in the United States as well as in Germany. But insofar as educational credentials contributed to elite status and its income concommitants, they were degrees from only some faculties and some kinds of colleges. Holders of medical degrees found these easily convertible into elite socioeconomic status, and bearers of Ivy League degrees had some advantages over others. But generally the status differences within the group of university credentialled widened much more than in Germany. Librarians, social workers, accountants, and nurses sought to liberate themselves from their academic "betters," to lay claim to distinct occupational turfs, and then to upgrade the credentials required for entrance so as to buttress their claim to professional status.[58] Thus credentialism also came to flourish once it became an American game. But its effect on changing social status rankings remained limited in a situation where almost all could play the game, and where the borderlines between theoretical and "practical" education, professional or technical occupations, and benchmarks of social rank generally remained more fluid and substitutable than in Europe.

III. Qualifications and Social Security Entitlements in the United States and West Germany

From the citizen's perspective the welfare state era is conceptualized as offering not only a wider variety of benefits, but also less conditional entitlement to them. National citizenship, when linked to control by national bureaucracies and adjudication by a national judiciary, is presumed to facilitate a conversion of political claims into *de jure* entitlements, which are uniform because they can eclipse ascriptive and parochial conditions. The initiation of national social security legislation in Germany in the 1880s and in the United States in the 1930s laid the basis for the growth of one bundle of more uniform citizens' entitlements. An important reason why it did so was that, in contrast to public benefits which were remodeled rather than newly initiated, such as education and health, these programs were increasingly either directly administered or very tightly supervised by national bureaucracies.

A. Bureaucracy, Social Security, and Entitlements

It is because the United States lagged in the introduction of such legislation that it sometimes ends up being classified with countries like Paraguay and Afghanistan in policy diffusion studies.[59] Moreover, it subsequently did not, in a diverse continental setting, follow the pattern of integration pursued by the European systems. Its federal system retained many "low stateness" attributes; its subnational units retained more options in the utilization of federal programs; and its judiciary remained less inclined to give priority to uniformity criteria in assessing policy implementation. In this section we shall contrast it with the capabilities of the more thoroughly bureaucratized German system that developed certain advantages for many citizens through its ability to link equality to security goals through a more legally structured benefit system.

Although those American programs that are totally administered by federal agencies, such as social security pensions, usually have nationally uniform benefit rates, benefit levels in education and social assistance have varied by factors of 4:1 among American states and localities. German per capita school spending or social assistance payments do not vary nearly as much, though they too exhibit something of a north-south gradient. The combination of a more developed social security system and a more extended unionization of the labor force has inhibited a polarization between those who have both good wages and security benefits and those who have neither.

Greater regional equalities in Germany can be seen as the consequence of an historical development through which the national bureaucracy reduced the relative significance of local governments and associations as intermediaries with significant discretionary administrative power. The degree to which national legislation relied on the latter agencies decreased perceptibly. Thus the sickness insurance law of 1883 made membership compulsory for certain kinds of workers, but left great administrative discretion in the hands of local sickness funds which became the program administrators. This element of self-administration remained a component of subsequent legislation, but decreasingly so. With the adoption of the 1927 unemployment insurance law, "self-administration remained a concept with scarcely any real social reference structure."[60] Central control of implementation tightened. In 1900, a visit to provincial insurance offices by officials from the Interior Ministry led quickly to a decline by one-third in invalidity pensions applications approved by these offices.[61] The power of the central government authorities made feasible a control on entitlement recognitions that proved difficult to replicate in later American programs relying on intergovernmental cooperation, especially regarding "positive" controls.

Even the decentralized programs, like sickness insurance, were incorporated within a nationally uniform system of rules and procedures which reduced opportunities for lower-level decision sharing and participation. Where the 1883 law had contained only 83 paragraphs, leaving plenty of room for rule making by the sickness funds, the corresponding sections in the 1911 Reich Insurance Law (RVO) contained no fewer than 370 paragraphs. The RVO created a uniform judicial apparatus for the entire German social insurance system, relying on technically and professionally trained *Beamten*. In this context, the sickness funds could not continue to ignore credentials in their staff recruitment, with the result that they too introduced training programs and examinations in 1925. Abolished by the Nazis, the funds were reestablished after the war. This pattern, together with the 1951 shift to equal employer-employee representation on the funds, contributed to a marked decline in utilization of the self-administration opportunities. Whereas in 1914 there were contested elections in 66 percent of the local sickness funds, by 1927 this occurred in only 27 percent; and by 1959, only 2 out of some 800 sickness funds held contested elections.[62]

B. Social Stratification and Employment Controls

Given their differential pattern of benefit entitlements, the two systems developed different ways through which to classify beneficiaries as their programs approached universality. This can be illustrated with reference to the German invalidity insurance program and the higher education system of California, both of which were by the 1960s offering benefits to over 80 percent of their potential clientele. In the German invalidity insurance program the courts came to distinguish among claimants on the basis of whether their previous levels of training and education entitled them to one of two kinds of pensions. In California, which had developed a three-tier system of junior colleges, state colleges, and state universities, observers noted "an unmistakable process of self-selection and recruitment by social background into the three-tier system, with occupational prospects appropriately linked to quality levels."[63] Though these stratification mechanisms operated at different points in the life-cycle, we can compare them as to the stringency of selection processes.

German law distinguishes sharply between relatively uncredentialed claimants for employment invalidity (*Erwerbsunfähigkeit*) benefits, who have to let themselves be assigned to any employment on the general labor market which is compatible with their state of health, and applicants for occupational invalidity (*Berufsunfähigkeit*) benefits, for whom the test of employability relates only to open positions at their approximate level of education and training.[64] The latter program's stronger guarantees originated in a 1911 law change that gave white-collar employes special status. In 1919 an arbitration court decision determined "that it is not acceptable that a former dancer in the Royal Ballet be assigned work in an office or in domestic work, but could only be assigned to a position which was socially nearly equivalent to her previous occupational position."[65]

German insurance authorities and social courts subsequently developed the so-called "three-level theory,' in accordance with which the credentialed white-collar and skilled worker applicants could not usually be directed toward unskilled jobs even though they might be quite suitable in terms of physical capability. This adjudication "caused the unskilled workers to be disadvantaged in relation to the skilled workers, and most probably disadvantaged the workers as a whole in comparison to the white-collar employees." The unskilled were those who "in their youth— for reasons for which they may or may not have been responsible—had not pursued or concluded a training or apprenticeship program, and who, therefore, in their old age would generally have no claim on an 'occupational' invalidity pension."[66] Somewhat similar distinctions have also been maintained in other branches of the German social security system, as in unemployment insurance and sickness insurance, where white-collar sickness funds have generally been able to offer better cost-benefit ratios than those enrolling manual workers.

Clearly the California system, and similar ones in other states, tend somewhat to perpetuate social stratification patterns since middle-class children tend to have both the higher grades and the motivation to go directly from high school to a state university where their chances of achieving higher professional status are better. But the American stratification system differs in that gate keeping to the higher institutions remains more open and in that the labelling attached to those who attend the lower-prestige institutions is less clear-cut and generalized. For men of similar social backgrounds, the selectivity of the colleges they attend affect future incomes, but bear no significant relationship to occupational status. The dependence of occupational status on socioeconomic background "only modestly inflates" the effects of higher education on the former.[67] In some state university systems only five percent of the variance in later earnings of alumni are attributed to the type of institution attended.[68] While attendance at community colleges serves a "cooling out" function for many, it enables many others—in California some 15 percent of high school graduates—to reach a university-level institution through the two-year institutions.

But while Californians could count on the greater permeability of the educational system to reduce inequalities of opportunity, they could not rely upon public social insurance mechanisms to guarantee security of occupational status. The American social security programs do not contain the equivalent of the German occupational invalidity program, and their social adjudication has not hinged so strongly as the German one on the principle of *Zumutbarkeit*. As one German writer explains it, "In the Federal Republic an invalidity pension is paid even if the insured could earn as much or more, but only in an occupation that enjoys lower social prestige, a shift to which entails downward social mobility. This protection of 'social prestige' is completely alien to the American preconceptions."[69]

While most social security programs serve to contain social decline, American attempts to define the attributes of security give less priority and emphasis to preventing downward social mobility than do German ones. Although the social prestige ranking of occupations is not too different in the two countries, the role of the more inclusive American higher education system in allowing occupations to seek to improve themselves by raising their credentialing standards has served to blur distinctions. Thus American sociologists write about the "semi-professions," in ways that Germans find it difficult to. A more official reflection of the tendency to diminish reliance on a stratified classification system occurred when the 1965 edition of the U. S. *Dictionary of Occupational Titles* dropped the categories "skilled," "semi-skilled" and "unskilled," because the terms were thought to carry confusing secondary socioeconomic connotations.[70]

In the Federal Republic, social court judges could continue to rely on a lexicon of skilled occupations, which has been published by the Federal Labor Ministry since 1954, in determining what job shifts might constitute "significant social decline." In effect, this has sometimes put judges in the position of seeking to control the social stratification system, causing one critic to protest that administrative law experts expected "society to follow the adjudication of the social courts in deciding on what it regards as 'social decline.'"[71] The less conceptually developed American welfare law offers a contrasting provision "centered around specific risks, and each carries conditions of entitlement related to that particular risk." In the case of unemployment, the claimant must "demonstrate the fact that his unemployment is involuntary partly by registering for suitable job openings through the public employment offices." But "what constitutes 'suitable' employment in these circumstances is both a hazy and controversial aspect of entitlement."[72]

C. The Diminution of Entitlement Barriers

If one examines the quantitative measures of entitlement utilization, it appears that the United States and Germany became less dissimilar during the late 1960s and early 1970s when both countries managed to dismantle barriers that had previously inhibited growth of some public programs. In the United States the successful attack on the "second-class" citizenship status of blacks removed political blocks to the adoption of many programs, such as federal financing of health care and education. It also triggered a vast range of political and judicial challenges to inequalities of various kinds that had previously been seen as normal concommitants of the American "low-state" system.

In West Germany successful attacks on the normative and motivational barriers that had limited the utilization of secondary education were pursued under the slogan *"Bildung ist Bürgerrecht"* (education is a civil right). The social distribution of educational opportunities, which had virtually remained constant from 1890s through the 1950s,[73] finally began to change. Whereas in the 1950s observers could still remark on "the low proportions of Germans, compared to Americans, who chose to change their way of life by increasing the length of their schooling,"[74] this disparity rapidly diminished. But although education was found to have a relatively strong effect on position in the labor market (in contrast to findings produced for the U.S. by Jencks and others), the broadening of West German educational opportunities "did not itself contribute to significant intergenerational mobility."[75]

The German *Bildungsboom* was galvinated by a growing recognition of the disparity between highly developed income maintenance programs on the one hand, and underdeveloped educational opportunities on the other. Even social security specialists, such as the authors of the 1966 *Sozialenquéte,* noted that "the increasing demands for schematic income benefits have tended to place social services in a politically detrimental position," and that education goals had been repressed as a by-product of the push for "perfectionism in the pension system."[76] Social scientists debated whether welfare efforts or educational investments could contribute more toward easing "the social problem situation associated with the word symbol 'security,' " and concluded that "under the prevailing social conditions an increase in school and occupational training capacity would more readily contribute toward a solution of this problem than would an increase in welfare effort."[77] When the greatly increased number of students threatened to deprive some applicants of the opportunity to pursue university studies, the Constitutional Court in 1973 affirmed constitutional guarantees of participation in such existing public benefits "because the modern state makes the social security and cultural development of the citizen one of its central concerns."

The American Supreme Court, at about the same time, was abandoning previously employed distinctions between rights and privileges. In a 1970 case, *Goldberg v. Kelly,* the Court held that "it may be realistic today to regard welfare entitlements as more like property than a 'gratuity,' " and acknowledged that welfare "benefits are a matter of statutory entitlement for persons qualified to receive them." Thus for the first time the court recognized entitlements that were founded neither on constitutional nor on common law claims of rights, but only on state-fostered expectations founded on sources like state laws and regulations. The recognition of these new statutory entitlements protected claims to benefits, once they had been given by the state, against arbitrary withdrawal without due process of law.[78]

The American welfare state, previously characterized by very loose linkages between citizenship status and social entitlements, was subjected to an overall thrust that tightened, rationalized, and departicularized claim conditions, and universalized social entitlements through larger subcomponents of the system. More sweeping and generous interpretations of the "equal protection" clause of the Fourteenth Amendment buttressed this thrust. In California the state courts went so far as to hold unconstitutional the system of school financing through local property taxes, which strongly affected the social selection manifested in recruitment to the different branches of the three-tier higher education system. However, the U. S. Supreme Court, reviewing a similar case, would not concede that "an identifiable quantum of education is a constitutionally protected right." In thus refusing to raise the right to education to constitutional stature, it stopped short of the equivalent German court decisions. Tribe's comment on *Rodriguez v. San Antonio* acidly etched the court's rationale for the acceptance of inequality: "Increased distance from the less fortunate seems to be a major incentive for upward mobility. State legislatures currently allow the wealthy to purchase such distance. The Texas public education financing scheme went a step further and told the rich . . . to create their own secure haven of privilege and exclusion. Judicial disruption of this pattern of upward mobility would have represented redistribution of a fundamental variety."[79]

D. Benefit "Uptake" and Bureaucratic "Outreach"

Despite the convergences noted in the preceding section, we can still identify ways in which constraints on the extension of welfare state benefits reflect the bureaucratic and pluralist nature that we attributed to the two systems at the outset of this article.

One confining condition on the more pluralist American system relates to the coordination of policies aimed at the goals of economic security and equality of opportunity. This is illustrated if one seeks to identify reforms in the education system that were adopted concurrently with the breakthroughs on social security legislation in the 1930s. "The New Deal, for all its concern for welfare in the United States, did surprisingly little to improve public schooling . . . and effected virtually no change in the distribution of educational opportunities or in the manner in which education was financed and administered."[80] This finding is especially surprising in view of Janowitz's above-cited claim about the "centrality" of public education to American welfare notions. The latter may have to be qualified in terms of policy trade-off possibilities in various political epochs. What the New Deal did implement were several programs aimed at linking education and employment opportunities more directly, such as the Civilian Conservation Corps and the National Youth Administration, and it is significant that these were terminated as soon as unemployment became less of a problem.

Once the broad Social Security Act was on the books most subsequent income maintenance and social service programs were added to it, so that, as is noted earlier in this volume,[81] the most salient feature of the American welfare state development is that almost all measures were passed as amendments to the original Social Security Act. The decision to overcome the bitter resistance to health insurance by also adding the Medicare and Medicaid programs in this way may well have inhibited subsequent attempts to lay the basis for a more universal health insurance program.

Another distinction between the pluralist American federal system and the bureaucratically integrated German one is that the increased central government role in social service financing has not been very closely correlated with national uniformity of benefits. When state programs were federalized, as in the case of the supplementary security income program, greater uniformity could be approached. But the bulk of federal programs involved intergovernmental transfers, and here the more aggressive state welfare bureaucracies could claim disproportionate resources. Thus one reason why California was able to build up the large state revenue surplus that helped pave the way for the Proposition 13 tax revolt in 1978 was that the officials in Sacramento were able to grab over 30 percent of some federal grants-in-aid funds. "Ordinarily state officials had a clearer perception than did federal regional officials of what the Social and Rehabilitation Service headquarters (in Washington) would approve. 'We had a better pipeline than they did,' a California official recalled. 'It became a joke.'"[82]

In a period like the 1960s most welfare benefits were distributed more generously in most American states, partly because of favorable court rulings, partly because more people applied, but also because officials moved to interpret eligibility requirements in a more liberal direction. Whether the official responsiveness was in reaction to riots and other signs of protest is still under debate,[83] but it seems that almost all states liberalized their eligibility requirements for Aid For Dependent Children (AFDC) benefits in this decade. But then in the 1970s the turn toward more restrictive interpretations appears to have been more marked than in

Germany. Cycles between reform and reaction, between tendencies toward generosity and stringency, appear to be sharper in the more pluralist than in the more bureaucratic system.

One reason why social assistance is much less controversial in German than in American discussions is that it looms much smaller in relation to the normal social security expenditures. In expenditure terms it absorbs less than 5 percent of what is spent on social security (in 1975, 1 percent of GNP as opposed to 23.9 percent) whereas in the United States the more limited distribution of social security benefits contributes to making the ratio (2.8 percent vs. 8.7 percent GNP, 1975) more like 30 percent. American social assistance has more poor to take care of because the other income support nets are more widely meshed, leaving a larger poverty population eligible for assistance.

Recent American experience generated a high degree of controversy and open policy making that forced welfare administrators to adopt a variety of "outreach" programs to find and enroll those whose low income made them eligible for the various assistance programs for the aged, blind, and disabled. Public campaigns and the activation of local groups helped generate an "explosion" of participation rates in programs like Aid for Dependent Children (ADFC). In Germany at the same time the welfare bureaucracy, operating as usual within its normal tight policy-making circles, created much less controversy and achieved no significant increase in participation rates. There the welfare agency is not as a rule looking for problems; it does not begin to activate entitlements until "a person appears, makes himself heard and felt, takes upon himself the role of an applicant and steadily pursues his claim."[84]

The proportion of those eligible for social assistance who actually receive it in Germany is somewhere between 20 and 50 percent. This compares with American participation rates of 90 percent for AFDC, 50 percent for supplementary social assistance, and about 40 percent for food stamps. In terms of policy development benchmarks—legislative initiation under social democratic sponsorship, minimal deviation from national benefit rates, and administration by reliable bureaucracy—the German outcome could have been expected to be better than the American. But a passive institutionalization shaped by the encapsulation of the welfare administration within a traditional bureaucratic pattern makes the recipient bear the onus of proving his special condition vis-à-vis skeptical officials.

"The Social Democratic form of mass mobilization and a state structure more disposed toward preventive social action" would seem to make the West German welfare system—with its universality of entitlements, structural compactness and lesser use of pressure for recipients to get off the rolls—an instrument "worthy of the welfare state label." But Leibfried's comparative analysis of "outcomes" in public assistance policies in Germany and the United States shows that the inclusion of unorganized marginal social groups is less well achieved by the German program. Although German law and ideology holds out a greater and more secure promise of adequate security for all who are in danger of falling into poverty than in the American case, the "promise is only selectively fulfilled since the delivery system is for structural reasons unable to live up to these promises."[85]

IV. The Growth of Entitlement Utilization in
Germany, Britain, Sweden, and the United States

In the two preceding sections, I have utilized German-American contrasts to probe some more novel and complex ways of understanding welfare state development. Now we return in this section to a descriptive analysis including also the other two countries initially discussed, Britain and Sweden.

A. Measurements and Thresholds

The discussion of the differential development of entitlements to education and social security caused me to become curious about whether historical aggregate data about benefit utilization would reflect these differences over a long time span. How might the available data be presented to illustrate not only that the United States was advanced in education, and Europe in social security, but also to demonstrate lucidly to what degree these benefits were accessible and utilized at various points in time and how convergence tendencies could be illustrated and compared. I also sought a technique that would help to examine and describe how, as the consequence of differing proclivities described in Section 1, the three European systems differed from each other in the degree to which their citizens utilized entitlements to the two kinds of benefits.

In the figures presented below, I attempt to show graphically how the dynamics of welfare state development, as pursued generally in this volume and specifically in this essay, can be represented through national policy development profiles. Their construction was facilitated by my being able to draw on the refined measurements of historical participation in social security and educational programs developed by two contributors to this volume, Jens Alber and Peter Flora, as well as by Arthur Banks. In order to impose simplicity on the massive data base, I decided to employ four threshold criteria that could be utilized to discriminate, fairly and effectively, as to the degree to which potential beneficiaries—the labor force in the case of social security, the primary school enrollees in the case of the postprimary education—did in fact utilize these programs at various points in time.

With regard to social security development,[86] relevant thresholds (T/SS) were defined as follows:

- T/SS_1: Year when enrollment in one of the four major social security programs—accident, old age, sickness, and unemployment insurance—first encompassed 10 percent of the labor force;
- T/SS_2: Year when at least 25 percent of the labor force was first enrolled in three of the four major programs;
- T/SS_3: Year when at least 50 percent of the labor force was first enrolled in three of the four major programs;
- T/SS_4: Year when at least 60 percent of the labor force was first enrolled in all four major programs.

With regard to education development,[87] relevant thresholds were defined in this manner:

- T/E_1: Year when, largely as a result of growth and spread of primary education enrollment, adult illiteracy first declined below 20 percent;
- T/E_2: Year when secondary school enrollment first constituted at least 10 percent of primary school enrollment;
- T/E_3: Year when secondary school enrollment first constituted 25 percent of primary school enrollment;
- T/E_4: Year when university enrollment first constituted 10 percent of primary school enrollment.

Enrollment measures are based on all kinds of schools, so that they include students enrolled in private as well as public institutions.[88]

B. National Policy Development Profiles

A comparative look at the German and U. S. policy development profiles show that they do, indeed, reflect the policy choices and proclivities that we have been discussing from the perspective of entitlements. Whereas the American profile shows equivalent education thresholds being passed one or two generations before those on the social security scale, the reverse holds true for Germany. The German profile can be seen to have the shape of a cigar. Its breadth is determined by the relatively long interval between the achievement of the equivalent thresholds. One of the German data point pairs, that comparing the third thresholds, embodies the longest interval—forty-seven years—found in any of the pairs in all four profiles. In this case it illustrates that the date at which half the labor force was enrolled in three social security programs occurred almost two generations earlier than the time point at which secondary school enrollment was one-fourth as large as primary school enrollment. Conversely, the strong implementation thrust of the Bismarck period also gave Germany the shortest threshold interval (T_1 -T_2 , three years) on any social security scale.

The American profile is in spatial terms very much the converse of the German figure. Not only do the education thresholds lead the social

Figure 8.1
Policy Development Profile for Germany

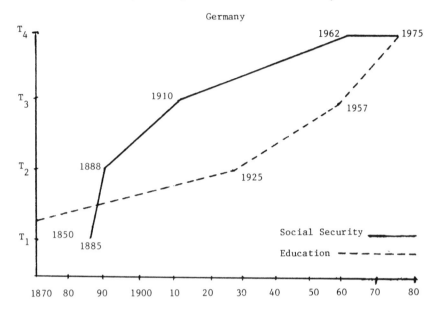

Figure 8.2
Policy Development Profile for the United States

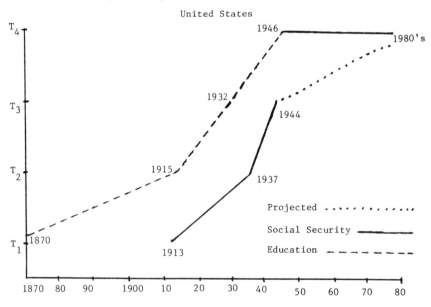

security ones, but the lag intervals are reciprocal. Where the German profile is broad in the middle, the American one is broadest at the ends. The interval between the first thresholds is the largest for any of the countries, forty-three years. The same holds for the fourth threshold distance, which is somewhere between thirty-two years and infinity, depending on when the United States passes what kind of general health insurance law. Earlier the United States shows something of a tendency for social security thresholds to coincide roughly with the preceding education threshold points, i.e., T/SS_1 (1913) coincides roughly with T/E_2 (1915), T/SS_2 (1937) with T/E_3 (1932), and T/SS_3 (1944) with T/E_4 (1946).

The discrepancy in utilization opportunities encountered by members of the primary school population and the labor force in any one generation can be seen to have been larger in the countries that were policy leaders in the early phases of welfare state development. This is most pronounced in the German case, where the average T/SS-T/E lag is thirty-three years, and where in one pairing the second education threshold is achieved a full fifteen years after the third social security threshold has already been passed.

The two systems that are labeled welfare state followers in Section I, Britain and Sweden, avoid this degree of policy extension bias. In both countries, education thresholds lag behind social security ones, but much less sharply. In the British case T/E_2 (1923) is almost simultaneous with T/SS_3 (1926) and T/E_3 (1946) almost dovetails with T/SS_4 (1947). This suggests that Britain, like Sweden, pursued a pattern of welfare state development in which education and social security entitlements were broadened on a more balanced basis. The relatively steep slope of the British policy lines reflects the relatively rapid transition to the welfare state there. The fact that the interval between the first and fourth social security thresholds encompasses the shortest time period of only thirty-nine years, bears out that the Beveridge reforms culminated a process that may be seen to have taken almost twice as long in Sweden and Germany. The straightness of the British educational development line reflects the fact that Britain did not attempt to match the radical expansion of educational capacity that Sweden undertook from the 1950s.

The slim Swedish policy development profile, shaped something like a cigarillo, may be interpreted as that of a policy follower that became an innovator. The uniqueness of the Swedish development is characterized by the profile tip produced as the consequence of the convergence of the education and social security lines around 1970. Evidently, the lead that Sweden took in Europe in pushing comprehensivization and university expansion resulted in the attainment of the fourth education threshold ahead of what mere projections might have led one to expect. More than other European nations, Sweden has sought to broaden the educational

Figure 8.3
Policy Development Profile for the United Kingdom

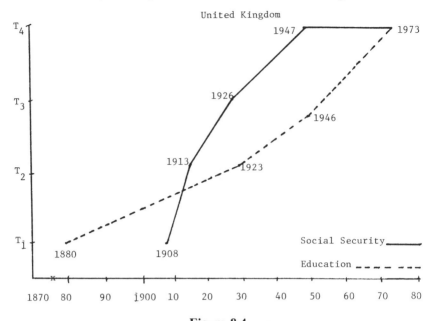

Figure 8.4
Policy Development Profile for Sweden

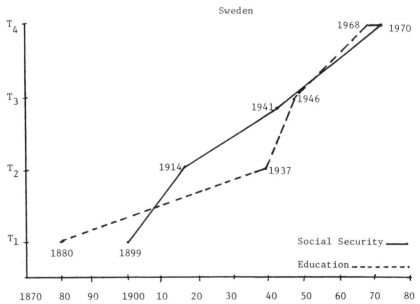

pyramid, while seeking techniques through which rapid growth of educational opportunity would not accentuate disparities between the most and the least educated.

In nineteenth-century settings Scandinavian associations and markets were less subject to bureaucratic control than in central Europe. With the decline of class distinctions, these societies were able to achieve higher degrees of social integration, which made more feasible the application of universal entitlement criteria. Sweden was the first country to introduce a universal social insurance system (1913); two generations later it was the first European country to operate a completely comprehensive secondary school system. The pervasiveness of public benefits and subsidies, both universal and selective, tended to create clienteles for welfare state programs in higher social strata which in other countries were more hostile to public sector expansion.

Opportunities for political participation and entitlement claims grew more *pari passu* in Sweden than in the other countries. Eligibility for social security programs were extended more quickly and smoothly up the social scale than in America, while postprimary educational utilization developed down the social scale more rapidly than in Germany. Thus Sweden managed during the twentieth century to develop a mix of social security and education programs that reduced the degree to which citizenship operates as an instrument of social stratification.

Notes

1. Heidenheimer 1973, p. 316.
2. Daalder 1966, p. 60.
3. Barker 1943, p. 68.
4. Stone 1975, p. xii.
5. Barker 1943.
6. Johanssen 1977.
7. Barker 1943. p. 83.
8. Huntington, 1968, Chapter Two.
9. Bailyn 1960, p. 107; Berlant 1975.
10. Berlant 1975.
11. Stokes 1950, p. 700.
12. Kaestle 1976; Berlant 1975.
13. Cremin 1976, p. 50.
14. Church 1976, p. 15.
15. Bendix 1968, p. 87.
16. Marshall 1963, p. 113.
17. Marshall 1963, p. 115.
18. Marshall 1963, p. 90.
19. Janowitz 1976, p. 34.
20. Welter 1962, pp. 189, 241.
21. Ringer 1978, p. 240.
22. Ibid.

23. Wiebe 1975, p. 142.
24. Church 1976, p. 343.
25. Jencks and Riesman 1968, p. 77.
26. Church 1976, p. 289.
27. Landes 1972.
28. Church 1976, pp. 289-90; my emphasis.
29. Brandes 1976, pp. 106-07.
30. Müller 1977, p. 28.
31. Lundgreen (1978: 107-10) questions this finding for the earlier period because of the criteria according to which Müller classified the various school types. But he too agrees that the reduction is evident for the post-1880 period. He also questions to what extent the conclusions that Müller derived from study of Berlin schools are applicable to Prussia. Further research on these questions is being pursued by a research group based at Bochum University.
32. Preuss 1975, p. 395.
33. Müller 1977, p. 54.
34. Keck 1977. We do not know how far we can generalize from this author's findings, since the diffusion of the Prussian model has not been examined in recent research.
35. Müller 1977, p. 55.
36. Church 1976, p. 184.
37. Calhoun 1973, p. 62.
38. Curoe 1926, p. 81.
39. Welter 1962, pp. 186-89.
40. Jarausch 1976.
41. Müller 1977, p. 287.
42. Gerhard 1977, p. 190.
43. Wiese 1902, p. 660.
44. Müller 1977, p. 283.
45. Müller 1977, p. 285.
46. Heidenheimer 1969, p. 334.
47. Ringer 1978.
48. Müller 1977, p. 279.
49. Selden 1960, p. 29.
50. Selden 1960, p. 53.
51. Gerhard 1977, pp. 184-89.
52. Church 1976, p. 296.
53. Jencks and Riesman 1968, pp. 82, 95.
54. Wilensky 1975, p. 5.
55. Bendix 1968, p. 257.
56. Scott 1914, p. 55.
57. Cremin 1976, p. 103.
58. Wilensky 1964.
59. Collier and Messick 1975, p. 38.
60. Leibfried 1977.
61. Tennstedt 1972, p. 35.
62. Tennstedt 1976, p. 402; Wirtschaftswissenschaftliches Institut, p. 123.
63. Wilensky 1975, p. 6.
64. Sozialenquete 1966, pp. 152-56.
65. Tennstedt 1976, p. 463.
66. Tennstedt 1972, p. 250.
67. Jencks 1979, pp. 167, 186.

68.   Sewell and Hauser 1975, p. 140.
69.   Doberschütz 1966, p. 103.
70.   Tennstedt 1972, p. 221.
71.   Tennstedt 1972, p. 213.
72.   Wickenden 1966, pp. 521-31.
73.   Kaelble 1975.
74.   Katona 1971, p. 162.
75.   Müller and Mayer 1976, p. 49.
76.   Sozialenquête 1966, pp. 245-46.
77.   Kaufmann 1970, p. 367.
78.   Tribe 1978, pp. 514-16.
79.   Tribe 1978, p. 1133.
80.   Church 1976, p. 350.
81.   Kudrle and Marmor, Chapter 3.
82.   Derthick 1975, p. 34.
83.   Gronberg 1977, pp. 140-150.
84.   Leibfried 1978, p. 68.
85.   Leibfried 1978, p. 69.
86.   For definitions and descriptions of programs, see Chapter Two, section IIA, above.
87.   The primary source utilized for educational statistics was Arthur Banks' *Cross Polity Time Series* that employs UNESCO data. Since certain classifications, appertaining particularly to the distinctions between primary and secondary schooling, are far from uniform, cross-checks were made with two other sources: B. R. Mitchell, *European Historical Statistics, 1750-1970*, (New York, Columbia University Press, 1975), and Peter Flora, *Indikatoren der Modernisierung* (Cologne: Westdeutscher Verlag, 1975). We found numerous instances where the threshold level years would have varied by a year or two. But we found only three cases where the threshold years would have varied by five years or more. These were: Germany T/E_3, 1957 (Banks), 1964 (Mitchell); England and Wales T/E_2 1933 (Banks), 1938 (Mitchell); and Sweden T/E_3 1946 (Banks), 1956 (Mitchell).
88.   We have considered the case for including only public school and university enrollments, just as the social security calculations were based only on public insurance programs. The main reason for not attempting to do so is empirical since the *public* or *private* classification of various school types, particularly in Britain, is ambiguous. Also, nonuniversal school types like Catholic primary schools would have been classified differently—as public schools in various German *Länder*, as private schools in the United States. Enrollment in private institutions is higher in the United States at the primary and tertiary levels, recently in the 15 to 20 percent range, than in the European countries, where it is minimal. But the private proportion of secondary school enrollment is less dissimilar. In 1965 to 1966 it was about 8 percent in the United States, about 10 percent in England and Wales, about 12 percent in Germany, about 3 percent in Sweden. *World Survey of Education*, Vol. V (Paris, UNESCO, 1971).

References

Anderson, Eugene and Pauline R. Anderson. 1967. *Political Institutions and Social Change in Continental Europe in the Nineteenth Century*. Berkeley, Calif.: University of California Press.

Bailyn, Bernard. 1960. *Education in the Forming of American Society.* Chapel Hill, N.C.: University of North Carolina Press.

Barker, Ernest. 1943. *The Development of Public Services in Western Europe 1660-1930.* London: Oxford University Press.

Bendix, Reinhard. 1968. *State and Society.* Boston: Little, Brown.

Berlant, Jeffrey. 1975. *Profession and Monopoly.* Berkeley, Calif.: University of California Press.

Brandes, Stuart D. 1976. *American Welfare Capitalism, 1880-1920.* Chicago: University of Chicago Press.

Calhoun, Daniel. 1973. *The Intelligence of a People.* Princeton, N.J.: Princeton University Press.

Church, Robert L. 1976. *Education in the United States.* New York: The Free Press.

Collier, David and Richard Messick. 1975. "Prerequisites versus Diffusion: Testing Alternative Explanations of Social Security Adoption." *APSR* 69: 1299-1325.

Cremin, Lawrence A. 1976. *Traditions of American Education.* New York: Basic Books, Inc.

Curoe, Phillip R. V. 1926. *Educational Attitudes and Policies of Organized Labor in the United States.* New York: Teachers College, Columbia University.

Daalder, Hans. 1966. "Parties, Elites, and Political Development in Western Europe." In *Political Parties and Political Development,* ed. Joseph LaPalombara and Myron Weiner. Princeton, N.J.: Princeton University Press.

Derthick, Martha. 1975. *Uncontrollable Spending for Social Service Grants.* Washington, D.C.: Brookings Institution.

Doberschütz, Klaus. 1966. *Die Soziale Sicherung des Amerikanischen Bürgers.* Berlin: Duncker & Humblot.

Fishlow, Albert. 1966. "Levels of Nineteenth-Century American Investment in Education." *Journal of Economic History* 26: 418-436.

Geissler, Heiner. 1976. *Die Neue Soziale Frage.* Vienna: Herder.

Gerhard, Dietrich. 1977. "The Educational Reforms in Germany and the United States at the End of the 19th Century, a Comparison." In *Gesammelte Aufsätze,* p. 190. Göttingen: Vandenhoeck and Ruprecht.

Goldschmidt, Dietrich. 1978. "Power and Decision-Making in Higher Education," *Comparative Education Review,* 22 (June): 212-241.

Gronberg, Kirsten A. 1977. *Mass Society and the Extension of Welfare 1960-1970.* Chicago: University of Chicago Press.

Heidenheimer, Arnold J. 1969. "Trade Unions, Benefit Systems and Party Mobilization Styles: Horizontal Influences on the British Labour and German Social Democratic Parties." *Comparative Politics* 1: 313-342.

Heidenheimer, Arnold J. 1973. "The Politics of Public Education, Health and Welfare in the USA and Western Europe: How Growth and Reform Potentials have Differed." *British Journal of Political Science* 3: 313-340.

Hofbauer, Hans and Paul Konig. 1973. "Berufswechsel bei männlichen Erwerbspersonen in der Bundesrepublik Deutschland." *Mitteilungen aus der Arbeitsmarkt - und Berufsforschung* 6, No. 1.

Huntington, Samuel. 1968. *Political Order in Changing Societies.* New Haven: Yale University Press.

Janowitz, Morris. 1976. *Social Control of the Welfare State.* New York: Elsevier.

Jarausch, Konrad. 1976. "Frequenz und Struktur: Zur Sozialgeschichte der Studenten im Kaisereich." Unpublished manuscript.

Jencks, Christopher and David Riesman. 1968. *The Academic Revolution.* New York: Doubleday.

Jencks, Christopher, et al. 1979. *Who Gets Ahead? The Determinants of Economic Success in America.* New York: Basic Books.

Johanssen, Egil 1977. "The History of Literacy in Sweden in Comparison with Some Other Countries." *Educational Reports Unea* 12.

Kaelble, Hartmut. 1974. "Sozialer Aufstieg in den USA und Deutschland, 1900-1960." In *Sozialgeschichte - Heute, Festschrift für Hans Rosenberg zum 70. Geburtstag,* ed. H. U. Wehler. Göttingen: Vandenhoeck & Ruprecht.

Kaelble, Hartmut. 1975. "Chancenungleichheit und akademische Ausbildung in Deutschland, 1910-1960." *Geschichte und Gesellschaft* 1 (1975): 121-149.

Kaestle, Carl F. 1976. "Between the Scylla of Brutal Ignorance and the Charybdis of a Literary Education." In *Schooling and Society,* Lawrence Stone, ed. pp. 177-191. Baltimore: Johns Hopkins University Press.

Katona, George, et al. 1971. *Aspirations and Affluence.* New York: McGraw-Hill.

Kaufmann, Franz-Xaver. 1970. *Sicherheit als Soziologisches und Sozialpolitisches System.* Stuttgart: Enke.

Keck, Rudolf W. 1977. "Die mittlere realistische Schule in der Epoche der Anpassung an Preussen von 1870 bis zur Weimarer Republik." In *Schule und Gesellschaft im 19. Jahrhundert,* ed. Ulrich Herrmann. Weinheim: Beltz.

Lacquer, Thomas. 1973. "English and French Education in the 19th Century." *History of Education Quarterly* 13: 53-60.

Landes, William M. 1972. "Compulsory Schooling Legislation: An Economic Analysis of Law and Social Change in the Nineteenth Century." *Journal of Economic History* 37: 54-89.

Leibfried, Stephan. 1977. "Die Institutionalisierung der Arbeitslosenversicherung in Deutschland." *Kritische Justiz* 31: 289-301.

Leibfried, Stephan. 1978. "Public Assistance in the United States and the Federal Republic of Germany—Does Social Democracy Make a Difference?" *Comparative Politics* 11: 59-76.

Lundgreen, Peter. 1978. "Die Bildungschancen beim Übergang von der Gesamtschule zum Schulsystem der Klassengesellschaft im 19. Jahrhundert." *Zeitschrift für Pädagogik* 24, No. 1: 101-115.

Marshall, T. H. 1963. *Sociology at the Crossroads and Other Essays.* London: Heinemann.

Mayer, Karl Ulrich. 1977. "Ungleiche Chancen und Klassenbildung." *Sociale Welt* 28, No. 4: 466-593.

Müller, Detlef K. 1977. *Sozialstruktur und Schulsystem.* Göttingen: Vandenhoeck & Ruprecht.

Müller, Detlef K., Bernd Zymek, Erika Kupper, and Longin Priebe. 1977. "Modelentwicklung zur Analyse von Krisenphasen im Verhältnis von Schulsystem und staatlichem Beschäftigungssystem." *Zeitschrift für Pädagogik* 14: 37-98.

Müller, Walter and Karl Ulrich Mayer. 1976. *Chancengleichheit durch Bildung: Untersuchungen über den Zusammenhang von Ausbildungsabschlüssen und Berufsstatus.* Stuttgart: Klett.

Preuss, Ulrich K. 1975. "Bildung und Bürokratie." *Der Staat* 14: 371-396.

Reich, Charles A. 1964. "The New Property." *Yale Law Journal* 73, No. 5.

Ringer, Fritz. 1978. *Education and Society in Modern Europe.* Bloomington: Indiana University Press.

Rokkan, Stein. 1975. "Dimensions of State Formation and Nation Building: A Possible Paradigm for Research on Variations Within Europe." In *The Formation of National States in Western Europe,* ed. Charles Tilly, pp. 562-600, Princeton, N.J.: Princeton University Press.

Scott, Jonathan French. 1914. *Historical Essays on Apprenticeship and Vocational Education.* Ann Arbor, Mich.: Ann Arbor Press.

Selden, William K. 1960. *Accreditation.* New York: Harper.

Sewell, William H. and Robert M. Hauser. 1975. *Education, Occupation and Earnings.* New York: Academic Press.

Sozialenquète-Kommission. 1966. *Soziale Sicherung in der Bundesrepublik Deutschland.* Stuttgart: Kohlhammer.

Stevens, Rosemary. 1971. *American Medicine and the Public Interest.* New Haven, Conn.: Yale University Press.

Stokes, Austin P. 1950. *Church and State in the United States,* vol. 1. New York: Harper.

Stone, Lawrence, ed. 1976. *Schooling and Society.* Baltimore: Johns Hopkins University Press.

Tennstedt, Florian. 1976. *Berufsunfähigkeit im Sozialrecht.* Frankfurt: Europäische Verlagsanstalt.

Tennstedt, Florian. 1976. "Sozialgeschichte der Sozialversicherung." In *Sozialmedizin in der Praxis, Handbuch der Sozialmedizin,* vol. 3, ed. Maria Blohmke. Stuttgart: Enke Verlag.

Tribe, Laurence H. 1978. *American Constitutional Law.* New York: The Foundation Press, Inc.

Vaughan, Michalina and Margaret Archer. 1971. *Social Conflict and Educational Change in England and France, 1789-1848.* Cambridge: Cambridge University Press.

Weber, Werner et al. 1965. *Rechtsschutz im Sozialrecht: Beiträge zum ersten Jahrzehnt der Rechtsprechung des Bundessozialgerichts.* Carl Heymanns Verlag.

Wechsler, Harold S. 1977. *The Qualified Student: A History of Selective College Admission in America.* New York: Wiley.

Weick, Karl E. "Educational Organizations as Loosely-Coupled Systems." *Administrative Science Quarterly* 21: 1-19.

Welter, Rush. 1962. *Popular Education and Democratic Thought in America.* New York: Columbia University Press.

Wickenden, Elizabeth. 1966. "The Social Welfare Law: The Concept of Risk and Entitlement." *University of Detroit Law Journal* 43: 517-530.

Wiebe, Robert H. 1975. *The Segmented Society.* New York: Oxford.

Wiese, Ludwig. 1902. *Das Höhere Schulwesen in Preussen.* vol. 4, ed. B. Irmer, 49.

Wilensky, Harold L. 1964. "The Professionalization of Everyone?" *American Journal of Sociology* 70: 137-158.

Wilensky, Harold L. 1975. *The Welfare State and Equality.* Berkeley: University of California Press.

Wirtschafts- und Sozialwissenschaftliches Institut des Deutschen Gewerkschaftbundes. 1977. *Sozialpolitik und Selbstverwaltung.* Cologne: Bund-Verlag.

Part Six

An End to Growth? Fiscal Capacities and Containment Pressures

Chapter 9

Trends and Problems in Postwar Public Expenditure Development in Western Europe and North America

Jürgen Kohl

Introduction

A widely shared concern of both political scientists and politicians is that Western democracies are confronting a fundamental crisis. In recent years, they appear to be more and more ungovernable because their governments are suffering under the burden of overload. There is consensus that this crisis is most clearly manifested in certain dilemmas of public choice, specifically the structural problems of budgeting public resources to meet public needs. Some neo-Marxist critics[1] refer to "the fiscal crisis of the (capitalist) state" that will eventually be transformed into a decisive "legitimation crisis" of (bourgeois) parliamentary democracy. Conservative and liberal critics,[2] on the other hand, blame exaggerated and unrestricted welfare state development for eliciting "the revolution of rising expectations" which is now exceeding the fiscal capacities of the state.

The origins of the present problems, according to both perspectives, lie in the policy-making structure of capitalist mass democracies. The rapid economic growth of the recovery period after World War II enabled Western democracies to increase public spending in almost all fields because of greater fiscal resources. Now, as the prospects for sustained economic growth diminish, political pressure is exerted on governments and parliaments to maintain and even expand the present level of public expenditures. Both former obligations and increased needs during economic crisis suggest that relative expenditure growth (public spending as a percentage of GNP) is disproportionately expanded when economic development slackens. Thus, public expenditure development is less a function of economic growth and is instead primarily determined by political and ideological factors.

Certainly, the general growth of public expenditures has been accompanied by structural shifts within them. For a better understanding of the prime determinants of these growth tendencies, one must differentiate between expenditure items to determine which are growing most rapidly and thereby shaping the general trend. Most authors, whether conservative or radical, agree that social expenditures have been the outstanding component in the secular rise of public expenditures, accounting for the larger share of general growth during past decades. Furthermore, it is significant to note the internal shifts within social expenditures between transfer payments (for purposes of income redistribution) and the provision of social services (such as health and education).

The sociopolitical mechanism underlying the disproportionate growth of social expenditures is often explained by the growing political power of the working class, represented by trade unions and (socialist) labor parties, which have first demanded social security and later income redistribution. After the institutionalization of social security systems, coverage has been extended and the relative levels of benefits raised repeatedly. Similarly, when private consumption reached a certain level of saturation, demands for superior public goods, especially in education and health care, have been advanced. Minimum standards for the provision of social services have been typically established as social rights and have maintained that identity even as basic standards have vastly increased. Moreover, since such demands are usually tied to the social goals of equality of opportunity and social justice, social spending is not easily reduced when economic resources decline. The fiscal problem is further compounded when increasing demands for public expenditures are not met by a corresponding willingness of the electorate to accept the necessary financial burden, such as higher taxes or social security contributions. While this tension exists in the provision of public goods in general, it is even more problematic in the case of social expenditures when claims are advanced for the sake of social justice or redistribution.

The logic of competitive politics holds that governments faced with the alternative of losing public support will tend to meet new demands without imposing new burdens. Various possibilities exist, which can be used in combination: increasing budget deficits to be financed by loans; cutting other expenditure items in favor of social transfer and social service expenditures; and, because no immediate pressure is exerted on behalf of them, reducing public investments. In all cases, the prospects for future economic development will be adversely affected.

These demands and expectations do not arise in all countries with equal intensity, nor do different political systems respond to the problems they pose in the same way. There are great differences between countries concerning, for instance, the organizational strength of the working class, ideological traditions, and existing program structures. Moreover, the political structure of interest articulation, aggregation, and representation varies greatly, so that even similar problems will probably lead to different political solutions regarding revenue and expenditure decisions. Last but not least, one must consider the role of political leadership in managing and responding to popular demands since this will lead to varying degrees of popular satisfaction.

For an appreciation of both present problems and future prospects of welfare state development, it may be helpful to compare and examine in greater detail the relevant empirical evidence. The above considerations have been formulated into the following questions for our analyses: First, what is the relationship between economic growth and public expenditure growth? Second, what is the significance of social expenditures as the driving force in public expenditure growth? Third, has the party composition of government influenced expenditure growth (and how)? Finally, what are some alternative political answers, as represented by fiscal policies, to the problems of expenditure growth?

The following analyses are based mainly on the series of OECD Statistics of National Accounts for 1950 to 1975. Within this framework, the public sector is broadly defined as all levels of government and the institutions of social insurance. This is a rather comprehensive definition of the consolidated public sector compared to a more narrow conception of the state excluding social security which typically prevails in budgetary statistics. Because the framework of national accounting does not always provide adequate functional classifications of expenditures, especially for social expenditures, we have established an additonal data set based on the Social Accounts series of the European Community covering the original member countries from 1962 to 1975.

I. Public Expenditures and the Constraints of Economic Growth

A. Trends in the Development of Total Public Expenditures

Total public expenditures are defined as the sum of central and local government expenditures plus social security outlays. On this basis, the size of the public sector varies considerably among the Western European (and

North American) nations, although all have experienced substantial expansion of the public sector in the postwar period.

Table 9.1
Trends in Total Public Expenditures, 1950-1975[3]

Country	public expenditures as % of GNP		average annual change	elasticity
	1950	1975		
Austria	25,0	40,3	+ 0,49	1,21
Belgium	26,3	44,9	+ 0,81	1,36
Denmark	19,4	47,5	+ 1,03	1,43
Finland	26,9	37,2	+ 0,55	1,19
France	28,4	42,4	+ 0,38	1,17
Germany	30,8	45,6	+ 0,45	1,17
Italy	27,8	43,1	+ 0,67	1,26
Netherlands	27,0	54,3	+ 1,04	1,32
Norway	25,5	46,5	+ 0,91	1,27
Sweden	37,5	51,0	+ 0,82	1,25
Switzerland	20,8	27,4	+ 0,66	1,45
United Kingdom	30,4	46,1	+ 0,53	1,22
United States	27,4	36,2	+ 0,37	1,32
Canada	26,8	41,2	+ 0,55	1,24

At the beginning of the period, public expenditure/GNP ratios ranged from about 20 percent to 30 percent, the latter mark reached only by the European big powers of the United Kingdom, France, and Germany.[3] As a consequence of the general rise of expenditures, the 1975 levels ranged from an exceptionally low 30 percent in Switzerland to more than 50 percent in Sweden and the Netherlands.

The differing paces of development have led to significant changes in the rank order of countries. Those departing from high initial levels have expanded at comparatively moderate rates, while in Sweden, Denmark, Norway, and the Netherlands, countries with low 1950 levels, the rise has been extremely rapid. From an initial level of 20 to 25 percent, the public expenditure/GNP ratio has increased at a rate of about 1 percent per year, thus doubling within a quarter of a century. A rising public expenditure/ GNP ratio means that public expenditures have grown faster than total economic output; this is even the case using constant prices, that is, when the usually higher inflation rates in the public sector are accounted for. This is even more striking since almost all of the countries have experienced rapid economic growth of more than 4 percent per year in the postwar period.[4]

This well-established phenomenon of an increasing share of economic output devoted to public expenditures does not however satisfactorily answer how economic growth and public expenditure development are functionally related in the short run. While longitudinal studies have confirmed that rising public expenditures are positively associated with gains in real output, it is unlikely that all countries followed the same developmental path or experienced the same short-term development. Instead, when public expenditures are compared on the basis of similar levels of real income, we can expect that significantly different levels will prevail (see, for instance, the comparatively low public expenditure levels in the United States and Canada, despite high income levels). While explanations for such deviations must consider different political structures, ideologies, and the relative position of nations in the developmental process, we can expect that deviations can also be systematically explained. One example of this is that latecomers in economic development are induced to spend higher proportions of GNP for public expenditures in order to catch up with the pioneer countries. In this case, a negative correlation between these two variables might result in crossnational comparison although the positive relationship would still hold for the long-term development of each country.[5]

In order to understand short-term changes in economic development and public expenditure behavior, several different, even contradictory propositions could be plausible. First, it could be assumed that what has been confirmed in the long run is equally true of short-term mechanisms, specifically, that public expenditure growth is simply a function of growing real output. This makes it possible to spend a larger share for public purposes without reducing existing levels of private consumption. (This hypothesis suggests a strong positive correlation between the respective growth rates.)

However, it is possible that changing economic conditions affect public revenues first (above all, direct taxes and social security contributions), so that public expenditures will change only after a time-lag. (This hypothesis suggests a strong positive correlation when the time-lag is properly considered.)

According to countercyclical fiscal principles, it could be expected that public expenditures will grow rapidly when economic growth rates are depressed and vice versa. The rationale here is that the need for additional expenditures, particularly social services, is increased in times of economic depression and crisis, and conversely, certain emergency measures, such as deficit spending, become unnecessary when the economy recovers. (This hypothesis implies a strong negative correlation.)

A fourth proposition suggests that public expenditures (and particularly social expenditures) grow irrespective of economic conditions, or at least fluctuate more and more autonomously. The underlying assumption is that economic necessities and/or opportunities are secondary to political factors as determinants of public expenditure. This does not necessarily imply that social expenditure growth is completely unrestrained, but that it may be expanded by rising popular demands as well as reduced by a welfare backlash in public opinion. (This hypothesis implies a zero correlation.)

Finally, it should be pointed out that there are no inherent contradictions between these mechanisms of short-term fluctuations and the long-run tendency for public expenditure levels to positively correlate with economic growth. While *annual* growth rates may be inversely related or virtually independent of each other, the *average* growth rates of public expenditures may nevertheless exceed those of economic growth.

The results of the correlation and lag analysis are summarized in Table 9.2. This information lends support to the first hypothesis that revenues and expenditures correspond immediately to changes in economic circumstances. The relationship between the respective growth rates from 1950 to 1975 is, without exception, positive and on the average relatively strong. It is somewhat stronger for current revenues than for total expenditures (.74 and .63, respectively). While these findings obviously contradict the hypothesis of countercyclical spending behavior as well as the autonomous growth of expenditures, the time-lag hypothesis cannot be completely dismissed. A comparison of the correlation coefficients shows that on the average the relationship is strongest within the same year, but that a positive relationship still exists after one year and only disappears after two. We should be aware, however, that the relationship between economic growth and public expenditure growth is not always consistent across countries. This may be due to the fact that public budgets are comprised of many heterogeneous expenditure items whose relative importance changes over time. Thus, we must differentiate the various components to identify specific relationships.

B. Expenditure Trade-offs: Public Consumption vs. Social Transfers

Public consumption expenditures (for the provision of public services including defense) and transfer expenditures (for the redistribution of cash

Table 9.2
Correlations Between Annual Growth Rates of GNP,
Current Revenues, and Total Expenditures

Country	current revenues			total expenditures		
	lag 0	lag 1	lag 2	lag 0	lag 1	lag 2
Austria	+ .78	+ .80	- .08	+ .88	+ .58	- .30
Belgium	+ .89	+ .68	+ .47	+ .58	+ .85	+ .82
Denmark	+ .54	+ .58	+ .37	+ .50	+ .63	+ .62
Finland	+ .78	+ .58	+ .20	+ .70	+ .62	+ .50
France	+ .86	+ .59	- .23	+ .74	+ .60	- .25
Germany	+ .87	+ .45	- .23	+ .63	+ .44	- .05
Italy	+ .75	+ .45	+ .12	+ .43	+ .47	+ .55
Netherlands	+ .62	+ .50	+ .25	+ .68	+ .24	+ .18
Norway	+ .78	+ .56	- .13	+ .63	+ .58	+ .08
Sweden	+ .81	+ .19	- .21	+ .26	- .09	+ .13
Switzerland	+ .56	+ .59	+ .42	+ .90	+ .39	+ .03
United Kingdom	+ .72	+ .66	+ .51	+ .84	+ .77	+ .66
United States	+ .64	- .07	+ .21	+ .29	+ .69	- .16
Canada	+ .82	+ .40	+ .07	+ .69	+ .64	+ .40
Average	+ .74	+ .50	+ .12	+ .63	+ .53	+ .23

income) form the two largest budget shares in the public sector and are of roughly equal size. But by a closer look at Figure 9.1, two different patterns can be discerned.[6] These are the Scandinavian pattern (Denmark, Sweden, Norway, and Finland), largely followed by the United Kingdom and Ireland, where public consumption expenditures prevail, and the Continental pattern (France, Italy, Belgium, the Netherlands, and Luxemburg), where more resources are devoted to transfer expenditures. Germany and Austria are somewhat between, but are moving closer to the Scandinavian pattern in recent years. These patterns proved sufficiently stable when tested at successive points in time.

It is suggested that these patterns reflect two different approaches to public policy, and to social policy in particular. The Continental pattern emphasizes the redistribution of cash income relegating final consumption decisions to individual preferences. While this may be an effective way to

Figure 9.1

Patterns of Public Expenditures in Western Europe (1974)[6]

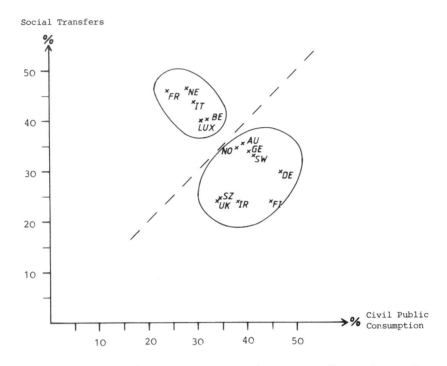

achieve income maintenance or greater income equality, cash transfers encourage reliance on the market provision of social services and thereby reinforce private modes of producing and delivering such services. Governments preferring this approach sometimes explicitly rely on the principle of the superiority of market production, even for social services such as health care.

The Scandinavian pattern, on the other hand, favors the public provision of services whereby collective choice more directly shapes the structure of supply and the mode of control. This approach seems especially suitable to effect changes in the quality or kind of services and to counterbalance disadvantages of private market provision. Whether the public provision of services leads to an improvement in services depends, among other things, on productivity and cost controls in nonmarket production. This in turn is largely service-specific.

There are not only different patterns in the relationship between transfer and public consumption expenditures, but the two also react very differently to economic changes. This is revealed by a correlation and lag analysis presented in Table 9.3. Compared to total public expenditures (see Table 9.2), the strength of the positive relationship remains generally the same for civil public consumption expenditures (that is, when defense, transfer, and public investment expenditures are excluded), and it decreases in the same way when time-lags are introduced. Thus, in support of the first proposition, the expenditures devoted to general administrative purposes and the provision of economic, environmental, and social services appear to be directly related to economic development. They are expanded in periods of prosperity and restricted when economic growth declines.

Table 9.3
Correlations Between Annual Growth Rates of GNP,
Civil Public Consumption, and Social Transfers

Country	civil public consumption			social transfers		
	lag 0	lag 1	lag 2	lag 0	lag 1	lag 2
Austria	+ .90	+ .51	– .18	+ .76	+ .86	– .04
Belgium	+ .59	+ .75	+ .65	+ .41	+ .72	+ .59
Denmark	+ .59	+ .58	+ .65	+ .35	+ .58	+ .48
Finland	+ .71	+ .72	+ .55	+ .52	+ .61	+ .57
France	+ .75	+ .29	– .61	+ .74	+ .36	– .03
Germany	+ .64	+ .41	– .12	+ .06	+ .27	+ .15
Italy	+ .30	+ .23	+ .21	+ .16	+ .36	+ .55
Netherlands	+ .82	+ .18	+ .21	+ .30	+ .31	+ .18
Norway	+ .47	+ .38	+ .17	+ .21	+ .44	– .19
Sweden	+ .70	+ .76	– .07	+ .05	– .06	– .08
Switzerland	+ .68	+ .64	+ .65	+ .10	+ .35	+ .60
United Kingdom	+ .91	+ .75	+ .70	+ .52	+ .59	+ .56
United States	+ .15	+ .27	+ .44	– .22	+ .36	+ .69
Canada	+ .52	+ .65	+ .41	+ .17	+ .36	+ .68
Average	+ .62	+ .51	+ .26	+ .30	+ .44	+ .35

Social transfers to individual households are much less closely related to economic fluctuations, and they tend to follow the time-lag pattern suggested by the second hypothesis since the average correlation coefficient is highest at the one-year time-lag. This may be explained by the fact that in most countries social security regulations, especially old age pension schemes, provide for earnings-related benefits tied to wage or price indices. We should be aware, however, that in four countries (Sweden, Germany, the Netherlands, and Norway) there is absolutely no relationship between economic growth and the growth of social transfers to households (the explained variance ranges from zero to one-fifth) and that for five other countries (Italy, Denmark, the United Kingdom, Switzerland, and Finland) the relationship is relatively weak (with an average explained variance of about one third). Insofar as this can be interpreted to mean that social transfer expenditures tend to fluctuate independent of changing economic circumstances, the fourth hypothesis is supported. Finally, in neither case are growth rates inversely correlated as would be expected if governments strictly followed the principles of countercyclical fiscal policy.

II. The Role of Social Expenditures in Expenditure Growth

A. Social Transfers

Disaggregating budget components is once again appropriate for explaining the general growth pattern of public expenditures. Social expenditures are of crucial importance because a great part of present political and economic problems is often attributed to accelerated welfare state development and its financial burdens.

Efforts to quantitatively assess the significance of social expenditures must resort to approximations. The category of social transfers is a good example of this, since social security benefits that have traditionally formed the core of social expenditures are comprised from 80 to 90 percent of transfer payments.[7] Their development and growing importance is illustrated by Table 9.4

By 1975, social transfers have risen to levels of more than 10 percent of the GNP in all countries (except Finland) whereas in 1950, only Germany and France had surpassed this level. In 1975, the most advanced level was attained by the Netherlands (26 percent) followed by France, Italy, and Belgium. But relative growth, as indicated by the income elasticities, has also been considerable in the United States and the Scandinavian countries. They started at very low levels (about 5 percent) and have almost tripled their transfers/GNP ratio. From the mid-sixties on, an acceleration of these growth tendencies can be observed in almost all countries (cf. Table 9.11).

Table 9.4
Trends in Social Transfer Expenditures, 1950-1975

Country	social transfers as % of GNP 1950	social transfers as % of GNP 1975	average annual change	elasticity
Austria	7,8	13,9	+ 0,21	1,25
Belgium	9,6	18,9	+ 0,38	1,44
Denmark	5,8	15,0	+ 0,31	1,46
Finland	5,8	8,8	+ 0,17	1,25
France	11,3	20,0	+ 0,29	1,23
Germany	12,4	16,7	+ 0,10	1,13
Italy	9,3	19,6	+ 0,47	1,43
Netherlands	6,6	26,1	+ 0,74	1,63
Norway	4,9	16,0	+ 0,38	1,41
Sweden	6,3	16,6	+ 0,39	1,45
Switzerland	5,9	10,2	+ 0,33	1,60
United Kingdom	5,7	11,1	+ 0,24	1,36
United States	3,3	11,5	+ 0,39	1,97
Canada	5,8	10,4	+ 0,22	1,36

In the framework of national accounting, transfer expenditures are usually not considered part of the public sector's contribution to the GNP, but form part of the disposable income of private households, after the redistribution process. Regarding transfers then as "publicly supported private consumption" and comparing them to private final consumption reveals a rapid increase at even higher rates than the social transfers/GNP ratio increase. The share of private consumption in the final use of the GNP is on the decline everywhere by an average of more than 10 percentage points since 1950.[8] This means that in most countries, one-fifth to one-fourth of private consumption is financed by public budgets through social transfer payments. The share of "pure" private consumption (total private consumption minus social transfers) has fallen below the level of 50 percent of the GNP.

Despite the current variations in the level of resources devoted to social transfer expenditures, their growth rates have been consistently higher than those for total public expenditures (cf. also the income elasticities given in Tables 9.1 and 9.4). As a result, they have gained additional importance in the consolidated budgets of all countries (except Germany). In those countries that followed the Continental pattern (France, Italy, the Netherlands), transfers accounted for more than 70 percent of the total expenditure growth (cf. the average increases of the respective ratios). This is partly explained by the fact that defense expenditure shares (which are included in public consumption) have gradually, but considerably declined from the mid-fifties to levels of less than 10 percent in 1975. This decrease has to some extent compensated for the increase in *civil* public consumption (which can be considered as the production costs of public goods and services), so that only small differences appear between civil public consumption and transfer expenditure growth when compared at current prices. But differences are again pronounced when compared at constant prices because the former are usually subject to higher rates of cost inflation than cash transfers which are usually deflated by the consumer price index.

B. Total Social Outlays

But if inter-country comparisons of social expenditures are restricted to transfer expenditures only, the picture is likely to be distorted. The total outlays for health, for instance, also include employee wages and investment expenditures, in addition to subsidies and transfers. The comparison may be extremely misleading unless differences in institutional arrangements of services are taken into consideration.[9] For this reason, a comparison of the level and structure of social expenditures based on the EEC concept is presented in Tables 9.5 and 9.12. It is essential to note that social expenditures are defined here as all expenditures for social risks or needs irrespective of their economic nature (i.e., whether they are spent as cash transfers, as reimbursements for private outlays, or as employee wages for the provision of certain services in kind).

Because of this more comprehensive definition, compared to the narrow concept of social transfers, the GNP shares are in general substantially larger and inter-country differences are less pronounced. But the basic trend is confirmed again: while in 1962 the social expenditures ratio did not exceed 20 percent of the GNP in any of the original member countries, it had crossed this benchmark by 1975 in practically all of them. The rate of increase, however, has been very different for the individual countries: extremely rapid in the Netherlands which started from the lowest level in 1962 and now holds the top position with a ratio twice as high as the former one, but very slow in France which only climbed from 16 percent to 20 percent over a 12-year period.

The differential rates of change reveal another interesting feature: In the 1960s, a trend toward convergence and greater harmonization, and a

Table 9.5
Social Expenditures as Percentage of Gross Domestic Product, 1962-1975

Year	Germany	France	Italy	Nether-lands	Belgium	Luxem-burg	United Kingdom	Ireland	Denmark
1962	17,5	16,3	14,3	13,7	15,5	15,7			
1963	17,7	17,2	15,1	15,5	15,7	16,0			
1964	17,8	17,4	15,5	15,8	14,9	16,2			
1965	18,2	17,9	17,4	16,9	16,3	17,1			
1966	18,7	18,2	18,1	18,2	16,5	17,6			
1967	20,2	18,4	17,8	18,9	16,9	19,3			
1968	20,2	18,6	18,9	19,3	17,8	18,8			
1969	19,8	18,3	18,9	19,9	17,8	17,7			
1970	19,9	18,3	18,9	20,6	17,2	17,7			
1970	21,4	18,9	18,8	20,7	18,5	16,0	15,7	12,7	19,4
1971	21,9	19,1	20,2	22,0	18,9	17,8	16,1	13,0	20,6
1972	22,7	19,2	21,7	23,1	20,3	18,2	16,8	12,9	21,0
1973	23,2	19,6	21,0	23,7	20,5	16,9	16,6	15,3	21,8
1974	24,7	20,0	22,6	25,6	21,6	16,3	17,3	17,1	24,5
1975	27,9	22,7	23,7	28,3	24,4	23,9	19,2	20,4	27,6

leveling of inter-country differences seemed to emerge in accordance with the hopes and political objectives associated with the formation of the European Economic Community.[10] In the seventies, this trend is somewhat reversed, widening the gap between the leading countries (the Netherlands and Germany) and the laggards (France, Belgium, and Luxemburg). This divergence has probably been reinforced by the incorporation of new members with Denmark at the top and the United Kingdom and Ireland at the bottom.

The differences are even more pronounced when expressed in absolute terms. For instance, social expenditures per capita in Germany, Denmark, and the Netherlands are twice the level of those in the United Kingdom and Italy.[11] This strongly suggests that attainment of large per capita increases in social expenditures has been facilitated by fairly effective economic performance. Those countries suffering most from economic difficulties have remained at low absolute levels, despite their efforts to raise relative expenditure levels.

C. Determinants of Social Expenditure Growth

In order to achieve a more precise understanding of the prime determinants of social expenditure growth, expenditures are subdivided here into the functional categories health, old age, invalidity and occupational injuries, unemployment, and family (cf. Table 9.12). Such functional classifications should be approached cautiously because national social security institutions do not cover a similar range of problems nor can the benefits they provide be attributed to just one single function. Therefore, the task of converting national statistical series and assigning identical functions cannot be solved unambiguously.

Despite these reservations, some conclusions concerning the average structure and the direction of change may be drawn: Expenditures for health services and old age (including survivors') pensions are the most important items in all countries. Taken together, they account for two-thirds of all social expenditures in most cases. Expenditures for old age, still the largest single item, range from 30 percent to almost 50 percent, while health expenditures cluster around 30 percent. Expenditures for invalidity and occupational injuries seem to vary greatly between countries, but this is probably due to differing institutional arrangements and statistical difficulties rather than political priorities.

Despite their political salience, expenditures for unemployment represent only a small portion of social expenditures. They show a distinctly upward trend in all countries in recent years, undoubtedly due to the increasing inability of Western economies to absorb potential members of the labor force. But interestingly enough there is only a low association between unemployment rates and unemployment expenditures when tested cross-nationally. This probably suggests differing priorities for governmental action and/or highly different standards and requirements for benefits.[12]

Family allowances and related measures are on the decline in most countries, particularly in those following the "Romanic" pattern that traditionally gave high priority to family policy. In France they declined from almost 30 percent to 20 percent and in Italy from more than 20 percent to about 10 percent within a decade. Family-related expenditures are stabilizing now at a lower limit of about 10 percent, while somewhat higher levels are still maintained by some predominantly Roman Catholic countries (France, Ireland, Belgium).[13]

The trend in expenditures for old age pensions and survivors' benefits is closely linked to demographic factors such as changes in the age structure, longevity, and mortality rates. While these conditions vary somewhat from country to country, on the average this expenditure item requires a fairly constant share in social expenditures, but of course a larger share in the GNP.

Health expenditures have exhibited the most rapid increases during the last decade and gained additional importance in all countries. In contrast to the outlays for pension, invalidity, or occupational injuries' insurance, which are almost exclusively cash transfers to private households, an increasing part of health expenditures is not for income maintenance during sickness, but for the provision of medical services. Because of the comparatively high rate of cost inflation that affects the direct public provision of services, an important part of rising health expenditures must be attributed to this factor.

In short, we can conclude that the development of social expenditures is conditioned mainly by three sets of factors:

Demographic shifts, particularly changes in the age structure of the population creating greater demand for social services. It is plausible to assume that, given certain standards for individual benefits, health expenditures will develop at the rate of growth of the total population, old age expenditures at the growth rate of the population group aged 65 years or more, and family allowances and related grants at the rate of change of the younger population group under twenty. All these expenditures must be financed mainly by taxes and contributions of the gainfully employed labor force. Since in almost all Western European countries the labor force is growing at a much lower rate than the other population groups, total outlays will *ceteris paribus* exceed the receipts. This eventually results in the necessity to raise the relative burden on the active labor force, or to cut certain services or transfer payments.[14]

Cost inflation, resulting from differential productivity gains on the supply side. Because the production of public goods and services is subject to low productivity gains (compared to the industrial production sector) and at the same time lacks the supply-demand equilibrium provided by market production, rising nominal expenditures are required just to maintain the same level of performance. This applies primarily to health and educational services that are extremely labor-intensive and must be controlled for when attempting to infer real improvements in services from an increase in social expenditures.

"Real" improvements, in standards and quality of services. Such improvements have been numerous in practically all fields of social policy. The coverage of established social security schemes has been extended, for instance, to include additional population groups. In addition, the level of benefits compared to previous earnings has been raised, or the eligibility requirements have been reduced. The quality of health services is improved, for instance, when new risks are covered by health insurance or when medical care is intensified and made more effective.

Obviously, this last set of factors is largely dependent on political decision making and subject to political controversy. Therefore, it is expected, that governments with different political and ideological commitments will influence social expenditure growth in particular and public expenditure growth in general. Although demographic and cost inflation factors unfortunately cannot be controlled for in the following analyses,[15] it is assumed that they probably affect expenditure development in different countries in a similar way. Thus, we shall turn to an analysis of governmental influence on public expenditures in order to explain further the differences in growth rates.

III. Party in Power and Public Sector Development

It has been clearly demonstrated in the preceding discussion that there are impressive differences between Western European countries with regard to the development of public expenditures, despite the similarity of general growth tendencies. They started at different levels after the war, experienced differing paces of development during the last decades and have now arrived at considerably different expenditure levels. These variations must now be examined against sociopolitical factors that might have encouraged or impeded public expenditure growth.

The sociopolitical mechanisms leading to increased state activity and expenditures have been briefly sketched in the introduction. Taking regard to national variations in political conditions, we can now venture some more specific hypotheses. Different expenditure levels after the Second World War, for instance, may be due, among other factors, to the degree of war involvement that required (and made possible) extraordinary efforts to raise resources. Once the machinery for extracting resources was built up, revenues could easily be directed to other expenditure purposes. The social security institutions developed earlier are probably of major importance in explaining social transfer expenditure levels. Similarly, the older ideological traditions of liberal and authoritarian rule and the corresponding conceptions of the responsibilities of the state have probably exerted lasting influences on the size of state bureaucracies and public budgets. Likewise, the different approaches to social service provision outlined above have had an impact on the emphasis placed upon transfer as opposed to public consumption expenditures. However, the following considerations may serve as a background for our analysis of welfare state development in the postwar decades and our understanding of the impact of political and ideological structures.

Increased welfare spending is most favored by the lower strata of the population both because of their urgent need for income maintenance measures and their potential gains from income redistribution while the middle and upper classes typically resist such attempts. The political articulation and aggregation of these interests and demands are, of course, structured by the opportunities for political organization and by the existing party system. While other social cleavages may be important, these economic interests will take precedent in the programs and the political rhetoric of the socialist or labor parties on the one hand and conservative and liberal ones on the other. Religion-based parties, common in Western Europe, are more difficult to assess, depending on whether traditional or social reformist tendencies prevail.

Because socialist parties traditionally stood for progressive taxation, both to advance social justice and to mobilize the fiscal resources needed to carry out social reforms, it is assumed that they also favor increasing the levels of total expenditures. Conversely, conservative and liberal parties are expected to oppose not only welfare state development, but increased activity beyond the classic functions of the state in general and interventions in the capitalist economy in particular. Therefore, they are expected to keep expenditure levels and increases as low as possible.

We can hypothesize then that countries with a large, strongly organized working class will lead in welfare spending and eventually in public expenditure increases in general.[16] But party strength expressed as the number of electoral votes is not directly translated into political power since electoral systems and parliamentary rules of representation intervene. Moreover, participation in government is the decisive threshold since ultimately executive power and the command of a parliamentary majority will most effectively determine budget decisions.

For this reason, the party composition of government has been selected for special attention from the complex network of causal factors leading to public expenditure decisions. For the following analysis, governments in the ten countries under consideration have been classified according to their ideological stance and their basis of parliamentary support.[17] Five types are distinguished: (1) Right: "pure" conservative majority cabinet, (2) Center-Right: conservative-dominated coalition cabinet, (3) Center: conservative-socialist coalition or coalition without a clearly dominant party, (4) Center-Left: socialist-dominated coalition cabinet, (5) Left: "pure" socialist one-party cabinet.[18]

To discern variations in the spending behavior of different types of government, factors that may have affected the spending behavior of all governments over time must be controlled. In order to eliminate such general influences, the following procedure has been adopted: first, European average increases of the total expenditure and social transfer ratios have been calculated for each year from 1950 to 1975; second, for each country and each year, the two growth rates have been classified as lying above or below the European averages; third, for each type of government in each country, a standardized ratio has been derived by dividing the number of years with increases above the average by the number of years in office; finally, for each type of government the respective ratios in the individual countries have been aggregated to derive an average ratio.

Tables 9.6 and 9.7 show these ratios and the corresponding percentages indicating the propensity of different party governments toward overproportional increases in total expenditures and social transfer expenditures respectively. A few generalizations are suggested by these results. With respect to total expenditures, "pure" socialist or socialist-dominated governments seem to increase their expenditures more rapidly than "pure" conservative governments. However, the strongest propensity toward disproportionate increases is found with Center governments (mostly conservative-socialist coalitions). The difference between Center-Right and Center-Left/Left governments is only small.

The growth pattern of social transfer expenditures is somewhat different. Social transfers most rapidly increased under Center-Right and Center coalitions. While conservative majority governments again show the smallest increases, leftist governments also remain below the average. The most remarkable difference is that between pure conservative and conservative-dominated Center-Right governments. Thus, the rank orders with respect to total expenditures (TE) and social transfers (ST) are the following:[19]

TE: Center > Center-Left/Left > Center-Right > Right
ST: Center-Right > Center > Center-Left/Left > Right.

The overall pattern—Center and Center-Right coalitions with the greatest propensity to increase and pure conservative governments with the

Table 9.6
Increases in Total Public Expenditures by
Party Composition of Governments, 1950-1975

Country	Right	Centre–Right	Centre	Centre–Left/Left
Austria	1/4 25 %		6/15 40 %	1/6 17 %
Belgium		4/6 67 %	4/6 67 %	1/4 25 %
Denmark		6/8 75 %		8/17 47 %
France	1/4 25 %	5/13 38 %	5/7 71 %	
Germany	2/4 50 %	3/12 25 %	1/3 33 %	4/6 67 %
Italy		9/20 45 %		
Netherlands		7/12 58 %	10/13 77 %	
Norway		2/5 40 %		13/20 65 %
Sweden				8/15 53 %
United Kingdom	6/17 35 %			4/8 50 %
Average	10/29 34 %	36/76 47 %	26/44 59 %	39/76 51 %

Table 9.7
Increases in Social Transfer Expenditures by Party Composition of Governments, 1950-1975

Country	Right	Centre-Right	Centre	Centre-Left/Left
Austria	1/4 25 %		7/15 47 %	0/6 —
Belgium		4/7 57 %	4/11 36 %	0/4 —
Denmark		4/8 50 %		7/17 41 %
France	1/4 25 %	6/13 46 %	4/7 57 %	
Germany	1/4 25 %	4/12 33 %	1/3 33 %	2/6 33 %
Italy		11/20 55 %		
Netherlands		11/12 92 %	10/13 77 %	12/20 60 %
Norway		4/5 80 %		15/25 60 %
Sweden				15/25 60 %
United Kingdom	5/17 29 %			2/8 25 %
Average	8/29 28 %	44/77 57 %	26/49 53 %	38/86 44 %

least—suggests that the dynamics of coalition governments override left and right differences. As long as conservative parties command a majority, they tend more than any other type of government to restrain the growth of public expenditures in general and of social transfers in particular. But the necessity to build coalitions in order to gain or to preserve executive power requires compromises, and the attempt to reconcile competing political priorities by alloting resources to each of them may even accelerate the growth of expenditures. The strongest tendency to increase total expenditures is found in conservative-socialist coalitions where socialist inclinations to expand state activities find additional support in the necessities of coalition building.

In addition to this interpretation it is further suggested that there are ideological differences between the parties classified as conservative or right, between the British Conservatives and the French Gaullists on the one hand (representing pure conservative governments) and the Christian Democrats in Germany and Italy for instance (which were the leading parties of Center-Right coalitions). The religion-based social reformist tradition of the latter may result in a greater willingness to spend larger sums for social purposes, particularly cash transfers for social security. This interpretation is supported by the outstanding performance of Center-Right and Center coalitions with regard to social transfer expenditures.

It would be misleading, however, to conclude from this evidence that socialist governments spend less for social purposes. They only spend less (or more precisely, increase less) for social *transfer* expenditures. The preference for direct public provision of social services reflected in the Scandinavian pattern where socialist governments have dominated in the postwar period, suggests that a considerable part of their social expenditures is probably hidden under the label of "civil public consumption." This would then explain the high level of total expenditure growth under leftist governments.

IV. Fiscal Responses to Problems of Expenditure Growth

Apart from inherent complexities and ambiguities, the concept of *government overload* as it has been developed and frequently discussed in recent years[20] applies at least partially to the problems posed by public expenditure growth. For if *overload* is understood essentially as a problem of imbalances between basic elements of the policy process, then imbalances between public revenues and expenditures can be seen as the fiscal aspect of the problem.

The perennial political task of budgeting can be described as searching for and maintaining a feasible balance between citizens' demands for public goods and services (which require public spending) and their willingness to pay for them (through taxes). Hence, government overload results when either demands are not satisfactorily met by public expenditures in accordance with given resources or when public expenditures are more or less responsive to articulated demands, but exceed available resources. In this view, a government's ability to maintain a proper balance between demands and resources is reflected in the surplus/deficit of the budget. The strategic options to be employed by political decision makers then are to restrain demands and/or expenditures, to increase resources by raising taxes, and to improve the institutional capabilities of transforming inputs into outputs.

Two specific aspects can be distinguished for testing the general hypothesis of overloaded fiscal capacities: First, it is implied that a widening gap between total public expenditures and revenues will evolve over time. In response to rising expectations and popular demands, governments have committed themselves to certain standards of public goods and services in the past. Especially when economic conditions worsen, increasing demands on the polity to maintain established levels of public services are coupled with growing difficulties in raising the required resources. In this situation, governments are likely to choose the most comfortable alternative for the short run: financing an ever increasing share of expenditures by borrowing.

Second, the articulated demands of pressure groups and the electorate in general predominantly concern the issues of social security and the provision of social services (as demonstrated by the overproportional increases of social expenditures). Thus, a rising share of revenues is needed to meet these demands for consumptive and transfer expenditures. On the other hand, public investments, such as in infrastructure and communications, are less attractive to the electorate and hence relatively neglected. Because the policy of deficit spending cannot continue unrestricted without eventually damaging the state's finances (public debt) and the economy as a whole (inflation), public investments are expected to be reduced, at least in the middle range trend.

In order to subject both propositions to empirical tests, these ratios are defined as indicators: (1) total deficit ratio (total expenditures/current revenues), (2) current deficit ratio (current expenditures/current revenues). Their development is shown in Figure 9.2.[21]

To appreciate the results, it must be understood that the surplus or deficit of the budget is largely a function of economic fluctuations. Deficit spending and surplus saving may even be used as policy devices to stabilize the economy. Therefore, the comparatively high irregular fluctuations exhibited should not be mistaken as indicators of instability. The crucial question is, instead, whether a trend can be detected despite these oscillations.

Figure 9.2
The Balance of Public Revenues and Expenditures
in Western Europe, 1950-1975

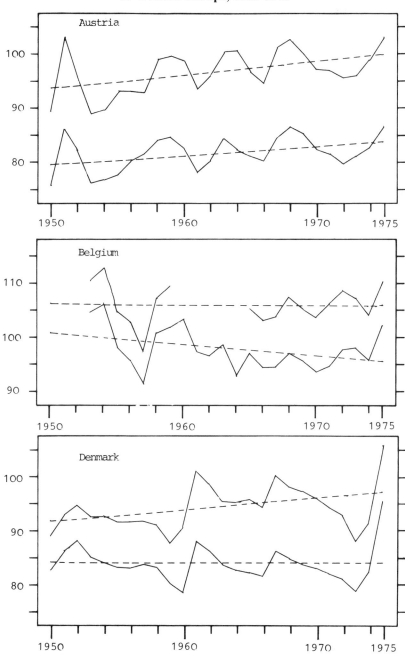

Figure 9.2
(Continued)

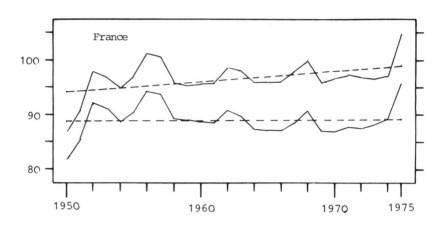

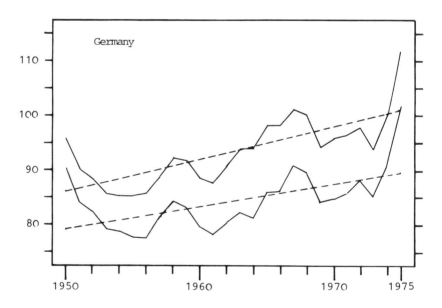

Upper line: Total deficit ratio
Lower line: Current deficit ratio
The regression lines are marked with dashes

Figure 9.2
(Continued)

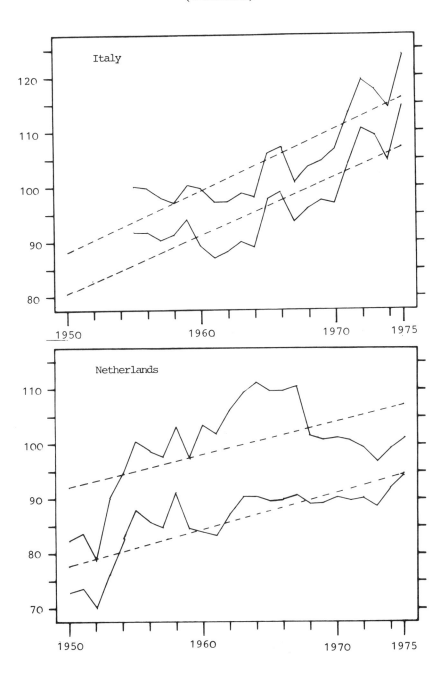

Figure 9.2 (Continued)

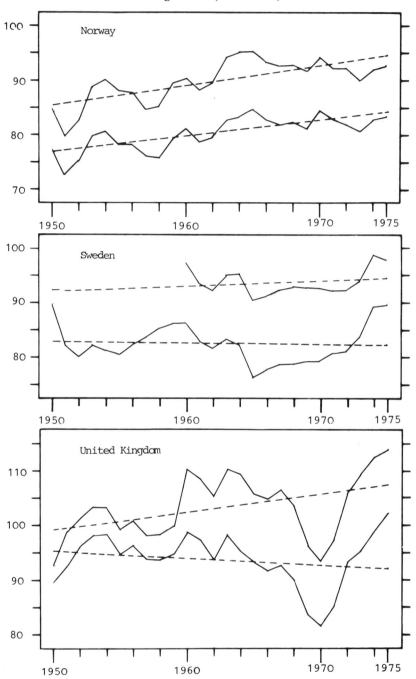

Figure 9.2 (Continued)

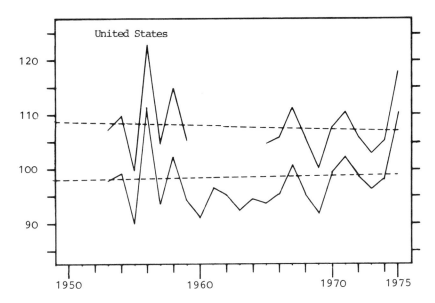

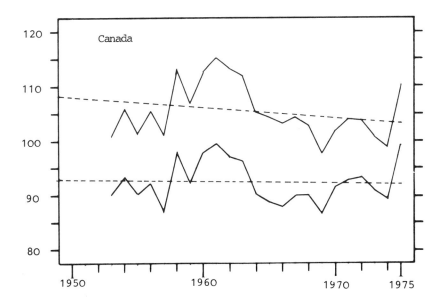

The *b* weights of the time-series regressions for both indicators, showing the average annual changes in deficit ratios, and the resulting differences between them, indicating a broadening or narrowing margin of public investments, are given in Table 9.8.

Table 9.8
Trends in the Balance of Revenues and Expenditures, 1950-1975

Country	total deficit ratio b_1	current deficit ratio b_2	margin for investments $b_1 - b_2$
Austria	+ 0,26	+ 0,17	+ 0,09
Belgium	- 0,01	- 0,20	+ 0,19
Denmark	+ 0,21	- 0,01	+ 0,22
France	+ 0,19	+ 0,02	+ 0,17
Germany	+ 0,60	+ 0,41	+ 0,19
Italy	+ 1,12	+ 1,06	+ 0,06
Netherlands	+ 0,61	+ 0,67	- 0,06
Norway	+ 0,37	+ 0,30	+ 0,07
Sweden	+ 0,09	- 0,03	+ 0,12
United Kingdom	+ 0,33	- 0,12	+ 0,45
United States	- 0,07	+ 0,15	- 0,22
Canada	- 0,20	- 0,04	- 0,16

The comparative evidence reveals certain interesting and partly unexpected features. Indeed, almost all countries follow an upward trend in the total deficit ratio indicating that on the average expenditures have grown at a faster rate than revenues. Whereas in the beginning of the postwar period, deficits were reported for only three countries (Belgium, the United States, and Canada), the trend growth rates have been high enough so that by 1975, the balance line has been surpassed by ten out of twelve countries.

Thus, the hypothesis that governments will increase budget deficits in the middle-range trend can be considered sufficiently confirmed.

In contrast to the second hypothesis, the trend growth rates of current deficits are generally smaller than those of total deficits. Therefore, the trend curves of both ratios slightly diverge in nine out of twelve cases. This is taken as proof that the propensity to increase budget deficits has not led to large-scale reductions of public investments. On the contrary, public· investment expenditures have been expanded and thereby have· contributed to increased deficits. What may be maintained at best is that government ability to expand the investment share in the budget is impaired to a certain extent by disproportionately increasing current deficits. The rank order correlation coefficient between the respective b weights given in Table 9.8 is Rho = -.42, but the correlation with regard to total deficits is insignificant (Rho = + .13).

How do higher deficit levels fit with rising shares of public investments? If it is correct that public investments have less appeal to voters than social expenditures, it must be concluded that political action has not automatically and exclusively been a response to mass demands. A more accurate argument then would contend that governments in the pursuit of their self-interest will search for compromises between the articulated demands of the citizens and the perceived and anticipated requirements of the economic system. The task of rendering popular demands and economic requirements compatible cannot be solved unambiguously, hence leading to a great variety of political responses and precarious solutions. This proposition can be further substantiated by some empirical observations.

Public expenditures have increased in general, and so have public deficits. But have deficits increased most in those countries where expenditure growth has been most rapid? According to the logic of the original hypotheses, one would expect high degrees of association, especially with regard to social transfers because these are considered the prime determinants in expenditure growth. Coefficients are supposed to be somewhat lower in the case of total deficits because of the hypothesized decline in investment shares. But when countries are ranked according to the average increases in expenditure ratios and in public deficit ratios, no significant overall relationship is apparent.[22]

Some contrasting examples stand out. Italy and Germany, those countries that show a distinct trend toward increasing their budget deficits, have experienced only moderate total expenditure growth. The Scandinavian countries, on the other hand, reported most rapid shifts in expenditure levels but kept relatively stable balances, especially with regard to current deficits. Belgium even succeeded in raising its expenditure level considera-

Table 9.9
**Rank Order Correlations Between Average Increases
in Public Expenditures and in Deficit Levels**[22]

	Total deficits	current deficits
Total public expenditures	+ .29	+ .05
Social transfer expenditures	+ .17	+ .28

bly without further increasing deficits (though admittedly staying at a high level). Only the Netherlands and Italy seem to fit the hypothesized mechanism to a certain extent: disproportionate increases in social transfers that are not matched by equivalent revenue increases have led to rapidly increasing current deficits that in turn only allow for minimal increases in public investments.[23] The United States and Canada are deviant cases for several reasons: contrary to the Western European countries they have not increased total deficits in the middle-range trend, but have reduced investment shares. While they fit the *fiscal overload* hypothesis in one respect (narrowing investment margin), they do not confirm it in the other (increasing total deficits). Western European and North American experiences thus suggest that it is particularly difficult to maintain stable budget balances *and* to keep or even expand the level of public investments. Rather, they point to two alternative responses to the problem of expenditure growth: increasing total deficits *or* decreasing investment shares. While the first option still allows for expanding public investments, the latter approach makes it possible to keep or even reduce deficit levels. The alternative chosen is supposed to reflect differences in budgeting priorities between the Western European and the North American countries (although the decisions may partly be influenced by the high deficit levels already attained in the United States and Canada).

It must be admitted that when only the last five-year period is examined, most countries have experienced tremendously increasing budget deficits. But one should not arbitrarily jump to the conclusion that this marks a decisive change in trend or acceleration. Again with the remarkable exception of Italy, the trend curves have changed little when an earlier analysis of the period 1950 to 1970 was extended up to 1975. This indicates that in most cases recent increases in deficits have not yet exceeded the magnitudes of normal oscillations around the middle-range trend.

Conclusion

The preceding discussion has shown that the baleful scenario of growing overload is by no means inevitable. The possibility should not be dismissed outright, however. Certain tendencies have been identified that point to continued increases in public expenditures: the rising costs of the provision of general administrative and social services caused by their low productivity gains and the demographic shifts likely to aggravate further the burdens of social security.

While it is hard to imagine that total public expenditures will continue to rise at rates similar to past decades, there is no clear indication of a final "limit to growth." Those countries that have reached the highest expenditure levels to date do not exhibit symptoms of stagnation, while others are still far from those advanced levels that have nevertheless proved politically feasible. It is particularly difficult to specify a functional ceiling in the case of social transfer expenditures because they do not diminish the shares of income available for overall private consumption, but only redistribute income between households. Desired levels are largely a matter of political choice, and national differences in this regard are unlikely to disappear.

The appropriate level of public expenditure will certainly remain a highly controversial problem, and any solution will require effective political leadership. Today, demands for limitation or eventual reduction of the public sector's share, for cutbacks in welfare expenditures and a reprivatization of public services are widespread. The recent phenomena of tax revolts are a major theme of the next chapter by Harold Wilensky. But it is also obvious that the quality of life depends on public goods and services as well as on private ones. It is therefore anticipated that a limitation of social expenditures, which usually implies a reduction of benefits and services for larger and especially poorer population groups, will be met by resistance.

There are different political answers to the question of the appropriate level of public expenditures. Independently of these answers, however, the question remains whether, given the inherent tendencies toward further expenditure growth, we can improve public services through increasing their efficacy as well as their responsiveness to perceived needs. Will these current problems, demands, criticisms, and endeavors lead "toward a new welfare state?" This question will be explored more deeply by Hugh Heclo in the concluding chapter.

Table 9.10
Total Public Expenditures as Percentage of GNP

Year	Austria	Belgium	Denmark	Finland	France	Germany	Italy	Nether-lands	Norway	Sweden	Switzerland	United Kingdom	United States	Canada
1950	25,0		19,4		28,4	30,8		27,0	25,5			30,4	27,4	26,8
1951	28,2		21,3		29,3	30,6		27,1	23,4			31,6	26,6	27,9
1952	29,0		22,4		32,1	31,3		27,1	25,3			32,9	24,9	27,1
1953	29,2	26,3	22,6		33,0	31,1		28,9	27,4			32,2	28,2	27,8
1954	27,6	26,1	23,0		32,0	30,6		28,7	27,2			31,4	27,1	27,2
1955	27,5	24,7	23,6		32,2	30,0	27,8	28,5	26,8			30,2	29,0	27,5
1956	28,8	24,8	23,7		34,3	30,2	29,3	29,9	26,7			29,8	27,6	29,7
1957	29,5	24,4	24,4		34,3	31,7	29,2	32,5	28,4			29,3		29,7
1958	31,5	26,8	24,8		33,3	33,1	29,5	33,4	29,7			30,1		31,1
1959	31,4	28,2	24,0		33,8	33,5	31,5	31,6	31,1			30,5		31,0
1960	30,7		25,0	26,9	32,5	31,7	29,6	34,3	31,9	37,5	20,8	32,2		30,4
1961	31,0		27,2	26,4	33,7	32,3	28,3	34,7	31,7	37,4	22,1	33,0		29,5
1962	32,8		28,1	27,8	35,0	34,0	29,3	35,8	33,7	38,7	23,3	33,6		29,3
1963	33,8		28,7	30,2	35,6	35,0	30,3	38,1	35,2	41,1	24,2	33,8		30,4
1964	34,6		28,5	30,4	35,6	34,7	31,0	38,8	35,1	41,1	25,5	33,5		32,3
1965	33,8	32,3	29,9	31,5	36,1	35,0	33,3	40,0	36,4	35,4	25,3	35,2	28,3	33,2
1966	34,3	33,4	31,7	32,2	36,0	35,4	33,5	42,2	36,7	37,2	26,1	36,0	29,6	33,6
1967	36,2	34,5	34,2	33,5	36,5	37,1	32,9	43,8	38,1	39,1	26,5	38,4	31,6	35,8
1968	36,8	36,3	36,2	34,1	37,6	36,4	34,5	42,6	37,8	41,3	26,2	39,0	31,8	36,7
1969	36,3	36,1	36,2	32,7	36,5	36,0	34,2	43,0	39,5	41,9	27,4	38,1	31,5	37,4
1970	35,8	36,5	40,0	32,0	38,5	35,9	35,4	44,4	41,0	42,8		38,1	32,9	36,1
1971	36,2	37,8	42,2	33,4	38,0	37,0	38,4	46,6	42,9	44,9		37,7	33,0	38,0
1972	36,3	38,9	41,8	34,4	37,8	37,8	40,3	47,1	44,7	46,0		39,4	32,8	41,1
1973	36,6	39,1	40,3	32,9	38,1	38,6	39,3	47,6	44,8	45,6		39,9	32,2	
1974	38,0	39,5	44,0	34,3	38,7	41,5	39,3	50,5	44,8	49,0		44,6	33,8	
1975	40,3	44,9	47,5	37,2	42,4	45,6	43,1	54,3	46,5	51,0		46,1	36,2	

Table 9.11
Social Transfers as Percentage of GNP

Year	Austria	Belgium	Denmark	Finland	France	Germany	Italy	Netherlands	Norway	Sweden	Switzerland	United Kingdom	United States	Canada
1950	7,8		5,8		11,3	12,4		6,6	4,9	6,3		5,7		
1951	8,6		6,4		11,7	11,3		6,7	4,5	5,6		5,3		
1952	9,9		6,6		11,8	11,6		7,2	5,1	5,5		5,7		
1953	10,4	9,6	6,4		12,4	12,0		7,2	5,6	6,2		5,9	3,3	5,8
1954	9,9	9,2	6,2		12,7	11,8		7,2	5,8	6,3		5,7	3,9	6,6
1955	9,4	8,8	6,7		13,1	11,6	9,3	7,1	6,0	7,3		5,8	3,8	6,4
1956	9,8	8,6	6,8		13,3	11,8	10,1	7,1	5,9	7,5		5,7	3,9	5,8
1957	10,0	8,6	7,6		13,5	13,1	10,2	8,9	6,5	7,7		5,7	4,3	6,5
1958	10,5	9,9	7,8		13,2	13,9	10,5	10,1	7,1	8,5	5,9	6,5	5,2	8,0
1959	10,7	10,6	7,5		13,2	13,3	11,7	9,7	8,0	8,5	5,8	6,8	4,9	7,9
1960	10,5	11,2	7,3	5,8	12,9	12,5	10,7	10,2	8,4	7,7	3,9	6,2	5,1	8,1
1961	10,9	10,9	7,5	6,1	13,5	12,5	10,3	10,4	8,5	7,7	4,2	6,3	5,6	6,9
1962	11,9	11,2	7,7	6,5	14,6	12,7	10,8	11,0	9,2	7,8	4,4	6,6	5,4	6,8
1963	12,2	11,4	8,0	6,8	15,4	12,6	11,5	12,6	9,6	8,4	4,3	7,0	5,4	6,5
1964	12,2	10,8	7,6	6,5	15,6	12,7	11,4	12,6	9,7	8,5	5,2	6,9	5,2	6,3
1965	12,2	12,2	8,3	7,0	16,1	12,8	13,3	13,9	9,8	9,6	5,3	8,2	5,4	6,1
1966	12,5	12,8	9,0	7,4	16,2	13,1	13,5	15,0	10,0	9,9	5,4	8,4	5,5	6,0
1967	13,1	13,0	9,9	7,9	16,4	14,3	13,4	16,8	10,6	10,6	5,8	9,0	6,2	6,9
1968	13,5	14,0	10,8	7,9	16,7	13,8	14,3	17,2	11,5	11,3	5,7	9,5	6,6	7,4
1969	13,4	13,7	10,8	7,6	16,5	13,3	14,3	17,9	12,2	11,8	6,7	9,5	6,8	7,6
1970	13,0	14,1	11,6	7,4	16,9	12,6	15,4	18,5	13,8	11,8	6,2	9,5	7,9	8,1
1971	13,3	14,2	12,1	8,1	17,0	12,7	16,8	19,8	14,8	13,1	6,2	9,4	8,7	8,7
1972	13,1	14,9	12,4	8,5	17,2	13,2	17,7	20,9	15,7	13,8	6,2	10,4	8,7	9,4
1973	12,9	15,5	12,2	8,0	17,4	13,3	17,2	21,6	16,1	13,9	8,1	10,1	9,0	9,1
1974	12,8	16,0	13,2	8,3	17,8	14,2	17,2	23,5	15,5	16,4	8,5	10,8	9,9	9,5
1975	13,9	18,9	15,0	8,8	20,0	16,7	19,6	26,1	16,0	16,6	10,2	11,1	11,5	10,4

Table 9.12
Functional Structure of Social Expenditures
(Functions as Percentage of All Social Expenditures)

Year	Germany	France	Italy	Nether-lands	Belgium	Luxem-burg	United Kingdom	Ireland	Denmark
1. Health									
1962	26,8	20,5	19,1	25,5	13,3	15,6			
1963	25,9	20,7	19,8	24,1	14,2	16,0			
1964	25,1	21,7	22,0	25,1	16,8	15,4			
1965	25,8	22,1	21,2	24,6	21,8	16,3			
1966	26,6	23,0	23,2	25,1	20,2	16,7			
1967	25,7	23,7	24,2	24,8	19,4	16,4			
1968	27,2	22,9	23,5	28,8	20,7	17,0			
1969	27,3	24,5	24,5	30,2	23,0	17,3			
1970	27,7	24,7	26,4	29,8	22,3	17,2	26,4	28,7	28,6
1971	29,1	25,2	25,5	30,9	22,9	18,0	26,0	28,4	28,0
1972	29,6	26,8	26,4	31,3	22,5	17,6	25,9	29,1	28,9
1973	30,9	26,9	26,6	31,1	23,6	18,2	25,5	27,5	31,0
1974	31,0	27,1	30,3	31,1	23,2	19,5	25,4	26,9	30,5
1975	29,6	26,5	27,1	30,4	23,1	22,9	25,8	31,8	29,3
2. Old age									
1962	43,3	32,3	32,5	45,4	40,1	57,8[1]			
1963	44,4	32,5	34,5	43,0	38,9	57,6			
1964	44,6	33,6	35,2	43,4	39,8	59,7			
1965	44,2	35,1	36,2	45,7	37,1	59,0			
1966	44,5	36,2	36,9	44,3	38,6	58,8			
1967	45,1	36,9	36,6	43,3	37,4	60,5			
1968	45,6	38,5	35,9	41,8	38,4	59,8			
1969	46,3	38,3	36,9	41,9	38,0	60,4			
1970	45,6	40,4	34,8	40,7	37,8	60,9	47,0	36,9	36,3
1971	44,2	40,3	36,8	39,7	37,7	60,5	46,9	36,8	35,2
1972	44,1	39,7	35,4	37,9	37,6	63,3	48,1	36,7	34,1
1973	43,8	39,9	35,3	38,1	40,1	63,1	49,3	35,2	35,5
1974	43,8	40,6	33,7	37,3	39,9	62,2	49,0	34,5	33,6
1975	41,7	40,8	34,2	36,4	38,4	52,2	45,5	32,2	32,6
3. Invalidity									
1962	11,1	8,0	11,0	6,3	10,7	8,6[1]			
1963	10,9	8,0	12,0	8,2	10,7	8,7			
1964	10,8	8,1	12,3	8,7	10,5	7,8			
1965	10,6	8,2	14,2	8,5	10,1	7,8			
1966	10,5	8,2	15,9	9,2	11,3	9,2			
1967	10,2	8,0	16,3	10,2	11,7	8,1			
1968	9,9	7,5	16,7	8,3	10,9	8,0			
1969	9,4	7,4	18,0	8,9	10,5	7,7			
1970	12,6[2]	7,2	17,7	11,9	10,5	7,8	9,3	10,2	14,3
1971	11,5	7,1	17,7	12,4	11,2	7,6	9,1	11,4	14,5
1972	12,2	7,1	19,1	13,2	10,9	7,4	9,8	10,9	14,5
1973	11,9	6,9	19,4	14,2	11,0	7,3	10,5	13,0	14,0
1974	11,5	6,9	18,1	15,0	12,1	7,6	11,0	13,6	13,1
1975	10,8	6,2	20,9	15,8	11,7	15,1	11,4	9,7	12,4

Table 9.12
(Continued)

Year	Germany	France	Italy	Nether-lands	Belgium	Luxem-burg	United Kingdom	Ireland	Denmark
4. Unemployment									
1962	1,1	0,4	2,7	4,1	4,8	0,0			
1963	1,8	0,7	2,4	5,6	5,4	0,0			
1964	1,2	0,6	1,7	3,5	4,6	0,0			
1965	1,0	0,7	2,1	3,5	4,5	0,0			
1966	0,9	0,5	1,6	3,8	4,5	0,0			
1967	1,9	0,7	1,2	4,5	6,3	0,0			
1968	1,5	1,0	1,2	4,7	6,1	0,0			
1969	1,8	0,9	0,8	4,3	5,2	0,0			
1970	0,5	1,0	1,1	3,3	4,3	0,0	4,3	5,7	3,0
1971	0,6	1,1	1,2	3,1	4,4	0,0	5,6	5,4	4,2
1972	0,8	1,1	1,7	4,2	4,7	0,0	4,7	5,6	2,5
1973	0,7	1,1	1,8	4,0	5,0	0,0	3,5	4,8	2,2
1974	1,6	1,3	2,0	4,6	4,5	0,0	3,6	5,1	6,4
1975	3,6	2,7	2,8	6,0	7,1	0,2	5,8	7,1	9,4
5. Family allowances									
1962	7,4	29,1	24,1	14,4	19,8	13,6			
1963	7,6	27,9	21,6	15,4	20,7	13,6			
1964	8,6	27,0	20,4	16,0	20,6	13,3			
1965	9,1	26,3	18,5	14,9	19,9	13,5			
1966	9,0	25,3	16,4	15,2	20,5	12,9			
1967	8,3	24,4	15,9	14,9	20,4	12,4			
1968	7,6	24,0	15,8	14,4	20,5	12,7			
1969	8,0	23,2	13,6	14,0	19,8	12,1			
1970	9,8	19,5	12,9	14,0	19,1	11,6	10,8	17,1	16,4
1971	9,7	19,3	13,5	13,4	17,8	11,6	10,0	16,3	16,6
1972	9,0	18,8	10,2	12,9	16,8	11,1	8,9	15,7	16,4
1973	8,3	18,9	9,2	12,3	16,0	10,8	10,4	17,8	15,3
1974	7,9	18,0	11,7	11,6	15,5	10,4	10,2	18,3	14,2
1975	10,2	19,6	11,8	11,6	14,9	9,3	10,6	17,3	13,7

Notes

1. See O'Connor 1973.
2. See Janowitz 1976.
3. The complete time-series are given in Table 9.10; the figure for 1950 refers to the first year for which data were available. *Annual average change* refers to increases in public expenditure/GNP *ratios* and gives the *b*'s of a time-series regression analysis. Interestingly, the actual values for recent years are mostly above the estimated values, indicating an acceleration of growth. *Elasticity* refers to *relative* growth of public expenditures as compared to economic growth. Values greater than unity thus indicate overproportional increases in public expenditures.
4. "Nominal" and "real" growth of public expenditures have been analyzed in greater detail by Garin-Painter 1970.
5. With regard to social expenditure development, see the evidence presented in *Indikatoren der sozialen Sicherheit* 1971.

6. In order to eliminate certain distortions arising from the fluctuating shares of defense expenditures and other than social transfers, the shares of civil public consumption and of social transfers are examined here and in Table 9.3. The figures given refer to 1974 in general, otherwise to the latest year for which data were available.

7. The time-series for "social transfers" has been compiled from the OECD series on "current transfers to households" and, later, the sum of "social security benefits" and "social assistance grants."

8. For a comparative graphical presentation of the respective time-series, cf. Flora, Alber, and Kohl 1977, p. 744.

9. Cf. the stupendous examples with regard to the organization of health services given by Garin-Painter 1970, pp 48ff.

10. See Organization for Economic Cooperation and Development 1970, pp. 74ff. and *Indikatoren der sozialen Sicherheit* 1971, pp. 106f.

11. Such comparisons of absolute expenditure levels presume that converting national currencies into a common unit by their official exchange rates gives a fairly accurate impression of their purchasing power. Figures are taken from the Social Accounts series published by the Statistical Office of the European Communities.

12. The respective unemployment rates are to be found in *Jahrbuch der Sozial-statistik* 1968ff; see also Mittelstädt 1975.

13. This might reflect certain statistical inadequacies, to the extent that only direct transfers are taken into account but no tax credits that can be used as an alternative policy device.

14. For empirical evidence on the evolution of the population structure in the countries of the European Community, see *Indikatoren der sozialen Sicherheit* 1971, pp. 70f.

15. Such analyses of expenditures on income maintenance controlling for the contribution of demographic changes, of changes in coverage of programs, and in transfer ratios (benefit levels) have been carried out in Organization for Economic Cooperation and Development 1976.

16. See Wilensky 1975, pp. 65ff.

17. Finland and Switzerland are excluded from the original sample, because of the complexities of their governmental systems which made it difficult to classify them, as well as because only incomplete time-series were available. The standard data sources used for classifying the types and periods of governments are Spuler 1964, 1966 and von Beyme 1970. In addition, the documentation in the annual volumes of the "Archiv der Gegenwart" and the "Europa-Archiv," part III, has been used for updating the classification to the seventies. In this work, I could rely on earlier efforts done by Jens Alber for which I am grateful. Governments have been classified as follows:

Country	Right	Center-Right	Center	Center-Left/ Left
Austria	66-69		50-65	70-75
Belgium	50-53	58-60	61-65	54-57
		66-67	68-73	
		74-75		
Denmark		51-53		50
		68-71		54-67
		74		72-73

Country	Right	Center-Right	Center	Center-Left/ Left
France	69-72	59-68	50-57	
		73-75		
Germany	58-61	50-57	67-69	70-75
		62-66		
Italy	50-53	54-75		
Nether-		59-64	50-58	
lands		67-72	65-66	
			73-75	
Norway		66-70		50-65
				71-75
Sweden				50-75
United	52-64			50-51
Kingdom	70-73			65-69
				74-75

18. Because only small differences with regard to their spending behavior were apparent between "pure" socialist and socialist-dominated coalition governments and because of the small number of cases, these are treated in the following analysis as a single type of government.

19. These ordinal relationships were confirmed in more than two-thirds of all cases when examined within the single countries. Given the small number of cases, this seems to be sufficient proof that they are not mere random results caused by aggregation.

20. See Rose 1977, Peters 1977, and other papers presented at the same workshop on "Causes and Consequences of Government Growth."

21. *Public investment expenditures* are here defined to equal gross capital formation, i.e., depreciation and capital transfers are neglected. *Total expenditures* are defined correspondingly and are not identical, therefore, with the concepts usually applied in budgetary statistics. For details concerning budget concepts in the OECD countries, see Wasserman 1976.

22. Spearman rank correlation coefficients (Rho) are calculated between the *b*'s for total resp. social transfer expenditures (cf. Tables 9.1 and 9.4) and the *b*'s for the deficit ratios (cf. Table 9.8).

23. A closer look at the actual figures for the Netherlands (cf. Figure 9.2) shows, however, that increases in deficit ratios were highest in the fifties when investments too were expanded. The current deficit ratio has remained stable in the sixties so that the reduction of investments can hardly be considered a reaction to expanded consumptive expenditures.

References

von Beyme, Klaus. 1970. *Die parlamentarischen Regierungssysteme in Europa.* Munich: Piper.

Flora, Peter, Jens Alber, and Jürgen Kohl. 1977. "Zur Entwicklung der westeuropäischen Wolfarrtsstaaten." *Politische Vierteljahresschrift* 18, 4: 1977, pp. 707-772.

Garin-Painter, Mary. 1970. "Public expenditure trends in OECD countries." In

Organization of Economic Cooperation and Development, Economic Outlook (Occasional Studies), pp. 43-56. Paris: OECD.

Janowitz, Morris. 1976. *Social Control of the Welfare State.* New York, Elsevier.

Kommission der Europäischen Gemeinschaften, Generaldirektion Soziale Angelegenheiten. 1971. *Indikatoren der sozialen Sicherheit.* Brussels.

Mittelstäedt, Axel. 1975. "Unemployment Benefits and Related Payments in Seven Major Countries." In Organization of Economic Cooperation and Development, Economic Outlook (Occasional Studies), pp. 3-22. Paris: OECD.

O'Connor, James. 1973. *The Fiscal Crisis of the State.* New York: St. Martin's Press.

Organization for Economic Cooperation and Development. 1970. *Expenditure Trends in OECD Countries, 1960-1980.* Paris: OECD.

Organization for Economic Cooperation and Development. 1976. *Public Expenditure on Income Maintenance Programmes.* Paris: OECD.

Peters, B. Guy. 1977. "The Dimensions of Overload: A Preliminary Empirical Inquiry." Paper presented to the ECPR Workshop. Berlin.

Rose, Richard. 1977. "Governing and 'Ungovernability.' A Sceptical Inquiry." Paper presented to the ECPR Workshop. Berlin.

Spuler, Bertold. 1964. Regenten und Regierungen der Welt (Minister-Ploetz), Pt.II, Vol.4, Neueste Zeit 1917/18-1964, Würzburg: A.G. Ploetz 1964 (2nd ed.) Vol.1, 1, Nachtrag 1964/65. Würzburg: A.G. Ploetz, 1966.

Statistisches Amt der Europäischen Gemeinschaften. 1968. *Jahrbuch der Sozialstatistik 1968.* Luxemburg.

Statistisches Amt der Europäischen Gemeinschaften. 1970. *Jahrbuch der Sozialstatistik 1970.* Luxemburg.

Statistisches Amt der Europäischen Gemeinschaften. 1972. *Jahrbuch der Sozialstatistik 1972.* Luxemburg.

Statistisches Amt der Europäischen Gemeinschaften. 1977. *Sozialkonten 1970-1975.* Brussels.

Wasserman, Mark 1976. "Public Sector Budget Balances." In Organization for Economic Cooperation and Development, Economic Outlook (Occasional Studies), pp. 37-51. Paris: OECD.

Wilensky, Harold L. 1975. *The Welfare State and Equality: Structural and Ideological Roots of Public Expenditures.* Berkeley, Calif.: University of California Press.

Chapter 10

Leftism, Catholicism, and Democratic Corporatism: The Role of Political Parties in Recent Welfare State Development

Harold L. Wilensky

Contemporary welfare states in Europe and America must function under conditions of slow economic growth, inflation, unemployment, energy shortages, and rising aspirations for equality and security—a recipe for political trouble.[1] The puzzle is that countries sharing these problems, as well as similar levels of taxing and social spending, vary greatly in the political protest they generate. In a recent paper,[2] I tried to solve this puzzle by developing a model of *democratic corporatism*, modified by the presence or absence of *old party dominance*. Variations in these attributes of structure help explain national differences in tax-welfare backlash.

By democratic corporatism I mean the capacity of strongly organized centralized economic interest groups interacting under government auspices within a quasi-public framework to produce peak bargains involving social policy, fiscal and monetary policy, and incomes policies—the major interrelated issues of modern political economy.[3] The measure is *corporatist-technocratic linkages* indicated by the centralization of government and the centralization of labor federations and, by inference, the centralization of employer federations.[4] Such structure for policy deliberation is a relatively effective consensus-making machine; it permits high levels of taxing and social spending with only weak or moderate political protest.

By old party dominance (or "old party system") I mean a party system dominated by one or two parties facing few significant opposition parties that to some extent operates within a long tradition of constitutional order. The measure is the age of the largest party in 1965.[5] Where one party or a stable set of coalition parties dominate a party system for decades, reaching accommodations internally and permitting little overt expression of discontent, diffuse unrest is bottled up. In the deep crisis of 1965-75, it spills over and finds expression in the form of tax-welfare backlash movements and new parties.[6]

In general, these attributes of structure must be combined with the "right" tax policy if a nation is to get away with lavish social spending without provoking strong, organized popular resistance. That policy is to avoid overreliance on the most painfully visible taxes (property taxes on households and income taxes) in favor of less visible taxes (consumption taxes and social security payroll taxes). The strongest antitax, antiwelfare, antibureaucratic movements, I found, flourished in countries with the greatest reliance on visible taxes, whatever their level of spending and taxing (e.g., the United States, a lean spender, and Denmark, a big spender).[7] Subsequent events, such as the spread of the spirit of California's Proposition 13, seem to confirm that analysis.

The two measures of these complex ideas—corporatism and old party dominance—are unrelated ($r = -.08$). I concluded that:

> There are two roads to the containment of mass discontents centered on taxes, social spending, and bureaucracy. A strong corporatist democracy which relies on invisible taxes dampens tax-welfare backlash, whether it has an old dominant party (Belgium, Netherlands) or not (France, Italy, Israel, Austria). And a young party system that provides several channels for party opposition and which relies on invisible taxes, also dampens backlash, whether it has strong corporatist-technocratic linkages (France, Italy, Israel, Austria) or not (West Germany, Japan, Ireland, New Zealand).[8]

The model is pictured in Figure 10.1.

The role of the working class in this previous analysis was ambiguous. Both the size of the working class and an aggregate measure of the strength of working class (left vote, voter turnout, union membership ratios) were irrelevant as sources of welfare effort; they were insignificant in regressions containing the crucial determinants of social security expenditures as a fraction of gross national product (SS/GNP)—age of population and corporatist-technocratic linkages. Further, as a determinant of tax policy or welfare backlash, working-class strength was ambiguous.

> When played against corporatism as a source of reliance on visible taxes, working class strength either drops out or it *increases* reliance on visible

Figure 10.1
An Initial Model Explaining Tax-Welfare Backlash

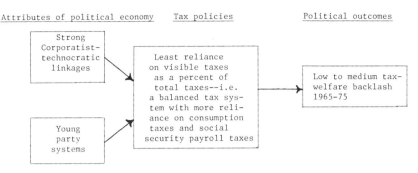

taxes. These figures could reflect the penchant of Left parties for progressive income taxes, but such an interpretation may be too simple. First, country-by-country examination of the effect of Communist Party vote suggests that the presence of a strong CP opposition is quite consistent with an avoidance of visible taxes. Among our 19 rich democracies, Italy and France rank 18th and 19th in reliance on visible taxes, while Finland ranks 9th. . . . This accords with some observers' claim that in these few countries with a large Communist vote, the CP does not bother much with tax structures, despite their objective importance for equality. Furthermore, it is possible that Left parties—CP and non-CP alike—are only mildly interested in the major sources of taxes and their visibility or invisibility, progressivity or regressivity; they are instead preoccupied with nationalization of industry, participation of workers (a popular theme of the non-CP Left), and other social policies. If Left parties mention taxes, they tend to advocate stiffer wealth and corporation taxes, relatively meager sources of revenue. Finally, if we take the viewpoint of a non-Left government facing strong Left opposition, avoidance of visible taxes both permits and necessitates freer spending—a kind of welfare counter-punch to the Left threat.[9]

This paper attempts to resolve these ambiguities by going beyond both old versus young party system and crude measures of working-class strength to consider the ideological stance and power of two mass-based types of political parties—Left and Catholic. It aims to integrate political party dominance into my model of democratic corporatism and thereby come closer to an understanding of whether and how political parties influence social policy.

I began with an hypothesis about the political role of the working class in welfare state development among rich countries: "Whether the working class is organized along socialist lines (strong socialist movements in the past and great electoral strength in the present, as in Italy, Sweden, and France) or along religious, linguistic or other lines (as in the Netherlands and Belgium) is irrelevant. What counts is the strength of the collective push for equality."[10] In view of the ambiguous results, I had the hunch that the original hypothesis was substantially true but our measures were weak, so I elaborated it by taking account of political parties with substantial working-class base. We devised measures of left party dominance and Catholic party dominance.

Because these two types of political parties seek a broad popular base, almost always including the working class, the present analysis is an indirect but more sensitive test of the role of the working class in welfare-state development, as well as a direct test of the impact of political party ideology and power. It shows that since World War I, leftism and Catholicism under some circumstances have had some effect on a country's tax system, welfare effort, and welfare output—as well as the political response to all three. Specifically, this paper explores the relative strength of Catholic and left party dominance in explaining variations among nineteen rich democracies in welfare effort measured by social security expenditures as a fraction of the GNP in 1966 and 1971; welfare output, here measured only by social security spending per capita; degree of reliance on painfully visible taxes; and the political response to spending and taxing, measured by tax-welfare backlash from 1965 to 1975.[11] In general, Catholic power (wherever Catholic parties exist) shapes welfare state development much more than left power. But both have surprisingly similar effects on the structure of modern political economies; they both foster corporatism.

I. Political Party Dominance and Welfare State Development

Although there has been extensive discussion of whether left power makes any difference in the direction of social change, social policy, and policy outcomes, the few attempts to tackle this difficult question systematically and comparatively have suffered from vague concepts or weak measures. And no one has systematically dealt with Catholic party dominance in relation to both leftism and social policy.

The ideology of left parties commits them to social policies aimed at economic redistribution. While it is thus plausible to assume that left party power is positively correlated with welfare effort and output in rich Western democracies, many social scientists question the validity of this traditional assumption. Some argue that shifts in the locus of power in modern government from legislatures to the executive and within the executive to technocrats in the bureaucracy have undermined the power of political parties. These trends have often been analyzed in terms of the development of a neocorporatist political economy where policy is determined by the interplay of administrative leaders, staff experts, and their interest-group constituents (cf. Wilensky, Schmitter, Heisler).[12] Similarly, theorists of industrial society and the capitalist state have played down the importance of ideological differences among the major parties in modern democracies or modern societies (Kerr, Miliband).[13] In contrast are students who accent the persistence of party power and, to a lesser extent, party ideology. They suggest that in many countries political parties have substantial power within bureaucracies (Daalder)[14] and that while less ideological and more inclusive than in earlier periods, parties are still clearly based on class interests (Lipset).[15] Thus, the debate over the impact of left party power upon economic redistribution and social welfare is far from resolved, even if everyone agrees that such parties in action have not made revolutionary changes.

Empirical studies of the relationship between left party power and the development of social welfare have used both longitudinal and cross-sectional data. Longitudinal studies have generally focused on the history of social policy in one or a few countries. They attempt to identify periods of critical innovation, such as the post-World War I period in Austria, the 1930s in Sweden and the United States, or the years just after World War II in Britain. The role of political parties in these policy innovations, and by implication the whole development of the welfare state, is then scrutinized. An excellent example of this approach is Charles Gulick's massive work on the growth of social programs in Austria in the decade after the First World War.[16] But however convincing such detailed historical case studies may be, the untangling of cause and effect in the genesis of policy in one or two cases presents formidable difficulties. For example, in his comparative study of the development of three income maintenance programs in Britain and Sweden, Hugh Heclo stresses the incremental influence of a variety of parties and the crucial role of the civil service. He therefore sees social policy as a piecemeal, ad hoc, largely unplanned process—a "random walk" in the face of great uncertainty—rather than a series of dramatic breaks with the past.[17] In this web of interconnected influences it is difficult to single out the contributions of individual parties, even in such seemingly clear-cut cases as the Swedish Social Democrats of the 1930s.[18]

Although they lack the subtlety of case studies, cross-sectional aggregate investigations permit a more systematic analysis of the impact of left party power. Unfortunately such studies are rare, their findings inconsistent. Early large-scale comparative studies of the effects of political variables on social policy include a cross-national study by Phillips Cutright[19] and an extensive literature, reviewed by Fry and Winters, on differences among the American states.[20] These studies generally found that political as compared to socioeconomic variables were weak explanations of various policy outcomes. Such findings have been supported by Pryor, Parkin, Jackman, Wilensky and Fried.[21]

Other recent studies have reasserted the importance of political variables in general and left party power in particular.[22] Especially relevant are Hibbs' cross-sectional and longitudinal study showing that left party power is associated with egalitarian policies or consequences of low unemployment and high inflation and Hewitt's findings that socialist power in the advanced industrial countries produces greater income equality—in contrast to both Jackman's and Parkin's findings that socialist party strength has little or no influence on economic equality.

These inconsistent results partly stem from different choices of independent and dependent variables, as well as from different measures of the same variables. More important are the hazards of inadequate concepts and measures. For instance, although both Jackman and Cutright deploy sophisticated techniques of analysis and are clear and cautious in presenting findings, both use a dubious measure of economic equality: intersectoral inequality as a surrogate for inequality among individuals or households.[23] Studies that use more direct measures of income inequality for similarly large samples of nations, such as Hewitt's, find that political variables are more important than socioeconomic variables as sources of equality.[24] More persuasive and consistent, however, are findings that relative to economic growth or its correlates, political ideologies or experience with representative government are weak explanations of public expenditures in general (Pryor) or social security spending in particular (Wilensky).[25]

Before asserting that left party power is a determinant of any outcome, one must develop clear concepts and sensitive measures of party power. No quantitative study to date is persuasive on this point. The most severe limitations include the measurement of party power in terms of popular vote (Peters) or representation in the legislature (Hewitt, Jackman).[26] Because of vast national variations in political structure and electoral procedures, size of vote is a poor guide to power. Similarly, the use of legislative representation leads to an overestimate of left party power in Japan, Switzerland, and France.[27] In my view, considering the long-term ascendancy of the executive and the differences between presidential and parliamentary systems, the best single measure of party power is instead representation in the executive branch of government. Although Hibbs also applies this criterion, he fails to distinguish among degrees of strength, relying instead on "percentage of years Socialist-Labor parties in executive (1945-69),"[28] thereby exaggerating the power of left parties in France and Italy.[29] In addition, various authors such as Hibbs, Hewitt, and Jackman restrict their studies to socialist parties, thereby obscuring the essential similarities between them and the Democratic Party in the United States during the period studied—a likeness which they themselves recognize.[30] Finally, all three authors ignore the Communist party, which for purposes of understanding macroeconomic domestic policy can be misleading, although maybe necessary for analysis of positions on participatory democracy, foreign policy, and civil liberties.

In order to remedy these shortcomings and clarify this complex debate, we have developed a measure of left party power and, because of its obvious and enduring importance, a comparable measure of Catholic party power.

II. New Concepts and Measures of Left and Catholic Party Dominance

We first measured left party dominance and then used the identical procedure for gauging Catholic party dominance, producing a government by government score for every left and every Catholic party in the nineteen countries from 1919 through 1976 whenever competitive politics prevailed. A long concept and coding memo is not included here, but the complexities are mentioned below and further summarized in the Appendix.

Party dominance is defined as a large amount of party power continuously exercised over a substantial period of time. To permit the most favorable test of the idea that party dominance makes a difference for social policy, we focus on three dimensions of dominance: (1) degree of control or influence left or Catholic parties have had in their countries' governments; (2) the number of times such parties have been thrown out; and (3) the total number of years of left or Catholic power. By keeping amount and continuity of power separate, we leave open the question of what counts most: the possession of power, however brief, or the continuity in office that permits program planning. By distinguishing between continuity as long duration and continuity as few interruptions of tenure, we can determine whether the sheer number of years in office is more important than security of tenure.

We coded party power from the post-World War I period because by then reasonably stable national identities were established for all nineteen rich democracies in the sample. Before World War I the Austro-Hungarian Empire was still intact, Finland was a principality of Russian Czars, and all of Ireland was under Westminster's control.

To measure left and Catholic party dominance, we had to determine the position of parties on a scale of leftism or Catholicism, to operationalize the concepts of party power and continuity of power, and to decide how to deal with caretaker and nonpartisan governments, with war years, and with the special case of Israeli statehood.

The Ideological Stance of Left and Catholic Parties

In my approach to the likely role of ideologies anchored in Catholic and socialist traditions, movements, and parties, I assumed considerable overlap of values. For instance, the values invoked to defend the welfare state comprise a veritable smorgasbord. They have included equality (social democrats, Marxian socialists, modern liberals), efficiency, economic prosperity, and equality of opportunity ("efficiency socialists" such as the Fabians), harmony and social justice (Socialists and Catholic humanists alike), political order, hierarchy, and the prevention of revolution (Bismarck and the Catholic Church as well as contemporary establishment Communists).[31] Nevertheless, there are some central themes that distinguish left parties from others, and, less surely, Catholic parties from others.

It is often argued that the Left-Right ideological distinction lacks utility either because policy positions are simply means to win power and are thus ephemeral or because there is no single dimension of political conflict. In contrast, when we classify parties as "Left" we assume the following:

- that left party positions are more-or-less stable and coherent, partly because the parties need to recruit and maintain a stable core of constituents including a majority of the working class.
- that socioeconomic issues focused on equality, while not exhaustive, are central in the political conflict between left and nonleft parties.

Specifically, leftism involves a commitment to use the apparatus of the state to redistribute national income toward lower strata, or at least toward the lower half of the income distribution. Left or Labor parties have historically advocated increased economic, political, and social equality. However, our variable refers to ideological stance, not to actual behavior in office (egalitarian policies or not) or social base (working class or not).

The ideological stance of Catholic parties is more difficult to delineate because of its greater diversity and the vagueness of party platforms and manifestos. Writers seeking to reveal a shared ideological perspective among European Catholic parties have had to emphasize such overarching values as personalism, pluralism, attention to the common good (rather than to a particular group or class), and "subsidiarity" or the idea that intervention by a higher political authority is justified only when a particular need cannot be met by a lower social group or unit of government.[32] This general set of values has not provided Catholic parties with specific principles to serve as guidelines for concrete policy. Positions on such matters as state ownership of industry, welfare policy, and political alliances have varied widely within parties, between countries, and across time. Thus, Einaudi writes of the Italian Christian Democrats' "complex ideology," which attempts "to gain permanent roots by being the image of many cross currents and of conflicting interests."[33] Of the French MRP Goguel remarks that its doctrine "consists essentially of an interpretation of history linked to a conception of man and society. A doctrine relating to civilization as a whole, it is not directly an economic doctrine."[34] Similar observations have been made regarding the Dutch, German, and Belgian Catholic parties, often with a critique of their opportunism.[35] But if the ideology of Catholic parties cannot be defined positively, it emerges clearly in terms of what it opposes: it stands as an alternative to both nineteenth-century liberalism and socialism, its two major ideological enemies. In contrast to liberalism, Catholic parties generally favor an active role of the state. But as opposed to collectivism, they view such intervention only as a means of harmonizing the conflicting interests of rival groups, whose basic independence the Catholics wish to safeguard. Within this ideological framework there is room for both social Christian principles, which lean toward egalitarianism, and an emphasis upon organic hierarchy. Again, their diversity suggests that Catholic party programs should be defined mainly in terms of what they oppose.

The ideological openness of Catholic parties has corresponded to a willingness to seek membership and support outside Catholic circles—a major source of strength. This "catch-all" tendency has been most apparent in the Federal Republic of Germany. Thus, in West Germany after World War II, CDU party leaders explicitly sought to open their doors to non-Catholics in order to gain a broad consensus; in fact, Protestants played an important role in founding the CDU organizations in Berlin. This ecumenical tendency did not become strong in the Belgian Christian Social party and the Dutch Catholic People's party until the mid-1950s. Although old ethnic-linguistic-regional cleavages in Belgium are increasingly salient (Francophones in Wallonia and Brussels vs. the Flemish in Flanders and Brussels), they have not prevented the continuation and even expansion of Catholic-Socialist collaboration, nor the emergence of a broader social base for a Catholic party.[36] Similarly, by the mid-1970s the Dutch Catholic party, reflecting a long-term weakening of the confessional-political blocs ("pillars"), moved toward merger with its Protestant counterparts; together they now form the Christian Democratic Appeal.

In short, "Catholic parties" here refers to anticollectivist, antiliberal themes in party ideology, not to an exclusively Catholic base of support.

For various reasons we excluded fascist parties despite their occasional similarities to Catholic and left parties.[37] We also excluded periods of nondemocratic rule in Germany, Italy, Austria, and Japan and in nations occupied by any one of these countries during World War II.

Measuring Left and Catholic Party Dominance

Party dominance is measured by the amount and continuity of participation in government in our sample nations from 1919 (or the closest date to the beginning of competitive party politics in an independent nation) through 1976. By amount, we mean control of key offices and institutions in government. By continuity, we mean a small number of interruptions in power and long tenure. The Appendix and a coding chart summarize the coding scheme. In systems with a strong president—Finland, France, the United States—we modified our scoring system.

Party continuity in office is measured by both the number of years in office (duration) and the number of interruptions in office. The main issues here concern how long a party must be in power to be counted; how long an interruption must last to count as a break in continuity; whether caretaker governments are considered as interruptions; and the nature of interruptions in presidential systems. We excluded insignificant periods of party power (less than six months); and insignificant interruptions (less than six months). In Finland we counted interruptions in control of the cabinet, but not the presidency, while in the United States we counted interruptions in occupancy of the presidency. We excluded caretaker governments and classified nonpartisan and national unity governments by the left or Catholic party power evident in these extraordinary coalitions.

War years are counted for countries which were both unoccupied and maintained democratic, competitive party politics during wartime. We date Israel from 1927, when the Jewish Agency, a kind of shadow cabinet for the future government, was established.

Of course, both left and Catholic party dominance can be seen in more places than the top political positions of government. Our measure leaves out other bases of power such as positions in bureaucratic agencies, wealth, popular support, organizational strength, and leadership capacities. However, these would be correlated with access to top power positions. Thus, despite the gradual breakup of traditional parties, perhaps accelerating since the mid-1960s, our measures probably capture a crucial source of power in modern democratic societies—party dominance of government.

III. Leftism and Catholicism as Sources of
Welfare Effort, Output, and Tax-Welfare Backlash

With these ideas and measures in hand, we can now explore the impact of left and Catholic party power on taxes, welfare effort and output, and resulting political responses.[38] I shall first present the bare findings concerning the effect of each type of political party, then integrate party dominance into my model of democratic corporatism. We shall see that both Catholicism and leftism have encouraged the development of a corporatist political economy, although they have opposite effects on tax-welfare backlash. I shall close with clues in my data suggesting that under conditions of intense Catholic and left competition, with accompanying discontinuities of left rule, social spending escalates.

Left Party Power

Left Power and Spending

During the entire period since World War I or the shorter period after World War II, cumulative left power has had no effect on welfare effort or output. For instance, left party power from 1919 to 1976 has no significant correlation with SS/GNP in 1966 (r = -.12), SS/GNP in 1971 (r = .04), or SS per capita 1971 (r = .30). In regression experiments including the major determinants of welfare effort—percentage of population aged sixty-five or more and corporatist-technocratic linkages—no measure of left power has any significant explanatory effect. Whatever influence left parties have is indirect and weak.

Left Power and Backlash

Similarly, no measure of left power has a significant direct effect on backlash. However, leftist party turnover, being thrown out two or more times since 1919, approaches significance as a source of backlash (r = .36), a finding I shall explore when I deal with the effect of discontinuities in any type of party power.

Left Power Taxes and Backlash

Left party power *does* increase reliance on painfully visible taxes. For instance, when played against two major determinants of tax visibility in 1965—old party dominance, which increases reliance on visible taxes, and corporatism, which decreases such tendencies—left party power still inspires reliance on visible taxes.

Dependent	Independent Variables	Beta	p
Tax Visibility	Old Party Dominance	.50	.01
1965	Corporatist-technocratic linkages	–.29	.09
	Left Party Power 1919-76	.47	.01
Multiple R² = .64			

Thus, leftism, like old party dominance, increases backlash indirectly through tax visibility (see Figure 10.2 and Tables 10.3 and 10.4). If there is any difference in the effect of old and left parties, it may be in the types of discontent they activate, not in the ultimate outcome. Old party dominance, that is, a party system dominated by one or two established parties facing only two or three opposition parties, bottled up mass discontent which by 1965-75 had spilled over. By preventing the organization of many splinter parties, old dominant parties can obscure mass discontent. Perhaps the gradual accumulation of left power instead encourages the sharper articulation of working-class interests, raises working-class hopes—along with tax visibility—and thereby frightens the middle or upper class. This interpretation is consistent with Table 10.3 where we find countries such as Denmark, Norway, Finland, the United States and the United Kingdom with strong cumulative left power from 1919 to 1976, high tax visibility in 1965, and medium to high backlash during 1965-75. In that league only Sweden is an exception: it has successfully dampened backlash, despite its early love affair with heavy income taxes.

These possible differences in the locus of backlash inspired by left vs. old parties, however, are not the main story. For Table 10.4 indicates a substantial overlap in left party dominance (1946-76) and old party dominance (Sweden, Norway, Finland, Denmark, the United States, the United Kingdom, and New Zealand evidence both), yielding a high average backlash score (see column 6). Whether old or left or old-left parties dominate, the intervening process is the adoption of higher income taxes and property taxes on households, a likely road to political trouble.

Catholic Party Power

Catholic Power and Spending

In contrast to leftism, cumulative Catholic power since World War I increases welfare effort (for 1966, SS/GNP r = .74; for 1971, r = .60). Catholic power and social security spending per capita, however, are unrelated (for 1966, r = .28; for 1971, r = .23). In both multiple regressions and cross-tabulations containing the most important sources of welfare effort—population sixty-five and over, corporatism, and avoidance of visible taxes—Catholic power holds up as a direct or indirect determinant of big spending. For instance, when they are in the same equation, Catholic power is even more important than the proportion of the aged as a predictor of welfare effort in 1966.

Dependent Variable	Independent Variables	Beta	p
SS/GNP 1966	Catholic Party Power 1919-76	.55	.01
	Persons 65 and over as percent of total population 1966	.51	.01

Multiple R^2 = .79

Catholic power also retains its significance in predicting 1971 SS/GNP, although in this regression it does not exceed the influence of the aged population.

Figure 10.2
Old Party Dominance and Left Power Increase Backlash Indirectly
Through Encouraging Reliance on Visible Taxes. Catholic Power Has
the Reverse Effect, Also Indirect*

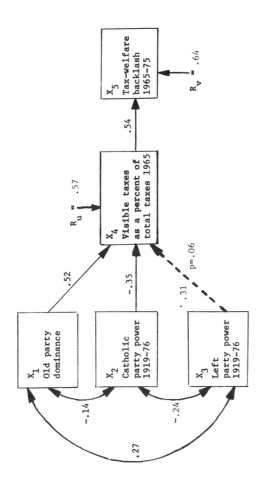

*Solid lines indicate relationships with p ≤.05. If we substitute 1971 tax
data, Left party power does not even approach significance as a predictor of
tax visibility.

Catholic Power, Taxes, and Backlash

Catholic party power decreases reliance on visible taxes (r = -.50 for 1965 and -.52 for 1971). In fact, no country scoring high on cumulative Catholic power scores high on tax visibility. We would expect, then, that the mobilization of antitaxing, antispending, antibureaucratic sentiments in movements and campaigns would not be prominent in these countries. Figure 10.2 provides support.

Controlling for a powerful determinant of visible taxes, old party dominance, we see that Catholic power dampens tax-welfare backlash through the avoidance of visible taxes ($P_{54} P_{42} = -.19$); conversely, left power increases backlash by encouraging visible taxes ($P_{54} P_{43} = .17$).

In sum, left party power alone is not directly related to either backlash or welfare effort (SS/GNP). Indeed, successful left parties increase backlash indirectly by agitation for the most painfully visible taxes. As we shall see, only in the rare cases of uninterrupted rule ("left dominance") does left party power reduce backlash and even then it has little or no effect on spending when we control for any other major source of welfare effort. However measured, left power is a poor second to Catholic power as an explanation of welfare effort or backlash.

Neither leftism nor Catholicism increases per capita social security spending. This is instead a product of affluence—GNP per capita with its demographic and bureaucratic correlates—and of corporatist-technocratic linkages.

Thus, with more sensitive measures of left party dominance we have settled one issue posed earlier: left power *does* tend to increase reliance on visible taxes and thereby increase tax-welfare backlash. (As left ideologues have claimed, visible taxes may be on the average more progressive than less visible taxes, but this varies greatly by nation and the exact structure of taxes and tax collection.) In contrast, Catholic power, like corporatism, is associated with avoidance of visible taxes and hence the reduction of backlash.

IV. Leftism, Catholicism, and Corporatism:
Interaction Effects and the Problem of Time Order

With this broad sketch of the differing effects of left and Catholic power behind us, we are now able to integrate the findings into my model of democratic corporatism. (Attributes of political economy result in tax policies which shape welfare effort and backlash.) We shall see that corporatism retains its influence only under some conditions of political history and economic policy. Its effect is direct and strongest for spending and taxing but is both indirect and less strong for backlash.

Table 10.1
Strong Corporatism and Strong Catholic Power
Each Foster Strong Welfare Effort in 1971.
Tax Visibility Has No Independent Effect.

	Strong Corporatism				Weak Corporatism			
	Strong Catholic Power 1919-76*		Weak Catholic Power 1919-76*		Strong Catholic Power 1919-76		Weak Catholic Power 1919-76	
	High Tax Visibility	Low Tax Visibility	High Tax Visibility	Low Tax Visibility	High Tax Visibility	Low Tax Visibility	High Tax Visibility	Low Tax Visibility
	No case	Belgium 20.7 Netherlands 24.0 Italy 22.8 Austria 23.1	Denmark 24.0 Finland 16.4 Sweden 23.8	Israel 11.8 France 17.8 Norway 19.6	No case	Germany 21.3	U.S. 11.7 Switzerland 11.4 UK 14.5 Australia 9.3 Canada 15.8 New Zealand 10.5	Japan 6.3 Ireland 12.7
Av. SS as % of GNP		22.7	21.4	16.4		21.3	12.2	9.5

*Catholic power for 1919-76 or for 1946-76 yields an identical classification. If we substitute 1965 tax visibility in this Table, the results are very similar.

Spending and Taxing

Table 10.1 gives us a better look at particular countries. It shows that strong corporatism and Catholic power each foster strong welfare effort in 1971, while tax visibility, our old standby for inhibiting welfare state development, has little independent effect. Only big-spending Denmark and Sweden, non-Catholic visible taxers, are exceptions.

When we add left power to the picture, however (Table 10.2), we discover two interaction effects. Strong corporatism, weak left party power, and low tax visibility together foster big spending in 1966, as illustrated by France, Italy, Austria, and the Netherlands (column 4). As for Catholicism, the six top spenders in 1966 are Austria, West Germany, France, Italy, Belgium, and the Netherlands, all of which score low in tax visibility, while all but France score high in Catholic power.[39]

In a cross tabulation with tax visibility and left power since 1919, corporatism appears to shape even per capita social spending for 1971. But this could be because the "high corporatist" countries are generally those with older populations. A multiple regression analysis, however, shows that if we control for the percentage of the population aged sixty-five and over and tax visibility, corporatism retains its independent influence.

Dependent Variable	Independent Variables	Beta	p
SS per Capita 1971	Persons 65 and over as percent of total population 1970	.51	.01
	Tax visibility 1971	.50	.02
	Corporatist-technocratic linkages	.47	.03

Multiple R^2 = .58 Controlling for both GNP per capita 1970 (ability to pay) and age of population 1970 (demand for social security) corporatism still retains its independent influence on SS per capita.

This is not to say, however, that a country with many aged citizens is not prone to more corporatist structures in its search for solutions to its fiscal burdens. Consistent with findings on spending, corporatism (in cross tabulations not reported here) remains a source of heavy total taxes in 1965 (and the r = .69). No other political variable has a consistent effect. Only the absence of strong Catholic power combined with weak corporatism yields a low tax burden.

Corporatism, Leftism, Catholicism, and Backlash

When we explain backlash, in contrast to taxes and welfare effort and output, corporatism has no consistent effect. The apparent interaction in

Table 10.2
Strong Corporatism, Weak Left Party Power 1919-1976 and Low Tax
Visibility in 1965 Together Foster Strong Welfare Effort in 1966.
Catholic Power Helps. Left Power and Tax Visibility Alone
Have No Effect

	Strong Corporatism				Weak Corporatism			
	Strong Left Power 1919-76		Weak Left Power 1919-76		Strong Left Power 1919-76		Weak Left Power 1919-76	
	High Tax Visi-bility	Low Tax Visi-bility	High Tax Visi-bility	Low Tax Visi-bility	High Tax Visi-bility	Low Tax Visi-bility	High Tax Visi-bility	Low Tax Visi-bility
	Denmark 13.9	Israel 8.0	No case	France 19.3	US 7.9	New Zealand 12.0	Switzer-land 9.5	Canada 9.4
	Norway 12.6	*Belgium 18.6		*Italy 19.2	UK 14.3		Austra-lia 9.2	*Germany 19.6
	Finland 13.1			*Austria 21.4				Japan 6.1
	Sweden 16.5			*Nether-lands 18.3				Ireland 11.2
Av. SS as % of GNP '66:	14.0	13.3		19.6	11.1	12.0	9.4	11.6

*Strong Catholic party power, 1919-76.

Table 10.3 suggests that left party power fosters visible taxes and thereby intensifies backlash (columns 1 and 5). Further,Catholicism combined with weak left power and low tax visibility dampens backlash (columns 4 and 8). Corporatism, whatever it is combined with, has no independent effect. The findings hold for either tax visibility date (1965 and 1971, and for left party power either since World War I or after World War II.

The Affinity of Catholicism and Corporatism

Catholic power (where it appears) is not only a more important source of welfare state development than left party power, but as one might expect, Catholicism is one historical root of corporatist democracy and has similar effects. There are already hints of this above. Corporatism, Catholicism, and low tax visibility have all turned up as sources of strong welfare effort. And corporatism and Catholicism each foster strong welfare effort, controlling for the other (see Table 10.1), although in multiple regression experiments the two never survive together; statistically speaking, they are substitutes for one another.

We can now try a direct test of the relation of Catholicism and corporatism in my scheme—path diagrams with cumulative Catholic party power as antecedent. At first glance the time order is a problem. Because one component of corporatism is centralization of government (which facilitates or necessitates the centralization of labor and employer federations), it could be argued that corporatist-technocratic linkages are as old as Catholic party power. However, Catholic parties, once formed, can and do build upon the ancillary institutions of the Catholic Church, which are much older than the centralized state. Catholic party dominance thus taps an older social-political complex. Further, while highly centralized governments may precede the creation of Catholic parties, the fully developed corporatist-technocratic linkages caught by our measures are a quite recent development.

We have, then the following simple model:

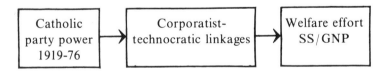

The Affinity of Catholicism and Leftism

That Catholicism is conducive to corporatism, democratic or not, is not surprising. That left party dominance would have effects similar to those of Catholic party dominance is not so obvious.

Political history provides abundant illustration of the functional equivalence of Catholicism and leftism, including many episodes of ideological

Table 10.3

Left Party Power 1919-1976 Fosters Visible Taxes in 1965 (or 1971) and Thereby Increases Tax-Welfare Backlash. Corporatism Has No Independent Effect. Catholic Power Combined with Weak Left Power and Low Tax Visibility Dampens Backlash.

Strong Corporatism				Weak Corporatism			
Strong Left Power 1919-76**		Weak Left Power 1919-76		Strong Left Power 1919-76		Weak Left Power 1919-76	
High Tax Visibility	Low Tax Visibility	High Tax Visibility	Low Tax Visibility	High Tax Visibility	Low Tax Visibility	High Tax Visibility	Low Tax Visibility
Denmark 5	Israel 1	No case	France 3	USA 5	New Zealand 5	Switzerland 4	Canada 3
Norway 3	*Belgium 2		*Italy 1	UK 4		Australia 2	*Germany 0
Finland 3			*Austria 0				Japan 0
Sweden 2			*Netherlands 2				Ireland 0
Average Backlash 3.3	1.5		1.5	4.5	1	3	.8

*Strong Catholic party power since WWI.

**If we substitute recent left power for cumulative left power the result is very similar. If we use tax visibility in 1971, the result is very similar.

and structural convergence. Although Catholic parliamentary groups, drawing on medieval and romantic themes, have often been conservative or reactionary, the rise of social Christian and particularly Catholic workers movements in Belgium, the Netherlands, Germany, Italy, and France pushed European Catholic politicians toward the left. For many decades they have increasingly emphasized support of free labor unions, labor legislation, social security, and an economic order based on industrial self-government and worker participation in management, ownership, and profits, with close collaboration between unions and employer associations. Opportunities for alliances with leftists opened up. For instance, in Germany during the 1920s a Catholic Minister of Labour, Fr. Heinrich Brauns, was responsible for vanguard progressive social legislation; the context was intermittent coalition between the SPD and the Center Party. Similarly, after World War I Belgium saw a variety of coalition governments: Catholic-Liberal-Socialist, Catholic-Liberal, Catholic-Socialist. But through them all, as Fogarty suggests, "the Catholic Party remained the pivot, and a steady stream of political and social reforms came forward."[40]

What contemporary socialists and Catholics have in common, aside from their desire to attain and maintain power, is a traditional humanistic concern with the lower strata, which has its roots in the early modern era. In the continental Catholic case, we find that Catholic humanists of the sixteenth century had considerable influence on the approach of urban businessmen and lawyers to their urban crisis and their poor, both "deserving" and "underserving." Lyon provides one of many examples of a religious coalition for welfare reform dominated by Catholics. In 1532, the French cleric and humanist Jean de Vauzelles urged the notables of Lyon to introduce sweeping new welfare measures including training and education for poor children, the recognition of the right of unemployables to support, a central treasury administered by laymen, and so on.[41] The contemporary expression of this Christian concern is evident in passages on welfare, poverty, and labor in the "social" Encyclicals of Popes Leo XIII, Pius XI, and John XXIII, as well as in the activism of social minded priests.

Thus, the data suggest that cumulative Catholic power and cumulative left power have similar effects on the direction of the political economy of rich democracies. Since World War I those countries with strong corporatist-technocratic linkages either have strong Catholic or left party power or both, except for France. Both Catholicism and leftism apparently foster strong corporatism—a finding that would please contemporary students of Italian politics who see Communist and Christian Democrats sharing the same bed.

Figure 10.3
Catholic Power and Left Power Each Foster Corporatism Which Fosters
Strong Welfare Effort, Controlling for Age of Population*

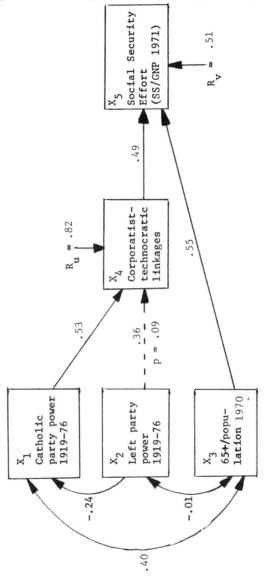

*Solid lines indicate relationships with p ≤ .05. Similar results
with the same levels of significance were obtained with 1966
SS/GNP and 1966 age data.

Even controlling for the most consistently powerful proximate cause of welfare effort, age of the population, Figure 10.3 shows that left power and Catholic power alike increase social security spending *indirectly* through their positive influence on corporatism (P_{54} P_{41} = .26 and P_{54} P_{42} = .18), although the path from leftism to corporatism is weak.

If we turn now to Table 10.4 we can pinpoint the countries that account for the results of the path diagram and search for exceptions.

Note that there are only five cases of strong Catholic party power—Italy, Germany, Austria, the Netherlands, and Belgium—and that their power has been relatively stable. Since World War I, during years of democratic experience, Germany and Belgium had only two interruptions of Catholic party influence, Austria and Italy only one, and the Netherlands none. Morever, of the five countries with strong Catholic party power, four are also strong in corporatism and low in tax visibility. Germany is the partial exception: it is low in tax visibility but is as yet more or less weak in corporatism.[42]

If Catholic party power is found with a corporatist political economy, does the absence of Catholic power mean the absence of corporatism and a concomitant reliance on visible taxes? In Table 10.4, of the fourteen countries low in Catholic party power, five score high in corporatism. France and Israel—corporatism without Catholicism— are partial exceptions to the pattern; they avoid visible taxes but score above average in corporatist-technocratic linkages. And France, however anti-clerical, has not only a long Catholic cultural tradition but in fact experienced a period of Catholic party power as well. At the beginning of the First Legislature of the Fourth Republic, the Mouvement Populaire Republicain was the largest non-Communist group in the Assembly.[43] Nevertheless, the scores of France are low over the long pull.

There remain the three clear exceptions: Sweden, Norway, and Finland. If Denmark were more corporatist, we could include it. And if Norway did not rank fourteenth of our nineteen countries in its reliance on "visible" taxes in 1971 and Finland ninth, we could label the whole a Scandinavian pattern of strong corporatism with heavy reliance on visible taxes. If any separate pattern exists, it points in another direction and once again suggests the functional equivalence of Catholicism and leftism. Excluding the marginal case of France, all the exceptions—Israel, Sweden, Norway and Finland—have a history of strong, cumulative left party power whether it is dated from post-World War I or post-World War II. Where Catholicism cannot leave its mark, leftism can, with corporatist democracy the end product in either case.

In short, there is an affinity between Catholicism, corporatism, heavy taxing through least visible means, and generous (or, as fiscal conservatives would have it, profligate) spending. If we consider deviations from this

Table 10.4
The Interaction After World War II of Left Party Power, Catholic Party Power, Corporatism, Tax Visibility, and Tax-Welfare Backlash

Low Left Party Power 1946–76

	Low Catholic Party Power Corp.	Back-lash		High Catholic Party Power Corp.	Back-lash
France	9.0	3	Italy	8.0	1
[v]Australia[°]	1.0	2	W. Germany	1.0	0
[v]Switzerland[°]	1.0	4			
[v]Canada[°]	0	3			
Ireland	0	0			
Japan	0	0			
Av. Scores:	1.8 Corp.	2 Bklsh.		4.5 Corp.	.5 Bklsh.

High Left Party Power 1946–76

	Low Catholic Party Power Corp.	Back-lash		High Catholic Party Power Corp.	Back-lash
[v]Sweden[°]	8.7	2	Netherlands	12.3	2
Norway[°]	8.7	3	Belgium	8.7	2
[v]Finland[°]	7.7	3	Austria	7.0	0
Israel	7.0	1			
[v]Denmark[°]	5.7	5			
[v]USA[°]	0	5			
[v]UK[°]	0	4			
[v]New Zealand[°]	0	1			
Av. Scores:	4.7 Corp.	3 Bklsh.		9.3 Corp.	1.3 Bklsh.

[v]High tax visibility 1971

[°]Presence of old party dominance (age of largest party in 1965 is sixty years or more).

pattern in the context of the direction of recent change in the political economies of rich democracies, we can find suggestions of conformity to the model. Although a case by case examination of process is beyond the scope of this paper, it appears that West Germany is becoming more corporatist; that Israel, without its extraordinary military burden, would spend more on social programs; and that the deviant countries, which in 1971 were still relying heavily on visible taxes, are with varying speed moving toward greater tax balance (Sweden, Denmark). We would then have two patterns: Catholic, corporatist, heavy taxers and spenders with balanced tax structures; and leftist, corporatist, heavy taxers and spenders with balanced tax structures. That some convergence of these two patterns has already occurred is suggested by the cases of Austria, the Netherlands, and West Germany, which have joined Belgium since World War II in combining high cumulative Catholic power and high or marginally high cumulative left power (see Table 10.4). Presumably if *Eurocommunism* takes hold or if a Center-Left coalition emerges, Italy and France would join the not-so-paradoxical pattern of enduring Catholic and socialist influence in democratic corporatist affairs.

V. Conclusion: The Effects of Party Continuity and Competition on Spending and Backlash

These data suggest that the more intense the competition between Catholic and left parties, the more left parties in power will spend. It would be useful to consider the number of interruptions in either left or Catholic power as an indicator of Catholic-left competition. But because Catholic parties have remarkably stable tenure in office, we cannot make any inferences about the effect of competition on their spending polices.

Consider, for example, the cases of the Italian Christian Democrats, the Belgian Social Christians, and to a lesser extent the Austrian People's party—all of which, at least until the mid-sixties, dominated their country's postwar politics. With such stability among powerful Catholic parties, we must settle for interruptions of left rule as our measure.

There are three clues that the number of times the left was thrown out indicates Catholic-left competition and results in more spending. First, there is a significant correlation between interruptions of left party power and social welfare effort in 1966 (the same relationship approached significance in 1971, r=.33). Second, the country with the highest number of left party interruptions, Belgium with six such occasions, also has a stable Catholic party; even with its intense ethnic-linguistic divisions, the Social Christians have dominated except for the years 1954-58. The country tied for second place, Germany with four left interruptions, has a similarly stable Catholic party, while France, with left parties thrown out three times, has a Catholic party which has at least held office. In these cases, interruptions of left party power appear to be good indicators of left Catholic competition. Finally, there is a significant positive relationship between left party interruptions since World War II and tax-welfare backlash, $r=.47$ (the relationship for the whole period also approaches significance: $r=.37$. See Appendix, Tables 10.5 and 10.6).

It is difficult to test directly the notion of competitive escalation of social spending because so few countries score high in both left and Catholic party power. For the entire period from 1919 to 1976, only Belgium scores high on both. In the post-World War II period three countries (Belgium, Netherlands, and Austria) evidence strong Catholicism and leftism. Germany is a marginal case where Catholic power is high and left power medium. Since there are only six countries with positive Catholic party scores, it is impossible to sift out an independent interaction effect by means of regression analysis. Thus, support for any remarks on Catholic-left interaction rests on the evidence in Tables 10.2 and 10.4.

Although limited, the data are consistent first with the idea that except in rare cases of long-term continuous rule (Sweden, Austria), left parties with a substantial mass base increase popular expectations, make promises beyond their capacity to deliver, and thereby increase backlash. (There is no relation between left power and actual social security spending.) Second, the data suggest that frequent alternating victories and defeats of left parties escalate their interest in spending their way to more stable power, whether from desire or necessity. With Catholic power so continuous, we cannot know what effect their frequent defeat might have.

These relationships also provide clues to the question of whether amount and duration of power count more or less than the continuity in office that permits planning. Apparently, for left parties, continuous power (few interruptions) generally permits the kind of planning that holds *down* spending while sheer amount of power and years exercised under intense competition has the reverse effect (for left power, the correlations approach zero; for Catholic power they are strongly positive).[44] In short, stable tenure and sheer amount of power without continuity may have opposite effects on social policy.

The analysis so far leads to these speculations: Old party dominance bottles up mass discontent, whatever it does for welfare state development.[45] Left party dominance, in contrast, has a dampening effect on both mass expectations and the pace of spending. Put another way, the long, stable, comfortable rule of left parties slows the adoption of new programs or the rapid expansion of old ones while simultaneously keeping high hopes in check. Old party dominance in the mid-sixties may have led to a subsequent burst of backlash; but continuous rule of leftist persuasion has not had the same result. Instead it is the discontinuities of rule, under conditions of intense Catholic and left competition, that may deepen the "crisis" of the welfare state.

Appendix on Methods

Details on methods and most measures and sources are in Wilensky (1975, pp. 121-147 and 1976, pp. 48-73). New measures used in this paper are summarized below.

Left party dominance. Defined in text. For eight of our nineteen nations and for the Weimar period of Germany we have used the classification scheme employed by De Swann, *Coalition Theories and Cabinet Formations* (1973), with minor changes. For the other eleven we used monographic literature and sourcebooks (partial bibliography is appended).

The classification of center parties as left or non-left is ambiguous in some cases, most notably those of the French Radicals and many Catholic parties. Because these parties are divided into highly diverse factions, some with a clearly leftist orientation, and because these factions shift in influence, it could be argued that we should ask which branches of the party are in the government at a given time. Thus, the Radicals in the French Cartel des Gauches in the early 1920s and the Belgian Social Christians in coalition with the Socialists after World War II could conceivably be classified as left. (For the Belgian case, see Henig, ed., p. 83.) However, for the small reduction in error to be achieved by trying to classify the ideology of each faction each year, the cost is high. Anyway, the research focus is left *party* power. Therefore we coded center parties as non-left, ignoring the leftist faction within them.

Amount of left power. From low to high we scored as follows:

0. A score of "0" is given for each year in which left parties did not meet the minimum criterion for left party power (see "1" below).
1. A score of "1" is assigned for each year that the left party has substantial, but not major or dominant power in the government.
2. A score of "2" is assigned for each year that a left party is the major party in the government without being dominant.
3. A score of "3" is given to a left party for each year that it is either the sole member of a majority government or the dominant partner in a coalition government.

Figure 10.4 summarizes this coding scheme.

Figure 10.4
Coding Scheme for Left and Catholic Party Dominance

Proportion of Total Seats in Assembly Held by the Government

Up to 1/2 (minority government)

Proportion of government's seats in legislature occupied by Left party*

	0 up to 1/3	1/3 up to 1/2	1/2 up to 2/3	2/3 - 1
	No Left* PM Left PM		No Left PM Left PM	
	0 1	1	1 2	2

1/2 or more (majority government)

Proportion of government's seats in legislature occupied by Left party*

	0 up to 1/3	1/3 up to 1/2	1/2 up to 2/3	2/3 - 1
	No Left PM Left PM	No Left PM Left PM		
	0 1	1 2	2	3

*Substituting Catholic for Left reproduces the coding scheme for Catholic party dominance.

Presidential systems: For Finland, France, and the United States we modified our scoring system. In Finland, a left party receives a score of 1 for each year it holds the presidency. Then it receives an additional 1 point per year for being a minor partner in a coalition (see criterion 1 above); or an additional 2 points per year for being either the major or dominant partner in the coalition (see criteria 2 and 3 above). This makes for a possible score of 3 per year, as in parlimentary systems. For the United States we assign a score of 2 for each year the Democrats occupied the presidency and a score of 1 for each year the Democrats controlled both houses of Congress. For France, in the years prior to the Fifth Republic we use the normal scoring for non-presidential systems; for Fifth Republic France, when the power of the presidency was enhanced, we would assign 2 points for every year that a left party holds the presidency and left parties would receive 1 point for each year they collectively hold a majority of seats in the legislature—a guide only to the future because neither left nor Catholic parties in fact received any score since de Gaulle took over in 1958.

Thus, in both parliamentary and presidential systems there is a possible score of 3 points per year for left party power. Whenever possible, we dated the exact month of changes in government; in those few cases where we could not locate the precise date of cabinet change, we used the date of election, which in parliamentary systems usually corresponds closely to changes in government (the resulting error is probably trivial). To obtain a final score, we add up the yearly scores over the whole time period under consideration. (But to analyze the relative effects of amount of power, number of years in office, and frequency of interruptions, we keep these separate.)

Duration of left power. Number of months in office, excluding insignificant periods mentioned in the text.

Number of left interruptions. Number of times a party with a power score of 1, 2, or 3 lost office for six months or more.

Measures of Catholic party power: amount, duration, and number of interruptions. We included among Catholic parties all those that fall under the definition given in the text. The scoring of Catholic party power was based on the same criteria as those used for the left parties.

Left party dominance 1919-76. We then created an index for the whole period and one for the post-World War II period combining left party power and number of interruptions in order to single out those left parties that exercised "sufficient" power with few interruptions. For the period since 1919, sufficient power meant a score of 30 (West Germany) and above; low interruptions meant 2 or fewer. For the post-World War II period, sufficient power was defined as 21 (Australia) and above; low interruptions meant 1 or 0. For both periods, countries with sufficient power and low interruptions received a score of 1; all other countries received a score of 0. For the period since 1919, Sweden, New Zealand, Norway, the Netherlands, Israel, and Austria received a score of 1. For the post-World War II period, Sweden, West Germany, Israel, and Austria received scores of 1.

Catholic party dominance 1919-76. We did not create a Catholic party dominance variable (that would combine amount of power and number of interruptions) for either the entire period or the post-World War II period because Catholic parties had significant power in only five countries and their power was seldom interrupted. In place of quantitative analysis based on such a variable we have relied on case by case examination.

Distribution of interruptions to party power.

> *Left 1919-76:* Belgium: 6; Denmark, West Germany, Finland, United Kingdom: 4; U.S.A., Australia, France: 3; Sweden, New Zealand, Norway, Netherlands: 2; Austria: 1; Switzerland, Canada, Israel, Italy, Japan, Ireland: 0.
>
> *Left 1946-76:* Belgium: 4; Denmark, Finland: 3; U.S.A., Australia, New Zealand, France, Norway, United Kingdom, Netherlands: 2; Austria: 1; Sweden, Switzerland, Canada, West Germany, Israel, Italy, Japan, Ireland: 0.
>
> *Catholic 1919-76:* West Germany, Belgium: 2; France, Austria, Italy: 1.
>
> *Catholic 1946-76:* Belgium: 2; West Germany, France, Austria: 1; Italy: 0.

All of the left and Catholic party variables together numbered 32. Because we would not use all of these in this analysis, we reduced them to 8 according to two criteria. First, if 2 variables were highly correlated we chose the one that made most theoretical sense. For example, power and duration for both left and Catholic parties were highly correlated. For left parties for the whole period, the correlation was .95; for Catholic parties, .98. In this case, we used the measure of amount of power, since it incorporated much more information. Second, we eliminated variables that were not conceptually independent of other variables. For example, interruptions of Catholic party rule is correlated .78 with Catholic party power because 13 countries never had significant Catholic party participation in government. Thus, their rule could not be interrupted—but this could hardly be considered an indicator of Catholic party dominance.

The correlations of several of these measures for each of two time periods appear in Tables 10.5-10.8.

Table 10.5
Zero Order Correlations Among Components of Left Dominance, 1919-1976: Old Party Dominance. Corporatism, Backlash, Welfare Effort and Output and Tax Visibility in Nineteen Countries

	(1)	(2)	(3)	(4)	(5)	(6)	(7)	(8)	(9)	(10)	(11)	(12)	(13)
(1) Left party power '19–'76	1.00												
(2) Left party interruptions '19–'76	.24	1.00											
(3) Left party duration '19–'76	.95	.34	1.00										
(4) Left party dominance '19–'76	.52	-.23	.57	1.00									
(5) Old party dominance	.27	.22	.26	-.11	1.00								
(6) Corporatist-technocratic linkages	.24	.18	.42	.45	-.08	1.00							
(7) Tax-welfare backlash	.25	.37	.17	-.28	.70	-.01	1.00						
(8) SS/GNP 1966	-.12	.41	.09	.17	-.22	.59	-.18	1.00					
(9) SS/GNP 1971	.04	.33	.24	.25	.13	.69	.06	.93	1.00				
(10) SS per capita 1966	.22	.54	.32	.12	.23	.39	.31	.69	.73	1.00			
(11) SS per capita 1971	.30	.37	.39	.15	.46	.42	.36	.52	.77	.86	1.00		
(12) Tax visibility 1965	.53	.20	.46	.06	.65	-.22	.54	-.37	-.07	.14	.33	1.00	
(13) Tax visibility 1971	.38	.21	.30	-.01	.60	-.47	.47	-.41	-.21	.07	.17	.85	1.00
	(1)	(2)	(3)	(4)	(5)	(6)	(7)	(8)	(9)	(10)	(11)	(12)	(13)

Note: For underlined correlations p ≤ .05

Table 10.6

Zero Order Correlations Among Components of Left Dominance, 1946-1976: Old Party Dominance, Corporatism, Backlash, Welfare Effort and Output, and Tax Visibility in Nineteen Countries

	(1)	(2)	(3)	(4)	(5)	(6)	(7)	(8)	(9)	(10)	(11)	(12)	(13)
(1) Left party power '46-'76	1.00												
(2) Left party interruptions '46-'76	.25	1.00											
(3) Left party duration '46-'76	.91	.27	1.00										
(4) Left party dominance '46-'76	.47	-.44	.57	1.00									
(5) Old party dominance	.27	.31	.25	-.24	1.00								
(6) Corporatist-technocratic linkages	.34	.31	.56	.17	-.08	1.00							
(7) Tax-welfare backlash	.23	.47	.13	-.45	.70	-.01	1.00						
(8) SS/GNP 1966	-.01	.23	.23	.29	-.22	.59	-.18	1.00					
(9) SS/GNP 1971	.17	.22	.41	.24	.13	.69	.06	.93	1.00				
(10) SS per capita 1966	.25	.26	.33	.28	.23	.39	.31	.69	.73	1.00			
(11) SS per capita 1971	.34	.13	.44	.29	.46	.42	.36	.52	.77	.86	1.00		
(12) Tax visibility 1965	.53	.11	.40	.05	.65	-.22	.54	-.37	-.07	.14	.33	1.00	
(13) Tax visibility 1971	.31	.19	.12	-.12	.60	-.47	.47	-.41	-.21	.07	.17	.85	1.00
	(1)	(2)	(3)	(4)	(5)	(6)	(7)	(8)	(9)	(10)	(11)	(12)	(13)

Note: For underlined correlations p $\leq$ .05

Table 10.7

Zero Order Correlations Among Components of Catholic Dominance, 1919-1976: Old Party Dominance, Corporatism, Backlash, Welfare Effort and Output, and Tax Visibility in Nineteen Countries

	(1)	(2)	(3)	(4)	(5)	(6)	(7)	(8)	(9)	(10)	(11)	(12)
(1) Catholic party power '19–'76	1.00											
(2) Catholic party interruptions '19–'76	.78	1.00										
(3) Catholic party duration '19–'76	.98	.70	1.00									
(4) Old party dominance	-.14	-.26	-.12	1.00								
(5) Corporatist-technocratic linkages	.45	.22	.50	-.08	1.00							
(6) Tax-welfare backlash	-.40	-.35	-.37	.70	-.01	1.00						
(7) SS/GNP 1966	.74	.69	.74	-.22	.59	-.18	1.00					
(8) SS/GNP 1971	.60	.43	.61	.13	.69	.06	.93	1.00				
(9) SS per capita 1966	.28	.41	.29	.23	.39	.31	.69	.73	1.00			
(10) SS per capita 1971	.23	.24	.25	.46	.42	.36	.52	.77	.86	1.00		
(11) Tax visibility 1965	-.50	-.57	-.46	.65	-.22	.54	-.37	-.07	.14	.33	1.00	
(12) Tax visibility 1971	-.52	-.55	-.50	.60	-.47	.47	-.41	-.21	.07	.17	.85	1.00
	(1)	(2)	(3)	(4)	(5)	(6)	(7)	(8)	(9)	(10)	(11)	(12)

Note: For underlined correlations $p \leq .05$.

Table 10.8

Zero Order Correlations Among Components of Catholic Dominance, 1946-1976: Old Party Dominance, Corporatism, Backlash, Welfare Effort and Output, and Tax Visibility in Nineteen Countries

	(1)	(2)	(3)	(4)	(5)	(6)	(7)	(8)	(9)	(10)	(11)	(12)
(1) Catholic party power '46-'76	1.00											
(2) Catholic party interruptions '46-'76	.58	1.00										
(3) Catholic party duration '46-'76	.97	.59	1.00									
(4) Old party dominance	-.26	-.12	-.22	1.00								
(5) Corporatist-technocratic linkages	.38	.28	.49	-.08	1.00							
(6) Tax-welfare backlash	-.43	-.30	-.40	.70	-.01	1.00						
(7) SS/GNP 1966	.72	.65	.75	-.22	.59	-.18	1.00					
(8) SS/GNP 1971	.56	.41	.61	.13	.69	.06	.93	1.00				
(9) SS per capita 1966	.25	.37	.27	.23	.39	.31	.69	.73	1.00			
(10) SS per capita 1971	.20	.18	.22	.46	.42	.36	.52	.77	.86	1.00		
(11) Tax visibility 1965	-.56	-.48	-.54	.65	-.22	.54	-.37	-.07	.14	.33	1.00	
(12) Tax visibility 1971	-.59	-.45	-.59	.60	-.47	.47	-.41	-.21	.07	.17	.85	1.00
	(1)	(2)	(3)	(4)	(5)	(6)	(7)	(8)	(9)	(10)	(11)	(12)

Note: For underlined correlations p $\leq$ .05

Notes

1. This is an entirely revised version of a paper presented at the Council for European Studies SPG/HIWED workshop, "The Historical Development and Current Problems of Welfare States," Luzern, July 22-27, 1977. It is a part of a forthcoming book on the politics of taxing and spending, based on research made possible by the support of the National Science Foundation (Grant SOC77-13265), the German Marshall Fund, the Russell Sage Foundation, and the Institute of International Studies and the Institute of Industrial Relations of the University of California, Berkeley. I am grateful to Val R. Lorwin and Arnold J. Heidenheimer for critical readings, to Timothy L. McDaniel for a creative contribution to the conceptualization, measurement and coding of party power, and to Theodore M. Crone, Philip K. Armour, Jeffrey Haydu, Harry Katz, Anne T. Lawrence, Paul M. Lewis, and Alison E. Woodward for research assistance.
2. Wilensky 1976.
3. *Ibid.*, pp. 21-23.
4. *Ibid.*, pp. 23-24, 54-56.
5. *Ibid.*, pp. 36-37, 52-56.
6. *Ibid.*, pp. 36-43.
7. *Ibid.*, pp. 14-21.
8. *Ibid.*, pp. 44-45.
9. *Ibid.*, p. 31.
10. Wilensky 1975, pp. 65-66.
11. For detailed discussion of concepts and measures of these dependent variables, see Wilensky 1975, pp. 121-134 and 1976, pp. 48-70.
12. Cf. Wilensky 1967, pp. 173-191 and 1976; Schmitter 1974; and Heisler 1974, pp. 63-65.
13. Kerr et al. 1964, pp. 226-228; Miliband 1969, pp. 63-70.
14. Daalder 1966a, pp. 60-6l.
15. Lipset 1964, pp. 344-346.
16. Gulick 1948.
17. Heclo 1974, p. 320.
18. *Ibid.*, p. 296.
19. Cutright 1967a and l967b.
20. For a review of this literature, see Fry and Winters 1970, pp. 508-511.
21. Pryor 1968; Parkin 1971; Jackman 1975; Wilensky 1975; and Fried 1976.
22. Fry and Winters 1970; Peters 1974; Hibbs 1977; Hewitt 1977; and Hicks, Friedland and Johnson 1978.
23. For a detailed review of evidence and measures on economic inequality, see Wilensky 1978.
24. Hewitt 1977.
25. Pryor 1968 and Wilensky 1975.
26. Peters 1974; Hewitt 1977; and Jackman 1975.
27. Hewitt 1977, p. 459.
28. Hibbs 1977, p. 1473
29. In his discussion, Hibbs does note that the representation of French and Italian socialists has been marginal but in his code both score about one-third, much higher than West Germany (19 percent) and much closer to the United Kingdom (about 48 percent) than their executive power warrants.
30. Hibbs 1977, p. 1475 and Hewitt 1977, p. 451.

31. Cf. Wilensky 1975, pp. 15ff.
32. De Swann 1973, p. 139; Fogarty 1957 *passim*; Vignaux 1943; and Pius XI *Quadragesimo Anno* 1930, par. 79-80.
33. Einaudi and Goguel 1952, p. 28.
34. *Ibid.*, p. 123
35. See, for example, Heidenheimer 1960, p. 44.
36. Cf. Lorwin 1966 and 1971.
37. Cf. Linz 1976 and Mayer 1971.
38. The methods for testing hypotheses in this paper remain the same as those described in Wilensky 1975, pp. 22 ff., 121-138; and 1976, pp. 48-70: examine the zero order correlations, run regression experiments, construct path diagrams to test causal models, then examine cross tabulations of three independent variables at a time with each dependent variable, listing country scores. Because regression techniques make rigorous assumptions about measurement on an interval scale, linearity, and the absence of interaction effects, I view them as complementary confirmation of the cross-tabulations in Tables 10.1-10.4, which pinpoint deviant cases and locate interaction effects obscured by correlational techniques. The multiple regressions and path diagrams, however, capture small differences obscured by the dichotomies of the tables. Together, regressions and cross-tabulations give us more confidence in the conclusions than either method used alone.
39. An identical table substituting left power since post-World War II for 1919-76 suggests that only corporatism increases 1966 welfare effort. No combination of left power since World War II and 1965 tax visibility has any effect. Similarly, corporatism shapes welfare effort for 1971, but again, no combination of left power since World War II and 1971 tax visibility has an effect.
40. Fogarty 1957, p. 299.
41. Davis 1968.
42. My measure of corporatism, as I noted in Wilensky 1976, p. 51, does not capture some tendencies in the German political economy. Structurally, while the DGB is relatively weak, and there are important elements of decentralization in government, it can be argued that functional equivalents of corporatism would justify a higher score: industry-wide bargaining by moderately centralized unions informally coordinating their strategy, the growing professionalization of union staffs, the wage leadership of the Metal Workers, the presence of a big employer association, much centralized bargaining in the health industry, etc. During the decade of "Konzertierte Aktion" especially, German unions traded off wage restraint for other non-wage gains (e.g., the growth of workers councils). Cf. Lembruch 1978 and Streeck 1978. However, no one argues that Germany has developed corporatism to the level of the Netherlands, Sweden, or Austria by any definition. In relation to my model of corporatism, the German case is ambiguous. And if we scored it higher, it would strengthen all the major findings of my study (e.g., the relationship between Catholicism, corporatism, less visible taxes, and low backlash).
43. MacRae 1967, p. 103.
44. This is consistent with the finding that the only measure of left power that decreases backlash since World War II is left party dominance—sufficient (medium to high) power continuously exercised. It is a dummy variable with only Sweden, Austria, and Israel scoring "1," the rest "0."
45. Wilensky 1976, pp. 37-43.

References

Bentwich, Norman D. 1960. *Israel Resurgent.* New York: Praeger.

Burns, James MacGregor. 1963. *The Deadlock of Democracy.* Englewood Cliffs, N.J.: Prentice Hall.

Camp, Richard L. 1969. *The Papal Ideology of Social Reform: A Study in Historical Development 1878-1967.* New York: Heinemann.

Cronin, John F. 1950. *Catholic Social Principles.* Milwaukee: Bruce.

Cutright, Phillips. 1967a. "Inequality: A Cross-National Analysis." *American Sociological Review* 32: 562–578.

Cutright, Phillips. 1967b. "Income Redistribution: A Cross-National Analysis." *Social Forces* 46: 180–190.

Daalder, Hans. 1966a. "Parties, Elites, and Political Developments in Western Europe." In *Political Parties and Political Development,* ed. Joseph LaPalombara and Myron Weiner, pp. 43-77. Princeton, N.J.: Princeton University Press.

Daalder, Hans. 1966b. "The Netherlands: Opposition in a Segmented Society." In *Political Oppositions in Western Democracies,* ed. Robert A. Dahl, pp. 188-236. New Haven, Conn.: Yale University Press.

Davis, Natalie Zemon. 1968. "Poor Relief, Humanism, and Heresy: The Case of Lyon." *Studies in Medieval and Renaissance History* 5: 215–275.

De Swaan, Abram. 1973. *Coalition Theories and Cabinet Formations.* San Francisco: Jossey-Bass.

Ehrmann, Henry. 1976. *Politics in France.* 3rd ed. Boston: Little, Brown.

Einaudi, Mario and Goguel, Francois. 1952. *Christian Democracy in Italy and France.* Notre Dame, Ind.: University of Notre Dame Press.

Elvander, Nils. 1974. "In Search of New Relationships: Parties, Unions, and Salaried Employees' Associations in Sweden." *Industrial and Labor Relations Review* 28: 60–74.

Engelmann, Frederick C. 1966. "Austria: The Pooling of Opposition." In *Political Oppositions in Western Democracies,* ed. Robert Dahl, pp. 260-283. New Haven, Conn.: Yale University Press.

Fogarty, Michael P. 1957. *Christian Democracy in Western Europe, 1820-1953.* London: Routledge & Kegan Paul.

Fried, Robert C. 1976. "Party and Policy in West German Cities." *American Political Science Review* 70: 11–24.

Fry, Brian and Winters, Richard. 1970. "The Politics of Redistribution." *American Political Science Review* 64: 508–523.

Gulick, Charles. 1948. *Austria from Hapsburg to Hitler.* Two vols. Berkeley, Calif.: University of California Press.

Heclo, Hugh. 1974. *Modern Social Politics in Britain and Sweden.* New Haven, Conn.: Yale University Press.

Heidenheimer, Arnold J. 1960. *Adenauer and the CDU: The Rise of the Leader and the Integration of the Party.* The Hague: Nijhoff.

Heisler, Martin. 1974. "Patterns of European Politics: the 'European Polity Model.'" In *Politics in Europe,* ed. Martin Heisler, pp. 27-91. New York: David McKay.

Henig, Stanley, ed. 1969. *European Political Parties.* New York: Praeger.

Hewitt, Christopher. 1977. "The Effect of Political Democracy and Social Democracy on Equality in Industrial Societies: A Cross-National Comparison." *American Sociological Review* 42: 450–464.

Hibbs, Douglas. 1977. "Political Parties and Macroeconomic Policy." *American Political Science Review* 71: 1467–1488.

Hicks, Alexander, Friedland, Roger and Johnson, Edwin. 1978. "Class Power and State Policy: The Case of Large Business Corporations, Labor Unions and Government Redistribution in the American States." *American Sociological Review* 43: 302–316.

Huntington, Samuel P. 1968. *Political Order in a Changing Society.* New Haven, Conn.: Yale University Press.

Jackman, Robert. 1975. *Politics and Social Equality: A Comparative Analysis.* New York: John Wiley & Sons.

Kerr, Clark et al. 1964. *Industrialism and Industrial Man.* New York: Oxford University Press.

Kirchheimer, Otto. 1966. "The Transformation of the Western European Party Systems." In *Political Parties and Political Development,* ed. J. LaPalombara and M. Weiner, pp. 177–201. Princeton, N.J.: Princeton University Press.

Langdon, Frank. 1967. *Politics in Japan.* Boston: Little Brown.

Lehmbruch, Gerhard. 1978. "Corporatism, Labour, and Public Policy." Unpublished paper presented at the Ninth World Congress of Sociology, Uppsala, August 1978.

Linz, Juan J. 1976. "Some Notes Toward a Comparative Study of Fascism in Sociological Historical Perspective." In *Fascism: A Reader's Guide,* ed. Walter Laqueur, pp. 3–121. Berkeley, Calif.: University of California Press.

Lipset, Seymour Martin. 1964. "The Changing Class Structure and Contemporary European Politics." In *A New Europe?,* ed. Stephen Graubard, pp. 337–369. Boston: Beacon.

Lorwin, Val R. 1966. "Belgium: Religion, Class, and Language in National Politics." In *Political Oppositions in Western Democracies,* ed. Robert Dahl, pp. 147–187. New Haven, Conn.: Yale University Press.

Lorwin, Val R. 1971. "Segmented Pluralism: Ideological Cleavages and Political Cohesion in the Smaller European Democracies." *Comparative Politics* 3: 141–175.

Lorwin, Val R. "Labor Unions and Political Parties in Belgium." *Industrial and Labor Relations Review* 28: 243–263.

MacRae, Duncan. 1967. *Parliament, Parties, and Society in France, 1946-1958.* New York: St. Martin's Press.

Maier, Charles S. 1975. *Recasting Bourgeois Europe: Stabilization in France, Germany, and Italy in the Decade After World War One.* Princeton, N.J.: Princeton University Press.

Mayer, Arno. 1971. *Dynamics of Counterrevolution in Europe, 1870-1956.* New York: Harper and Row.

Miliband, Ralph. 1969. *The State in Capitalist Society.* London: Quartet Books.

Nousiainen, Jaakko. 1971. *The Finnish Political System.* Cambridge, Mass.: Harvard University Press.

Parkin, Frank. 1971. *Class Inequality and Political Order.* New York: Praeger.

Perlmutter, Amos. 1970. *Anatomy of Political Institutionalization: The Case of Israel and Some Comparative Analyses.* Harvard University: Center for International Affairs.

Peters, B. Guy. 1974. "Income Redistribution: A Longitudinal Analysis of France, Sweden, and the United Kingdom." *Political Studies* 22: 311–323.

Pius XI. 1930. Encyclical *Quadragesimo Anno.* Washington, D.C.: National Catholic Welfare Conference, 1942.

Pryor, Frederick. 1968. *Public Expenditures in Communist and Capitalist Nations.* Homewood, Ill.: Irwin.

Reynaud, Jean-Daniel. 1975. "Trade Unions and Political Parties in France: Some Recent Trends." *Industrial and Labor Relations Review* 28: 208–225.

Rokkan, Stein. 1966. "Norway: Numerical Democracy and Corporate Pluralism." In *Political Oppositions in Western Democracies,* ed. Robert Dahl, pp. 70-115. New Haven, Conn.: Yale University Press.

Schlesinger, Arthur M., Jr. 1958. *The Coming of the New Deal.* Boston: Houghton-Mifflin.

Schmitter, Philippe C. 1974. "Still the Century of Corporatism?" In *The New Corporatism: Social-Political Structures in the Iberian World,* ed. F.B. Pike and T. Stritch, pp. 85-131. Notre Dame, Ind.: University of Notre Dame.

Schwartz, Mildred. 1974. "Canadian Voting Behavior." In *Electoral Behavior,* ed. R. Rose, pp. 543-619. New York: Free Press.

Stjernquist, Nils. 1966. "Sweden: Stability or Deadlock?" In *Political Opposition in Western Democracies,* ed. Robert Dahl, pp. 116-146. New Haven, Conn.: Yale University Press.

Streeck, Wolfgang. 1978. "Organizational Consequences of Corporatist Cooperation in West German Labor Unions: A Case Study." Berlin: International Institute of Managment, discussion paper.

Vignaux, Paul. 1943. *Traditionalisme et Syndicalisme.* New York: Editions de la Maison Francaise.

Wilensky, Harold L. 1967. *Organizational Intelligence: Knowledge and Policy in Government and Industry.* New York: Basic Books.

Wilensky, Harold L. 1975. *The Welfare State and Equality.* Berkeley, Calif.: University of California Press.

Wilensky, Harold L. 1976. *The 'New Corporatism,' Centralization, and the Welfare State.* London: Sage Publications.

Wilensky, Harold L. 1978. "The Political Economy of Income Distribution: Issues in the Analysis of Government Approaches to the Reduction of Inequality." In *Major Social Issues: A Multi-Disciplinary View,* ed. Milton Yinger, pp. 87-108. New York: Free Press.

Chapter 11

Toward a New Welfare State?

Hugh Heclo

> . . . recent writings from all sides make it abundantly clear that the ideals which inspired the achievement of a "welfare state" are now no longer universally shared. Comprehensive notions of a "welfare state" based on complete "equality of citizenship" no longer receive universal assent (or lip service). Against a background of recurring fiscal crises, "paying for services" has replaced "fair shares for all" as a current political slogan.

The preceding comment epitomizes much of the current feeling that basic changes are underway in democratic government and social policy. Yet the writings to which this author refers are not part of the present "crisis of the welfare state" literature. Professor Asa Briggs was, in fact, describing the situation at the end of the 1950s—a period of time that many observers now identify as marking the outset of a new and enthusiastic burst of welfare spending and programming.[1] If nothing else, glancing over one's shoulder in this way may help temper some of the assumptions about the uniqueness of our own times. Perhaps it is a natural vanity for every writer to see himself as standing on the edge of a decisive historical moment. Every now and then it is useful to imagine that the opposite may be true. Perhaps there is no wave of future, only many small ripples; no decisive watersheds, only a variety of slippery slopes. The incrementalism that we see everywhere in public policy may actually be one of the most radical forces for change.

This chapter tries to look at our present circumstances in light of the past, hoping in this way to gain some perspective on what the future of the welfare state might portend. Have we in some sense reached the end of that familiar if muddled line of development that has characterized postwar social policy in the democracies? Have the customary forces so changed or the regenerative powers of our normal social politics become so depleted that present problems point toward a new kind—or perhaps no kind— of welfare state in the future?

My answer to the question of whether or not there is a movement toward a new welfare state is yes and no. The following pages develop four main arguments:

1. Democratic welfare states have moved through three general stages in the last 100 years, each with somewhat different ways of relating politics, the economy and social policy.
2. Because of unexpected circumstances, particularly postwar economic growth, the welfare state in its most recent phase took on a peculiar and unsustainable quality.
3. Consequently, some redefinition of the democratic welfare state is inevitable.
4. Yet changes will not be simple or unidirectional. In particular, changes will not merely reflect the currently fashionable theories of overloaded government, fiscal crisis, welfare backlash, and tax revolts. Rather, the emerging reformulation will involve a struggle to find new means of pursuing those basic values that have always underlain development of the democratic welfare state.

Table 11.1 presents the basic points in schematic form. Inevitably, an account of this nature does much injustice by simplifying many variations among countries and policies. Since a good deal of the texture of this variation is described in earlier chapters, attention here will focus on what seem to be the broad, widely shared features of development.

I. Stages of Welfarism

The historic record of welfare states during the last 100 years suggests three somewhat overlapping phases, each building on what had gone before. The first period can best be described as an era of *experimentation*. Beginning in roughly the last third of the nineteenth century, there occurred an unprecedented upsurge in national legislation directed at one or another kind of social betterment. As we have seen in preceding chapters, the most obvious example was the invention and diffusion of a new technique called social insurance. However, there were also manifestations of a new policy activism in areas such as public education, hospital organization, mental treatment, unemployment relief, and many others. Without being too doctrinaire about the exact time limits of this phase in each country, it appears that social policy experimentation continued into the World War I years (when many programs were disrupted and reformu-

lated) and on into the 1920s (when demobilization and economic dislocations precipitated any number of new collective provisions).

Experimentation was reflected in several ways. More than at any time
since, there was a good deal of chopping and changing in programs. The
number of those entitled to a particular benefit went not only up but also
occasionally down; major programs were started with high hopes, only to
be abandoned. In Germany, for example, the proportion of the labor force
covered by work injury insurance reached over four-fifths in the early 1890s
but was under three-fourths in the early 1900s; the proportion covered by
sickness insurance was higher in the period from 1910 to 1912 than it was in
the crisis period of 1932 to 1933. In Britain the 1908 pension system was
created and hailed as a major breakthrough, only to be substantially
abandoned in later years. In Scandinavia a host of official commissions
proposed pushing social insurance programs first this way and then that.
Comparable shifts took place at the state and local government level in the
United States when progressive reformers initiated their own varying
versions of the welfare-state-in-embryo.

Experimentation was also indicated by the abundance of arguments and
counter-arguments over fundamentals. Should policies inquire as to
whether those in need are deserving or underserving, or just poor? Are
compulsory government programs legitimate? Where are the proper boundaries of public activity? Is social policy a temporary expedient for reliev-
ing particular, disadvantaged groups or is it an enduring feature for the
nation at large? If policy can be thought of as having a constitution (rules
identifying basic parts and their relation), then the years from 1870 to 1930
mark the period of great constitutional debate for the modern welfare state.

I am not suggesting that these questions were ever fully resolved, then or
now, but in the era of experimentation the basic premises of government
action were open to a relatively great deal of wide-ranging and intermin-
able argument. More than that, there was a sense of excitement. It is
impossible to read in the early literature of the welfare state without
catching the flavor of this excitement—the enthusiasm with which social
insurance developments in other countries were reported, the fascination
with the technical details of various proposals, the assurance that fundamental changes were about to take place in government's impact on
society.

In essence, what was occurring amid all these arguments, tentative
commitments, and false starts was an effort to move beyond established
ways of thinking about the economy, social responsibility, and democratic
politics. In economic terms, experimentation coincided with a spreading
and periodically intensifying international business cycle. Social and economic disruptions were immense and nationwide throughout the Western

Table 11.1
Stages of the Welfare State

	Experimentation (1870s-1920s)	Consolidation (1930s-1940s)
Economics:		
events	international diffusion of business cycle; dislocations of industrialization	depression, wartime planning, destruction, reconstruction in austerity setting
reactions	relief of distress via ad hoc exceptions to 'laws' of political economy	integration of social expenditures with doctrines of demand management
Politics:		
events	workers movements, suffrage extensions, growth of mass parties	discrediting opponents of national government activism
reactions	policy innovations seeking to accomodate Liberal,Conservative and Socialist principles	all-party governments in war; emerging consensus on postwar reconstruction
Social Policy:		
form	innovation and volatility in programming;'constitutional' argument on boundary problems	unification of previous experiments
contents	dispensations for the deserving poor and working class;social insurance invented	**remedies for** risks shared by all citizens
value choices	attempts to reconcile liberty,equality, and security	demonstrations that the 3 values are mutually-reenforcing

Table 11.1
(Continued)

Expansion (1950s-1960s)	Reformulation (1970s-?)
unexpected, sustained economic growth	unexpected combinations of recession and inflation
intensified commitment to full employment;growthmanship as solvent of economic tradeoffs	ad hoc attempts to subordinate social policy to a new sense of scarcity
political bidding and group competition for painless policy growth	political disaffection; electoral volatility;distrust in traditional appeals
declining necessity for political commitment and consensus building; 'end of ideology' ideology	competition to reduce expectations and avoid unpopularity;neo-liberal attacks on tax,spending and bureaucracy issues
filling gaps and extending inherited approaches	reopening 'constitutional' issues; inadvertent extension in boundaries of social policy
compensations to preserve rising living standards; group struggle for relative shares of increases	marginal slowdowns in spending and programming; low-cost substitute means to seek same social goals
denial that important value choices are at stake	new recognition of 'tragic' choices; search for positive-sum relationships

world. Market fluctuation was essential to the economic order and the juggernaut of growth. Yet the emerging industrial system also needed a stable, disciplined work force; the turmoil created by market fluctuations worked in the opposite direction.

In social terms, traditional relationships were strained and breaking. The new industrial system tore at bonds of reciprocal duty that had tied class to class, occupation to occupation, person to person in agrarian societies. Yet there was also a moral base in Western society that carried an obligation to care about what was happening to others. Rationalizations offered by the "laws" of political economy competed with the humane impulse to relieve suffering and invent some form of social betterment that could prevent its recurrence. Young socialists, businessmen of conscience, churchmen and women, members of workers' fraternal organizations, journalists and many others puzzled over the paradox of affluence—the persistence of grinding poverty and misery in the midst of all the new industrial wealth.

In political terms, experimentation coincided not only with unprecedented extensions of voting and other political rights, but also with the advent of new sources of collective power in the industrial work force. Watching the growth of unions and socialist groups, those in the existing citadels of power adopted a variety of defensive strategies, some repressive, some accomodating demands for political participation, some yielding ground on distributive issues. Reformers continued to insist that those in power do something about the worker problem, or "social question" as it came to be called. Rarely were these pressures and reactions as simple as they now seem in retrospect.[2]

It would be artificial and unnecessary to try and choose *one* dominant motive among all the forces at work—self-defense of class interests versus reformers' moral zeal, economic versus political forces. The point is that here was a combination of forces capable of initiating a new era of experimentation on a variety of policy fronts. Three key values—liberty, equality and security—appeared to be at odds in the late nineteenth century. Trying to resolve the tensions among these values tended to push each of the prevailing bodies of political opinion into an activist orientation toward government and social policy, although each in a somewhat differing way. Calling for order, conservatives were driven to think about new means of advancing security for workers who would otherwise be open to the blandishments of agitators. Proclaiming political liberties, liberals were forced to confront the material deprivations that rendered individual liberty a meaningless formality. Hovering in the background, the young socialist movements were soon under pressure to support immediate relief measures that could be interpreted as steps toward their egalitarian goals.

Experimentation did not start from a clean slate. It largely responded to preexistent poor law traditions that prevailed throughout Western nations.

The poor law was localist, often improvised, and unreliable in the face of major economic downturns. Reacting to this legacy, policy innovators tended to search for national approaches that would standardize, plan for, and guarantee resources to deal with major kinds of economic and social adversity. The poor law was highly discretionary in its operations and stigmatizing. Experimentation sought policies that would be nonjudgmental and fairly automatic in helping the victims of socioeconomic forces that were beyond their control. Being highly pragmatic people, policy experimentators rarely couched the debate in theoretical terms. Implicitly, however, theirs was a tremendous theoretical contribution to modern social policy. Their search, if not their particular policy answers, was vital in spreading a commitment to the view that appropriate public policies *could* reconcile fundamental values of liberty, equality and security. It is this view more than anything else that eventually formed the leading premise of the democratic welfare state.

Yet the immediate results in this period of social policy were experiments, not the welfare state. The invention and diffusion of social insurance techniques late in the nineteenth century was obviously a portentious event. At a stroke it offered a workable model of a public policy that was national, standardized, and non-stigmatizing. However, there were many other types of experimentation. Major efforts at poor law reform were launched in many Western nations. Some of the first extensive efforts at housing reform and urban development policies were undertaken. Better organized charity movements were directed at first one type of social problem and then another. Solutions to poverty through better health or education were heralded, forgotten, and revived.

Despite their bewildering complexity, all of the experiments in government activism tended to have a common point of reference. Social policy was generally regarded as a dispensation. Economically, whatever was done about the social or worker problem was a dispensation from the sound "laws" of political economy. Regardless of any other arguments for activist policies, few people contended that social interventions were good economics (an exception were early advocates of action to improve the public health of the nation).

Politically too the new policies were a kind of dispensation. As earlier chapters show, no single party can claim exclusive rights of parentage for the welfare state; everyone was in on the act of conception, although some more than others at different times and places. Denying they were catering to the mob, conservatives could claim that minor infringements on private property rights were a dispensation from conservative principles necessary for protecting the social order. Liberals could claim that any paternalism or risk of state interference with individual freedom was remote if all one was doing was to relieve the destructive, illiberal conditions prevailing among the distressed. Once they arrived in office later in the period of experimentation, socialists could treat ameliorative reforms as a dispensation from their ultimate program, that is, pending arrival of a truly socialist order. Almost everyone could suspend a little of their ideology in order to do a little good.

Quite apart from the economics or politics of it, to do good was also a form of social dispensation. The policy experiments were mainly seen as a question of what some people were doing for other people. Those who enjoyed the benefits of education would help those who did not. Those who knew about proper health or housing would tell others who did not. In the tradition of charity, those better-off would give a little bit to relieve the suffering. Again, social insurance was something of a portentious exception, since it was one program where individuals were said to be helping themselves through contributing to state insurance premiums. But even here the spirit of social dispensation could be found. Almost nowhere can one find a worker's movement that initiated or enthusiastically supported early social insurance proposals. Rather, social insurance was a program created by experts and policy middlemen who believed they knew what was good for ordinary wage earners and their families. Few if any of the experimentators assumed that the same medicine would be good for the middle and upper classes.

Obviously there is no one moment when the era of experimentation ended. But with the Great Depression and World War II, experimentation gradually gave way to a more generally agreed structure of welfare state activities. In fascist dominated countries this development was seriously distorted (largely through the distruction of liberal social values and independent intermediary groups, but even here the immediate postwar years saw a return to patterns familiar in the Western democracies.) Social insurance was the centerpiece of the welfare state structure. It was, after all, one area where policy makers could feel confident that they possessed a social policy technique that was capable of solving a social problem: contributory benefits did cope with the threat of income insecurity on a variety of fronts. But close by were also new, if more vague, commitments to social improvement through employment, housing, education, and health policies. Certainly there were precedents for programs in all these fields. What was missing in the *era of consolidation*, compared with that of experimentation, was the tentativeness. In other words, there was generally a great deal less argument about fundamentals and private/public boundary problems; less reversibility in programs once established; less varied proposals and greater acceptance of the existing "constitution" of social policies. That the national government should and could act was taken for granted. Excitement shifted away from the discovery of new policy ideas and toward the challenge of erecting a coordinated structure of programs in the welfare state itself.

Consolidation does not mean that a single, uniform set of programs was created everywhere, although after the end of hostilities in 1945 a few countries such as Britain did erect "the" welfare state into something of a policy ideology. Consolidation, like experimentation, was a variable phenomenon, and it too had its economic, political, and social aspects.

In economic terms, consolidation occurred as the new Keynesian economics and full-employment goals became accepted in governing circles. Rarely did this happen quickly or dramatically enough to rate a newspaper headline, but it happened all the same, in one nation after another. The tremendous events of this period—struggling with the depression, organizing for war, planning for postwar reconstruction—left a residue of presumptions that were all the less noticable because so widely shared. The economy not only could and should be managed, but it should also be guided by, above all, a social goal called full-employment. Spending for social purposes could serve economic purposes of increased production, investment, and stable fiscal policy. Social policy was not only good economics, but the economic and social spheres of public policy were integrally related with each other.

The same events helped create consensus on many political assumptions about social policy. The depression undercut faith in any party program that relied entirely on the private sector to solve social problems. National government activism became not only politically acceptable but widely expected on issues of social policy as well as economic management. Almost all political factions in the victorious democracies had participated in government wartime management; politicians from many sides also participated in planning postwar reconstruction. The question was not whether some extensive, permanent system of state activity called the welfare state was necessary. The question was how to bring it all together.

Obviously the variations were considerable. In countries such as Britain and Sweden, emphasis was placed on the provision of common services, social solidarity, and comprehensive income maintenance programs. War-torn continental nations put greater stress on reconstruction, while affirming that this rebuilding process combined economic and social policy goals. In the United States, World War II (unlike World War I) brought with it a permanent growth in national government spending, employment, and responsibilities. But consolidation in social policy was only partial. Truman initiatives in health, education, housing, and so on met far less success than European counterparts and were vastly complicated by the uniquely American problem of civil rights. The U.S. population had not suffered the kind of dislocations and physical devastation that prevailed in Europe.

(Memories of depression unemployment were one thing shared on both sides of the Atlantic, but here there was a successful U.S. policy initiative in the form of the 1946 Employment Act.) Neither did World War II create a government coalition in the United States that could, as in many European countries, erect the basic structure of welfare programs with a minimum of political opposition. Above all, attention to the social agenda was soon overwhelmed in the United States by national security and foreign policy issues. Only the United States was in a position to respond with credible power, and the communism issue eventually blighted Truman's domestic initiatives. In this sense, Western Europe's lead in consolidating the welfare state was underwritten by the stultification of U.S. social policy.

Yet whatever these differences in national emphasis, all of the efforts at consolidation had certain broad things in common. Most important was a rejection of the older dispensation approach. Social policy was no longer seen as a dispensation from economic laws, an exception to political principles, or an act of largesse from one's betters. The austerities of depression and war tended to turn into reality what had often only been paid lip service during the previous decades of experimentation: a rough equality of sacrifice and sense that everyone was vulnerable. The prevailing assumption, created by hard experience, was now that collective social policy arrangements were required for everyone's good and not merely for the working class or some special group of deserving poor. In country after country, World War II carried in its wake a commitment to social services and income maintenance programs that would have been unthinkable to the turn of the century reformers.

What did consolidation mean? In general it did not mean a large number of unexpectedly new ideas in social policy. Rather it entailed a gradual bringing together of selected ideas from an earlier period into an affirmation of the effectiveness of democratic government as social manager. The result of consolidation was hardly some fixed solution or set of social priorities. Quite the opposite. What came to be labelled as the welfare state was an arrangement for living with mutually inconsistent priorities, a system of tolerated contradictions. Which should have priority, adequacy or equity in social insurance programs? Centralized standards for equality or local freedom of choice that produced inequalities? Economic security, or the liberty to succeed or fail on one's own? Planned social services or market exchanges?

Despite rhetorical flourishes at the time, the fact is that no Western democracy, not even any particular program, answered such questions in anything like a consistent way. New social policies might emphasize basic levels of adequacy, security, and equality, but they did not (in policy analysts' English) "prioritize" anything. This ambiguity, together with its political ramifications, helps account for the difficulty of intellectually coming to grips with the welfare state in any neat, rationalistic way. Politically, the welfare state was an amalgam of extraordinarily diverse ideas and interests: of crusading liberalism, with its confidence in the possibilities of social betterment, human progress, and secular individualism; of traditional conservatism, with its stress on paternalistic steps to safeguard institutions and social order against radical change; and of the more recently arrived socialism, with its faith in the benign power of government to undertake collective responsibilities.

Looked at from the nineteenth century, it would have seemed an impossible combination of perspectives. Viewing it through the eyes of those who had endured the turmoil of the interwar and war years we can see how well balanced such a mixture of ideas might be. It tended to achieve for the postwar democracies the kind of mutual check and balance among principles that had served so well in the creation of representative government two centuries earlier. The experimentors had sought ways to make liberty, equality, and security compatable. The consolidators acted in the faith that these three widely shared values were each necessary to the other; no final choice was necessary. And their resulting actions were generally accepted.

The era of consolidation ended in the late 1940s and early 1950s when it became clear that the back of any serious political opposition had been broken. In some nations this outcome was expressed by means of transitions in government, when successor parties not only refused to dismantle but continued to build on what had been done before.[3] Sometimes it happened via continued frustration at the polls, when it became clear that outright opposition to the existing consolidation would ensure continued defeat.[4] In either case, there was a generally accepted feeling that something permanent and positive was in place. Whether or not it was actually called a welfare state (and a country such as the United States strongly resisted the term), few people considered it likely or desirable to return to a prewar, predepression approach to social policy. Argument now shifted to filling gaps and expanding at the margins. In a few years some scholars were contending that there was a "decline of ideology" throughout the Western democracies.

The year after the mid-1950s have constituted a third phase that might be labelled as *expansion*. Of course, as earlier chapters have shown there had been extensions of social programs throughout the twentieth century. The term expansion is used here to suggest that, although social policy coverage and costs have grown for generations, the most recent stage represents a growth that has been largely within the structure of welfare state activities that was consolidated during and shortly after the depression and World War II. To see our current situation in clear perspective, we need to examine this expansionary stage more closely.

II. Subversion Through Economic Growth

Growth in social policy during the last twenty-five or so years has been largely a question of filling gaps and extending inherited approaches within the existing welfare state structure. This is suggested by the fact that one need add almost no new categories or functions in order to display the growth in programs and spending during this period. (The United States is something of an exception, since some consolidation is still underway in areas such as health insurance, family policy, and labor market programs.)

The leading indicator of this expansion is government spending. The information in Jürgen Kohl's chapter clearly shows how much the Western democracies have had in common since the early 1950s. Government tax extractions grew faster than economic resources; total expenditures grew faster still. In every country the result has been a gradually increasing share of national economic product absorbed by the public sector. The result has also been growing government deficits, although not to unprecedented levels and not to such an extent that the most recent years portend a long-term trend toward bankruptcy. (Nor does this mean, as Kohl demonstrates, that those nations that have increased spending the most have the greatest deficits; there is no correlation.) The largest single driving force behind the public sector has been increased spending for social policy, and without a relative decline in rates of defense spending to offset some of the social spending increases, total budgets would have been even larger. Of all social spending, government transfers have been the fastest growing component, to the point where central governments are now major distributors of consumers' income. This trend of increased public transfers has been fairly continuous despite periodic economic ups and downs, and to a significant extent leads to an exaggerated view of how far government is impinging on the private sector in the command over goods and services.[5] These trends are common not only in Western Europe but throughout the developed democracies, including a so-called welfare state laggard such as the United States.[6]

Taken together, all of these incremental increases suggest something of the expansionary trend in the welfare state with which the current generation is familiar. What is perhaps the most important point about this expansion is usually taken for granted, its setting in a context of unprecedented, sustained economic growth. Obviously there have been occasional slowdowns and in a few countries at a few times outright reverses in economic performance. But compared with all of the pre-World War II years—back in fact to the earliest point economic statistics become available in pre-industrial Europe—the last 25 to 30 years have represented a uniquely smooth upward curve of economic growth.[7]

We tend to forget now that this successful economic performance was largely unexpected. The basic structure of the welfare state (national social insurance programs, general social services, Keynesian fiscal management, and so on) was consolidated amid memories of profound insecurity in the past and fears of continued disruptions in the future. Expectations of poor economic performance, for example, pervaded discussions leading up to the U.S. Employment Act, British Beveridge plan, Swedish national insurance system, and German programs for *wiederaufbau* in the 1940s. The period of consolidation had been, as T.H. Marshall termed it, an austerity society of rationing, price controls, and pervasive expectations that the boom and bust syndrome following World War I was about to repeat itself.[8] Perhaps more than anything else, it was this sense of common danger and vulnerability that made the security-equality-liberty aims of the new welfare state seem consistent and integral to the functioning of both society and the economy.

Sustained economic growth facilitated continued expansion of social spending. But gradually and indeliberately it also undermined the premises of the welfare state that policy makers thought they were creating at the end of World War II. It did so in at least three ways.

First, while the dangers of social insecurity remained, they became less shared. Major dislocations such as depression and war had struck every social group; minor fluctuations in a period of overall growth touched only certain sections. Recessions left a minority of workers unemployed, but most workers were untouched. More than that, the very nature of social need to which welfare policies were responding in an age of affluence was individualized rather than a collectively shared experience. Health crises, single-parenthood, distress in old age—these might affect vast numbers of people, but by their nature the problems struck only isolated families and created no sense of shared experience. Asked about poverty, a majority of affluent Europeans could say either that there were really no poor people in their town (53%) or that if there were the respondent did not see them (37%). Likewise Americans were probably inclined to see poverty as a problem of blacks because, even though there are more than twice the number of whites as blacks living below a poverty level, only 12% of poor whites were concentrated in poverty neighborhoods in metropolitan areas, compared with approximately 40% of poor blacks.[9]

None of this means that collective provisions failed to be made. Sustained economic growth provided a bonanza with which spending for social purposes could be expanded, particularly in the area of income transfers. But the benefits, like the problems, have been largely individualized. Social insurance, which dominates the expansion in public spending, is a case in point. During the transitions from experimentation, to consolidation, and on to expansion, social insurance programs have performed a remarkable historical task. These programs more than any others have managed to bridge the gap between the older tradition of self-help and the newer responsibilities for collective distribution. In the United States, for example, social insurance accounted for about 10% of total individual income during 1976. Every income group shared in some part of its benefits (even the top fifth of family income units received almost 12% of total social insurance payments). Yet social security also had the greatest effect of all national programs in lifting families above poverty level incomes.[10] However since the program manifests itself only in terms of individuals' own monthly payments, this extraordinary accomplishment produces little sense of collective achievement in the welfare state. Likewise, during the 1973-75 recession (the most severe since the Great Depression) income maintenance programs as a whole prevented the income of those below the poverty level from dropping significantly in the aggregate. The one thing about this major social policy accomplishment that was widely shared was grumbling that personal taxes were too high.

Sustained economic growth undermined the presumptions of the postwar welfare state in a second way. Seen less as a response to shared problems, the benefits to be derived from the welfare state came to be regarded as a means for calculating differential gains. For every increase in one group's income and consumption, there were always other groups that could make a legitimate claim to keep pace. The alacrity with which basic pension systems created in the 1940s shifted into a variety of forms of constant updating was one expression of the more general tendency. Growth facilitated evaluations of comparative performance. Comparison facilitated identification of new individual and group inequities. New inequities facilitated expansion in social programs. In effect, sustained growth put the welfare state as a social justice machine into competition with the economy as an inequity producing machine.

This compensatory dynamic cut several ways, all corrosive of the social solidarity that had inspired the austerity welfare state. Rather than as the expression of a larger public interest, government was put in a position to be perceived as little more than an aimless device for tallying the secondary (postmarket) distribution of income. The ongoing struggle for shares of this new and growing distribution process helped mobilize new groups and create new cleavages among old groups. This did not destroy traditional group and class conflict but it certainly helped, in the longer run, to disorganize it. In the end, corrosion went deeper than the fact that affluence heightened different groups' sense of relative deprivation (vis-à-vis both primary and secondary distribution processes). As Fred Hirsch eloquently argued, success in distributing more material goods throughout society increasingly focussed competition on positional goods that could not be distributed more widely without diminishing their value.[11] In all these ways, increasing national wealth tended to undermine the faith in compatable values. Security in a period of growth implied differential gains, not equality; liberty implied meeting a quantitatively and qualitatively expanding set of wants, not basic needs.

Finally, sustained growth subtly threatened welfare state premises by gradually devaluing the political commitment necessary to sustain social policy. Economic growth, with its virtually automatic increases in tax revenues, tended to make social policy expansion almost costless in political terms. In the era of austerity, consolidating the welfare state had required strong political backing, something that was a long time in coming until depression and war eventually mobilized these forces. In an era of affluence, passive acquiescence could suffice; politically the welfare state could expand on the basis of more for everybody. Higher benefits, wider coverage, more services could be afforded, if not this year, then in succeeding years' fiscal dividends. Government budgets and deficits might grow, but then so would people's incomes. Those who saw an "end of ideology" in this period were, in a limited sense, right. Welfare state politics could lie in repose while the engine of economic growth did its work.

As the political price of social policy declined, the need to build and maintain a strong, positive political coalition behind the expanding welfare state diminished. Historically—in the Western democracies as much as in Bismarck's original social insurance plans—welfare state proposals had been used by politicians as a means of helping them solve political problems. Expansion during the period of economic growth removed most of this political imperative. It was possible to have policy without pain. Politicians did not have to strive mightily to build a working consensus, even though expansionary changes were occurring that would have been astonishing a generation earlier. More and more, social policy was assumed to be aimed exclusively at solving social problems; any investment in confronting, debating, and resolving political problems (who is losing and gaining? what are the implications for personal liberty? what rights and duties are owed by whom? is it worth it?) could be minimized.

As a result of these three forces, the recent expansion stage actually operated at two levels. On the surface, familiar programs and functions of the welfare state were merely growing along with (although somewhat faster than) the economy. But a deeper level, key premises of modern social policy were being eroded. It is not that many people questioned whether values of liberty, equality, and security were compatible with or necessary to each other. That is the point: any commitment to struggling with the inevitable tensions among such values went soft. Expansion of the austerity welfare state in a context of sustained affluence was producing not just more of the same but implicitly a newer way of thinking about the welfare state. Instead of shared risks and vulnerability, its ethic was based on piecemeal compensation for anyone who lagged behind others' gains. The emerging system was not simply a return to the older dispensation approach because virtually everyone could claim to be entitled to one or another kind of compensation. The course being followed was politically easy but perilous. Since policy commitment was justified on the basis of solving social problems (and much less on strong political commitment to certain values), and since no one knew how to guarantee such solutions, few groups had trouble showing that their needs were going unmet. Thus the late 1960s witnessed a restatement of the nineteenth century paradox of affluence but this time with everybody joining in as claimants for justice and improved public policies. Students were oppressed. Poverty persisted. Women were suppressed. Capital wasn't getting a fair return. Jobs weren't meaningful. Workers weren't getting their share of the expanding product. The disabled were discriminated against. In short inequality was redis-covered. Economic growth was not enough. The welfare state would have to do more.

By a strange twist, the more social policy became dominant in the economy and helped absorb its product, the more it became viewed as a mere appendage to the economy, whose growth was taken for granted. In an earlier period of risk and austerity, consolidators of the welfare state had been inclined to see social policy as a support to their none-too-strong capitalist economies, just as the new policies of fiscal management were integral to any aims of social policy. In our own wealthy postwar period, social policy increasingly came to be regarded as a kind of luxury good produced by the ever-rolling surpluses of economic growth. The 1970s were to be a different story.

III. The New Pessimism

The previous section argued that expansion of social policies in an era of sustained economic growth tended to subvert essential features of earlier welfare state conceptions. Instead of deliberately coordinating the two spheres, policy makers increasingly treated the welfare state as an appen-dage of economic performance. It was a neat separation: economic policy would be concerned with increasing output as smoothly as possible; social policy would follow along and focus on redistributing that output so as to compensate those who fell behind. Hence the growing prominence of income transfer programs (although obviously many other forms of non-cash programs were also expanding). After a generation or more of expansion, the democratic welfare states had produced a policy system that was admirably attuned to—and presumed—continuous economic growth. Politically it was a low cost system whose operation generated minimum conflict and maximum, if somewhat passive, support. Economically it was in rough harmony with conventional thinking about fiscal management. Socially, it avoided raising difficult questions about social values. Commitments on the welfare state rose as commitment to it fell.

What happened in the 1970s was the kind of disillusionment that might be expected from a one/two punch: an unsettling rediscovery of inequality by the end of the 1960s followed by a stalling of the economic growth machine in the 1970s. A postwar policy structure that was accustomed to expansion had to accomodate economic reverses that were as unexpected as economic success had been to the pre-1950s policy makers. In a twinkling (or so it will probably seem historically), complacency about the momentum of the welfare state gave way to doom-mongering by many in the intellectual elite, people who were once the strongest champions of activist social policies.

The indictment against the welfare state that gained currency involved one or more of the following three counts.

1. *Cost.* Social welfare spending (that is, expenditure for income maintenance, health, housing, education, and other social services) has accelerated dramatically, resulting in what is variously termed as a "bloated," "excessive," or "runaway" public sector. The complaints about welfare spending have become more politically noticeable throughout the Western democracies as taxes and social security contributions have increasingly hit moderate and even lower income groups. The fact is that the cost of the modern welfare state is not being covered by reckless use of government deficits and printing presses. The middle class is being heavily taxed and future cost will not be able to be met in a financially responsible way without a willingness to pay even higher taxes. It is that willingness that is increasingly being called into question.

2. *Ineffectiveness.* Critics claim that, for all of its expensive ambitions, the welfare state has failed to deliver on too many of its promises. At a minimum there are legitimate complaints that government programs have been extraordinarily inept at delivering money and social services to people who actually need them. At a maximum, there is a sense of disillusionment that government is perversely impotent; welfare programs seem incapable of altering social conditions in the way intended (toward increased equality) and in trying to do so have produced undesirable consequences that were not intended (incentives for client dependency and bureaucratic snooping for example). Hence both liberals and conservatives have been able to find

common cause in citing the shortcomings of contemporary social policy. The complaints can be heard directed at all sorts of programs: education policies that do not equalize opportunity but do provide a means for the acquisition of new inequalities; subsidized health services that provide more formal access but only to highly unequal qualities of care; antipoverty programs that do more for the professional middlemen than for the poor; job-training programs that only entrench the disadvantages of those already at the bottom of the labor market, and so on and on.

3. *Overregulation.* While criticized as relatively impotent in achieving social objectives, the growing welfare state bureaucracies are also able to arouse fears of excessive government power. In a sense, it is not particularly difficult to design government programs that would deliver cash benefits, health care, or other social services in an effective way—that is, providing what is intended to whom it is intended. Totalitarian systems have shown how solutions can be imposed on all those groups—professionals, consumers, local governments, political entrepreneurs, and others—that in democratic regimes are in a position to interfere with the effective power of government planners. For critics of the contemporary welfare state, increased effectiveness purchased at the price of such antidemocratic solutions is hardly attractive. Their real worry is that a satisfactory threshold of effectiveness in welfare administration may be attainable only after passing well beyond the limits of democratic processes, which imply widespread participation, diversity, and checks on government power. Thus, frustrated by its own ineffectiveness, democratic government is tempted to achieve its ever more ambitious social goals by imposing solutions, invading individual privacy, and bureaucratizing the initial impetus for human compassion with a host of welfare rules and regulations. Or in trying to arbitrate competing group claims, welfare bureaucracies may overlook the interests of those who are not organized to exert pressure. In this way a well-intentioned kind of arbitrariness can develop, forcing human diversity into whatever formula (e.g., quotas) happens to facilitate political-bureaucratic management of the prevailing group demands for compensation.

In essence the new pessimism of the 1970s revived the view—so long out of favor—that there were inherent contradictions among the basic values surrounding the democratic welfare state. It was expensive, so expensive that costs of social policy were themselves posing a threat to individuals' economic security. It was ineffective, generally in providing high standards of service and particularly in making inroads into the gross inequalities of market-oriented societies. And it was dangerous, threatening to pursue welfare at the expense of individual liberty. The welfare state's past achievements were said to be overpriced, its unattained goals were disappointing, and the requisites for its future success implied a disturbing concentration of power. None of these indictments was entirely new, but with the sharpest economic downturn since the depression (not enough to create a shared sense of mass suffering but enough to upset the routines of compensation) criticisms of the welfare state acquired special force in the 1970s. Intellectuals have followed with a variety of explanations for the apparent disorders of the welfare state, or as it is more recently labelled, welfare capitalism.

One set of theories views expansions of social policy as essentially a form of side payments to keep the lower orders in line. While this class conflict view has a long lineage, the more recent versions have attempted to show that the need for capital accumulation requires the payment of larger and larger amounts of hush money to economically exploited groups, leading to larger public deficits and eventual crisis.[12]

A second line of interpretation—a demand push model—sees the problem in terms of uncontrollable growth in the welfare state produced by an unrestrained pressure for benefits and unwillingness to face up to the associated costs. The exact routes differ (some emphasizing demands for welfare spending, others union power, and still others full employment goals that lead to persistent overstimulation of the economy), but all these excesses of democracy theories point toward the same end: a breakdown of representative government.[13]

A third variant of the new pessimism interprets disorders of the modern welfare state in terms of a supply-pull problem: government bureaucracies with a vested interest in continued expansion; professional service providers dedicated to the extension and never-ending refinement of "needs"; a system of economic production that massages the public maw into higher and higher levels of immiserating consumerism.[14] This line of thinking leads to a variety of strategies for rediscovering, living with, and indeed revelling in facts of scarcity.

It hardly needs to be said that these three sets of ideas are not entirely consistent with each other. Some evidence, or at least persuasive arguments, can be found to support each, and it would be foolish to deny that some version of all these pressures has existed throughout (but also before) the postwar period. Yet it appears to me that the welfare state is more complex, its motive processes more dynamic than is credited by any version of the new pessimism. Pure amplification and self-destructive expansion is not what has happened in recent years. New directions of class self-defense (if that is one's vehicle for interpretation) have been discovered; demands being pushed have changed; some supply-pulls have been redirected. Even as the intellectuals were launching their well-reasoned forebodings, the actual behavior of governments and publics was contradicting the view that either were in the grip of one or another set of inexorable forces.

As the 1970s progressed, the record tended to show the Western democracies behaving in a manner exactly the opposite of what the welfare state critics should have predicted.[15] Almost nowhere could parties be found trying to outbid each other in promises to continue rapid expansions in social policy spending. Almost everywhere they engaged in a competition to avoid unpopularity and reduce expectations. In nation after nation governments chose to fight inflation as a first priority rather than to reflate and fight unemployment., For example, in West Germany the Social Democratic government gave wide publicity to its promise not to reflate until inflation was beaten (then at 4%!). In Great Britain, the conventional model of a collectivist welfare state, the socialistic Labor government maintained itself in power with anti-inflation policies that tolerated a rate of unemployment higher than at any time in the postwar period. Similarly in the United States, the revival of the Democrats' fortunes in 1976 can hardly be traced to efforts at promising more than George McGovern had in 1972; by that token it should have been Sargent Shriver who won the 1976 primaries rather than a man promising to cut the bureaucracy and balance the budget by 1981. Preliminary evidence suggests that as the 1970s continued, social spending and public budgets grew but at a somewhat slower rate than during the previous decade and that in some countries spending "shortfalls" (i.e., expenditures below what had been planned) were more common than unexpectedly large public budgets.[16]

What about public attitudes that were supposedly immured in expectations of ever-continuing growth in the economy and public policy? The 1970s provided an interesting experiment to test the demand-push theory of public pressure for expanding the welfare state. Survey information for the United States and Western Europe shows a considerable willingness in the general public to act sensibly and lower expectations in response to (and in anticipation of) unfavorable events.[17] At least three kinds of process appear to have been at work throughout the Western democracies during this time of economic troubles and declining confidence in leaders and social institutions. First, people tended to compartmentalize satisfactions. Considerable dissatisfaction with the performance of the economy and government could exist while ordinary people continued to feel generally satisfied with their lives and the things closest to them. In the second place, people were inclined to lower the base for comparing how well things were going. Even at the peak of the boom in the 1960s, only a minority of Americans and Europeans expected prosperity to continue growing as it had in the past; in the 1970s people appeared ready to compare their situation with a more pessimistic baseline that was lower than a high level of prosperity. Finally, people were highly flexible in their expectations for the future, adjusting their view of coming good or bad times as circumstances seemed to require.

In short, experiences in the 1970s seem to have modified the priorities that politicians promised, the political behavior that voters rewarded, and the expectations that people carried around in their heads. It is such manifest responsiveness to experience that, more than anything else, undercuts the new pessimism and any theories of uncontrollable growth or breakdown in democratic welfare states.

In the 1970s—a period of recession, inflation, and unemployment in unique combination—the welfare state's social programs did not wither away. Instead these programs helped policy makers cope with the unsettling economic and environmental conditions in a relatively humane manner. Hundreds of thousands of families were protected from the worst effects of their breadwinners' unemployment. Millions of dollars were spent to see to it that treatment of people's health problems was not abandoned simply because of a downturn in the economy. Billions of dollars, francs, marks, and so on were transferred to see to it that those most vulnerable—the aged, young, and disabled—were not left in the front lines during the battle with inflation and its attack on living standards. Nowhere is there evidence of major welfare state programs being dismantled. What can be seen here and there among the Western democracies are efforts to slow down some expenditures' growth rates, to institute more cost controls, to refrain from undertaking major new social policy commitments, or to stretch out their implementation over time (the U.S. health insurance debate is a good example). To judge all of this as a sign of democratic excess or failure of capitalism depends on criteria derived not from social science but from one's policy preferences.

To summarize, the rapid expansion of social policies during the postwar period was vastly facilitated by a degree of persisting economic growth that was as unexpected to the welfare state's founders as to its critics. But this growth also undermined the conception of integrated economic and social policy—and ultimately the balance of liberty, equality, and security values—on which they had based their plans. Without any deliberate decision to do so, social policy came increasingly to be seen as a residual luxury supported by the nation's economic surplus. When it became clear in the 1970s that this surplus could not be assured, critics turned on the democratic welfare state as never before, citing its activity as a primary drain on the forces of economic progress and/or human betterment.

And yet there is clearly good reason to think that these pessimistic claims are off target, particularly in light of the moderate, cost-conscious government and public reactions to the serious economic disturbances of the 1970s. What events of the 1970s cast doubt upon was an unreflective view of social policy into which countries, and democratic politics, had drifted in the postwar period. Far from strengthening the welfare state, the politically cheap expansion of programs actually tended to devalue the commitment to social policy and transform it into a predicate of economic growthmanship and mass consumerism. The welfare state and its underlying values have never depended on uncontrollable public spending, big bureaucracy, or ever more unrealistic political bidding. Looking back now we can see that during much of the postwar period, social policy was set on a course that made it somewhat superficial and certainly vulnerable to any future economic downturn. But there is little reason for thinking that such a course is immutable. Indeed, my prediction is that the 1980s will produce lusty evidence to the contrary. These years will show the strength of the underlying welfare state commitment—an affirmation of the importance of *and* a refusal to choose absolute priorities among the basic values of individual liberty, social equality, and economic security.

Notes

1. See Briggs 1961.
2. See for example the discussions of various nations' "distribution crises" in Grew 1978.
3. Thus despite some Republican hopes, the Eisenhower administration did not demolish social security and other New Deal programs. Likewise, the return-ing Churchill government did not, apart from a few mainly symbolic changes, repudiate what the prior Labor government had done. In France, the Gaullists of the Fifth Republic, having lost power once, were at pains later in the 1950s to preserve continuity with Fourth Republic social policies.
4. Sweden and West Germany offered contrasting versions of the same point. In Sweden, where Social Democrats were in power, center and right opposition parties were soon persuaded to drop unpopular criticisms of the socialists' welfare state programs (though the opposition parties remained unsuccessful for many years). In Germany, it was the Social Democrats who were in opposition and in the 1950s felt the need to accomodate their socialist program to the welfare state that had been consolidated by Christian Demo-crats in the immediate postwar years.
5. Since transfer spending is usually counted as part of government expenditure in the numerator but not counted in the denominator of GNP (or national income), ratios of spending to GNP often overstate the extent of collective governmental command over resources.
6. Nutter 1978.
7. Brown 1968; see also Garraty 1977.
8. Marshall 1961.
9. A variety of such surveys are discussed in Rose 1977.
10. In 1976 an estimated 20.2 million families were in poverty before public transfer payments. After social insurance benefits the number was reduced 45% to 11.1 million. "Welfare" in the form of other cash assistance only reduced the number by a further 10% to 9.1 million; in-kind transfer pay-ments led to an additional decrease of 19% to 5.3 million families. Congres-sional Budget Office 1977.
11. Hirsch 1976.
12. The most familiar version is O'Connor 1973. For a more general survey see Jessop 1977.
13. The more prominent examples are Brittan 1975; Buchanan and Wagner 1977.

14. Again there is an impressive array of pessimistic viewpoints, some of which go much further than any simple supply side model. See Ophuls 1977; Illich 1977. Without too much injustice one could say that Robert Heilbroner (*Business Civilization in Decline*) and Daniel Bell (*The Cultural Contradictions of Capitalism*) attempt to synthesize the second and third schools of thought.

15. This seems to be the general thrust of David Cameron's various findings, as in for example, Cameron 1978a and Cameron 1978b. Taking a longer time frame the picture seems, contrary to the new pessimism, reassuringly multivariate. Governments of the left appear more responsive than others to changing economic circumstances and use a greater variety of tools, but they are also the governments of high interest rates and do not exhibit any unusual proclivity toward big budget deficits. See Cowart 1978.

16. In the United States for example, the ratio of total government spending to GNP rose 27% during the 1950s, 21% during the 1960s, and only 6% during the 1970s. In real terms, government consumption of goods and services (note the exclusion of transfer payments) rose from 19% of GNP in 1940 to 25% by 1970, but by 1977 had fallen back to 20%. This and other points of scepticism about the case made by neoconservatives are raised by Musgrave 1979. See also Plotnick 1977; and Hartman 1978. Britain's spending shortfall "problem" is described in *The London Times,* March 11, 1978.

17. In addition to note 8 *supra,* see especially Katona 1971.

References

Briggs, Asa. 1961. "The Welfare State in Historical Perspective." *Europaisches Archiv fur Soziologie* 2, 221-258.

Brittan, Samuel. 1975. "The Economic Contradictions of Democracy." *British Journal of Political Science* 5.

Brown, E.H. Phelps and Margaret. 1968. *A Century of Pay.* New York: Macmillan.

Buchanan, James M. and Wagner, Richard E. 1977. *Democracy in Deficit.* New York: Academic Press.

Cameron, David. 1978a. "The Expansion of the Public Economy." *American Political Science Review* 71.

Cameron, David. 1978b. "Taxes, Deficits, and Inflation." Paper prepared for the Brookings Institution Project on the Politics and Sociology of Global Inflation.

Congressional Budget Office. 1977. "Poverty Status of Families under Alternative Definitions of Income." *Background Paper No. 17.*

Cowart, Andrew T. 1978. "The Economic Policies of European Governments." *British Journal of Politics* 8.

Crozier, Michael and Huntington, Samuel. 1975. *The Crisis of Democracy.* New York: New York University Press.

Garraty, John. 1977. *Unemployment in History.* New York: Harper and Row.

Grew, Raymond, ed. 1978. *Crises of Political Development in Europe and the United States.* Princeton: Princeton University Press.

Hartman, Robert W. 1978. "The Spending Shortfall." In Joseph Peckman et al. *Setting National Priorities: The 1979 Budget.* Washington, D.C.: The Brookings Institution.

Hirsch, Fred. 1976. *The Social Limits of Growth.* Cambridge: Harvard University Press.

Illich, Ivan. 1977. *Toward a History of Needs.* New York: Pantheon Press.

Jessop, Robert. 1977. "Recent Theories of Welfare Capitalism." *Cambridge Journal of Economics* 1.

Katona, George et al. 1971. *Aspirations and Affluence.* New York: McGraw-Hill.

Marshall, T.H. 1961. "The Welfare State: A Sociological Interpretation." *Europaisches Archiv fur Soziologie* 2.

Musgrave, Richard A. 1979. "Budget Size and the Leviathan Syndrome." Paper presented to the American Political Science Association Convention, Washington, D.C.

Nutter, Warren G. 1978. *Growth of Government in the West.* Washington, D.C. American Enterprise Institute.

O'Connor, James, 1973. *The Fiscal Crisis of the State.* New York: St. Martin's Press.

Ophuls, William. 1977. *The Ecology and Politics of Scarcity.* San Francisco: Free-Press.

Plotnick, Robert. 1977. *Social Welfare Expenditures and the Poor.* Madison, Wis.: Institute for Research on Poverty.

Rose, Richard. 1977. "Ordinary People in Extraordinary Circumstances." *Studies in Public Policy No. 11.* Glasgow, Scotland: Center for the Study of Public Policy, Strathclyde University.

Rose, Richard and Peters, Guy. 1978. *Can Government Go Bankrupt.* New York: Basic Books.

Contributors

JENS ALBER, research fellow at the European Institute, Florence, and university assistant at Cologne University, holds degrees from the Universities of Konstanz and Mannheim. He is the author of *Die Entwicklung sozialer Sicherungssysteme im Licht Empirischer Analysen* (1979) and *Vom Armenhaus zum Wohlfahrtsstaat: Modernisierung und die Entwicklung der Sozialversicherung in Westeuropa* (1980).

PETER FLORA is professor of sociology at the University of Cologne and the European University Institute, Florence. He directed the project on Historical Indicators of Western European Democracies. He is author of *Modernisierungsforschung, Indikatoren der Modernisierung* and *Quantitative Historical Sociology,* and editor of the forthcoming handbook *State, Economy and Society in Western Europe 1815-1975,* which is comprised of data collected by the HIWED Project.

HUGH HECLO, professor of government at Harvard University, was previously affiliated with the Brookings Institution, M.I.T., and the University of Essex. He is the author of *Modern Social Policies in Britain and Sweden: From Relief to Income Maintenance* (1974), *Comparative Public Policy* (1975), and several volumes dealing with bureaucracies in Britain and the United States.

ARNOLD J. HEIDENHEIMER, professor of political science at Washington University, St. Louis, has been visiting professor at the Universities of Berlin, Bergen, London, and Stockholm. His publications include *Comparative Public Policy: The Politics of Social Choice in Europe and America* (1975), *Political Corruption: Readings in Comparative Analysis* (1978), and *The Shaping of the Swedish Health System* (1980).

HARMUT KAELBLE, professor of economic and social history at the Free University of Berlin, has held visiting appointments at Harvard and Oxford Universities and the Maison des Sciences de l'Homme. His publications include *Industrielle Interessenpolitik in der Wilhelminischen Gesellschaft* (1967), *Probleme der Modernisierung* (coauthor, 1978), and *Historical Mobility Studies* (1980).

JURGEN KOHL, assistant for social policy in the sociology department at the University of Bielefeld, received his Ph.D. degree from Mannheim University. He is the author of *Staatsausgaben in West-Europa* (1980) and a contributor to *Soziologischer Almanach* (1979).

FRANZ KRAUS, research assistant with the HIWED Project, is a student at the University of Mannheim.

ROBERT T. KUDRLE, associate professor at the Humphrey Institute of Public Affairs at the University of Minnesota, has published studies of economic policies and is a contributor to *National Health Insurance: Conflicting Goals and Policy Choices* (1980).

STEIN KUHNLE, lecturer in sociology and research associate in comparative politics at the University of Bergen, is the author of *Patterns of Social and Political Mobilization: A Historical Analysis of the Nordic Countries* (1975) and a contributor to *Acta Sociologica* (1978).

THEODORE MARMOR, professor of political science and public health and chairman of the Center for Health Studies at Yale University, has taught at Harvard and the Universities of Chicago, Minnesota, and Wisconsin. He is the author of *The Politics of Medical Care* (1970).

HAROLD L. WILENSKY, professor of sociology at the University of California at Berkeley, has taught at the Universities of Chicago and Michigan. His publications include *Intellectuals in Labor Unions* (1956), *Organizational Intelligence: Knowledge and Policy in Government and Industry* (1967), and *The Welfare State and Equality* (1975).

Index

SUBJECTS

409

NAMES